Explicit Instruction
Effective and Efficient Teaching

Anita Archer
Charles Hughes

About the Authors

ANITA ARCHER, PhD, is an educational consultant to school districts on explicit instruction, the design and delivery of instruction, behavior management, and literacy instruction. She has taught elementary and middle school students and is the recipient of 10 awards honoring her excellence in teaching and contributions to the field of education. Dr. Archer has served on the faculties of San Diego State University, the University of Washington in Seattle, and the University of Oregon in Eugene. She is nationally known for her professional development activities, having presented in every state over the course of her 40-year career. Dr. Archer is coauthor, with Dr. Mary Gleason, of numerous curriculum materials addressing reading, writing, and study skills.

CHARLES HUGHES, PhD, is Professor of Special Education in the Department of Educational and School Psychology at The Pennsylvania State University and Adjunct Senior Scientist at the University of Kansas Center for Research on Learning in Lawrence. Prior to joining the Penn State faculty in 1985, Dr. Hughes worked in schools for 14 years as a general and special education teacher, a state-level consultant, and an educational diagnostician. His research interests focus on the development and validation of self-instructional strategies to help students with learning and behavior problems manage their academic and classroom behaviors. He has published over 100 articles, books, book chapters, and curriculum materials and has served as President and Executive Director of the Council for Exceptional Children's Division for Learning Disabilities and editor of the Council's journal *Learning Disabilities Research and Practice*.

Preface

As educators, we all have the same goal: to help our students make the maximum possible academic gains in a positive, respectful environment that promotes their success and nurtures their desire to learn. One of the greatest tools available to us in this pursuit is **explicit instruction**—instruction that is systematic, direct, engaging, and success oriented. The effectiveness of explicit instruction has been validated again and again in research involving both general education and special education students. While it has proven to be very helpful for normally progressing students, it is essential for students with learning challenges. Explicit instruction is absolutely necessary in teaching content that students could not otherwise discover. For example, without explicit input, how would an individual discover the sound associated with a letter, the quantity associated with a number, the steps in an efficient math algorithm, the order of operations in algebra, the process for sounding out words, the construction of a persuasive essay, the elements in scientific inquiry, or a spelling rule for dropping the final *e*? Explicit instruction is helpful not only when discovery is impossible, but when discovery may be inaccurate, inadequate, incomplete, or inefficient. For example, a student may generate a strategy for taking notes on text, but the strategy may be laborious and the notes incomprehensible. This student would benefit from explicit instruction on a more effective alternative. Another student may have a cursory idea of a concept through reading text, but may need explicit instruction to ensure that the nuances of the concept are understood.

The goal of this book is to empower teachers in the use of explicit instruction, given that it is both an *effective* and *efficient* procedure for teaching our children. We begin in Chapter 1 with a review of the basic elements, principles, and research on explicit instruction. In Chapters 2, 3, and 4, explicit instruction is applied to skills and strategies, vocabulary and concepts, and rules—three types of content that all educators teach and that students have difficulty discovering independently. Within these chapters, basic instructional procedures are presented and illustrated with example lessons representing many content areas, grade levels, and student populations (special education and general education). In Chapter 2, a general model of instruction including the steps of modeling, prompted or guided practice, and unprompted practice (referred to as **I do it. We do it. You do it.**) is introduced and applied to the teaching of skills and strategies in which students perform some behavior (e.g., sounding out a word, writing a coherent paragraph, completing a science experiment). Chapter 3 focuses on research-validated practices for selecting and teaching vocabulary terms and their underlying conceptual base, using both examples and non-examples. Chapter 4 concentrates on the importance of using examples and non-examples when teaching rules or lawful (If–Then) relationships.

Although teachers are certainly empowered when they understand the explicit instructional steps involved in teaching this content, there is so much more to teaching than developing lesson plans. In Chapter 5, we focus on establishing an environment and climate that supports both teachers and students. We provide suggestions for organizing the physical space and for establishing and introducing classroom rules, guidelines, procedures, and routines. When these systematic actions are taken, the resulting environment will be more peaceful and productive.

Perhaps the most important aspect of explicit instruction is the delivery of lessons. A teacher can design a perfect lesson plan, but if this plan is delivered in a manner that fails to involve or engage students, learning will not occur. Because effective delivery of instruction is paramount in explicit instruction, two chapters are dedicated to this topic. Chapter 6 presents scientifically validated procedures for gaining responses in small or large groups, with abundant examples to enliven the procedures. Chapter 7 extends the discussion of delivery skills with an emphasis on monitoring students' responses, providing feedback on correct and incorrect responses, and maintaining a brisk pace that helps to engage students.

Chapter 8 concentrates on a topic too seldom discussed and implemented in classrooms: appropriate practice, including initial, distributed, and cumulative practice implemented as independent work or homework. If skills, strategies, vocabulary, concepts, or rules are briefly introduced without adequate subsequent practice, the result is that students are "overexposed and underdeveloped," lacking the level of mastery and automaticity needed for effortless performance.

In keeping with the book's focus on explicit instruction, we have marshaled the same procedures in writing each of the chapters. Each teaching procedure is explained, then modeled with example items and lessons and in some cases contrasted with non-example lessons, and finally practiced through the application exercises. However, it is difficult to capture in print the dynamic, interactive nature of instruction. For this reason, we have established a companion website (*www. explicitinstruction.org*) where you can watch or download video clips of lessons

illustrating the book's procedures. Other materials, such as additional example lessons and application exercises, are also posted on the website.

You may be wondering: How does this book fit into a series titled *What Works for Special-Needs Learners*? The answers are **intervention and prevention**. First, explicit instruction is at the heart of scientifically based **interventions** for specialneeds learners in all of the content areas covered in previous books in this series: word recognition, reading comprehension, writing, and mathematics. Research (see Chapter 1) has made it very clear that interventions for special-needs students, whether intensive or strategic, require well-organized, explicit instruction that is unambiguous if they are to thrive academically. Second, explicit instruction is also at the heart of **prevention**—those actions taken in our schools to reduce the number of students requiring strategic or intensive interventions and to promote achievement gains across students. Given that the research supporting explicit instruction is equally strong in regard to teaching academic skills, strategies, and concepts in general education classes (especially in the areas of reading, writing, and mathematics), initial instruction must be clear, explicit, and engaging so that all students can thrive.

Our desire in writing this book is to support *you*, the teachers, who have the very demanding task of delivering instruction on a daily basis, knowing that the fate of children's academic growth is truly in your hands. As you read these chapters, including the embedded example lessons, you will find that they reinforce much of what you already know. Be sure to acknowledge your current knowledge. In some cases, you will be reminded of a practice that you are currently not using but could include or reinstate within your daily teaching. Finally, we hope to expand your knowledge of effective and efficient teaching, for it is our strong belief that "how well you teach = how well they learn."

As you will see, effective and efficient explicit instruction requires that we attend to the details of instruction because the details do make a significant difference in providing quality instruction that promotes growth and success. Thus, we must remember our English teacher's mantra: Don't forget to dot your *i*s and cross your *t*s. (Did you miss the designer's humor in creating the cover?)

With deep respect and humility, we thank you for your dedication to children and our shared profession.

ANITA ARCHER
CHARLES HUGHES

Acknowledgments

Both of us have had the gift of rich professional careers, extending over many decades. During that time, countless teachers, professors, researchers, educators, writers, collaborators, and speakers have contributed to our knowledge, practice, and vision, making detailed and accurate acknowledgments difficult. The impetus for penning this book came from the thousands of preservice and inservice teachers we have instructed, and especially from their positive feedback about the benefits of explicit instruction for their students' learning.

In the course of writing this book, numerous individuals have supported our efforts. We are grateful to Dr. Rachel Wannarka for her insightful editing of early versions of several chapters and to Dr. Steve Graham, coeditor of this series, for his invaluable analysis of the original manuscript, leading to a much more cogent text. Finally, we would like to acknowledge the contributions of Dr. Mary Gleason, who carefully edited all of the chapters and checked the examples for teaching efficacy. Her brilliance and exceptional knowledge of instruction is woven into the fabric of this book.

Contents

Contents

Contents   xiii

CHAPTER 1

Exploring the Foundations of Explicit Instruction

In the quest to maximize students' academic growth, one of the best tools available to educators is **explicit instruction**, a structured, systematic, and effective methodology for teaching academic skills. It is called **explicit** because it is an unambiguous and direct approach to teaching that includes both instructional design and delivery procedures. Explicit instruction is characterized by a series of supports or **scaffolds**, whereby students are guided through the learning process with clear statements about the purpose and rationale for learning the new skill, clear explanations and demonstrations of the instructional target, and supported practice with feedback until independent mastery has been achieved. Rosenshine (1987) described this form of instruction as "a systematic method of teaching with emphasis on proceeding in small steps, checking for student understanding, and achieving active and successful participation by all students" (p. 34). In this chapter, we establish the foundation for the remaining chapters by exploring the following topics: (1) elements of explicit instruction, (2) the underlying principles of effective instruction, and (3) the research evidence supporting explicit instruction. We also respond to possible concerns about an explicit approach to teaching.

ELEMENTS OF EXPLICIT INSTRUCTION

Educational researchers (e.g., Brophy & Good, 1986; Christenson, Ysseldyke, & Thurlow, 1989; Gersten, Schiller, & Vaughn, 2000; Hughes, 1998; Marchand-

1

Martella, Slocum, & Martella, 2004; Rosenshine, 1997; Rosenshine & Stevens, 1986; Simmons, Fuchs, Fuchs, Mathes, & Hodge, 1995; Swanson, 2001) have identified a range of instructional behaviors and elements characteristic of an explicit approach to teaching. These 16 instructional elements are listed and briefly described in Figure 1.1. They are illustrated in more detail in subsequent chapters of this book.

FIGURE 1.1. Sixteen elements of explicit instruction.

1. **Focus instruction on critical content.** Teach skills, strategies, vocabulary terms, concepts, and rules that will empower students in the future and match the students' instructional needs.

2. **Sequence skills logically.** Consider several curricular variables, such as teaching easier skills before harder skills, teaching high-frequency skills before skills that are less frequent in usage, ensuring mastery of prerequisites to a skill before teaching the skill itself, and separating skills and strategies that are similar and thus may be confusing to students.

3. **Break down complex skills and strategies into smaller instructional units.** Teach in small steps. Segmenting complex skills into smaller instructional units of new material addresses concerns about cognitive overloading, processing demands, and the capacity of students' working memory. Once mastered, units are **synthesized** (i.e., practiced as a whole).

4. **Design organized and focused lessons.** Make sure lessons are organized and focused, in order to make optimal use of instructional time. Organized lessons are on topic, well sequenced, and contain no irrelevant digressions.

5. **Begin lessons with a clear statement of the lesson's goals and your expectations.** Tell learners clearly what is to be learned and why it is important. Students achieve better if they understand the instructional goals and outcomes expected, as well as how the information or skills presented will help them.

6. **Review prior skills and knowledge before beginning instruction.** Provide a review of relevant information. Verify that students have the prerequisite skills and knowledge to learn the skill being taught in the lesson. This element also provides an opportunity to link the new skill with other related skills.

7. **Provide step-by-step demonstrations.** Model the skill and clarify the decision-making processes needed to complete a task or procedure by thinking aloud as you perform the skill. Clearly demonstrate the target skill or strategy, in order to show the students a model of proficient performance.

8. **Use clear and concise language.** Use consistent, unambiguous wording and terminology. The complexity of your speech (e.g., vocabulary, sentence structure) should depend on students' receptive vocabulary, to reduce possible confusion.

9. **Provide an adequate range of examples and non-examples.** In order to establish the boundaries of when and when not to apply a skill, strategy, concept, or rule, provide a wide range of examples and non-examples. A wide range of examples illustrating situations when the skill will be used or applied is necessary so that students do not underuse it. Conversely, presenting a wide range of non-examples reduces the possibility that students will use the skill inappropriately.

10. **Provide guided and supported practice.** In order to promote initial success and build confidence, regulate the difficulty of practice opportunities during the lesson, and provide students with guidance in skill performance. When students demonstrate success, you can gradually increase task difficulty as you decrease the level of guidance.

(cont.)

FIGURE 1.1. *(cont.)*

11. **Require frequent responses.** Plan for a high level of student–teacher interaction via the use of questioning. Having the students respond frequently (i.e., oral responses, written responses, or action responses) helps them focus on the lesson content, provides opportunities for student elaboration, assists you in checking understanding, and keeps students active and attentive.

12. **Monitor student performance closely.** Carefully watch and listen to students' responses, so that you can verify student mastery as well as make timely adjustments in instruction if students are making errors. Close monitoring also allows you to provide feedback to students about how well they are doing.

13. **Provide immediate affirmative and corrective feedback.** Follow up on students' responses as quickly as you can. Immediate feedback to students about the accuracy of their responses helps ensure high rates of success and reduces the likelihood of practicing errors.

14. **Deliver the lesson at a brisk pace.** Deliver instruction at an appropriate pace to optimize instructional time, the amount of content that can be presented, and on-task behavior. Use a rate of presentation that is brisk but includes a reasonable amount of time for students' thinking/ processing, especially when they are learning new material. The desired pace is neither so slow that students get bored nor so quick that they can't keep up.

15. **Help students organize knowledge.** Because many students have difficulty seeing how some skills and concepts fit together, it is important to use teaching techniques that make these connections more apparent or explicit. Well-organized and connected information makes it easier for students to retrieve information and facilitate its integration with new material.

16. **Provide distributed and cumulative practice. Distributed** (vs. massed) **practice** refers to multiple opportunities to practice a skill over time. **Cumulative practice** is a method for providing distributed practice by including practice opportunities that address both previously and newly acquired skills. Provide students with multiple practice attempts, in order to address issues of retention as well as automaticity.

As noted earlier, effective and explicit instruction can be viewed as providing a series of instructional supports or scaffolds—first through the logical selection and sequencing of content, and then by breaking down that content into manageable instructional units based on students' cognitive capabilities (e.g., working memory capacity, attention, and prior knowledge). Instructional delivery is characterized by clear descriptions and demonstrations of a skill, followed by supported practice and timely feedback. Initial practice is carried out with high levels of teacher involvement; however, once student success is evident, the teacher's support is systematically withdrawn, and the students move toward independent performance. The 16 elements of explicit instruction can also be combined into a smaller number. Rosenshine and Stevens (1986) and Rosenshine (1997) have grouped these teaching elements into the six teaching functions outlined in Figure 1.2.

FIGURE 1.2. Six teaching functions.

1. Review
  a. Review homework and relevant previous learning.
  b. Review prerequisite skills and knowledge.

2. Presentation
  a. State lesson goals.
  b. Present new material in small steps.
  c. Model procedures.
  d. Provide examples and non-examples.
  e. Use clear language.
  f. Avoid digressions.

3. Guided practice
  a. Require high frequency of responses.
  b. Ensure high rates of success.
  c. Provide timely feedback, clues, and prompts.
  d. Have students continue practice until they are fluent.

4. Corrections and feedback
  a. Reteach when necessary.

5. Independent practice
  a. Monitor initial practice attempts.
  b. Have students continue practice until skills are automatic.

6. Weekly and monthly reviews

UNDERLYING PRINCIPLES OF EFFECTIVE INSTRUCTION

In addition to the explicit instructional elements outlined in Figures 1.1 and 1.2, several underlying principles of effective instruction have emerged from educational research conducted over the past 30+ years. These **principles** of instruction can be viewed as the underpinnings of effective, explicit instruction, while the **elements** of explicit instruction can be seen as methods to ensure that these principles are addressed in designing and delivering instruction.

In their review of teacher effectiveness research, Ellis and Worthington (1994) have identified and described these principles, and their delineation serves as the basis for this section of the chapter. The principles are briefly listed in Figure 1.3, followed by a detailed explanation of each principle. Ways in which the 6 principles and the 16 elements described earlier in the chapter interact during instruction are elaborated in subsequent chapters concerning lesson structures for teaching basic skills and strategies, concepts and vocabulary, and academic rules, as well as in the chapters describing effective delivery of instruction.

FIGURE 1.3. Principles of effective instruction.

1. **Optimize engaged time/time on task.** The more time students are actively participating in instructional activities, the more they learn.

2. **Promote high levels of success.** The more successful (i.e., correct/accurate) students are when they engage in an academic task, the more they achieve.

3. **Increase content coverage.** The more academic content covered effectively and efficiently, the greater potential for student learning.

4. **Have students spend more time in instructional groups.** The more time students participate in teacher-led, skill-level groups versus one-to-one teaching or seatwork activities, the more instruction they receive, and the more they learn.

5. **Scaffold instruction.** Providing support, structure, and guidance during instruction promotes academic success, and systematic fading of this support encourages students to become more independent learners.

6. **Address different forms of knowledge.** The ability to strategically use academic skills and knowledge often requires students to know different sorts of information at differing levels: the declarative level (*what* something is, factual information), the procedural level (*how* something is done or performed), and the conditional level (*when and where* to use the skill).

Engaged Time/Time on Task

The instructional variable of time has two interrelated aspects: how much time is spent teaching and how much time is spent learning. Although these two aspects interact, it is important to note that increasing instructional time alone does not always lead to an increase in time that students spend learning or in the total amount learned. Thus the *quantity* of instruction can be seen as a necessary but not sufficient component of learning; the combination of *quantity* and *quality* of instruction is the key to student success.

Several terms used in the teacher effectiveness literature are related to instructional and learning time. Understanding these terms is a prerequisite to understanding the research findings in this area.

Available Time

Available time is the amount of time available for all activities during the school day/year. For example, if school hours run from 9 A.M. to 3 P.M. there are approximately 6 hours of available time per school day. Of course, other activities (lunch, taking attendance, etc.) automatically reduce the amount of time available for academic instruction/activities.

Allocated Time

Allocated time is the amount of time dedicated for instruction in academic content (i.e., how much time a teacher allots or schedules for instruction in content areas, such as language arts, math, etc.). Some research in this area indicates that allocated time makes up about 70% or approximately 4 hours of the school day, with the remainder used for noninstructional activities. Increasing allocated time appears to have a slight positive impact on student achievement (Anderson, 1976; Walberg, 1986).

Engaged Time/Time On Task

Engaged time/time on task is the amount of time students are actively engaged in a learning task (e.g., listening to the teacher, solving a problem, listening to other students respond, taking notes, reading). Some research indicates that students are engaged during less than half of the time allocated for instruction, or approximately 2 hours per day (e.g., Anderson &

Walberg, 1994; Haynes & Jenkins, 1986). The positive correlation between engaged time and achievement, while stronger than for allocated time, is still relatively modest.

Academic Learning Time

Academic learning time (ALT) is the amount of time students are *successfully* engaged in academic tasks at the appropriate level of difficulty (i.e., not too hard or not too easy). There is some indication that ALT occurs, on average, for only a small percentage of the day (i.e., about 20% of allocated time or 50 minutes per day) in many classrooms (Fisher et al., 1978). Such a small percentage is unfortunate, given the strong link between ALT and achievement. It is worth noting that many elements of explicit instruction and many teaching techniques that we describe in the remaining chapters of this book focus on increasing ALT. That is, they are designed to promote teaching appropriate tasks and increasing the amount of time students are engaged in these tasks at a high level of success. In addition to methods discussed later in the book, some relatively simple and straightforward ways of increasing both quantity and quality of instructional time are presented in Figure 1.4. In Figure 1.5, you will see how one teacher uses these guidelines to increase the amount of ALT in her classroom.

High Levels of Success

As noted above, increasing engaged time has a positive impact on student learning. However, it is when students are *both engaged and successful* that they learn the most. Merely engaging in a task or performing a skill is not useful if the percentage of errors is too high; in essence, students are spending their time practicing errors. Although student errors or incorrect responses are most likely to occur during initial instruction, you can make learning more efficient for students by minimizing and correcting these errors as soon as they occur. High success rates are positively correlated with increased learning outcomes; conversely, low rates of suc-

FIGURE 1.4. Ways of optimizing instructional time.

1. **Increase allocated time and time spent teaching in critical content areas.**

2. **Ensure an appropriate match between what is being taught and the instructional needs of students.** Consider the importance of the skill and the level of difficulty. Verify that students have the prerequisite knowledge to learn the skill.

3. **Start lessons on time and stick to the schedule.**

4. **Teach in groups as much as possible.** Teaching students in large and small groups increases both ALT and the amount of instruction for each student, as compared to other instructional arrangements such as one-to-one instruction or seatwork. Seatwork is useful for practicing newly acquired skills to build retention and fluency, but it is not a substitute for well-designed group instruction.

5. **Be prepared.** Often instructional time is lost because teachers don't have their teaching materials organized and ready for instruction. Thus they must spend time gathering their thoughts and materials that they could be using for teaching.

6. **Avoid digressions.** When teaching, stay on topic and avoid spending time on unrelated content. This is not to say that using appropriate humor or providing anecdotes or analogies to illustrate and illuminate content should be avoided, but rather that doing so should serve an instructional purpose.

7. **Decrease transition time. Transition time** refers to moving from one instructional activity to another. Often instructional time is lost through inefficient and disorganized transitions.

8. **Use routines. Routines** refer to the usual or unvarying way activities are carried out in the classroom. Routines save time because both students and teachers know how and what they are supposed to do without having to think or ask about it. In relation to instructional activities (e.g., group instruction, seatwork, cooperative groups), students know how and when they can get needed materials, ask for help, and so on. These routines are typically taught at the beginning of the year and reinforced as the year progresses. (Routines are discussed in detail in Chapter 5.)

cess are correlated with negative outcomes (Berliner, 1980). Brophy and Evertson (1976) analyzed the research on teacher effects (which we expand upon later in this chapter), and posited that optimal rates of correct responding should be about 80% during initial instruction and approximately 90–95% when students are engaged in independent practice.

In order for high rates of success to occur during instruction, several design and delivery factors must be considered. Briefly, some of the factors that increase level of success include teaching material that is not too difficult (although scaffolding procedures allow teachers to teach skills that otherwise might be too advanced or difficult for students to learn through more minimally guided teaching approaches), clear presentations, dynamic modeling of skills and strategies, supported practice, active participation, careful monitoring of student responses, and immediate corrective feedback.

FIGURE 1.5. Case study: Analyzing instructional time.

Ms. Talbot, a special education teacher, has decided she wants to increase the amount of time spent on academic instruction, now that she is aware of how important this principle is to student learning. To begin this process, she examines the amount of time she currently devotes to each academic area during the day. Although her current schedule of instruction is fairly full, she decides that she can increase the daily allocated time for language arts if she adds 10 more minutes. This will result in 30 hours of additional time that can be used for academic instruction over the course of the school year.

Ms. Talbot is also aware that merely allotting time for instruction is insufficient by itself, and that many things can get in the way of using the time optimally (i.e., keeping students engaged successfully). To begin the process of optimizing the use of allocated time throughout the school day, she spends the next week collecting some data: the number of transitions that take place between activities, how long they take, how much of that time is spent in nonacademic activities (e.g., students' asking questions about where things are or what they should do), whether she starts and ends her lessons on time, and so on. At the end of the week, she can readily see that there is a fair amount of "wasted" time.

She decides to develop and teach more routines, so that students throughout the school day know exactly what to do when it is time for the next instructional session (e.g., put away materials from the last activity, get out materials for the next activity). She also begins to make a concentrated effort to start each instructional session on time. She estimates that just doing these things will increase the potential amount of time students are actively engaged in academic activities by about 10 minutes a day or approximately 30 hours a year.

Because Ms. Talbot is aware that instructional time for each student can be increased by grouping whenever this is practical, she examines how she arranges instruction during the day. She notices that she spends a fair amount of her instructional time working one-on-one with her students. Although they certainly need this level of individualization to some extent, she also sees that she can increase the amount of instruction they get through grouping by skill level. She changes how she spends her time teaching by teaching in groups for half of the class period, working with individual students who need some "boosting" for a third of the period, and using the rest of the time for other arrangements such as well-designed peer and group activities. Because of these changes, students in her classes are now receiving more instruction than in the past.

Content Coverage/Opportunity to Learn

Content coverage refers to the amount of content actually presented (vs. time allocated) to students. Put another way, the more content that is covered well, the greater the potential for student learning. To distill this principle even further, we could say, "The more you teach, the more they learn." A number of decisions affect the quality and quantity of content coverage, including *what to teach, how to teach it*, and *how it will be practiced.*

Decisions about *what to teach* can be characterized as curricular decisions. You can increase content coverage by deciding what is important for your students to learn. Thus you can examine your curriculum, select critical skills and objectives, and discard or at least deemphasize those that are less critical. For example, you may decide that certain math skills (e.g., alternative bases, Roman numerals) may not be the most important skills to teach, and thus you may choose to spend more time covering more essential skills (e.g., computation, problem solving, measurement).

In addition, content coverage can be maximized when teachers focus on skills, strategies, concepts, or rules that will generalize to many other items or situations. For example, instead of teaching the pronunciation of each word as a specific entity, a teacher can introduce letter–sound associations and decoding strategies that can be applied to many words. Similarly, in preparing students for reading a passage, a teacher can examine the list of vocabulary terms and decide to stress terms necessary for passage comprehension and terms that would be encountered in the future, only briefly introducing the remaining words. Likewise, a social studies teacher may choose to introduce a "Big Idea" concerning historical events (**Problem–Solution–Effects**) and guide students in using this scheme to analyze numerous events (Kame'enui & Carnine, 1998). This teacher may also systematically introduce learning strategies for doing common classroom tasks, such as reading passages or writing a section summary.

In addition to decisions about *what* should be taught, content coverage is influenced by *how* skills are taught and practiced. Although this is essentially what this book is about, several instructional considerations are directly related to content coverage, and most of these considerations are related to *efficiency*. The more direct and parsimonious the delivery of instruction is, the more content can be covered. There are different ways that academic content can be taught; however, some instructional methods take more time, which has a negative impact on content coverage. For example, if the objective for a group of students is to learn how to write the letters of the alphabet, giving them dried lima beans, paper, and glue for the purpose of forming letters, while possibly fun, is less efficient and effective in meeting this objective than using explicit instruction procedures. Avoiding digressions, decreasing transition times, and increasing opportunities for students to learn by requiring frequent responses will also increase content coverage.

Grouping for Instruction

Students achieve more in classes in which they spend much of their time being directly taught by their teacher (Rosenshine & Stevens, 1986). Generally, group instruction has been found to be the most effective and efficient approach to teaching basic skills. Teacher-led group instruction most likely has this positive impact on achievement because it increases such effective teaching elements as clear explanations, modeling, practice, feedback, and frequent responding.

The instruction, whether in general education or specialized settings, need not be delivered to the whole class; small-group instruction is often more effective. Brophy and Good (1986), in their analysis of instructional grouping in general education, concluded that breaking a larger class into smaller groups is necessary when the class is heterogeneous in terms of skill level (a common occurrence in today's classrooms) and when students are beginning to learn academic skills.

Breaking a large class into smaller groups allows for more practice and repetition, as well as for closer monitoring. Later research on students with special learning needs (Elbaum, Vaughn, Hughes, Moody, & Schumm, 2000) found that instruction in groups of 6–8 was generally more effective than smaller or larger groups or one-to-one instruction. For example, if a special education teacher spends 60 minutes on math instruction using a tutorial approach and has 12 students in her resource class, on average each student would receive 5 minutes of instruction. If the teacher is able to form two skill-level groups for instruction, each student will receive about 30 minutes of instruction. In addition, students who are taught in groups rather than tutored have more opportunity for peer interactions and more practice in academically related skills, such as turn taking, listening to others, and making contributions.

Grouping for instruction is typically accomplished by putting students into groups based on their instructional needs and current functioning level. Although heterogeneous (mixed-functioning-level) groups have some advantages for certain instructional outcomes, grouping by academic skill level allows students to learn the skills most appropriate for them, thus increasing their success. This form of grouping should be used flexibly and should always be based on individual students' needs, which may change over time.

Scaffolding Instruction

Scaffolding in an instructional context is analogous to the scaffolding used when constructing a building. A lot of scaffolding is used as construction begins, but as the building begins to take shape, the scaffolding is removed in stages until the building stands on its own. Also, the purpose of scaffolding in both construction and instruction is the same: to allow individuals to do a task that could not be done without using it at first.

Through deliberate, careful, and temporary scaffolding, students can learn new basic skills as well as more complex skills (e.g., learning strategies, complex math operations, strategies for writing longer products), maintain a high level of success as they do so, and systematically move toward independent use of the skill. Scaffolding addresses several areas of learning difficulty exhibited by many students (especially those with disabilities), including attention problems, working memory deficits, and poorly organized knowledge (Swanson, 1999; Swanson & Siegel, 2001). The amount of initial support needed and the rate at which the support is withdrawn will vary, depending on students' needs. When scaffolding, teachers typically provide high levels of initial guidance and then systematically reduce support as students respond with greater accuracy. As guidance is reduced, students are required to perform with increasing independence until they are able to perform the skill on their own.

Scaffolding instruction can be applied by using several elements of explicit instruction:

1. Taking a complex skill (e.g., a multistep strategy) and teaching it in manageable and logical pieces or chunks.
2. Sequencing skills so that they build on each other.
3. Selecting examples and problems that progress in complexity.
4. Providing demonstrations and completed models of problems.
5. Providing hints and prompts as students begin to practice a new skill.
6. Providing aids such as cue cards and checklists to help students remember the steps and processes used to complete tasks and solve problems.

In summary, scaffolding is an effective approach for ensuring success and building confidence for students while they learn, because it provides the needed support that helps bridge the gap between current abilities and the instructional goal (Rosenshine, 1997).

Addressing Different Forms of Knowledge

Students often need to understand information at differing levels in order to use the information or knowledge strategically. Thus students should be provided instruction that targets different levels or forms of knowledge when appropriate. Although various taxonomies of knowledge exist (e.g., Bloom, 1956; Gagne, 1985; Kame'enui & Simmons, 1990), we focus on three forms of knowledge as categorized and described by Ellis and Worthington (1994). The first level is **declarative knowledge**, which can be characterized as factual-level knowledge, or *what* something is. Here are some examples of declarative knowledge forms:

u When asked to name a letter, can do so accurately. u When asked what sound a letter makes, can say the sound. u When asked what 6 times 4 is, can say/write the correct product. u When asked what the months of the year are, can say them in order.
u When asked to tell the parts of an essay, can respond with "Introduction, body, and conclusion."
u When asked the meaning of *concentrate*, can accurately define it and provide examples of the word's use.

Procedural knowledge relates to *how* something is done. It involves knowing how to perform skills or steps in a process or strategy, such as the steps in solving a long-division problem. Some additional examples of procedural knowledge forms include being able to do the following:

u Fill out a check.
u Solve two-digit multiplication problems. u Determine the main idea of a paragraph. u Write a persuasive essay.

u Determine the pronunciation of a multisyllabic word. u Take well-organized notes on a lecture.

Conditional knowledge refers to knowing *when* and *when not* to use a particular skill or strategy. Some examples of conditional knowledge include these:

u Being able to decide when to use a question mark to end a sentence. u Knowing when to borrow from the next column in a subtraction problem. u Knowing which reading comprehension strategy to use, based on the genre (narrative vs. expository material). u Writing a product that reflects the desired topic, audience, and purpose.

Our purpose for presenting and describing these forms of knowledge is to stress that you not only should teach what something is, but, whenever appropriate, should also teach how something is done and when to do it. When you convey all three forms of knowledge to your students, they are much more likely to become independent, self-regulated learners.

How to Use the Six Principles

The six principles we have just finished discussing are highly correlated with student achievement. In Chapters 2–4, we describe how the elements of explicit instruction and the principles of effective instruction are applied and addressed during explicit lessons.

In discussing these *elements* and *principles*, we have constructed a number of lists. It can be tempting to treat these lists of instructional design and delivery procedures in a "cookbook" fashion (i.e., to follow the steps of the "recipe" exactly as presented). However, it is important to view these procedures in a more fluid manner. That is, not all elements are necessary in all instructional situations, and not all elements are used to the same degree for each skill or strategy taught. Just as master chefs do, master teachers rely on their knowledge of their "customers" to alter how they do things. For example, the amount of support provided via scaffolding will vary, depending on what is being taught (e.g., complex vs. simple skills, new content vs. familiar content) and to whom it is being taught (not all students need the same amount of explicitness or support). It is overly simplistic to attempt to reduce the act of teaching to merely using a specified set and sequence of steps. Effective teachers always supplement the recipe by adding their personality, humor, creativity, and enthusiasm. However, if key ingredients are left out of the recipe, the result can be disastrous. Consider what may happen if a teacher is teaching a group of students to use a new and relatively complex strategy, and the teacher omits verification of prerequisite skills, clear demonstrations of the strategy, supported initial practice, and multiple independent practice attempts with corrective feedback. This is definitely a recipe for disaster!

A CONVERGENCE AND ACCUMULATION OF EVIDENCE SUPPORTING EXPLICIT INSTRUCTION: A SUMMARY OF SELECTED RESEARCH

The purpose of this section is to summarize research from studies about the effectiveness of using an explicit approach to teach academic skills; this research was conducted in general education as well as special education classrooms. We present findings from several literature reviews of effective teaching behaviors published over the last 30+ years. In addition, we briefly summarize the findings of one of the largest educational studies conducted in the United States, which examined the effectiveness of various educational programs designed to help economically disadvantaged students. Our intent is not to present an exhaustive review of all published studies, but rather to succinctly build a case that research over time and from various perspectives provides a strong base of support for using explicit instruction to teach academic skills and content.

Research in General Education

Teacher Effects Research

Jere Brophy and Thomas Good published a chapter in the *Handbook of Research on Teaching* (Wittrock, 1986) entitled "Teacher Behavior and Student Achievement." In this chapter, they reviewed studies conducted from 1973 through 1983 in which the link between teacher behavior and student achievement was investigated. This type of research is often referred to as **process** (teacher behavior)–**product** (student achievement) **research**. Their review included studies from major programs of process-product research conducted in general education classrooms. This body of research included observational, correlational, and experimental methodologies; however, all studies focused on the relationship between teaching behaviors and students' academic outcomes. Typically, researchers conducted correlational studies by selecting a variety of instructional procedures, administering pre- and postachievement tests to students, and then identifying the instructional procedures and elements used by the teachers whose students showed significant gains (Rosenshine, 1997). In experimental studies, teachers were provided training in the use of procedures identified as being highly related to achievement in the correlational studies, to see whether their students would perform better on academic assessments. In most cases, students of the teachers who were using explicit instruction techniques had higher achievement scores than students in control classes.

Brophy and Good's (1986) integration of the findings across dozens of studies identified some overarching instructional variables highly related to student achievement, including several discussed earlier: engaged time, content coverage, and level of success. Another consistent finding was that the instructional elements (teaching behaviors) identified in this chapter typically resulted in better student achievement. Brophy and Good summarized their conclusions about effective teacher behaviors by stating:

> The second [theme] is that students learn more efficiently when their teachers first structure new information for them and help them relate it to what they already know, and then monitor their performance and provide corrective feedback during recitation, drill, practice, or application activities. For a time, these generalizations seemed confined to early grades or to basic rather than more advanced skills. However, it now appears that they apply to any body of knowledge or set of skills that has been sufficiently well organized and analyzed so that it can be presented (explained, modeled) systematically and then practiced or applied during activities that call for student performance that can be evaluated for quality and (where incorrect

or imperfect) given corrective feedback. (1986, p. 366)

Others (e.g., Gage & Needles, 1989; Rosenshine & Stevens, 1986) have reviewed this era of teacher effects research and reached much the same conclusion: A structured, explicit, and scaffolded approach to instruction has a positive impact on student academic achievement.

Project Follow-Through

One of the largest general education studies conducted in the United States, Project Follow-Through, was originally intended to extend the efforts of preschool Head Start programs for economically disadvantaged students into elementary school (Watkins, n.d.). However, due to budget cuts, the focus of this project changed to one of identifying effective approaches/programs for teaching this population of students. The study was conducted over multiple years during the 1960s and 1970s and included tens of thousands of students across the country. The effectiveness of 12 programs was examined.

The researchers themselves categorized these programs based on the description and primary instructional emphasis provided by the program developers. Programs were categorized as (1) **basic-skills,** (2) **cognitive-conceptual,** and (3) **affective–cognitive** models. Basic-skills models emphasized directly teaching basic academic skills. Cognitive-conceptual models included intellectual skill development, learning to learn, problem solving, and other developmental approaches (e.g., Piagetian); affective–cognitive models emphasized self-esteem, problem solving, self-concept, and developing positive attitudes toward learning. All students in the study were administered a variety of measures that focused on the acquisition of either basic skills, problem-solving abilities, or self-concept.

According to Watkins (n.d.), the overall results indicated that in terms of measures of basic academic skill improvement,

"The Direct Instruction model had an unequivocally higher average effect on scores in the basic skills domain than did any other model." Siegfried Engelmann and his colleagues at the University of Oregon developed Direct Instruction (see Adams & Engelmann, 1996, for a description and summary of research on Direct Instruction that includes Project Follow-Through). We offer Project Follow-Through results as support for a direct, explicit approach to teaching; however, it is important to point out that although Direct Instruction includes the majority of the elements of explicit instruction and is based on such principles as increasing on-task behaviors, high levels of success, and content coverage, it is distinguished from explicit instruction by its emphasis on curriculum design (Stein, Carnine, & Dixon, 1998). Aside from this curriculumbased distinction, the overlap of teaching procedures is extensive.

While it may not come as a surprise that one of the basic-skill models resulted in the largest improvements in academic skill performance, it should also be noted that Direct Instruction (along with a behavior analysis program) had the largest impacts on tests of affective measures; most models emphasizing affective development had average or negative impacts (Watkins, n.d.). Though certainly not confirmatory, these results lend support to the contention that success begets selfesteem and not the other way around.

Research in Special Education

Over the past 20 years, several published articles have synthesized various bodies of intervention research with students who have special needs, primarily learning disabilities. In this section, we summarize the findings of these publications as they relate to explicit instruction.

In 1989, Christenson et al. summarized findings of their research on instruction for students with mild learning disabilities. Their synthesis yielded a number of instructional factors that reinforced the need for well-organized and explicit methodologies for teaching academic content. These factors included (1) clear expectations about what is to be learned, (2) clarity of presentation, (3) multiple opportunities for student responses, (4) active teacher monitoring of these responses, and (5) frequent evaluation and feedback. Other factors identified were effective classroom management, creating a positive learning environment, allocating sufficient time for academic instruction, and ensuring a good match between instructional content and student needs.

Vaughn, Gersten, and Chard (2000) summarized findings of several research syntheses that were federally funded through the Office of Special Education Programs. Vaughn and her colleagues examined intervention research on a variety of topics, including instruction in written expression and reading comprehension, as well as grouping practices for students with learning disabilities. In the area of writing instruction, the authors analyzed 13 studies (all of which resulted in large effect sizes) and identified best practices in teaching expressive writing skills to these students. These practices included the following:

1. Explicit teaching of critical steps in the writing process, including models and prompts.
2. Explicit instruction in teaching writing conventions across multiple genres (e.g., persuasive essays, compare-and-contrast essays).
3. Guided feedback to students via teacher and/or peer feedback about the quality of their writing attempts.

When examining reading comprehension research, Vaughn et al. (2000) synthesized the results of two meta-analyses on the topic (Gersten et al., 1998; Mastropieri, Scruggs, Bakken, & Whedon, 1996). They concluded that instruction in reading comprehension "should be overt, and students should have multiple opportunities to practice the strategy under quality feedback conditions before they are expected to use the strategy on their own" (p. 105).

The last area investigated by Vaughn and colleagues dealt with the effects of instructional grouping arrangements (e.g., whole-group, small-group, pairs) on student achievement. They analyzed work by Elbaum and colleagues (e.g., Elbaum et al., 2000), who conducted a meta-analysis of 19 studies that looked at grouping methods and included students with disabilities. The highest effect sizes were associated with small-group instruction.

Kroesbergen and Van Luit (2003) concluded, based on their meta-analysis of over 50 studies of students with math disabilities, that explicit methods were more effective than less direct instructional methods such as discovery learning.

As part of a series of meta-analyses of intervention research, Lee Swanson (Swanson & Hoskyn, 1998; Swanson, 1999, 2001) attempted to identify instructional components or factors that predicted positive learning outcomes for students with learning disabilities. Based on an analysis of 180 published intervention studies, Swanson identified eight instructional elements that accounted for much of the impact of an intervention, regardless of the skill being taught (e.g., reading comprehension, writing skills). These instructional behaviors were similar to the ones described above. They include (1) skill sequencing, (2) segmenting (i.e., breaking down skills for instruction), (3) providing multiple practice attempts with accompanying feedback, (4) scaffolding by controlling task difficulty, (5) using smallgroup instruction, (6) asking questions/requiring frequent responses, (7) modeling, and (8) requiring students to do homework. In addition, Swanson found that cueing strategy use was an important instructional element.

Finally, several reviews of published intervention research focusing on the effectiveness of computer-assisted instruction (CAI) programs designed to teach academic skills to students with learning disabilities revealed similar findings. In addition to assessing the effectiveness of various CAI programss, the authors (Hall, Hughes, & Filbert, 2000; Hughes & Maccini, 1997; Maccini, Gagnon, & Hughes, 2002) analyzed instructional design and delivery features embedded in effective CAI programs. Again, instructional components included error correction procedures with elaborated and corrective feedback, teaching in small steps, clear demonstrations, prompted practice, use of wide ranges of examples and non-examples, and cumulative reviews and practice.

Recent Government Reports: General and Special Education

Three recent reports sponsored by the U.S. Department of Education have also identified explicit instruction as a well-supported instructional approach. In 2008, the National Mathematics Advisory Panel reported that explicit instruction has consistently shown positive effects on the math performance of students with mathematical difficulties, in the areas of both computation and problem solving. That same year, the Institute of Education Sciences published a report on improving adolescent literacy (Kamil et al., 2008), in which instructional methods were evaluated based on their level of evidence (e.g., strong, moderate, low), and this evaluation was used to make specific recommendations. The two recommendations that had the strongest level of evidence supporting their use were providing explicit vocabulary instruction and providing direct and explicit comprehension strategy instruction. The next year, a similar report (Gersten et al., 2009) was published identifying recommendations and the level of evidence supporting them in the area of teaching math skills to struggling elementary and middle school students. Again, the level of evidence for explicit instruction (e.g., modeling, guided practice, corrective feedback, and cumulative review) was rated as strong. It is important to point out that none of these reports stated that explicit instruction was the only way to teach. However, the conclusions were clear: Explicit instruction should be a consistent mainstay of working with students both with and without learning difficulties.

Comment on the Research

This section is not intended to be an exhaustive or detailed review of research supporting an explicit approach to teaching. However, it should be clear that such research does exist, has accumulated over decades, and comes from diverse types and areas of research. Despite ample supporting evidence, concerns about this form of instruction exist, and we would be remiss not to include some discussion of these issues.

RESPONSE TO POSSIBLE CONCERNS ABOUT EXPLICIT INSTRUCTION

We believe that a direct and explicit methodology is helpful to all students learning new skills and content, and is absolutely essential for struggling or disadvantaged learners. Nevertheless, it is important to address some of the more frequently voiced criticisms and concerns about aspects of explicit instruction. Fundamental issues about how to teach and how students learn have been debated for more than a century, and we don't believe we will settle the issues here. Having said this, we now discuss some criticisms related to explicit instruction, many of which are explored in other documents (e.g., Heward, 2003).

Guided versus Unguided Instruction

Terminology aside, perhaps the most basic question in

education is this: "What is the best way to teach students?" First, we believe that there is no one best way to teach. Instruction should be based on students' needs and guided by research rather than by a personal philosophy. With that said, the debate about instruction hinges primarily on how students learn and on what degree of structure and support they need to acquire important skills and knowledge. In some ways, instructional approaches can be put on a continuum of how much guidance and scaffolding are considered desirable in teaching new skills to novice learners (in terms of their knowledge about what is being taught) or intermediate learners. Explicit instruction can be placed at one end of this continuum, and constructivist or discovery approaches can be placed at the other end. In explicit instruction, scaffolding includes logical structuring of curricula (e.g., sequencing, segmenting), explaining fully what is to be learned, and providing the necessary supports and prompts as students begin to learn and apply new information. As noted earlier, approaches at the other end of this continuum are characterized by minimal teacher guidance and structure as students discover or construct essential information (Kirschner, Sweller, & Clark, 2006; Sweller, Kirschner, & Clark, 2007).

Kirschner and colleagues approach the issue of how much explicit guidance is needed for novice and intermediate learners to acquire knowledge and skills by presenting information about what is currently known regarding human cognition and learning, specifically in the areas of working and long-term memory. The results of research in this area indicate that expert problem solvers derive their ability and skills by drawing on their long-term memory of a topic. They know a *lot* about the topic; they can draw upon this knowledge and use it as they learn to solve problems, and thus are better able to "discover" solutions with minimal guidance or support. By contrast, novice or intermediate learners do not have similar stores of knowledge to draw on, and so they are much less able to learn new information and solve problems. The well-documented limitations of working memory—the length of time new, incoming information can be stored (30 seconds or less), as well as its capacity (5–7 "bits" of information)—during problem solving have deleterious effects for novice learners. Because they lack ready access to a well-developed and connected knowledge base in long-term memory, they are left with trying to take in and manipulate complex and novel information within the limited capacity of their short-term memory. For example, if a novice learner is given a problem to solve and is expected to examine the problem and discover a solution, but lacks an extensive, well-connected knowledge base on the topic, the limited capacities of working memory will result in so-called "cognitive overload." This overload hinders efficient learning, often results in errors, and ends in frustration. However, if novice and intermediate learners are given guidance through supports such as clear models or worked examples, the tax on working memory is significantly reduced; the more information and guidance provided, the less the working memory load, and this lessening allows students to focus on what is to be learned. If on the other hand, students do have a well-connected store of knowledge on the topic, a less structured and guided approach may be effective, given the unlimited capacity of long-term memory to be used during problem solving. It is interesting however, that Kirschner and his colleagues report that even for students with prior knowledge, high levels of guidance are as effective as unguided instruction.

Student-C entered versus Teacher- Centered Teaching

Proponents of constructivist approaches to teaching (e.g., problem-based learning, discovery learning) have created a false dichotomy by labeling explicit methods as "teacher-centered" and constructivist approaches as "student-centered."

The implication of these labels is that one approach is more concerned about students than the other. Proponents of constructivist approaches (e.g., Poplin, 1988; Steffe & Gale, 1995; Stainback & Stainback, 1992) contend that students should construct or discover knowledge themselves via exposure to information-rich environments, and that the teacher's primary role should be guiding students as they construct their own knowledge in response to experiential activities, rather than actively role structuring curricula and presenting content to students.

We believe that using the labels "teacher-centered" and "student-centered" to characterize these instructional approaches is misleading and is the result of constructivism proponents' efforts to cast their methodologies in a positive light (e.g., "Our approach is about the student") and explicit instruction methods in a less favorable light (e.g., "their approach is about what the teacher wants"). Such is not the case. Proponents of explicit instruction are equally focused on students. They understand, however, that many students struggle with learning when necessary guidance and support are not provided. We contend that appropriate use of explicit elements of instruction is indeed "student-centered," in that it incorporates what we know about how students learn new material and about the skills they need in order to be successful. In addition, if one looks closely at the applications of explicit instruction elements in the remaining chapters of this book, it should be apparent that all instructional decisions are based entirely on student needs and performance, rather than on a rigid adherence to "teacher-centered" techniques.

Decontextualized versus Contextualized Instruction

As described earlier, one element of explicit instruction is teaching specific and discrete skills and/or subskills. Concerns related to this element include the notions that teaching discrete skills trivializes education, that a "reductionist" approach (i.e., explicit teaching of skills) ignores the whole child, and that processes such as reading are greater than the sum of their isolated parts (e.g., subskills of reading such as phonemic awareness or decoding) (Heward, 2003). To address these concerns, we note first that in addition to the research supporting the effectiveness of explicit instruction, results reported by the National Reading Panel (2000) indicate that teaching phonemic awareness and phonics (to name a few subskills) does have a positive impact on students' overall reading ability (being able to read words in print accurately and fluently, as well as demonstrating comprehension). Second, we believe that teaching the discrete skills constituting an overall skill does have this potential pitfall—*if* the skills or subskills are not linked whenever possible to the overall skill. For example, teaching punctuation skills or sentencebuilding strategies in isolation, without providing opportunities to use these skills in the context of the overall writing process, would be likely to result in the socalled "splinter skill" phenomenon (whereby students do not generalize what they are learning).

Thus, while we acknowledge the *potential* for isolated skill instruction to result in students' inability to apply or generalize these skills to an overall skill set, we emphasize that this can be avoided by making sure students understand how the pieces (i.e., skills) fit and by bringing the pieces together through contextualized practice and expanded instruction. This helps students begin to broaden their understanding and application of skills in less guided and more exploratory activities.

Drill and Practice versus "Drill and Kill"

As noted several times in this chapter, providing numerous practice attempts for students as they learn new skills is a key element of explicit instruction and consistently appears as an important element in teaching students with learning difficulties (e.g., Swanson & Sachse-Lee, 2000). Because drill and practice are integral to learning, we devote an entire chapter of this book to guidelines for providing effective practice. Although we believe that judicious practice is critical for students to commit useful facts, rules, concepts and strategies to memory in order to use them fluently (i.e., accurately, fluidly, and with little thought), some educators (e.g., Kohn, 1998) have raised concerns about the use of drill and practice as learning tools. Among these concerns are that practice (via seatwork and homework) dulls creativity; indeed, practice for committing skills and facts to memory has been dubbed "drill and kill." Part of this contention appears to be based on the assumption that repeatedly practicing skills dulls the mind and does not lead to higher-order thinking or creativity. Instead, students should be given more enjoyable problems to solve on their own, whereby they construct their own knowledge. Through such activities, it is believed, students will become fluent and automatic on their own.

    We have found no research to back up this contention, although we agree with Heward (2003) that regular drill and practice can be "conducted in ways that render it pointless, a waste of time, and frustrating for children" (p. 191). However, when used appropriately, routine practice is an extremely powerful instructional tool that not only helps students learn and retain basic skills and facts in a fluent fashion, but has positive outcomes when students attempt higher-order strategies. As Heward points out, the ability to use basic skills in reading or math without having to stop and think about them allows students to allot more of their attention to solving more complex tasks. For example, if students are not fluent in basic math facts, their ability to solve complex math problems will be hindered: They must use their working memory to remember basic math facts, and thus will have less attention to focus on the problem-solving aspect of the task. Similarly, the positive relationship between reading words fluently (which comes from repeated practice and exposure to words) and comprehending what is read has been clearly documented (Chard, Vaughn, & Tyler, 2002; Kubina & Hughes, 2008). It appears that the adage "drill and kill" would be more appropriately stated as "drill and skill" or even "drill and thrill."

CHAPTER SUMMARY AND A FINAL CASE STUDY

This chapter has several purposes: (1) to define explicit instruction; (2) to describe 16 *elements* that work together to make instruction organized, transparent, and responsive to students' learning needs; (3) to address the underlying *principles* associated with achievement, such as the importance of optimizing academic learning time, level of success, and content coverage; and (4) to summarize decades of research that supports the use of these elements for teaching a range of students including those with learning difficulties, arriving at the same conclusion: Many students need explicit instruction in order to learn and apply academic skills.

In addition to providing a foundation for the remaining chapters, this chapter has been designed to undergird a story—a story of an effective teacher using the elements and principles of explicit instruction to maximize student achievement.

Mr. Davidson is one such teacher.

Mr. Davidson teaches general math to a group of 25 seventh graders, including 3 special education students. Before the present semester began, Mr. Davidson examined the math book adopted by his school district and determined those skills that would be emphasized and others that would be deleted or deemphasized; he also examined the prerequisites skills for each skill, strategy, or concept. In addition, Mr. Davidson identified a number of strategies that needed to be broken into smaller steps to ensure his students' success.

Knowing that time is of the essence, Mr. Davidson decided to use the following plan for daily lessons. To reinforce the use of the plan, Mr. Davidson designed a parallel lesson-planning form and displayed a poster with the plan in his classroom.

1. Have students complete five review items as a warm-up activity.
2. Review any additional prerequisites for the skill/strategy to be taught.
3. Establish the goal and relevance of today's lesson.
4. Model the new skill/strategy.
5. Provide guided practice with the new skill/strategy.
6. Introduce independent practice with the skill/strategy.
7. Provide small-group instruction to struggling students as needed.
8. Review the focus skill at the end of the period and assign homework.

To observe Mr. Davidson is to see a master teacher in action: His explanations are clear; his pace brisk; his monitoring continuous; his feedback positive, corrective, and immediate. Throughout the lesson, he constantly elicits responses: Students say answers together, share answers with their partners, solve problems on whiteboards and paper, and draw diagrams to illustrate concepts and strategies. As students write responses or share with their partners, Mr. Davidson moves around the room examining written responses, listening to explanations, and otherwise connecting with the students. Smiles abound from students and teacher alike, and occasional laughter can be heard by others out in the hall. But most importantly, an examination of student responses indicates that *learning*, not just teaching, is occurring in this classroom.

In the next chapters, we discuss how the elements and

principles of explicit instruction are translated into the design and delivery of academic lessons. As you will see, utilization of the 16 elements ensures that the principles of learning are addressed. For example, carefully structured lessons that include guided and supported practice result in higher levels of student success; teaching at a brisk pace allows more content to be covered; and eliciting increased numbers of student responses enhances student engagement.

CHAPTER 2

Designing Lessons

Skills and Strategies

Teachers of all grade levels teach students to *do* things: forming a manuscript letter, sounding out words, writing a coherent paragraph, keeping a record of assignments on a calendar, solving an algebraic equation, completing a science experiment, writing a persuasive essay, reading and comprehending text, and interpreting data on a chart. The term **skills** is often used as the overarching label for doing something well, whether it is as simple as forming a letter or as complex as writing an essay. Embedded in the broad realm of skills are **strategies**, which are systematic plans or approaches for solving a problem or completing a task that involve a series of sequential steps. For example, students can be taught a series of steps for completing a division problem (Divide. Multiply. Subtract. Compare. Bring down.) or for fixing up their reading comprehension when something does not make sense

(Reread. Look back. Read ahead. Restate in your own words.). Whereas all strategies provide students with a plan that they can execute in response to a problem or task, some strategies also include steps in which the students evaluate their performance or the outcome. This chapter focuses on how to explicitly teach students to **do** things, whether these are referred to as skills or as strategies.

In addition, we describe the overall structure and components of a prototypical explicit lesson and apply it to the teaching of skills and strategies. The lesson design addresses many of the instructional elements and principles associated with student achievement, as outlined in Chapter 1. The components of an explicit lesson presented here are similar to those suggested by numerous authors, though

23

the labels we use differ (Carnine, Silbert, Kame'enui, & Tarver, 2009; Engelmann & Carnine, 1982; Hunter, 1982; Rosenshine, 1995, 1997; Slavin, 2008). A typical explicit lesson is presented in three logical parts: **opening**, **body**, and **closing**. The **opening** of a lesson usually includes several activities that frame the lesson's purpose, as well as ensure that students have the prerequisite skills and knowledge to learn the new skill or content. The **body** of the lesson is where instruction on the new skill occurs, and the **closing** of the lesson provides a review and informs students about what is coming next. Although the lesson structure presented here may appear to be a fixed process of instructional design, it can be adapted, depending on the nature of the content you want to teach and the needs of your students. We are not suggesting that this should be the only form of instruction that you provide to your students. Although explicit lessons presented in large or small groups should be a mainstay of the school day, there is ample time for well-designed cooperative group and partner activities, projects, student presentations, and so on.

OPENING OF THE EXPLICIT LESSON

Gain Students' Attention

Gaining students' attention may seem to be an obvious thing to do before beginning a lesson, but we have seen many lessons begin while students are still talking, shuffling materials, or engaging in other nonacademic activities. If a lesson starts when students are not paying attention, they may miss critical information related to learning. This results in wasted instructional time and possible student errors.

Although there are many ways to gain attention, you should select a procedure and use it consistently. This "ritualizing" makes it clear to students exactly what they are supposed to do; by eliminating confusion about expectations, it saves valuable instructional time. A simple statement such as "Everybody, we are going to start our math lesson now" is actually communicating to students that they need to put away materials irrelevant to the math lesson, get out necessary math materials, and focus on the teacher. Initially it may take some time and instruction to establish a routine for beginning a lesson, but students soon learn to respond to "attention getters" with increasing promptness. *What* you say or do to get your students' attention really is less important than obtaining it before beginning the lesson.

As critical as it is to gain attention at the beginning of the lesson, it is equally important to repeat this process throughout the lesson whenever students are expected to make a response that takes their attention from you momentarily. For example, if your students have written down a math problem and solved it, you should regain attention with a cue such as this: "Look up here. Let's solve this problem together." In other words, gaining attention is a necessity throughout the lesson.

State the Goal of the Lesson

After gaining their attention, provide your students with

information about the goal of the lesson. This clearly lets the students know what they are going to learn. The statement can be fairly short: "Today you are going to learn how to write the lower-case manuscript letter *r*." Or it can be a little longer and bring in related skills recently learned: "We have been working on writing complete sentences. Today you are going to learn how to write a paragraph. A paragraph is a group of related sentences." These statements make explicit what the lesson is going to cover and help students (as well as you, the teacher) focus on the upcoming content.

Discuss the Relevance of the Target Skill

If you have been a classroom teacher for any length of time, you are familiar with the question "Why do we have to learn this?" This is certainly a valid inquiry. By discussing the relevance of the target skill, you can increase students' motivation for learning the skill and the probability that they will use the skill once it has been mastered. Along with identifying the *why*, your discussion could include *where* and *when* the new content can be used, as in this example:

> We have been learning how to tell time to the hour. Today you are going to learn how to tell time to 5 minutes. This is important because everything does not happen on the hour. For example, our reading class begins at 10:35, lunch is at 12:15, and PE begins at 2:10. Tell your partner some times or situations when it would be important to tell time to 5 minutes, not just to the hour. [Teacher moves around the room listening to students' examples, and then asks a number of students to share their examples.]

There are a few things to keep in mind about discussions of relevance. First, although students will ideally come up with *why*, *where*, and *when* they can use the skill, often they are unable to do so, given their lack of familiarity with the skill. In that case, you must directly convey the skill's relevance. For example, students learning to write complete sentences may not know why the skill is important. Second, a discussion of relevance is not always necessary if the skill you are teaching in the current lesson is similar to skills that have already been taught. If the day's lesson is on how to write a particular letter of the alphabet, and students have had previous lessons on writing other letters, the importance of writing legibly has probably been discussed several times and does not need to be repeated. Third, whenever possible, you should include in your discussion of the current skill's relevance the larger context for applying the skill. For example, when you are teaching a particular punctuation rule, the discussion of relevance might include why it is important to learn that particular rule, as well as a brief discussion about why correct punctuation is important when communicating through writing. Finally, like all aspects of explicit instruction, this discussion must involve the students; it should not be a one-way conversation. Even when you have imparted the relevance, you can involve students by having them retell the relevance to their partners.

Review Critical Prerequisite Skills

Frequently, students need to have mastered previous knowledge or skills before they are able to learn a new skill. Knowing whether your students have these prerequisite skills is critical to the instructional process. Without verifying students' prerequisite skills, you might begin instruction only to find that your students are unable to learn the new material; if so, time is wasted and errors are made. To put this another way, content coverage and level of success are both reduced.

One of the first steps in the instructional design process is to *identify* prerequisite skills that would be important to review during the opening of the lesson. Often skills are cumulative in nature, and thus identifying prerequisites is a process of identifying any recently taught skill(s). For example, if you are going to teach two-digit addition with regrouping in a particular lesson, it is important to verify that students can solve two-digit addition problems that do not require regrouping. It may also be prudent to ascertain that they understand place value, especially if this topic has not been taught or practiced recently. Other examples of prerequisite skills are found in Figure 2.1.

Once you have identified the prerequisite skills, review them during the lesson opening. The key principle to a good review is to *verify* that *all* students know how to perform the prerequisite skills. It is also important to distinguish a review from reteaching. A review typically consists of giving students a task requiring the use

FIGURE 2.1. Examples of prerequisite skills.

Skill to be taught	Possible skill(s) to review
1. Measuring to the nearest quarter-inch	1. Measuring to the nearest half-inch
2. Reading consonant–vowel–consonant–finale *e* (CVCe) words (e.g., *cave, make, like, mole*)	2. Reading consonant–vowel–consonant (CVC) words (e.g., *can, top, pin*)
3. Determining when to end a sentence with a question mark	3. Determining when to end a sentence with a period
4. Paraphrasing a main idea	4. Locating a main idea in a paragraph
5. Solving two-digit division problems	5. Solving one-digit division problems
6. Telling time to 5 minutes (e.g., 3:15, 8:45, 2:05, 10:50)	6. Counting by 5's, identifying hour and minute hands, indicating direction of hands' movement, telling time to the hour
7. Determining the perimeter of a rectangle	7. Concepts of perimeter, rectangle, and sides; the addition operation
8. Combining sentences by adding an adjective to the "start" sentence	8. Concepts of adjective and noun; use of the articles a or an before a noun

of the prerequisite skill(s) and seeing whether they can perform the task correctly. A review is *not*:

1. *Reteaching.* Reteaching is only done if needed. Reteaching takes time, and if it is unnecessary, valuable instructional

time is lost.

2. *Asking the students if they remember how to perform the skill.* Most students will merely nod their heads, but this does not verify that they can actually do it.

3. *Asking one or two students to come to the board and solve a problem.* Again, the goal of a review is to verify that *all* students can perform the prerequisite(s).

A review of prerequisites should be straightforward. As stated earlier, give all students in your instructional group a task that requires usage of the prerequisite skill(s), and then evaluate whether or not each student can do it. To take a few examples from Figure 2.1, you can give your students a few problems that require computing two-digit problems that do not require regrouping, give them a paragraph and have them underline the topic sentence, or present some CVC words to read in unison. A typical review might proceed like this:

> Before we work on how to add problems that require regrouping, let's review how to add two- and three-digit problems that *don't* require regrouping. Complete these problems. When you are done, put your pencils down and we will check them.

Sometimes students will have been assigned homework on a prerequisite skill, and a quick way to review is to go over the homework in the lesson opening. This type of activity kills two birds with one stone: It verifies knowledge of the prerequisite, and it allows timely evaluation and feedback to students about their homework performance. Though we have presented the components of the opening in a specific order, in many lessons you will find it easier to review the prerequisite skills, especially if these are embedded in homework, before rather than after introducing the goal of the lesson.

Application 2.1 provides an example of a fairly detailed lesson opening. However, openings will vary in content and length, depending on the target skill and needs of students.

Some openings will not need to be as long or detailed as this example; other openings will include additional information, such as instruction on the vocabulary terms necessary for the lesson or a preview of the tasks that students will be engaged in during the lesson (Hughes, Maccini, & Gagnon, 2003; Lenz, Alley, & Schumaker, 1987; Lovitt, 2000).

APPLICATION 2.1. Example: Opening of an Explicit Lesson

Directions: Carefully analyze this lesson opening, and write down any good practices that you identify. When you are done, compare your list of good practices to our observations (see *Feedback on Application Exercises*, page 253).

BACKGROUND INFORMATION

Group being taught: Sixth graders.

Prior instruction: In the past week, students have been introduced to the concepts of topic sentences and detail sentences. In addition, they have written expository paragraphs (paragraphs that explain).

Skill to be taught: Writing a sequential paragraph.

Goal of this lesson: Students will learn about the organization of sequential paragraphs.

Larger goal: Students will be able to write different types of paragraphs.

Prerequisite skills: Can determine a topic sentence and related details embedded in a paragraph.
Know the meanings of *sequence* and *sequential order.*

OPENING OF THE LESSON

Gain students' attention. Let's get started with our lesson. [Teacher pauses.]

State the goal of the lesson. We have been working on constructing well-written, coherent paragraphs. In the next few weeks, you are going to learn to write different types of paragraphs starting with sequential paragraphs. Sequential paragraphs tell events in order.

Review critical prerequisite skills. Let's review what we have learned about paragraphs. What do we typically begin a paragraph with? *A topic sentence.* Tell your partner the two things included in a topic sentence. [Teacher moves around room, listens to responses, and then calls on an individual.] What two things are included in a topic sentence, Jason? *A topic and what you want to say about the topic.* Perfect! Everyone, read the topic sentence on the board. *There are several advantages to growing up in a large city.* What is the topic? *Growing up in a large*

city. What does the author plan on telling about growing up in a large city? *The advantages.*
    What kind of sentences usually follow a topic sentence? *Detail sentences.* Think of a detail sentence that might follow this topic sentence. [Pause.] Share your detail sentence with your partner. [Teacher monitors and listens to a number of suggested detail sentences, coaching as necessary.] Look up here. Maria, what was your detail sentence? *City dwellers can attend plays, musical performances, and sporting events.* Great! Your detail sentence tells an advantage of growing up in a city. Jared, tell me your detail sentence. *A child living in the city has the opportunity to meet people with different backgrounds.* Yes, that would be an advantage of living in the city.
    Today you are going to begin learning how to write a sequential paragraph. [Teacher writes *sequential paragraph* on the board.] Please write *sequential paragraph* on top of your paper. We have used the word *sequential* in reading class. Tell your partner the meaning of *sequential.* [Teacher monitors.] Everyone, look here. Martin, report for you and your partner. *"Sequential" means in sequence or in order.* Yes, *sequential* means in order. In a sequential paragraph, several events are presented in order. A sequential paragraph tells what happens first, what happens next, what happens next, what happens next, and so on.
    Discuss the relevance of the target skill. There are many times when we might write a sequential paragraph. For example, if you are telling about what you did on vacation, you might write a ————. [Teacher signals for a group response.] *Sequential paragraph.* Yes, you might tell what happened first, second, third, and so on. If you were telling about a historical event, you might write a ————. [Teacher signals for a group response.] *Sequential paragraph.* Think about other times you might write a sequential paragraph. [Pause.] Please tell your partner some times you might write a sequential paragraph. [Teacher moves around the room, listening to students and coaching as needed.] Erin, when might you write a sequential paragraph? *If you were writing a story.* Yes, in a story you tell events in order. When is another time you might write a sequential paragraph, Jerome? *Well, if you were telling someone how to do something, you would have to tell what to do first, then next, until they were done.* I agree . . . we might write a sequential paragraph that tells directions. Fran, you and your partner had another idea. Please share. *If you were writing the steps in a science experiment, you would tell the steps in order.* Another terrific example.
    So there are many times that we need to write sequential paragraphs. Today we will look at examples of well-written sequential paragraphs. We'll also examine some poorly written sequential paragraphs and decide how we can improve them.

To summarize, the opening of a lesson provides students with a clear and focused idea of what is to be learned, how it will be learned, and why it is important to learn. In addition, the opening is used to verify that students are ready (i.e., have the prerequisite knowledge and skills) to learn the new content.

Then it is time to begin the instruction on the new skill or content.

BODY OF THE EXPLICIT LESSON

The body of the lesson is where instruction on the new skill or content occurs. Therefore, it varies a great deal, depending on what is being taught. However, when introducing a skill or strategy, the lesson body generally includes three processes: (1) **modeling or demonstrating the skill** (often referred to as **I do it.**), in which the teacher is showing students how to perform the skill); (2) **providing prompted or guided practice** (referred to as **We do it.**), in which the teacher is guiding students in performing the skill); and (3) **providing unprompted practice** (often referred to as **You do it.**), in which students perform the skill without teacher assistance. These three processes are used to show the students clearly what they are expected to learn, give them opportunities to practice the skill under conditions that promote high levels of success and confidence, and provide an opportunity to demonstrate that they can perform the skill independently at a high level of success *before* being assigned either seatwork or homework.

Modeling (I Do It.)

Modeling is a powerful instructional tool. If the skill you are teaching consists of steps to follow or actions to complete, the best way to begin instruction is to show students what they are supposed to do. Modeling consists of two components: **demonstrating** the skill and **describing** what is being done (i.e., the actions being performed and the decisions being made). The describing component of the model is often referred to as a **think-aloud**. Thinking aloud gives students access to the self-questions, self-instructions, and decisions that occur as a problem is solved or a task completed. In addition to "show and tell," a good model (1) is clear, consistent, and concise; (2) includes several demonstrations, depending on the complexity of the skill being taught; and (3) involves students. Let's examine each of the variables involved in creating and delivering an effective model.

Clear, Consistent, and Concise

Because the think-aloud helps students internalize and remember the steps and the decisions involved in using the new skill, it should include only the critical aspects of the problem-solving/task-completing process. Describing every possible thought or behavior will make it difficult or impossible for your students to remember the key steps. For the think-aloud to be effective, your description should be clear, and its wording should be concise and consistent.

To illustrate with a non-example, the following description of a simple skill— how to write a letter of the alphabet—violates the tenets of an effective model:

> Everybody, watch me as I demonstrate how to write a legible lower-case manuscript letter *h*. First I put my pencil on the top, solid line, and then I draw a straight line down to the bottom, solid line. Then I put my pencil on the line I just drew, right below the dashed line. Then I draw an arch until it hits the dashed line and then curve down to the bottom line. Watch me as I do it again. I start at the top line and then draw a vertical line down to the solid line. Then I put my pencil on the line and draw a curve up to the middle line and then go down.

Although this model is technically accurate in terms of writing the letter *h*, the description is too wordy. Remember, the teacher is expecting students to use these verbalizations as they initially write the letter (of course, after the skill becomes automatic, they won't need to use self-vocalization). A good think-aloud for this type of basic skill should only include a brief description of key actions. The more concise the think-aloud, the more likely students will be to remember the steps and processes. In addition, different words are used to describe the same steps in this model, which also decreases clarity. The first time, the phrase "straight down to the bottom, solid line" is used; the second time, students are directed to "draw a vertical line." The words "curved" and "arched" are used interchangeably, as are "middle" and "dashed." One phrase or word is not necessarily better than the other, as long as students have that word in their spoken vocabulary. The point is to select the best phrasing for the students and stick to it. The following is an example of a better model, one that uses consistent language, is brief, and focuses on the key actions:

> Everybody, watch and listen while I write the lower-case manuscript letter *h*. I start at the top, go down to the bottom line, curve up to the middle line, and then down to the bottom line. Watch again. Start at the top, go down to the bottom line, curve up to the middle, and then down to the bottom.

This model is briefer, more consistent, and much easier for students to remember than the non-example presented above. The second version of it is shorter than the first, though the same key words are used. With some skills, after the first one or two models, the think-aloud can be further simplified as long as the key action words remain. So if a third demonstration were necessary, the teacher's wording might be "Down, curve up, and down," which is much easier to remember!

Provide Several Models

Unless the new skill is very simple or similar to previously mastered skills, more than one model is often needed. The number of necessary demonstrations depends on the complexity of the target skill, the students' ease in learning new skills, their background knowledge in the academic area, and (to some extent) the amount of time the model requires. However, modeling should not be overdone. Often a teacher of struggling students will demonstrate repeatedly. Unfortunately, while the teacher is becoming more adept at the skill, the students are not. As soon as students demonstrate proficiency, guided practice should be initiated, and responsibility for performing the skill should be shifted from the teacher to the students.

Involve Students in the Model

After the first modeling of the skill or strategy, subsequent models can involve the students by asking them questions in which the answers rely on knowledge gained in the first model or on previously mastered background knowledge. For example, after modeling how to compute two-digit addition problems without regrouping, a teacher might say:

> Now I want you to help me do a problem. [Teacher writes 42 + 33 vertically on the board.] Which column do I add first? *The ones.* What is 2 plus 3? *5.* [Teacher writes 5 in the ones column.] What column do I add next? *The tens.* What is 4 plus 3? *7.* [Teacher writes 7 in the tens column.] What is 42 plus 33? *75.*

Note that the teacher is still the one performing the skill. At this point, students are answering questions about the content, not performing the new skill.

These questions and the information obtained from listening to student responses serve three key instructional functions: (1) keeping students involved and active in the lesson, (2) having students rehearse the critical content, and (3) verifying understanding. Because many students have difficulty listening passively for extended periods of time, keeping them involved is imperative. Asking students to "help" during the demonstration promotes increased attention and rehearsal of critical content.

Involving students in this manner and at this point in the lesson provides you with useful information. If your students answer the questions correctly, it verifies that they have an initial understanding of key steps involved in solving the problem, completing the task, or using the skill, allowing you to move on. If students respond incorrectly, you know what steps or processes are causing difficulty and can address these problem areas before proceeding to the next part of the lesson.

Involving students in the model typically takes the form of asking questions after you have demonstrated the skill or strategy one to three times. However, if students already know some of the subskills involved in the new skill, you can involve students earlier in order to reduce the time they spend just watching and listening. Let's go back to the example of adding two-digit numbers requiring regrouping. The teacher can involve students in the first model as shown here:

> Watch me while I show you the steps for solving two-digit addition problems that require regrouping. I want you to help me out with some of the things you already know. [Teacher writes 46 + 27 vertically on the board.] Read the problem. *46 plus 27.* Which column do we add first? [Teacher requests a group response.] *The ones.* That's right, the ones column. Add the ones in your head. [Pause.] Tell me the sum, everyone. *13.* Correct, it's 13.
>
> When the sum of a column is greater than 9, you need to regroup. When we regroup, we write the ones digit (the 3) under the ones column, and then we carry the tens digit (the 1) to the tens column and add that column. Now we've already added the ones column, so what column do we add next? *The tens.* Add 1 plus 4 plus 2 in your head. [Pause.] Tell me the sum, everyone. *7.* Correct. [Teacher writes 7 in the tens column.] Everyone, read the problem and the answer. *46 plus 27 equals 73.*

Here the teacher involves students in the first demonstration, asking questions about skills in which the students are already proficient. New content is modeled without asking questions. After the teacher demonstrates the strategy once or twice, the teacher then begins to ask questions about the new content. For example:

> u If the sum is greater than 9, what do I need to do? *Regroup.* u The sum of the ones column is 13. What number do I write in the ones column? *3.* u Where do I carry the one ten? *To the tens column.*

After several demonstrations, and when students are responding accurately to questions, it is time for students to practice the skill. However, as the next section on guided practice makes clear, students are not given a worksheet or task and asked to practice on their own. Instead, the teacher continues to work with the students.

Prompted or Guided Practice (We Do It.)

The purpose of initial practice activities in an explicit lesson is to provide students opportunities to become successful and confident users of the skill. Because high levels of success are associated with increased rates of learning, students often need teacher-provided supports as they begin to practice new or difficult skills. These supports or scaffolds are gradually withdrawn as students demonstrate success. The level of initial support and the rate at which it is withdrawn are based on student performance (i.e., level of success).

Typically, guided practice is provided through the use of prompts. These prompts can be viewed as *directions, clues, cues,* or *reminders* about what to do when performing the new skill. Prompts come in a variety of forms, with the highest level being **physical prompts** or guidance. Physical prompts are often used with students who have severe developmental delays, or for teaching purely motor tasks (such as tying a shoe or buttoning). For example, after modeling the formation of the letter *h* to a student with significant learning and motor challenges, the teacher might place his or her hand over the hand of the student who is gripping a pencil and guide the student in forming an *h* while saying, "Down, curve up, down." Similarly, when teaching the desired baseball swing, a coach might grip the bat held by a young player and guide the child in hitting the ball while saying, "Eye on the ball. Back, through, connect."

For the most part, **verbal prompts** are used in explicitly teaching academic skills. The teacher provides spoken prompts as students practice the new skill. Verbal prompts include explicit *directives* (tell them what to do), *questions* (ask them what to do), or *reminders* (remind them what to do). To illustrate verbal prompts, let's return to the earlier example of teaching students to solve addition problems that do not require regrouping. After modeling a number of problems, the teacher can guide the students in solving problems by asking them questions to prompt each step in the strategy. Note that the students are performing the skill even though the teacher is providing step-by-step guidance.

> [Teacher writes this problem on the board vertically: 34 + 21.] Write this problem on your paper. Be sure to line up the numbers in the tens and ones columns. [Teacher moves around the room, checking to make sure the columns are aligned.] What column do we add first? *The ones.* What is 4 plus 1, everyone? *5.* Write 5 in the ones column. [Teacher pauses.] What column do we add next? *The tens.* What is 3 plus 2, everyone?
>
> *5.* Write 5 in the tens column. [Teacher pauses.] What is 34 plus 21? *55.*

When using verbal prompts during guided practice, you should use wording parallel to that used during modeling, to prevent confusion. Similarly, when you are guiding students in doing additional items, the wording needs to be consistent, because you are reinforcing a cognitive routine that you hope students will internalize.

Visual prompts are written (e.g., on a poster, chalkboard, SMART Board, or individual cue card) and serve the same function as verbal prompts: to increase students' success as they practice a new skill. Examples of common visual prompts are posters that list steps in the scientific process, steps in the writing process (e.g., Pick a topic. Brainstorm. Outline. Write. Edit. Share.) or steps involved in comprehension monitoring (Reread. Look back. Read ahead. Restate in your own words.).

Visual prompts can be used in initial modeling of a skill or strategy, in guiding students as they practice the strategy, or later as reminders of the strategy steps. In the example found in Application 2.2, notice how the teacher uses a visual prompt (a strategy chart) during modeling and guided practice. Also, notice how similar wording is used across the modeling and guided practice portions of the lesson in order to promote success.

APPLICATION 2.2. ANALYSES OF LESSON OPENING, MODELING, AND PROMPTED OR GUIDED PRACTICE

Directions: Carefully analyze the modeling and guided practice steps in this lesson, reflecting on these questions:

1. What good practices occur during the opening of the lesson?
2. What positive practices are used during the modeling?
3. How does the teacher prompt students during prompted or guided practice?

Then compare your answers with ours (see *Feedback on Application Exercises*, pages 253–254).

BACKGROUND INFORMATION

Group being taught: Seventh graders in supplemental reading class.

Prior instruction: In past lessons, students have been taught how to use the wording of a question to formulate a partial answer. On the previous day, they have read an article about Gandhi.

Strategy to be taught: Students are being taught a comprehension strategy for responding to written short-answer questions. The strategy includes the following steps:

1. Read the item.
2. Turn the question into part of the answer and write it down.
3. Think of the answer or locate the answer in the article.
4. Complete your answer.
5. Reread your answer. Ask yourself: Does it make sense? Are all parts of the question answered?

Goal of this lesson: Students will learn a strategy for answering written questions in all of their classes.

Larger goal: To empower students with efficient and effective reading comprehension/study skill strategies that will enhance their academic performance.

Prerequisite skills: Can read the article accurately and turn questions into partial answers.

Note. Adapted from Archer, Gleason, and Vachon (2005). Copyright 2005 by Sopris West Educational Services. Adapted by permission.

OPENING OF THE LESSON

Gain students' attention. Let's begin.

State the goal of the lesson. Today you are going to learn a strategy for answering written questions. This strategy uses the skill of turning the question into part of the answer that we've focused on in past lessons.

Discuss the relevance of the target skill. There are many times when you need to write out answers in response to a written question. Usually when you write answers, you need to write a complete sentence or a paragraph. For example, after we read each article in our reading program, you will be writing answers to comprehension questions. However, you will also be able to use this strategy outside of school when you answer questions on a job application. Please list classes or situations where you have answered written questions. [Students record ideas as teacher monitors and writes ideas and corresponding student names on an overhead transparency.] Now share your ideas with your partner. If your partner has an excellent idea that you do not have, add it to your list. [Teacher monitors and continues to add ideas to the overhead transparency.]

Let's look at your classmates' ideas. [Teacher and students read ideas: science class, social studies class, English class, health class, state test, application to summer drama camp, Boy Scout badge documentation.] Yes, these are all situations in which you could apply the strategy for answering written questions.

Review critical prerequisite skills. Before we look at the strategy, let's review how to turn the question into part of the answer. [Teacher displays this question on screen: "Why was Gandhi's education in law critical to his later activities?"] On your paper, turn the question into part of the answer and write the partial answer. [Teacher monitors.] Read your partial answer to your partner. [Teacher monitors.] Chloe, read your partial answer. *Gandhi's law education was critical to his later activities in a number of ways.* Excellent partial answer. You used words from the question in your partial answer. Also, you clearly understood what the question is requesting. Aden, read your partial answer. *Gandhi's law education was important to later activities for the following reasons:* Again, an excellent partial answer.

BODY OF THE LESSON

Introduction to the strategy. Let's learn about the strategy for answering written questions. [Teacher points to the strategy.] Read Step 1. *Read the item.* Yes, first you would read the question carefully. Read Step 2. *Turn the question into part of the answer and write it down.* This is the skill that we have been practicing: using words from the question in the answer. Read Step 3. *Think of the answer or locate the answer in the article.* Sometimes you know the answer, but often you will need to look back in the article or chapter to locate an answer or additional examples to explain your answer. Read Step 4. *Complete the answer.* Now you are ready to complete your answer. Read Step 5. *Reread your answer. Ask yourself: Does it make sense? Are all parts of the question answered?* Of course, when you are done, you should reread your answer to be sure that it makes sense and is complete.

Modeling (I do it.). My turn to use the strategy. Read Step 1. *Read the item.* [Teacher displays question.] Read the question with me. *When Gandhi lived in South Africa, what were some of his acts of nonviolent resistance?* Read Step 2. *Turn the question into part of the answer and write it down.* This is my partial answer. [Teacher displays partial answer.] Read it with me. *When living in South Africa, Gandhi engaged in several acts of nonviolent resistance.* Notice that I used words from the question in the partial answer. Read Step 3. *Think of the answer or locate the answer in the article.* I am going to look back in the article. [Teacher looks at the article.] Here is one example: Gandhi refused to move to a third-class seat on a train and was finally thrown off the train. In the next section, the article tells about Gandhi refusing to get off a stagecoach even when he was beaten. Now I have ideas for the answer. Read Step 4. *Complete your answer.* [Teacher displays completed answer.] Read my completed answer.
When living in South Africa, Gandhi engaged in several acts of nonviolent resistance. In one incident, Gandhi purchased a first-class train ticket but was told to move to a third-class seat, which he refused to do. Read the final step. *Reread your answer. Ask yourself: Does it make sense? Are all parts of the question answered?* Read my answer again. *When living in South Africa, Gandhi engaged in several acts of nonviolent resistance. In one incident, Gandhi purchased a first-class train ticket but was told to move to a third-class seat, which he refused to do.* When I reread my answer, I realized that it did not make sense and was incomplete. The answer suggests that Gandhi engaged in several acts of nonviolent resistance, but I only provided one example. Here is my edited answer. Please read the entire answer.
When living in South Africa, Gandhi engaged in several acts of nonviolent resistance. In one incident, Gandhi purchased a first-class train ticket but was told to move to a third-class seat, which he refused to do. At another time, Gandhi refused to sit on the dirty footboard of a coach even when he was beaten. In both cases, he did not respond with violence. He did not fight, yell, or call the drivers names. Now the answer is complete.

Prompted or guided practice (We do it.). Tell them what to do. [Teacher displays this question on the screen: "Why was Gandhi able to practice law in Great Britain, South Africa, and India?"] Let's use the strategy together. Read the question with me. [Teacher and students read the question.] *Why was Gandhi able to practice law in Great Britain, South Africa, and India?* Turn the question into part of the answer and write it down. [Teacher moves around the room, monitoring and coaching.] Read your partial answer to your partner. [Teacher monitors.] Malcolm, read your partial answer. *Gandhi was able to practice law in Great Britain, South Africa, and India because . . .* Great, you used wording from the question in your partial answer. Think of the answer or look back in the article, but don't write anything down yet. [Teacher monitors.] Ones, then Twos, tell the answer to your partner. Begin with your partial answer. [Teacher monitors.] Dalsha, tell us your answer. *Gandhi was able to practice law in Great Britain, South Africa, and India because these three countries were part of the British Empire. The countries in the British Empire were all under the same rule of law.* Excellent. Everyone, complete your written answer. [Teacher monitors.] Reread your answer, and ask yourself if the answer makes sense and if you answered all parts of the question. If it doesn't make sense or all parts are not answered, fix it up. [Teacher monitors and provides feedback.] First Ones, then Twos, read your completed answer to your partner. Partners, listen carefully to be sure the answer makes sense and is complete. [Teacher monitors.]

Prompted or guided practice (We do it.). Ask them what to do. [Teacher displays this question on the screen: "Why was life difficult for Indians living in South Africa?"] Ones, tell your partner what we should do first to respond to this question. [Teacher pauses.] Isabella, what should we do first? *Read the item.* Everyone, read the question with me. *Why was life difficult for Indians living in South Africa?* [Teacher and students read the question.] Twos, tell your partner the next step in the strategy. [Teacher monitors.] Asher, what is the second step? *Turn the question into part of the answer and write it down.* Everyone, do that. [Teacher monitors and coaches.] Ones, then Twos, read your partial answer to your partner. [Teacher monitors.] Ones, tell your partner the third step in the strategy. [Teacher monitors.] Quentin, what is the step? *You have to either think of the answer or locate the answer in the article.* Yes, Quentin, that is the next step. Everyone, I want you to look back in the article so that you can add examples to your answer. [Teacher monitors.] Ava, what is the fourth step? *Complete your answer.* Everyone, please complete your answer. [Teacher monitors and coaches while students look back and write.] Finally, you need to reread your answer. Tell your partner what you should ask yourself as you reread your answer. [Teacher monitors.] Madison, what should you ask yourself? *Does the answer make sense? Are all parts of the question answered?* Reread your answer and fix it up if necessary. [Teacher monitors.] Please read your answer to your partner. Give feedback to your partner. [Teacher monitors.] Zachery, please read your answer to the class. *Life was difficult for the Indians who lived in South Africa because they were treated as racial outcasts. For example, South African whites considered Indians "inferior" because of their race. As a result, Indians faced many racial injustices, such as having to ride in the third-class section of a train or on the outside of a stagecoach rather than sit inside with white passengers.* Your answer is well formulated. You used words from the question, you answered all parts of the question, and the answer makes sense.

Prompted or guided practice (We do it.). Remind them what to do. [Teacher displays this question on the screen: "What kinds of nonviolent actions did Gandhi support?"] Read the item with me. *What kinds of nonviolent actions did Gandhi support?* Use the strategy to answer this question. Be sure that you include words from the question in your answer and that you look back in the article. When you are done, reread your answer to be sure that it is complete and makes sense. [Teacher monitors and coaches.] Read your answer to your partner. [Teacher monitors.] Jasmyn, please read your completed answer. *Gandhi supported a number of nonviolent actions in his campaigns against the British government, in both South Africa and India. These included refusing to fight back when attacked, distributing pamphlets, collecting* *names on petitions, organizing Indians to protest British practices in nonviolent ways, and refusing to move out of preferred seats on trains and stagecoaches.* Jasmyn, a carefully considered answer. You included wording from the question and located examples in the article to complete your response.

As mentioned earlier, prompts begin at a certain level of support and are gradually withdrawn (faded) based on student performance. The highest-level verbal prompt is essentially *telling* students what to do step by step as they work their way through a task or problem. For the first prompted practice item found in Application 2.2, the teacher tells the students everything they should do as they apply the strategy to answering the question, making it almost impossible for students to make a mistake. If the skill is not difficult for the students, it may not be necessary to start at such a high level of prompting. Use your knowledge about your students to determine whether high-level prompts are warranted.

If a high level of initial prompting is warranted, the next level of prompt in the fading process involves *asking* students what needs to be done rather than telling them. If you reexamine the teacher's prompting in response to the next item in Application 2.2, you will see that the directives have been replaced with parallel questions (actually a mix of directives and questions), with similar wording emerging. This prompt, which is still fairly high-level because of its step-by-step nature, requires the students to assume more responsibility for the skill performance.

When students can correctly answer the key questions about the strategy steps and perform the steps accurately, the prompt can be further faded, with the teacher's simply *reminding* students to carry out the critical behaviors. For example, in response to the final item in Application 2.2, the teacher reminds the students to turn the question into part of the answer and to refer back to the article.

As with the decision about what level to start prompting, the decision about how quickly to fade the prompt is based on the extent to which the students make correct responses. It may happen that you fade the level of prompting, only to find that several students are still making mistakes. In this case, the amount of support withdrawn may have been too large, and you may need to put back a little bit of the scaffolding as the students work through the next example or problem.

During prompted or guided practice, it is also useful to ask questions that promote and verify understanding. These questions usually come in the form of "why" or "how" questions. For example, the teacher asks individual students questions such as "Why is it useful to incorporate wording from the question into part of the answer?", "Why should you look back in the article?", and "Why should you reread your answer?"

During the guided practice part of an explicit lesson, it is important to monitor student responses closely, for two major reasons. First, since the fading process is based on student performance, it is critical to know whether students are being successful. Second, monitoring student responses allows you to provide corrective feedback, which is a critical aspect of learning. Both student monitoring and providing feedback are covered in more detail in Chapter 7. When students are performing the skill with high rates of accuracy, the third and final part of the body of the lesson occurs: unprompted practice.

Unprompted Practice (You Do It.)

The purpose of the unprompted practice in an explicit lesson is to determine whether students can perform the skill without any physical, verbal, or visual prompts. This initial attempt at independent practice is performed while students are still in the instructional group, so that you can monitor the students closely and give them any needed feedback. This process is straightforward: Provide students with several problems/tasks similar to the ones presented during the model and guided practice sections of the body of the lesson, and ask them to do them on their own. During unprompted practice, it is useful to have students do one item at a time, followed by checking their answers and providing feedback until they consistently perform accurately. If students are asked to do all the problems presented in unprompted practice before their answers are checked, some students may be practicing errors. When students practice errors, these errors can be very difficult to undo! After students have demonstrated that they can accurately perform the skill without prompts, you can then move to the final part of the lesson—"closing it up."

To summarize, the components of the body of a lesson on a skill or strategy are **modeling, prompted or guided practice,** and **unprompted practice** (or **I do it. We do it. You do it.**). During the modeling phase, you demonstrate and describe the skill, using wording that is clear, consistent, and concise while involving the students by asking questions. When providing guided practice, you support students with physical, verbal, or visual prompts that are gradually faded. Finally, you check understanding by providing and monitoring unprompted practice.

These three components of the explicit lesson body must be viewed not as a static procedure, but rather as a flexible procedure that is dependent on the complexity of the skill and the prior knowledge of the students. In many lessons, the three components may each be identified once in an entire lesson, but each component may also be repeated a number of times within a single lesson. For example, when teaching students to sound out words, a teacher may say:

> My turn to sound out this word: ssssaaaammm (**I do it.**). Sound it out with me: ssssaaaaammmm (**We do it.**). Sound it out by yourselves: *sssaaaaammmm* (**You do it.**). Say the word quickly. *Sam.*

The teacher may then repeat all three components of the instructional routine with one or more words, such as *man, map, sat*, and *fat*.

When you are teaching a more complex strategy, the three components may occur over many days. For example, on Day 1, you model a strategy for writing a paragraph. On Day 2, you repeat the model but involve the students by having them "help" you. On Day 3, you guide students in writing a paragraph using very deliberate verbal prompts to tell students what to do. On Day 4, prompted practice continues with your asking the students questions rather than telling them what to do. This prompted practice is repeated for up to three additional days, depending on the students' level of proficiency. On Day 8, you remind students of the strategy steps before they begin writing, and on Day 9, the students write independently, but still under your watchful eye.

CLOSING OF THE EXPLICIT LESSON

The closing of the lesson is brief. Typically the teacher begins with a short *review* of what was learned. For example, the lesson in Application 2.2 may end with the following review. Notice that the lesson review, like all parts of the lesson, is not static but interactive; it requires the students to answer questions on the material that has been taught.

> You have to answer questions in many classes, and you can use this strategy. After reading the question, you can turn the question into ? *Part of the answer.* Tell your partner a benefit of using wording from the question in your answer. [Teacher monitors.] After writing down the partial answer, what should you do next? [Teacher gives thinking time.] William? *You either think of the answer or locate the answer.* Great. Next you complete the answer and reread it. Tell your partner what you should ask yourself as you reread your answer. [Teacher monitors.] Amber? *You should ask yourself if your answer makes sense and if you answered all parts of the question.*

Following the brief review, often a short *preview* of what will be learned next is presented: "Tomorrow we will practice this strategy again with more difficult questions."

The final component of closing a lesson is assigning *independent work* designed to give the students more practice in the new skill and/or a previously taught skill. Not all lessons end with assigning seatwork or homework on the new skill. Many skills are too complex to teach in one lesson as illustrated above in the example of teaching a paragraph-writing strategy. Accordingly, if students are not ready to be assigned independent work on the new skill, it may be more appropriate to assign independent practice on previously taught skills.

If it is appropriate to assign independent practice during the close of the lesson (i.e., the students have shown that they can perform the skill with high rates of accuracy during unprompted practice), a couple of guidelines should be followed.

FIGURE 2.2. Structure of an explicit lesson.

Throughout lesson: Involve students. Monitor performance. Provide feedback.

First, if the independent work consists of the same task used during instruction (e.g., additional questions on the article, to be answered by using the strategy), you can simply ask students to complete the task at their seats or to complete it as

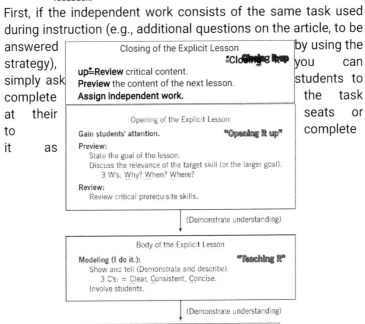

Closing of the Explicit Lesson

=Closing It up
up=**Review** critical content.
Preview the content of the next lesson.
Assign independent work.

Opening of the Explicit Lesson
Gain students' attention.   **"Opening It up"**
Preview:
  State the goal of the lesson.
  Discuss the relevance of the target skill (or the larger goal).
    3 W's: Why? When? Where?
Review:
  Review critical prerequisite skills.

(Demonstrate understanding)

Body of the Explicit Lesson
Modeling (I do it.):   **"Teaching It"**
  Show and tell (Demonstrate and describe).
    3 C's: = Clear, Consistent, Concise.
  Involve students.

(Demonstrate understanding)

Body of the Explicit Lesson

homework. If the task is somewhat different from what was done during the lesson, then it is advisable to go over the new format and explain the directions, as well as to verify that students understand the directions (rather than simply asking them, "Does everybody understand what to do?"). Also, depending on the task and the students, you may wish to model one item of the task and/or to have the students complete one while still in the group so that you can check for accuracy. The topic of providing appropriate independent practice (i.e., classwork and homework) is covered in greater detail in Chapter 8.

The steps in an explicit instruction lesson are encapsulated in the flow chart found in Figure 2.2. You can utilize the flow chart as you complete the following application activities. To illustrate how this lesson structure can be applied to various skills and strategies at different grade levels, we have provided three explicit lessons (Applications 2.3, 2.4, and 2.5). When you are examining the lessons, we suggest that you assume the role of the teacher, perhaps reading the lessons out loud or teaching them to a willing friend or colleague.

APPLICATION 2.3. MODEL LESSON: ALGEBRA LESSON ON PARENTHESES

Directions: Read the lesson out loud or teach it to a friend or colleague. Then go back and note any exemplary practices evidenced during the opening, the body, and the closing of the lesson. Finally, compare your observations to ours (see *Feedback on Application Exercises*, pages 254–255).

BACKGROUND INFORMATION

Group being taught: Eighth graders in beginning algebra class.

Prior instruction: Students have been introduced to the concepts of variable and expression and how to evaluate a simple expression.

Skill to be taught: Using first step in order of operations.

Goal of the lesson: Students will learn the first step in the order of operations: Solve the operations in the parentheses first.

Larger goal: Students will learn all components in the order of operations: (1) parentheses, (2) exponents, (3) multiplication/division left to right, (4) addition/subtraction left to right. They will learn a mnemonic device to help them remember the order of operations: (1) P̲lease, (2) E̲xcuse, (3) M̲y D̲ear, (4) A̲unt S̲ally.

Prerequisite skill: Can evaluate a simple expression.

OPENING OF THE LESSON

Gain students' attention. Students, please put all of your materials away except your math log, a pencil, and your math book. [Teacher pauses.] Look up here.

State the goal of the lesson and its relevance. Today we are going to continue our work with variables and expressions. You are going to learn how parentheses are used in expressions. This knowledge is critical in solving algebraic equations.

Review critical prerequisite skills. But first let's do a little review. Ones, tell your partner what a variable is. [Teacher monitors and calls on a student.] *A variable is a symbol that represents a number.* Yes, a variable is a symbol that represents a number. Look at the expressions 3 + x and t − 6. In the first expression, what is the variable, everyone? It's *x*. Yes, x is a symbol that represents a number. Everyone, what is the variable in the second expression? It's *y*. Correct.

Let's look again at the definition of an expression. [Teacher displays the definition on an overhead transparency.]

Expression:
  u mathematical
  statement u that may
  use
    ⓐnumbers
    ⓐvariables or
    ⓐboth

[Teacher displays the following items on author transparency.]

1. 2
2. X
3. <
4. 2 + 6 − y
5. ⑤

Check each of these items against the definition. On your paper, write the items that are expressions. [Teacher monitors and then asks individuals the following questions.] Why is 2 an expression? *It is a number.* Why is x an expression? *It is a variable.* Why is the heart not an expression? *It is not a mathematical statement. It is not a number or a variable representing a number.* Why is 2 + 6 − y an expression? *It contains both a number and a variable.* Why is the square not an expression? *It is not a mathematical statement. Also, it is neither a number nor a*

variable.
Wow, you really have mastered these concepts! Let's learn more about expressions.

BODY OF THE LESSON

Modeling (I do it.). [Teacher writes 5 r (6 + 3) on an overhead transparency.] Look at this expression. When an expression contains more than one operation, parentheses can be used to show which computation should be done first. So when we have an expression, we first look for parentheses and do the operation or operations inside the parentheses. In this problem, 6 + 3 is inside the parentheses, so I will do that operation first. What is 6 + 3, everyone? *9.* [Teacher writes *9* below 6 + 3.] After I have done the operation inside the parentheses, I can do the remaining operation. Everyone, what is 5 r 9? *45.* The value of this expression is 45.

Look at this expression. [Teacher writes (5 r 6) + 3.] Notice that it has the same numbers and operations as the previous problem. However, the parentheses are in a different location. First we do the operations inside the parentheses. What is 5 r 6, everyone? *30.* [Teacher writes 30 below 5 r 6.] Now I can do the remaining operation. What is 30 + 3? *33.* Notice that the expression has a different value when the parentheses are in a different location.

[Teacher writes 63 − (4 − 3) on the transparency.] Help me do this problem. Should I do the operations inside or outside of the parentheses first? *Inside.* What is 4 − 3? *1.* [Teacher writes 1 under 4 − 3.] Now, I can do the remaining operation. What is 63 − 1? *62.*

Prompted or guided practice (We do it.). Let's do some problems together. Please stay with me so we can do these items correctly. [Teacher writes (63 − 4) − 3 on the transparency.] Write this expression on your paper, but don't solve it. Do we do the operations inside or outside of the parentheses first? *Inside.* Write the answer to 63 − 4 on your paper. Put your pencil down to show that we can go ahead. [Teacher writes 59 below 63 − 4.] Check your answer. Now do the remaining operation. [Teacher monitors and writes 56.] So the value of this expression is 56. Notice that the expression has a different value than in the previous expression, when the parentheses were in a different location.

[Teacher writes 15 − (9 + 6) on the transparency.] Write this expression on your paper. Put your pencil down when you are done. Do we do the operations inside or outside of the parentheses first? *Inside.* Good, find the value of this expression. [Teacher moves around the room and monitors students. Then teacher writes the completed item on the transparency and has students check their work.]

[Teacher writes (15 − 9) + 6) on the transparency.] Write this expression on your paper. Do we do the operations inside or outside of the parentheses first? *Inside.* Find the value of the expression. [Teacher monitors and provides feedback.] Look at these two expressions. They had the same numbers and operations, but different values. You can see how important it is to do the operations within the

parentheses first.
[Teacher writes (35 − 5) − (4 + 2) on the transparency.] Copy this expression. Do
we do the operations inside or outside of the parentheses first? *Inside.* Yes, here you
have two sets of parentheses. Do the operations inside both sets of parentheses and
then subtract. Find the value of the expression.
[Teacher monitors and provides feedback.]
[Teacher writes (9 + 16) − (16 − 8) on the transparency.] Copy this expression
and find the value of the expression. Don't forget—parentheses first. [Teacher
monitors and provides feedback.] Terrific.

Unprompted practice (You do it.). Find the value of Item A. Put your pencil down
when you are done. [Teacher monitors and then provides feedback on the item. This
is repeated for Item B.] Now complete the remaining problems, and then we will go
over them. [Teacher monitors and then provides feedback to the group.]

A. (6 r 5) − 4
B. 6 r (5 − 4)
C. (5 + 6) r (8 − 2)
D. (13 − 3) r (10 − 5)
E. (9 r 2) − 8

CLOSING OF THE LESSON

Review. Today you learned the first step in an algebra strategy called the order of
operations. First, we do the operations that are inside the   . Everyone?
Parentheses. Yes, we always do the operations inside the parentheses before
those outside the parentheses.

Preview. Tomorrow we will learn about the second operation in the order of
operations: exponents.

Independent work. Please open your algebra book to page 5. Complete the items in
Set A. We will check your homework at the beginning of class tomorrow.

APPLICATION 2.4. MODEL LESSON: DETERMINING THE MAIN IDEA

Directions: Read the lesson out loud. Then go back and note how the teacher
involves the students during the opening, body, and closing of the lesson. Finally,
compare your observations to ours (see *Feedback on Application Exercises*, pages
255–256).

BACKGROUND INFORMATION

Group being taught: Fifth graders.

Skill to be taught: Determining the main idea in a paragraph in preparation for learning the paraphrasing strategy:

Step 1. Read a paragraph.
Step 2. Ask yourself, "What were the main idea and details in this paragraph?" Step 3. Put the main idea and details into your own words.

Lesson objective: When presented with a reading selection containing several paragraphs written at the students' reading level, students will be able to determine the main idea of each paragraph.

Larger goal: Students will be able to paraphrase the main idea and details of paragraphs in a reading selection written at the students' grade level.

Prerequisite skills: Read at the fourth-grade level or above; understand the meaning of *topic sentence.*

Note. Based on Schumaker, Denton, and Deshler (1984).

OPENING OF LESSON

Gain students' attention. Everybody, put everything away and get out your paraphrasing strategy folder.

State the goal of the lesson and its relevance. Today you are going to continue learning the paraphrasing strategy. In this lesson, we will focus on the second step of the strategy: You will learn how to determine the main idea in a paragraph. Determining the main idea will give you the "gist" of what the paragraph is about. It will be easier to remember the main idea than to try and remember all the information in the paragraph. Tell your partner how the paraphrasing strategy can help you. [Teacher monitors and calls on a student.] *It helps you understand and remember what you have read. Great. Being able to determine main ideas and details, and then put them into your own words, helps you understand and remember what you read better. Tell your partner when or where can you use this strategy. [Teacher calls on students and receives answers such as You could use the strategy in science, social studies, and health classes, or Whenever you are reading something factual.]* Excellent! Pretty much any time you have to read something and it is important to understand and remember the material, you can use the paraphrasing strategy.

Review critical prerequisite skills. Let's review what a topic sentence is. Here are two paragraphs. Each sentence is numbered. On your slate, I want you to write the number of the sentence in the first paragraph that you think is the topic sentence. When you are done, look up at me so I know you are ready to show your slate. Okay, let's see the slates. You all picked Sentence 1. Why? [Teacher calls on a nonvolunteer.] *The first sentence said what the paragraph is about.* Great answer!

[Teacher repeats this review for the second paragraph.]
BODY OF THE LESSON

Modeling. I am going to show you some steps to go through as you determine the main idea in a paragraph. Watch and listen carefully. [Teacher hands out copies of a passage containing several paragraphs about canoes, and displays the passage on a screen.] The first step of the strategy is to read the paragraph. Let's read the first paragraph together. [Teacher and students chorally read the paragraph.]

To locate the main idea, I will need to ask myself some questions and look through the paragraph. First, I ask myself, "What is this paragraph about?" This paragraph is about canoes. All of the sentences in the paragraph talk about canoes. Second, I ask, "What does it tell me about canoes?" It tells me how canoes look. Listen as I say the main idea. This paragraph tells about how canoes look.

If I am not sure how to answer these first two questions, I can look in two places to help me find the answers. First, I can look at the first sentence of the paragraph. Why would I look at the first sentence? [Teacher calls on a student.] *The first sentence is often the topic sentence.* Great. Yes, often the first sentence is the topic sentence, and the main idea is stated there. Then I can look in the other sentences to see if the keyword or words in the first sentence are repeated. For example, in this paragraph the word *canoe* is repeated, so I am pretty sure the paragraph is about canoes. Once again, this is the main idea of this paragraph: This paragraph tells me about the appearance of canoes. Repeat the main idea. *This paragraph tells me about the appearance of canoes.*

Everyone, read the second paragraph with me. [Teacher and students read the paragraph chorally.] Watch and listen again while I determine the main idea in this paragraph. First, I ask myself, "What is this paragraph about?" This whole paragraph is about Native Americans. Second, I ask myself, "What does it tell me about Native Americans?" I am not certain about what it told me about Native Americans. I can look in two places to help me answer these questions. First, I can look at the first sentence of the paragraph. It says, "Native Americans build canoes from parts of trees." That really helps me. I can also see if a key word or words are repeated. Yes, the words "Native Americans" is repeated three times, so I am sure that the paragraph is about. With this additional information, I can state the main idea. This paragraph tells how Native Americans canoes made canoes from parts of trees. Repeat the main idea. *This paragraph tells how Native Americans made canoes from parts of trees.*

[Teacher begins to involve students in modeling.] Okay, I am going to determine the main idea in the third paragraph, but this time I want you to help me. Let's start by reading the third paragraph out loud together. [Teacher and students read the paragraph.] Great reading!

Now in order to determine the main idea, what is the first question I ask myself? [Teacher calls on a nonvolunteer.] *What is this paragraph about?* So I ask myself what the paragraph is about. It is about dugout canoes. What question do I ask myself next? [Teacher calls on a nonvolunteer.] *What does it tell me about dugout canoes?* Very nice! So I ask myself what this paragraph tells me about dugout canoes. It tells me the process used to make dugout canoes. Listen to the main idea. This paragraph tells me the process used to make dugout canoes. Repeat the main idea. *This paragraph tells me the process used to make dugout canoes.*

If I was unsure about what the main idea is, what sentence should I look at? [Teacher signals for a unison response.] *The first sentence.* Great! Why do I look at the first sentence? [Teacher calls on a nonvolunteer.] *It is often the topic sentence.* When I look at the sentence I see it is talking about dugout canoes. What else can I look at to help me figure out the main idea? [Teacher calls on a nonvolunteer.] *You can see if key words are repeated.* Right again. I look for repetitions of the key words in other sentences. And I see that *dugout canoes* is repeated several times. Once again, listen to the main idea. This paragraph tells how dugout canoes were made. You have a good understanding of the procedure for determining the main idea in a paragraph. Now it is time for you to try it.

Prompted or guided practice (We do it.). Tell them what to do. Read the next paragraph and look up at me when you are done. Now let's determine the main idea. First, ask yourself, "What is the paragraph about?" What is the paragraph about, everybody? [Teacher signals for a unison response.] *Birch bark canoes.* That's right, it is about birch bark canoes. Next, ask yourself, "What does the paragraph tell me about birch bark canoes?" Ones, tell your partner what the paragraph tells about birch bark canoes. [Teacher calls on a nonvolunteer.] *It tells me how canoes were made from birch bark.* Good thinking!

Now let's assume you still need to think about what the main idea is. You will look at the first sentence. You do this because it is probably what kind of sentence? [Teacher signals for a unison response.] *A topic sentence.* Great, it is often the topic sentence. Now, look over the rest of the paragraph and see if any of the words in the topic sentence are repeated in the rest of the paragraph. [Teacher pauses.] What key words are repeated? [Teacher calls on a student.] *The word "bark" is repeated.* Think . . . what is the main idea of the paragraph? [Teacher provides thinking time.] Ones, tell your partner the main idea. Begin by saying: This paragraph tells . . . [Teacher monitors.] Anthony, state the main idea. *This paragraph tells how canoes were made from birch bark.* Yes, I agree. Write the main idea under the paragraph. [Teacher monitors.]

Prompted or guided practice (We do it.). Ask them what to do. Read the next paragraph and look up at me when you are done. Now let's determine the main idea. Ones, tell your partner: What question do we ask first? [Teacher monitors.] Grace? *What is the paragraph about?* Yes, that is the first question. Everyone, what is the paragraph about? [Teacher signals for a unison response.] *Canoes.* Yes, it is about canoes . . . but specifically about modern canoes. Twos, tell your partner what you should ask yourself next. [Teacher monitors.] Felix? *What does the paragraph tell me about modern canoes?* Ones, tell your partner what the paragraph tells about today's canoes. [Teacher calls on a nonvolunteer.] Ava? *It tells about various types of modern canoes.* Good thinking! Where would you look in the paragraph that might help you determine the main idea? [Teacher provides thinking time.] Ones, tell your partner the main idea. Begin by saying. "This paragraph tells . . . " [Teacher monitors.] Hamilton, state the main idea. *This paragraph tells me about different kinds of* *modern canoes.* Yes, I agree. Write the main idea under the paragraph. [Teacher monitors.]

Prompted or guided practice (We do it.). Remind them how to do it. Okay, let's do one more. Read the next paragraph and find the main idea. Remember to ask yourselves the two questions and, if you need to, look for clues about what the main idea is within the paragraph. Please write your main idea under the paragraph. [Teacher monitors.] Bryan, please state your main idea. *This paragraph tells how today's canoes are used recreationally.*

Great work. Who figured out the main ideas after asking the two questions? Did anybody have to look at the topic sentence and word repetitions to be sure?

Unprompted practice (You do it.). Everybody has done a good job of using the procedure to determine the main idea of a paragraph. Now I would like to see if you can do it entirely on your own. Here are four more paragraphs. Determine the main idea of the first paragraph, and write it underneath the paragraph. When you are done, put your pencil down so I know you are finished. [Teacher monitors and provides feedback to students. Teacher repeats with an additional paragraph, monitoring and providing feedback on the second main idea. Because of the students' accuracy on the first two main ideas, teacher then has them complete the final two items; teacher continues to monitor and provide corrective feedback.]

CLOSING OF THE LESSON

Review. Again, great work. You really know how to use the procedure to determine the main idea.

Twos, tell your partner why this is important to do. [Teacher monitors and then calls on an individual.] *You can remember the main idea . . . and it really makes you think about the paragraph.* Ones, tell your partner: What questions do you ask yourself to determine the main idea? [Teacher asks a nonvolunteer.] Marcus? *You ask yourself: What is the paragraph about? And what does it tell me about that topic?* If you have difficulty figuring out the main idea, where is one place you can look? [Teacher calls on another student.] *You can read the first sentence. You can also look for repeated key words.*

Preview. Tomorrow we will continue to work on learning the paraphrasing strategy. You will learn how to locate and determine details related to the main idea of a paragraph.

Independent work. For homework tonight, I want you to select one of your textbooks from any of your classes and determine the main idea for three consecutive paragraphs. For each paragraph, write down the main idea. Tomorrow I will check to see how you did, and we will discuss how the procedure worked for you.

APPLICATION 2.5. Model Lessons: Three Consecutive

SENTENCE-COMBINING LESSONS

Directions: Many skills and strategies need to be taught over a number of days. Thus the modeling, guided practice, and unprompted practice may not all occur in a single lesson. In the following three 15-minute lessons, students are learning how to combine two sentences. Read each of the three lessons. Then go back and reread the three lessons, noting how the teacher alters the opening, the body, and the closing, and speculating on why the changes are made. Finally, compare your observations with ours (see *Feedback on Application Exercises*, pages 256–257).

BACKGROUND INFORMATION

Group being taught: Seventh graders with learning disabilities in a writing class.

Prerequisite skills: Meaning of *adjective*; correct use of *a* and *an* before a noun.

Skill/strategy to be taught: Combining sentences that include adjectives.

Goal of lessons: Students will be able to combine two sentences by adding an adjective to the stem sentence.

Larger goal: Students will be able to combine two to five sentences in order to create longer, more sophisticated sentences and to reduce redundancy in their writing.

Prerequisite skills: Identifying adjectives. Using a and an/

Note. Adapted from Archer, Gleason, and Isaacson (2008). Copyright 2008 by Sopris West Educational Services. Adapted by permission.

DAY 1

Stimuli on transparency and students' papers

Lesson: Sentence combining.

Opening of the Lesson

Gain students' attention. Look up here. Let's begin.

State the goal of the lesson. At the beginning of our language arts class each day, we are going to practice combining sentences. You will learn how to combine two, three, four, or even five sentences into a single well-written sentence.

Discuss the relevance of the skill. When we combine sentences, we end up with longer sentences that are often more sophisticated, more mature, and more interesting to the reader. Also, combining sentences will often reduce redundancy in your paragraphs. *Redundancy* is the repeating of information.

1. Bristol Park has a vast, grassy <u>expanse</u> surrounded by <u>rows</u> of towering <u>trees</u> and fragrant <u>flowerbeds</u>.
2. In <u>spring</u>, multicolored tulips, yellow daffodils, and blue irises fill many <u>beds</u>.

Stimuli on transparency and students' papers

As we combine sentences, you will learn about the conventions of English and gain what is called "sentence sense"—the understanding of what

2. **Start: The tracks cover**
3. Add *a* or *an*:
   a. _____ rose
   b. _____ red rose
   c. _____ incredible rose
   d. _____ elegant rose
   e. _____ yellow rose
   f. artificial yellow rose

Sentence-Combining Items
1. **Start: Josh has a ^ train set with 80 feet of tracks.**
Add: The train set is electric.
Create:

sentences are and how they are structured. You will find that combining sentences is something you can do when you are editing paragraphs to improve the quality of your writing. Tell your partner one benefit of learning sentence combining. [Teacher calls on individual students.]

Review critical prerequisite skills. Our first sentence- combining activities involve

Lesson: Sentence combining.

adjectives—words used to tell more about nouns. In these sentences, I have underlined the nouns. If the noun has an adjective that tells about it, circle the adjective. [Teacher monitors and then gives feedback on the answers.]

the garage floor.
When we want to indicate that there is one thing, we place the article *a* or *an* in front of the noun. When do we use the

article *a*? [Teacher calls on a student.] *When the word begins* *with a consonant sound.* Right. When do we use the article and the word after the article sound right together.
[Teacher monitors and provides feedback.]
Now, let's combine sentences that include adjectives.

Body of the Lesson
Modeling (I do it.). Look up here. [Teacher directs students' attention to the overhead.] We are going to combine sentences. We will always begin with a "Start" sentence. Read the "Start" sentence with me. *Josh has a train set with 80 feet of track.* Now read the "Add" sentence. *The train set is electric.* The word

the article
an? [Teacher calls on a student.] *When the word begins with a* *vowel sound.* Find Item 3. Add the article *a* or *an*. Be sure that

Add: The tracks are winding.

Create:

electric tells about the train set. I underline the word *electric.* Now I want to add *electric* to the "Start" sentence. Because *electric* tells about the train, I am going to insert the word before *train.* [Teacher writes *electric* above the ^.] Now I have to change the article *a* to *an*, because electric begins with a vowel sound. Read the new sentence. *Josh has an electric train set with 80 feet of tracks.* Write the new sentence after "Create."

Prompted or guided practice (We do it.). Let's combine sentences together. Find Item 2. Read the "Start" sentence. *The tracks cover the garage floor.* Read the "Add" sentence. *The tracks are winding.* Underline *winding.* Now write your "Create" sentence. [Teacher monitors and then shows the "Create" sentence on the overhead.] Read the "Create" sentence. *The winding tracks cover the garage floor.*

Stimuli on transparency and students' papers	Lesson: Sentence combining.
3. Start: Buildings line the tracks. Add: The buildings are tiny. Create:	Find Item 3. Read the "Start" sentence with me. *Buildings line the tracks.* Read the "Add" sentence. *The buildings are tiny.* What word will we underline? *Tiny.* Write your "Create" sentence. [Teacher monitors and then shows the "Create" sentence on the overhead.] Read the "Create" sentence. *Tiny buildings line the tracks.*
4. Start: Josh pretends that the train delivers things to the buildings. Add: The buildings are miniature. Create:	[The same instructional procedures are repeated with Item 4.] The "Create" sentences form a paragraph. Let's read the paragraph. *Josh has an electric train set with 80 feet of tracks. The winding tracks cover the garage floor. Tiny buildings line the tracks. Josh pretends that the train delivers things to the miniature buildings.*

Closing of the Lesson

Review. You did an excellent job combining sentences. Tell your partner one good reason to combine sentences. [Teacher monitors and then calls on students.] *The sentences will be longer and better. You won't be repeating things in your paragraph. The sentences will be more mature . . . like older writers.*

Preview. Tomorrow we will continue combining sentences with adjectives.

DAY 2

Stimuli on transparency and students' papers	Lesson: Sentence combining
	Opening of the Lesson Look up here. Today we are going to combine sentences that include adjectives. Tell your partner some reasons that we might want to combine sentences. [Teacher calls on individuals.]
Sentence-Combining Items	**Body of the Lesson** 1. Start: Many people in Union City are immigrants.

Add: The immigrants are
            Cuban.

Create:

Prompted or guided practice (We do it.). Let's combine sentences together. Find item 1. Read the "Start" sentence. *Many people in Union City are immigrants.* Read the "Add" sentence. *The immigrants are Cuban.* What word will you underline? *Cuban.* Great. Write your "Create" sentence. [Teacher monitors.] Read your "Create" sentence to your partner. Be sure that it makes sense. [Teacher then shows the "Create" sentence on the overhead.] Read the "Create" sentence. *Many people in Union City are Cuban immigrants.*

2. **Start: Life in Union City is a change for them.**

   Add: The change is huge.

   Create:

3. Start: They had to leave many belongings behind.

Add: Their belongings are precious.

Create:

Find Item 3. Complete it. Don't forget to underline the word that you plan to add. [Teacher monitors.] Twos, read your "Create" sentence to your partner. Be sure it makes sense. [Teacher then shows "Create" sentence on the overhead.] Read the "Create" sentence. *They had to leave many precious belongings behind..*

Unprompted practice (You do it.). Find Item 4. Do

4. Start: However, they feel very welcome in their country.

Add: Their country is new.

Create:

this item on your own. [Teacher monitors.] Ones, read your sentence to your partner. [Teacher then shows the "Create" sentence on the overhead.] Read the "Create" sentence. *However, they feel very* then shows the "Create" sentence on the overhead.]

Read the "Create" sentence. *Life in Union City is a*

huge change for them. welcome in their new

country.

Now let's read the edited paragraph. *Many people in Union City are Cuban immigrants. Life in Union City is a huge change for them. They had to leave many precious belongings behind. However, they feel very welcome in their new country.*

Closing of the Lesson

You did an excellent job combining sentences with adjectives.

Find Item 2. Read the "Start" sentence. *Life in Union City is a change for them.* Read the "Add" sentence. *The change is huge.* What word will you underline? *Huge.* Great. Write your "Create" sentence. [Teacher monitors.] Ones, read your "create" sentence to your partner. Be sure that it makes sense. [Teacher

Stimuli on transparency and students' papers	Lesson: Sentence combining
2. **Start: Butterflies flit from flower to flower.** **Add:** The butterflies are colorful. **Create:** Unprompted practice	**(You do it.).** Find Item 2. Do this item on your own. [Teacher monitors.] Ones, read your sentence to your partner. [Teacher then shows the "Create" sentence on the overhead.] Read the "Create" sentence. *Colorful butterflies flit from flower to flower.*
3. **Start: White-footed mice scurry through the grasses.** **Add:** The grasses are tall. **Create:**	Do Items 3 and 4. [Teacher monitors and provides feedback.] Find Item 3. Ones, read your edited sentence to your partner. [Teacher displays the "Create" sentence on the overhead.] Read the new sentence. *White-footed mice scurry through the tall grasses.*
4. **Start: A hawk swoops down and grabs one of the mice.** **Add:** The hawk is red-tailed. **Create:**	Find Item 4. Twos, read your edited sentence to your partner. [Teacher displays the "Create" sentence on the overhead.] Read the new sentence. *A red-tailed hawk swoops down and grabs one of the mice.*

Now let's read the edited paragraph. *The meadow is a lively environment. Colorful butterflies flit from flower to flower. White-footed mice scurry through the tall grasses. A red-tailed hawk swoops down and grabs one of the mice.*

Closing of the Lesson

Tomorrow you will learn how to add two or more adjectives to a noun as we combine sentences.

CHAPTER SUMMARY

The structure of an explicit lesson as described in this chapter is based on researchbased instructional principles associated with student learning and achievement. The components of this type of lesson are designed to make optimal use of your instructional time, keep students engaged, and promote high rates of success through explicitness and scaffolding procedures.

The **opening** of the lesson makes it clear to students what they are learning as well as why they are learning it. In addition, you verify that students have the appropriate prerequisite skills to learn the new content, and you link the new content to the old. During the **body** of a lesson that introduces skills or strategies, you make the content explicit by starting off modeling for the students exactly how the skill is used, as well as key thought processes (e.g., self-instructions, self-questions). Involving students in the model verifies that they have a basic understanding of the skill, thus increasing the likelihood of success as they begin to practice it themselves under teacher guidance. Guided or prompted practice provides scaffolding as needed to ensure high rates of success. You then fade these prompts based on the students' performance as they move toward using the skill independently. Finally, students are required to demonstrate that they can solve the problem or perform the skill on their own, but in a situation where you can deliver any necessary corrective feedback or instruction. Then and only then should you provide independent practice, secure in the knowledge that your students have the proficiency they need to demonstrate their newly acquired skills with a high level of success. The lesson ends with a **closing** in which the critical content is reviewed.

Although neither the opening nor closing of a lesson changes dramatically with content other than skills and strategies, the body of the lesson is different when the focus is on teaching vocabulary and academic rules—the topics of the next two chapters. But before leaving this chapter, apply your knowledge again with Applications 2.6 and 2.7.

APPLICATION 2.6. IDENTIFYING POTENTIAL PROBLEMS AND GENERATING POSSIBLE SOLUTIONS

Directions: Below are some brief descriptions of teachers' behaviors during an explicit lesson. Identify any potential problems that may result from these instructional behaviors, and then state how they can be corrected (potential solutions). Compare your responses to the ones provided in *Feedback on Application Exercises*, pages 257–258.

1. When reviewing a prerequisite skill during the opening of the lesson, the teacher has three of eight students go to the board and solve the problems.
2. When discussing why the target skill for the lesson is important to know, the teacher tells them all the reasons.
3. When modeling the new skill of solving two-digit addition problems, the teacher demonstrates once and then asks everyone if they understand.
4. When modeling the new skill of solving two-digit addition problems with regrouping, the teacher demonstrates once and then moves into guided practice.
5. During guided practice, the teacher begins with a high-level verbal prompt (i.e., "tells") and then says,
"Great job, everybody. Do the next one on your own."

APPLICATION 2.7. DESIGNING AN EXPLICIT LESSON

Directions: Select a fairly simple academic skill to teach explicitly. Write a goal and a brief rationale for why the skill is important/useful for students to learn. Once you have a clear idea what you want students to be able to do after the lesson, think about and identify important prerequisites for learning the skill. Identify what kind of task you would have your students do as a review for one of these prerequisite skills. Then write what you would say and do as you model the skill for students. Next, describe how you would prompt the skill and how you would fade the prompt. Finally, describe the closing of your lesson.

CHAPTER 3

Designing Lessons
Vocabulary and Concepts

In Chapter 2, we have presented a flexible lesson design for teaching strategies and skills. In this chapter, we turn our attention to vocabulary terms and concepts; these are grouped together because they require similar instructional practices, in which the learner must discern whether or not to apply what has been taught. For example, while learning the vocabulary word *furious*, even though the underlying concept *mad* or *angry* is already known, the student must determine when a feeling could be labeled *furious* ("If your little brother destroyed your model airplane, you might feel *furious*.") and when it would not be called *furious* ("If your little brother gave you a model airplane for your birthday, you would not feel *furious*."). Similarly, while learning *perpendicular*, because both the word and the underlying concept are unknown, the learner must discriminate between examples of *perpendicular* (*two lines intersecting* at a *90-degree angle*) and nonexamples of *perpendicular* (e.g., two lines intersecting at a 40-degree angle), which have one attribute or part of the definition missing (a 90-degree angle). In fact, a vocabulary word or concept is not truly understood unless the learner has learned both when and when not to apply it.

There are many research-validated practices for expanding students' vocabulary, including embedding brief explanations of unfamiliar vocabulary as books are read aloud to students; teaching students word-learning strategies, such as determining the meaning of a word by using context clues and parts of words (prefixes, suffixes, roots); locating the meaning of the word in a glossary, dictionary, or online source; and encouraging wide reading. However, we are going to focus on explicit vocabulary instruction, for a number of reasons:

53

1. Students receiving explicit, engaging vocabulary instruction experience growth in vocabulary (Tomesen & Aarnoutse, 1998; White, Graves, & Slater, 1990).

2. When students receive intentional teaching of target words, their comprehension of text containing the target words improves (McKeown, Beck, Omanson, & Pople, 1985; Stahl & Fairbanks, 1986). Teaching vocabulary has been shown to increase students' comprehension of new content by 12 percentile points (Stahl & Fairbanks, 1986). Similarly, Jenkins, Stein, and Wysocki (1984) found that if words were taught before they were encountered in text, the ability to comprehend the words increased by a factor of 1/3.

3. In sixth grade and below, direct explanation accounted for about 80% of words learned, adding support for explicit vocabulary instruction (Biemiller, 2001).

4. Even in the upper grades, where more and more word meanings are gained from wide reading, explicit instruction on vocabulary words remains a critical component of vocabulary acquisition.

5. Explicit vocabulary instruction is particularly critical for struggling readers, who do not read extensively and have more difficulty using contextual cues to determine word meanings (Beck, McKeown, & Kucan, 2002).

Researchers have reached broad agreement as to the characteristics of effective vocabulary instruction (National Reading Panel, 2000; Stahl & Fairbanks, 1986). First, vocabulary instruction must go beyond the traditional procedure of having students copy a list of words, look the words up in the glossary, copy the definitions, and study the definitions. Second, vocabulary instruction, like all explicit instruction, must be unambiguous, involving a clear presentation of word meanings and contextual examples (Baker, Simmons, & Kame'enui, 1995). Next, multiple exposures to target words is necessary if vocabulary instruction is to have a measurable impact on vocabulary attainment and reading comprehension (Beck, Perfetti, & McKeown, 1982; Nagy, 1988; Stahl & Fairbanks, 1986). McKeown et al. (1985) found that 10 encounters with target words reliably predicted increased reading comprehension. To allow multiple exposures, sufficient instructional time must be allocated. Although 30 minutes per word would be excessive, 5–15 minutes of initial instruction may be necessary, depending on students' familiarity with a word, the difficulty of the concept, and the depth of understanding needed for comprehension (Jenkins, Matlock, & Slocum, 1989). In addition, instruction must provide information concerning a word's meaning (definitional information) and examples that illustrate how and when the word is utilized (contextual information) (Stahl, 1999). Finally, students must be actively engaged in word-learning instruction and subsequent review activities. These variables are woven into the example lessons provided later in the chapter. First, however, we discuss preparation for explicit vocabulary instruction.

PREPARATION FOR EXPLICIT VOCABULARY INSTRUCTION

Prior to introducing vocabulary, a teacher must do three things: (1) select appropriate vocabulary that will be the most useful to students both at this time and in the future; (2) determine how each word's meaning will be conveyed to students; and (3) develop examples to illustrate each word and, when helpful, non-examples to establish what the concept is not.

Selecting Appropriate Vocabulary for Explicit Vocabulary Instruction

Many, many vocabulary terms are available for instruction in all subjects (language arts, math, science, social studies, health, consumer science, art, physical education, music, etc.). In fact, the challenge is not a dearth of vocabulary terms, but rather an overwhelming number. As a result, you must carefully distinguish those words that will receive expanded, robust, explicit vocabulary instruction and ongoing review from those that will receive only a brief introduction, in order to facilitate immediate comprehension but not necessarily long-term retention. Even though the number of vocabulary terms you teach will probably depend on the difficulty of the words, the background knowledge of your students, the ease with which they learn new vocabulary terms, and the depth of understanding you believe they need, several authors have suggested that you teach 3–10 vocabulary terms in depth for each specific story, portion of a chapter, or body of knowledge to be introduced (see, e.g., Stahl & Fairbanks, 1986). Because working memory is limited, the number of vocabulary terms must be limited.

The task then becomes one of choosing which words merit

more instructional time for expanded (or elaborated), explicit instruction and subsequent review. Four guidelines will assist you in choosing the words. Use these guidelines when you are selecting vocabulary for elaborated instruction, or when you must decide which words in a prescribed list should receive elaborated versus brief instruction.

Guideline 1: Select Words That Are Unknown

Selecting words that students do not yet know seems like an obvious guideline, but curriculum materials occasionally suggest words that learners already know. These known words merit only a swift review or no instructional time at all. For example, a fourth-grade reading text listed the word *secret* for vocabulary instruction. By fourth grade, however, all students will have had a secret, heard a secret, betrayed a secret, and mastered *secret*. Thus *secret* should receive no instructional time.

Guideline 2. Select Words That Are Important to Understanding a Passage or Unit

Generally, vocabulary instruction is implemented to improve students' understanding of a narrative or expository passage, or a unit of knowledge in such subjects as math, science, or social studies. As such, the importance of the word to the passage or unit of knowledge should be considered. If comprehension of a third-grade story hinges on understanding the meaning of the word *contagious*, that word and its underlying meaning should be introduced. If a science chapter focuses on *photosynthesis* and *cellular respiration*, knowledge of those terms before reading the chapter will facilitate comprehension.

Guideline 3: Select Words That Students Will Hear, Read, Write, and Say in the Future

Select words that will be most useful to students later, as well as now. For example, to prepare students for hearing the story *The Grouchy Ladybug* (Carle, 1996) in kindergarten, a teacher selects these words for instruction: *ladybug, aphids, friendly,* and *grouchy.* The students will certainly have more opportunity in the future to utilize the words *friendly* and *grouchy* than *ladybug* and *aphids,* both of which can be taught very rapidly by using the pictures provided in the book.

Similarly, a middle school language arts teacher reviews an anthology selection and determines that these words require preteaching: *remote, malicious, presumptuous, composure, forester, hyacinths, Welsh rarebit, verge, distressed, contentment,* and *rheumatism.* Given the number of words and the limited instructional time, the list must be trimmed to a more reasonable number. The teacher first removes *distressed* as a word already known to students, and then removes *forester* because it can be easily understood, given their current knowledge (*forest*). Next, the teacher decides that passage understanding will not be compromised by lack of knowledge of the terms *hyacinths, Welsh rarebit,* and *rheumatism,* and decides to tell students the meanings of these words during passage reading. Explicit vocabulary instruction will be provided on *remote, malicious, presumptuous, composure,* and *contentment*—all words that students can utilize in the future.

Beck et al. (2002) suggest that different words have different levels of utility, and refer to these levels as **tiers**. Tier 1 words are common words, such as *food, chair, run,* and *table,* which are known to most students and require little if any instructional time. Tier 2 words are words that are used frequently by mature speakers and readers but are unknown to our students. Students generally understand the concept underlying each Tier 2 word but are unfamiliar with the new word. For example, students may not be familiar with the words *furious, infuriated,* or *enraged,* but may have a full understanding of the underlying concept, *mad* or *angry.* Tier 2 words in elementary classes may include *jubilation* (joy), *defraud* (cheat), *calculate* (figure out), *arrange* (lay out), *innocent* (not guilty). In elementary classes and classes serving students with special needs, Tier 2 high-utility words must be emphasized to optimize generalization to other settings and times. At the secondary level, Tier 2 words may include such words as *analyze* (study), *contrast* (see differences), *fundamental* (important or crucial), and *equivalent* (same). To meet the language demands of secondary classes, students must be facile with this type of word, often referred to as "general academic vocabulary." A useful tool for secondary teachers is the Academic Word List of 570 high-incidence, high-utility words that occur frequently in a wide range of academic texts (Coxhead, 2000). The list also includes the members of each word's family (e.g., the *concept* family includes *conception, concepts, conceptual, conceptualization, conceptualize, conceptualized, conceptualizes, conceptualizing,* and *conceptually*).

Generally, Tier 3 words are low-frequency vocabulary terms used in only one domain and taught in content-area classes. Examples of Tier 3 words may be *totalitarian* and *judicial review* in social studies; *foreshadowing* and *vignette* in language arts; *diameter, arc,* and *chord* in geometry; and *condensation, evaporation,* and *precipitation* in science. Although Tier 3 words are used less often than Tier 2 words, they have an important function because they strengthen background knowledge for content-area learning. Thus both Tier 2 and Tier 3 terms have a place in instruction, with Tier 2 words emphasized in elementary classrooms and Tier 3 in content-area classes. However, even in secondary content-area classes, where Tier 3 words are paramount, an attempt should be made to add a few generalizable Tier 2 words to vocabulary lessons to expand students' general academic vocabulary. For example, a high school history book lists these words for instruction before students read a chapter on the Middle Ages: *feudalism, fief, vassal, primogeniture, manorialism, serfs,* and *chivalry.* Though knowledge of these words would support comprehension of the chapter and provide a foundation of background knowledge, the students will not encounter these words in a variety of settings. To augment this list, the teacher may add *analysis*, a chapter word that will be useful in a variety of settings.

Guideline 4: Select Words That Are Difficult to Learn and Need Interpretation

Finally, you should use extra instructional time, explicitness, and review for words that students will probably find more difficult to learn. Many possible factors could increase the difficulty of a word; let's consider some of these, but you should not feel compelled to formulate a checklist to analyze every word.

WORDS THAT LABEL UNKNOWN CONCEPTS

If a target word labels an unknown concept, it is probably more difficult to learn than if the word refers to a known concept. For example, the following novel words will require a minimum amount of instructional time, because the students will already have synonyms for them in their personal lexicon: *crockery* (plates, cups, dishes), *ravenous* (very hungry), *numerous* (many), and *flawless* (perfect). Little instructional time will also be needed even if no single-word synonym was known, but the definition is very familiar: *residence* (a place where a person lives), *pester* (to bother someone again and again), and *humiliation* (a feeling of being ashamed or foolish). Unfamiliar words such as *succinct* or *ubiquitous* may appear difficult for intermediate students; however, these words are likely to take less instructional time, because the underlying concepts of "short and to the point" and "everywhere" are known. On the other hand, when both the word and the underlying concept are unknown, more instructional time is almost certainly required. Students will probably need elaborated instruction for these content-area words or terms:

Science: *angular momentum, dynamic friction, magnetic field, thermodynamics*
Social studies: *branches of government, checks and balances, ethnocentrism*
Health: *complex carbohydrates, lactose intolerance, antibiotic resistance, epidemic*
Mathematics: *cardinal number, denominator, parallelogram, tessellation*
Art: *asymmetry, complementary colors, impressionistic art, representational art*

As you have already deduced, vocabulary terms with unknown concepts are often members of Tier 3. However, the underlying concepts of some Tier 2 words may be unknown to students. For example, they may be unfamiliar not only with the words *concede* and *altruistic*, but also with their underlying concepts.

WORDS NOT ADEQUATELY ADDRESSED THROUGH PASSAGE CONTEXT CLUES

While reading connected text, students encounter many words whose meaning cannot be learned from context because the context supplies inadequate or no clues. If one of those words is critical to passage comprehension, you will need to provide in -depth instruction. However, when the chapter provides a clear definition of the target word, numerous examples, and an elaborated explanation, you can reduce the amount of preteaching (though some prior instruction will alert students to the importance of the word, thus increasing their attention to the meaning conveyed in the text).

WORDS RELATED TO ABSTRACT RATHER THAN CONCRETE CONCEPTS

A word referring to an abstract concept—one that exists in thought only—is much more difficult to learn than a concept that can be illustrated in a concrete fashion, with a picture, an actual object, or acting out. Consider these pairs of words taken from a middle school language arts anthology. The term *compulsion* may be more difficult to learn than *gnarled*, *transformation* than *brooch*, *incorporate* than *tourniquets*, and *devotion* than *roamed*.

WORDS THAT REFLECT COMPLEX CONCEPTS

In deciding whether a word is more difficult for students to learn, examine the word's complexity. Three variables are particularly important to determining whether a concept is simple or more complex: the number of attributes in the definition, the number of concepts included in the definition that must be understood, and the number of related concepts needed to understand the vocabulary term.

Attributes, in this context, are the parts of a definition that need to be in place in order for an example to represent a concept. As the number of attributes increases, the learner must consider each. The learner will also need to know the other concepts embedded in the definition. Examine the definitions for the following math terms, and consider the level of complexity for each.

variable u a letter or symbol
u stands for one or more
numbers

ordered pair u a pair of numbers u to
locate a point u on a coordinate plane
u first number tells how far to move
horizontally u second number tells
how far to move vertically

Variable is a relatively simple concept with just two attributes and only known concepts embedded in the definition. On the other hand, the concept of *ordered pair* is much more difficult. The definition contains numerous attributes and requires understanding of the concepts *point, coordinate plane, horizontally,* and *vertically.*

Complexity is increased not only with the number of attributes and embedded concepts, but also with the number of related concepts. For example, one textbook defines the term *branches of government* in the following way:

> *branches of government* u established in the
> U.S. Constitution u to divide the power of
> government u between legislative,
> executive, and judicial branches

To truly understand the term *branches of government,* students will need to understand the concepts embedded in the definition (*constitution, legislative, executive, judicial*), as well as many related concepts (*Presidency, Congress, House of Representatives, Senate, Supreme Court, constitutional, unconstitutional, republic, democracy, delegated powers, separation of powers, checks and balances, veto,* and *legislation*). Because of its complexity, the vocabulary term *branches of government* will require introduction before passage reading, discussion during passage reading, and discussion and expansion after passage reading.

WORDS THAT ARE DIFFICULT TO PRONOUNCE

Some words are more difficult to learn because students have not heard the words, the words are not pronounced as would be expected from the letters (irregular words), or the words are difficult to produce physically. Students will have more difficulty attaching meaning to a word and cognitively storing and retrieving that word's meaning if the word is difficult to pronounce; therefore, you will want to choose words for instruction that students need to practice pronouncing, as well words whose meanings they need to learn.

Neither kindergarten teachers nor high school chemistry

teachers should assume that students can easily pronounce words. This act of "assumicide" will surely stunt vocabulary attainment. Instead, you should be sure to include practice on the pronunciation of words in your vocabulary instruction, including modeling the pronunciation of the novel word, pronouncing it with the students a number of times as needed, and having them pronounce the word. This practice will also support the use of these new vocabulary words during discussions. If students are confident about the correct pronunciation, they are much more likely to use the word orally.

WORDS REQUIRING ADDITIONAL INTERPRETATION

Finally, attention must be given to other terms that might cause confusion for students, especially words with multiple meanings and idioms, phrases, or expressions that have meanings different from their literal interpretations. Consider the music student thinking of a *staff* as a group of teachers, the social studies student conceptualizing *division* as a math operation rather than a division of powers, or the math student believing that a *negative* number is a bad number. Similarly, without explicit instruction, students are likely to take idioms literally. For example, students might interpret the sentence "The experienced secretary really *knows the ropes*" to mean that the secretary enjoys rock climbing on weekends.

Every day, you must make decisions concerning which vocabulary terms to emphasize with extended time, instruction, and review. In fact, selecting the words may be the most important act in vocabulary instruction. Let's put these guidelines into practice using the examples in Applications 3.1, 3.2, and 3.3 from elementary and secondary classes. Read the directions, select the requested number of words for elaborated instruction, and then read our decisions and rationale. Recognize that these are professional decisions, so your conclusions may not match ours. As you select words, emphasize words that are **unknown, critical** to the content (even though you have not read the text), **useful in the future,** and more **difficult** to learn.

APPLICATION 3.1. VOCABULARY

SELECTION FOR PRIMARY READ-ALOUD

The book *Enemy Pie* by Derek Munson (2000) will be read to a second-grade class. While reading the story, the teacher will give students brief explanations of novel words. After reading the book, the teacher will provide elaborated, explicit instruction on four words. Using the four general guidelines for selecting words for elaborated instruction, choose four words from those listed just below. Then read our choices and rationales for these choices, below the word list.

Directions: Circle four words for elaborated, explicit vocabulary instruction.

perfect	*trampoline*	*recipe*	*disgusting*	*earthworms*
ingredients	*horrible*	*nervous*	*invited*	*relieved* *boomerang*

Situation: Read-aloud
Grade level: Second grade
Materials: *Enemy   Pie*   by ᵒⁿ
Derek Muns

Vocabulary term	Amount of instruction	Rationale
perfect	None or brief	Second graders probably know the meaning of *perfect*. They or someone in their class will have had a perfect paper. At most, you may do a quick review as you read the story.
trampoline	Brief during passage reading	*Trampoline* is not a Tier 2 word and has a concrete referent. During the reading of the story, you can simply point to the picture of the trampoline.
recipe	Brief during and after passage reading	*Recipe* may be unknown to second graders, is critical to passage understanding, and may be useful in the future. But it is not a difficult word to learn, given its association with food—a concept well known to second graders! While you read the story, give a short explanation, and then provide brief instruction after the story by presenting the word, its meaning, and a few examples. "This word is *recipe*. What word? *Recipe*. A recipe gives you special directions on how to make a food. If you make a cake, you need a cake recipe. If you make a pie, you need a pie

---

Recipe. If you make a meatloaf, you need a ~~meatloaf~~

Recipe."

Vocabulary term	Amount of instruction	Rationale
disgusting	Expanded	*Disgusting* is an excellent word for elaborated vocabulary instruction, as it may be unknown to second graders, is critical to passage understanding, and will be useful to the learners. Think of all the times second graders can use the word *disgusting*.
earthworms	Brief after passage reading	*Earthworms* is a compound word, making the instruction fairly straightforward. Have students read the two words in *earthworms*, and then show how the second relates to the first. "Read the two words in this compound word. *Earth worms.* To figure out the meaning of compound words, we look at the second word first. *Earthworms* are worms found in the earth."
ingredients	Brief during and reducing the after passage reading	You should teach *ingredients* right after *recipe*, thus amount of instructional time needed. The challenge with this word is not its meaning, as it is again connected to a mastered concept (food), but its pronunciation. As a result, the pronunciation should be practiced a number of times. "This word is *ingredients.* Say it with me. *Ingredients.* Say it three times. *Ingredients, ingredients, ingredients.* What word? *Ingredients.* When you read a recipe, you learn what to put in the food you are making. Each thing you put in the food is an *ingredient.* If a cake recipe tells you to put flour in the batter, the flour is an ———. *Ingredient.* If you put eggs in the cake batter, the eggs are an . *Ingredient.* If you put milk in the cake batter, milk is an . *Ingredient.*"
horrible	None	Second graders probably know the word *horrible.* They have probably read *Alexander and the Terrible, Horrible, No Good, Very Bad Day* (Viorst, 1972), and at some point someone may have informed them that they were horrible.

nervous	Expanded	*Nervous* is an excellent choice for extended instruction. The word is critical to the selection and useful in the future. Students can use the term to label their feelings and can use the word in their written stories.
invited	Maybe	Instruction on this word will depend on the group of students in the class and on the setting. In many settings, students may be familiar with this word because they've received party and sleepover invitations. In other settings, the children may not have been *invited* to a special event.
relieved	Expanded	*Relieved* is an excellent choice for elaborated instruction, as the word may be unknown, is critical to passage understanding, and will be useful to second graders. For instance, when a test is canceled, students can respond, "I am so relieved." It will be especially effective to teach *relieved* after *nervous*, thus showing the change in feelings when something difficult is over.
boomerang	Brief during passage reading	Of course, upon seeing this word, many of us may be tempted to leap into a 6-week unit on the indigenous population of Australia, but brief instruction will probably be wiser. Showing a picture and describing the use of the boomerang today should suffice.

APPLICATION 3.2. VOCABULARY SELECTION FOR FIFTH-GRADE CHAPTER BOOK

The teacher plans to provide elaborated, explicit vocabulary instruction on four words before students read Chapter 1 of *The Family under the Bridge* (Carlson, 1958/1986). Very brief instruction or no instruction at all will be provided on the remaining words. Before reading our comments, select four words from the list just below.

Directions: Circle four words for elaborated, explicit vocabulary instruction.

monsieur   cathedral   cowered   hidey-hole

hyacinths   can't abide dignity   Gypsy fastidious   loitering

adventure   quay

Situation: Reading first chapter in book.
Grade level: Fifth grade
Materials: *The Family under the Bridge*, Chapter 1 by Natalie Savage Carlson

Vocabulary term	Amount of instruction	Rationale

Vocabulary term	Amount of instruction	Rationale
monsieur	Brief	This word can be taught very quickly, as the students will already know the synonym *mister*. The instruction can focus on the pronunciation of the word.
cathedral	Brief or none	A brief definition such as "an important church," coupled with a picture will be adequate for *cathedral*.
cowered	Expanded instruction before passage reading	Although the term *cowered* is seldom used in oral language, it is used more often in literature to describe the action of characters. Also, the word is critical to passage understanding and is probably unknown to fifth graders.
hidey-hole	None	Students will have no difficulty inferring the meaning of *hidey-hole*, given the context and the structure of the word.
hyacinths	None	Students will find this word in a paragraph describing a flower cart. Thus the meaning is easily inferred from the context.
can't abide	Expanded instruction before passage reading	The term *can't abide* can be taught for a number of reasons. First, it expresses how Armand, the tramp, feels about children—an understanding central to the plot. It is also a term that fifth graders can use in speech and in writing.
dignity	Expanded instruction before passage reading	*Dignity* is used to describe how Armand responded to children mocking him, giving the reader insight into Armand's character. The term may be unknown to fifth graders but is certainly a useful word to master.
Gypsy	Brief	Many fifth graders will not be acquainted with this ethnic group. A *Gypsy* community is a very important factor in subsequent chapters, meriting brief instruction of the term *Gypsy*.
Vocabulary term	**Amount of instruction**	**Rationale**
fastidious	Maybe expanded	*Fastidiously* is used to describe one of Armand's actions. Although *fastidious* is not a common word, it will be of interest to fifth graders, if time permits.
loitering	Expanded instruction before passage reading	This is a perfect fifth-grade word. Think of all the times a teacher can use this word: "No loitering at the drinking fountain," "Let's move along . . . no loitering."
adventure	None	*Adventure* is a word that fifth graders will know.

quay	Brief	*Quay* is used throughout the book to label the structures along the banks of the Seine. Limited instruction should be adequate, given that this is a low-frequency word that has a very concrete reference. *Quay* should be introduced in relationship to *Seine*, which is never identified as a river. Google Images provides numerous pictures of the quays along the Seine in Paris. Showing students these pictures and other pictures of Paris will not only support students' vocabulary growth, but also enhance background knowledge and interest in the book.

APPLICATION 3.3. VOCABULARY SELECTION FOR MIDDLE SCHOOL SOCIAL STUDIES

Middle school students are preparing to read a chapter section entitled "The Five Themes of Geography" in their social studies book. Because the book and chapter are not available to you, which makes this selection task difficult, read through our comments to see how the selection guidelines can be applied to a content-area textbook.

Situation: Middle school social studies
Materials: *World Cultures and Geography* (2005), Chapter 2, Section I: "The Five Themes of Geography"

Vocabulary term	Emphasis	Rationale
theme	Expanded	Although the word *theme* is not listed in the chapter's suggested vocabulary, it should be taught for a number of reasons: It is the central concept in the chapter, it may be unknown, and it can be used in numerous instructional settings.
continent	None or brief review	Ideally, middle school students will have mastered this concept. The need for instruction can be assessed by asking students to list the continents.
location	None	*Location* is probably known to middle school students or can be quickly explained as "where a place is."
latitude	Review	*Latitude* has recently been taught but should be reviewed.
Vocabulary term	Emphasis	Rationale

longitude	Review	*Longitude* should also be reviewed.
absolute location	Expanded	The most powerful approach may be to teach *absolute* as a synonym for *exact*, and then to explain *absolute location* based on latitude and longitude. Knowledge of *absolute* can then be used to determine the meaning of *absolute temperature* and *absolute altitude*—vocabulary terms also found in the text. Another meaning of *absolute* (i.e., complete with no restrictions) can also be introduced and extended to *absolute power, absolute freedom, absolute proof, absolute justice, absolute truth, absolute monarch, absolute knowledge, absolute requirement*, and so forth.
relative location	Expanded	As with *absolute*, introducing the meaning of *relative* (comparison with something else, not exact) would have the benefit of generalization to terms such as *relative location, relative effectiveness, relative darkness, relative value, relative age, relative humidity*, etc. The adjective *relative* will be especially important to teach, given that many students upon hearing the word *relative* are thinking of aunts, uncles, cousins, and grandparents.

Determining How the Word's Meaning Will Be Conveyed

In addition to carefully selecting words for expanded, explicit vocabulary instruction, you will need to formulate a definition that clearly and accurately conveys the meaning of each word. Five possible methods for communicating the meaning of a word are (1) presenting a "student-friendly explanation" for the word; (2) guiding students in determining the critical attributes embedded in a glossary or text definition; (3) introducing the meaning of the word by exploring the meaning of the embedded prefixes, suffixes, and/or roots; (4) guiding English-language learners in recognizing cognates; or (5) a combination of these four methods. The procedure you select will depend on the grade level of your students, the subject you are teaching, and the language sophistication of your students. Let's explore the first four of these methods.

Present a "Student-Friendly Explanation" for the Word

When you are teaching students the meanings of words, particularly Tier 2 words, it is wise to use definitions that are easy to understand, contain only known words, and indicate how the words are used. These are often referred to as "studentfriendly explanations" (Beck et al., 2002). Perhaps, in preparing to introduce the vocabulary word *attention* to fourth graders, you locate this definition in a standard dictionary:

> *Attention*—(1) The act or state of attending through applying the mind to an object of sense or thought. (2) A condition of readiness for such attention involving a selective narrowing of consciousness and receptivity.

Although the definition is accurate, it is certainly inadequate for fourth graders or anyone who does not know the term *attention*. First, the word is defined by using a derivative (*attending*). In addition, there are numerous words that students may not know, including *object, sense, condition, readiness, selective, consciousness*, and *receptivity*. You will need to create a student-friendly explanation instead. One excellent strategy for creating student-friendly explanations is to look the word up in a dictionary designed for English-language learners. For example, this is the definition given in the *Longman Dictionary of American English* (2006):

> *Attention*—the act of listening or looking carefully

Often definitions presented in dictionaries for English-language learners are better than ones we could quickly generate. For this reason, every teacher should have a dictionary for English-language learners, such as *Collins COBUILD Student's Dictionary Plus Grammar* (2005) or the *Longman Dictionary of American English* (2006). Two prominent publishers of dictionaries for English-language learners have also placed their dictionaries online for free use by teachers and students: *Heinle's Newbury House Dictionary of American English* (*nhd.heinle.com*) and *Longman Dictionary of Contemporary*

English (*www.ldoceonline.com*). Whether you generate the definition or locate it a dictionary, it is useful to rephrase the definition by creating a sentence that indicates how a word is used: "When you give something your *attention*, you listen and look carefully."

Now it is your turn to create student-friendly explanations. Application 3.4 is an exercise to provide you with practice in doing this.

APPLICATION 3.4. CREATING STUDENT- FRIENDLY EXPLANATIONS

First, read the additional examples of dictionary or glossary definitions and accompanying studentfriendly explanations. Then read the remaining definitions and create student-friendly explanations. Some definitions will need significant revisions in order to transform them into student-friendly explanations; others will need little editing. Be sure that your student-friendly explanations are easy to understand, contain words that students know, and indicate how each word will be used. If you have a dictionary for English-language learners, use that as an aid. When you are finished, compare your student-friendly explanations with ours in *Feedback on Application Exercises*, page 259.

Setting and population	Vocabulary word: Dictionary or glossary definition	Student-friendly explanation
Second-grade read-aloud	*disgusting* (adj.)—to cause to feel disgust; to cause revulsion, repellent, offensive	If you think something is *disgusting*, is unpleasant or unacceptable. You REALLY dislike it. (Developed from definition provided in *Collins COBUILD Student's Dictionary*, 2005)

Setting and population	Vocabulary word: Dictionary or glossary definition	Student-friendly explanation
Fifth-grade reading group	*loitering* (v.)—to linger in an aimless way; spend time idly	You *loiter* when you stand or sit in a public place with no real purpose. When you just hang out, you loiter.
Ninth-grade global studies	*conglomeration* (n.)—(1) the act or process of conglomerating; (2) an accumulation of miscellaneous things	When a large group of different things are gathered together in an untidy or unusual way, it is a *conglomeration*. (Developed from definition provided in *Cambridge Advanced Learner's Dictionary*)

Second-grade read-aloud	*nervous* (adj.)—easily agitated, excited, or irritated; apprehensive
Fifth-grade reading lesson	
	cower (v.)—to crouch from something that menaces or dominates
Seventh-grade language arts lesson	*sublime* (adj.)—of such magnificence, grandeur, or exquisiteness as to inspire great veneration
Eleventh-grade science lesson	*empirical* (adj.)—based on, related to; verifiable by experience, experiment, or observation

Guide Students in Determining the Critical Attributes Embedded in a Glossary or Text Definition

Although student-friendly explanations work very well for Tier 2 words, another approach is useful when you are teaching content-area vocabulary, particularly Tier 3 words that represent the specific terminology for a body of knowledge. For these Tier 3 words, begin with the definitions provided within the text or glossary. Guide students in locating each word's definition in the text or glossary, breaking the definition into its critical attributes (parts), and recording the word and attributes in their vocabulary logs. For example, if your math text defines *perimeter* as "the measurement of the distance around a shape or object", students can break it down into three attributes:

perimeter

1. measurement
2. of distance
3. around a shape or object

All three attributes will need to be in place for something to be considered a *perimeter.* If something is not a measurement, not a distance, or not around a shape or an object, then it is not a *perimeter.*

This approach has several advantages. First, listing the word and critical attributes supports students cognitively as they analyze the meaning of more complex concepts. Second, students can use the list of attributes to determine whether something is an example or a non-example of the concept. Finally, students learn a strategy for recording words and definitions that they can use independently for new words, even when teacher-directed explicit instruction is not provided on those new words.

Introduce the Meaning of a Word by Exploring the Embedded Base Words, Prefixes, Suffixes, and/or Roots

Another viable method for introducing the meaning of a new word is to focus on the **morphemes** or meaningful units within the word. Many words have embedded base words, roots, prefixes, and/or suffixes that students can use to determine the meaning of the word. When teaching the word *action,* you can call attention to *act* and the noun suffix, *ion.* Similarly, *embarrassment* contains the base word *embarrass* and the noun suffix *ment, reconstruction* contains the base word *construct,* the prefix *re* meaning again, and the noun suffix *tion;* and *hydroelectric* contains the Greek root *hydro* for water. Of these elements, **prefixes** are particularly helpful in determining the meaning of words, for a number of reasons:

1. Prefixes are easy to identify at the beginning of words.
2. They have consistent pronunciation and spelling.
3. They consistently alter the meaning of a word (*heat* to *preheat, test* to *pretest*).
4. Twenty prefixes—*un, re, in* [*im, il, ir*] meaning "not"; *dis, en*

and *em; non; in* and *im*, meaning "in"; *over, mis; sub; pre; inter, fore; de; trans; super, semi, anti, mid;* and *under*—account for 97% of prefixed words (White, Sowell, & Yanagihara, 1989).

On the other hand, the meanings of **suffixes** are often very abstract and confusing (e.g., *ment* can mean "condition of," "quality of," or "state of"), with a few exceptions (such as *less, able,* and *ful*). What should be emphasized when teaching derivational suffixes is that they often change the base word's part of speech. For example, with the addition of *ion*, the verb *reflect* becomes the noun *reflection;* with the addition of *ly*, the adjective *quick* becomes the adverb *quickly;* with the addition of *al*, the noun *inspiration* becomes the adjective *inspirational.*

Greek and Latin roots (e.g., *astro* in *astronomy, astrophysics, astronaut,* and *astronomer*) can also be introduced as tools for determining the meaning of unknown words. However, several challenges should be noted:

1. Many Greek and Latin roots appear in only a small number of words.
2. Often the relationship between the original meaning and the modern usage is obscure, making generalization difficult.
3. Many have more than one spelling, hindering identification of the root in words.

Despite these challenges, secondary students should be introduced to Greek and Latin roots as they emerge in target vocabulary words. For example, a language arts teacher who is presenting the word *chronology* can use this opportunity to introduce the Greek root *chron*, meaning "time," and the suffix *ology*, meaning "the study of." Students can conclude, perhaps with a little teacher assistance, that *chronology* refers to the study of events in time. Similarly, in science, a domain in which many words contain Greek or Latin roots, the teacher can introduce *microscope* by providing the meaning of the prefix *micro* (small) and the Greek root *scope* (look at), allowing the students to conclude that a microscope is used to look at small things.

This approach has many benefits. First, students learn morphemes that can be generalized to other words. For example, after *chron* and *chronology* are introduced, the students can explore the use of *chron* in *chronicle, synchronize*, and *anachronism*. Second, students learn about various origins of English and its systematic foundations. Third, the study of prefixes, suffixes, and roots increases students' "word consciousness" (awareness of words) and interest in the English language. However, there is a major caveat: Frequently, the literal interpretation made from combining the meaning of the morphemes is not adequate to understand the modern use of a word. For example, the word *manufacture* contains *man*, meaning "hand," and *fac*, meaning "make." The literal interpretation would then be "the act of making something by hand," which is quite different from the word's current usage. An experienced teacher will want to pair this analysis with a student-friendly definition, such as "To *manufacture* things is to make them in a factory. Usually things are made in a factory by machines and people." In other words, you will want to use more than one method when presenting the meaning of a word.

Guide English-Language Learners in Recognizing Cognates

Another procedure for introducing a word's meaning is to utilize **cognates**, or words that are similar orthographically, semantically, and syntactically in two languages (Carlo et al., 2004; Hiebert & Kamil, 2005). In other words, the words have similar spelling, meaning, and use in the two languages. This is a particularly useful strategy for Spanish speakers who are learning English, because many words in both languages have origins in Latin. It is estimated that there are between 10,000 and 20,000 Spanish–English cognates, and that these cognates account for one-third of the words in academic textbooks (Nash, 1997). When examining the 570 words in Coxhead's (2000) Academic Word List, Lubliner and Hiebert (2008) determined that 70% were morphologically transparent cognates. Here are some examples of Spanish and English cognates:

English   Spanish
combination	*combinación*
university	*universidad*
splendid	*espléndido*

In the upper grades, Spanish speakers will encounter an increasing number of cognates as the number of words with Latin roots increases, especially in science and social studies. For example, students may meet these words in their studies:

English   Spanish
discrimination	*discriminación*
glacier	*glaciar*
culture	*cultura*

Despite the power of cognates for enriching the vocabulary of Spanish speakers who are acquiring English, teacher-directed instruction on the meanings is still necessary. First, even small changes in spelling, such as *pausa* to *pause*, reduce some students' ability to recognize English–Spanish cognates (Nagy, García, Durgunoglu, & Hancin-Bhatt, 1993), requiring the teacher to point out the similarities. Second, there are numerous cases of false cognates, in which the spellings are similar but the meanings differ. Consider these examples:

English   Spanish
carpet	*carpeta* (folder)
embarrassed	*embarazada* (pregnant)
exit	*éxito* (success)

Developing Examples and Non- Examples

Presenting students with a definition, even a student-friendly explanation, is not adequate for vocabulary attainment. Students will also need examples of the vocabulary term's use and, when the concept is more difficult, non-examples in order to establish firmly what the concept is and what it is not. These examples and non-examples can be **concrete**, **visual**, or **verbal**.

Designing Examples

Even though **concrete** examples are only occasionally possible, they are very powerful when their use is feasible. For example, if you are preparing students for a read-aloud of *Pumpkin, Pumpkin* by Jeanne Titherington (1990), showing students an actual *vine* will be more powerful than displaying a picture. Another way to make concepts concrete and to bring them alive is to act them out. As you teach *saunter*, you can move around the room demonstrating the concept. As you introduce words such as *despondent* and *jubilant*, you can show the emotions using facial expressions and body posture.

More often, you can use pictures and illustrations as examples and "talking points" for illustrating a concept. These **visual** examples can come from the current textbook, from other print material, or from the wealth of material available on the Internet. For example, in teaching the vocabulary term *anxiety*, photos downloaded from the Internet that show a student overwhelmed with homework or an anxious youngster giving a report in front of the class would be perfect focal points for a discussion of *anxiety*.

In many cases, you can provide visual examples by sketching them even when you doubt your artistic talent. For instance, if you are teaching *diameter*, draw a circle with a center point, and then add a line representing the diameter. It really is true: A picture is worth a thousand words.

Generally, you do not present concrete and visual examples alone; instead, you couple them with verbal explanations. In many cases, however, you can use a **verbal** example (a story or scenario) alone to illustrate a vocabulary term. As you teach the term *concentration*, for instance, you can provide the following verbal examples.

> When you look or listen carefully and with interest, you concentrate. When you look or listen carefully, you . *Concentrate*. For example, yesterday in the library, Matt read his book even when people were talking near him. He really knows how to ————. *Concentrate*. This morning, MacKenzie did her whole math paper without even looking up at the clock. MacKenzie really knows how to . *Concentrate*. If you sat down at the kitchen table and did your homework without stopping to watch TV or pet the dog, you would show that you can really . *Concentrate*.

Designing Non-Examples

When you are introducing a more challenging vocabulary term (especially if the underlying concept is difficult or unknown), or when you are checking understanding of any vocabulary term, you can use examples and non-examples to clarify the boundaries of the vocabulary term or concept. Use the following steps to design non-examples:

u *Step 1: Examine the definition provided for the term, and determine the critical attributes or parts of the definition.* Identifying the critical attributes of the concept is key to developing both examples and non-examples. The examples must include all critical attributes, but the non-examples should have one attribute missing.

Simple vocabulary terms may have only one critical attribute. For example, the term *furious* is defined as "very angry," *credulous* as "believing anything," or *dearth* as "any scarcity or lack." As illustrated earlier, more complex concepts may have numerous attributes. For example, in math class, this definition may be given for *diameter*: "When a line passes through the center point of a circle and the endpoints are on the circle, the line is a *diameter*." Therefore, the following attributes can be enumerated:

diameter u a line u passing through the center point of a circle u endpoints on the circle

Now it is your turn. Application 3.5 is designed to give you practice in determining critical attributes from definitions.

APPLICATION 3.5. Determining Critical Attributes from Definitions

---

For each definition after our additional examples below, determine the critical attributes. When you are done, compare them with our interpretations in *Feedback on Application Exercises*, page 259.

Definition	Critical attribute or attributes
conglomeration When many different things are gathered together in an untidy or unusual way, this group is a *conglomeration*.	*conglomeration* u many different things u gathered together u in an untidy or unusual way
contentious A *contentious* person is someone who is always ready to argue.	*contentious* u always ready to argue
independent variable An *independent variable* is a variable in an experiment that is changed on purpose.	
immigration *Immigration* is the process of people coming into a country with the intent to live and work there.	
retaliate When you harm someone in return for an injury or wrong he or she has done, you *retaliate*.	

u *Step 2: Design examples in which all attributes are present.* Whether you are using concrete, visual, or verbal examples, all critical attributes need to be evident in each example. Let's return to an earlier concept, *diameter*. You can draw a circle and a center point, and then a line representing the diameter, and explain: "A line is drawn through the center point, and the endpoints of the line touch the circle. This line is a *diameter*." In teaching *democracy*, you can say, "The United States has a system of government in which eligible citizens vote in free elections to elect representatives to our federal government. Thus we have a form of government called a *democracy*." For *furious*, you can utilize this example: "If your little brother drew pictures on your homework and you had to redo your homework, you might get very angry. You might be *furious*."

When you are teaching a new vocabulary term, you will want to provide a number of examples to ensure that students do not create a misconception. For example, if the only explanation of the word *survive* involves a family surviving a car accident, students may conclude that *survive* has something to do with a car accident. Similarly, if *perimeter* is only explained by using drawings of shapes on the overhead, students may not generalize the concept to the measure around a door, picture frame, or room.

u *Step 3: Design non-examples in which some, but not all, critical attributes are missing*. As suggested earlier, non-examples are used to establish the boundaries of the concept—what it is and what it is not. Non-examples, like examples, can be concrete, visual, or verbal, but in all cases at least one critical attribute is excluded. As illustrated in the example lessons in the next section, non-examples can be used to help introduce concepts (particularly more challenging, complex concepts) and to check students' understanding.

Now it is your turn to write examples and non-examples. Application 3.6 provides you with some practice in doing this.

APPLICATION 3.6. DESIGNING EXAMPLES AND NON-EXAMPLES

For each word and its list of attributes write one example and one or more non-examples. When you are finished, compare your examples and non-examples with those we have created (see, *Feedback on Application Exercises*, page 260).

Critical attribute or attributes	Examples	Non-examples
conglomerati on u many different things u gathered together u in an untidy or unusual way Ms. Martin has a basket near her front door containing newspapers, junk mail, dog bones, running shoes, makeup, and garden seeds. This is a	*conglomeration.* Ms. Martin has a huge basket of junk mail sitting near her front door. This would not be called a *conglomeration*, because all the items are the same. In every room in her house, Ms. Martin has a collection, including collections of shells, driftwood, rare books, teacups, ivory jewelry, and Chinese dishes. These would not be considered a *conglomeration*, because these things, though	different, have not been gathered all together. *contentious* u always ready to argue *independent variable* u variable in an experiment u changed on purpose *immigration* u people coming into
a country u with the intent to live and work there *sufficient* u		

Critical attribute or attributes	Examples	Non-examples
retaliate	No matter the issue or the person, Mrs. Regent is willing to argue. Mrs. Regent is *contentious*. Four groups of #3 hybrid corn were planted in the same soil with the same amount of sunlight, but were given different amounts of water. The *independent variable* was the amount of water. The amount of water	No matter the issue or the person, Mrs. Regent is open-minded and positive, wanting to learn other people's viewpoints. Mrs. Regent is not *contentious*. The amount of sunlight was not an *independent variable*, because it was not intentionally changed. The type of soil was not an *independent variable*, because it was not changed on purpose.

u   harm
someone u in
return   for   an
injury or wrong
he or she has
done

EXPLICIT VOCABULARY INSTRUCTIONAL ROUTINE

Once preparation for vocabulary instruction (selection of words, determination of method for conveying meaning, and generation of examples and non-examples) is complete, explicit instruction can begin. Throughout this book, we have emphasized the use of effective and efficient instructional routines that optimize students' learning and also support teachers in the daily delivery of instruction. In keeping with that theme, a simple yet powerful routine for teaching vocabulary terms is introduced in this chapter. This basic vocabulary instructional routine, similar to those proposed by other authors (e.g., Beck et al., 2002; Biemiller, 2001; Carnine et al., 2009; Diamond & Gutlohn, 2006; Frayer, Frederick, & Klausmeier, 1969; Marzano & Pickering, 2005), contains the following steps:

u *Step 1: Introduce the word.* The first step in the routine involves telling the students the pronunciation of the word or guiding them in decoding the word. As discussed earlier, if students cannot accurately pronounce the word, they will have more difficulty attaching meaning to the word, storing it cognitively, and subsequently retrieving it. If the word is difficult to pronounce, model the pronunciation and have the students repeat it a number of times. u *Step 2: Introduce the meaning of the word.* Next, introduce the meaning of the word, using one of the procedures explored earlier:

⊚Option 1. Provide a student-friendly explanation.

⊚Option 2. Guide students in analyzing the meaningful parts of the word.

⊚Option 3. Have students determine the critical attributes embedded in a glossary definition.

⊚Option 4. Assist English-language learners in recognizing cognates and transferring meaning from their first language to their emerging second language.

u *Step 3: Illustrate with examples.* The third step in this basic instructional routine is to illustrate the concept with a number of concrete, visual, or verbal examples, being careful to include all critical attributes in the examples.

u *Step 4: Check students' understanding.* Finally, you will want to check students' understanding of the concept by actively involving them in interacting with the word. Several procedures are particularly beneficial, including these:

⊚Option 1. Have students distinguish between examples and non-examples, and explain why the exemplar is either an example or a non-example.

⊚Option 2. Ask students to generate their own examples.

⊚Option 3. Ask students questions that require deep processing of the word's meaning beyond simply mimicking the definition.

To get a better sense of this instructional routine, carefully examine the lessons found in Figures 3.1 and 3.2. Notice that all four steps of the basic instructional routine are used in both lessons, with slight adaptations based on the nature of the concept being taught. For the lesson in Figure 3.1, the eighth graders are preparing to read an excerpt from a biography about Harriet Tubman. The teacher presents instruction on *elude*, a word critical to passage understanding. Notice that several examples are given, including some that directly relate to the use of the word in the passage, which enhances comprehension. Also, note that the depth of learning is increased by having students generate synonyms for *elude*. For the lesson in Figure 3.2, the teacher introduces the word *autobiography* by examining the morphemes in the word (*auto, bio, graph*). The teacher then reiterates the meaning, using a student-friendly explanation. After teaching *autobiography* according to the basic instructional routine, the teacher assists students in transferring the meaning of *auto* to other words.

Now it's your turn. Use Application 3.7 to design your own vocabulary lesson, to be taught according to the basic instructional routine.

APPLICATION 3.7. DESIGNING A VOCABULARY LESSON TO TEACH WITH THE BASIC INSTRUCTIONAL ROUTINE

Directions: Select a Tier 2 word that you could teach, using the basic instructional routine introduced in this section of the chapter. You may use one of the following words and its accompanying studentfriendly explanation, or you may choose your own word.

Word	Student-friendly explanation (Developed from definition provided in *Collins COBUILD Student's Dictionary*, 2005)
outrageous	If you describe something as *outrageous*, you are emphasizing that it is unacceptable or very shocking.
refusal	A *refusal* is the act of firmly saying or showing that you will not do, allow, or accept something.
lavish	If you describe something as *lavish*, you mean that a lot of time, effort, or money has been spent on it to make it as impressive as possible.

Let's now turn our attention to more complex concepts in which the word is unfamiliar and the underlying concept is not known. In this case, the basic instructional routine will be augmented to include not only examples of the concept, but non-examples that will better convey the boundaries of the concept (what it is and what it is not).

In Chapter 2, we have described three major steps in the body of an explicit instruction lesson, including modeling (**I do it.**), prompted/guided practice (**We do it.**), and unprompted practice (**You do it.**). If you were to reexamine the previous vocabulary lessons, you would discover that only two of the steps are used there: **I do it.** (introduce the word, introduce the meaning of the word, and illustrate with

FIGURE 3.1. Basic instructional routine: Middle school.

Setting: Eighth-grade language arts

Situation: Preparation for reading a portion of a biography about Harriet Tubman.

Step 1: Introduce the word.

[Teacher displays the word.] This word is *elude*. What word? *Elude*. We pronounce it as "e lüd." Say the word again. *Elude*.

Step 2: Introduce the meaning of the word.

Option 1. Provide a student-friendly explanation.

If you avoid someone or escape from them, you *elude* them. If you avoid someone or escape from them, you ____ . *Elude them*.

Step 3: Illustrate with examples.

If runaway slaves were able to hide from patrollers who were hunting for them, the slaves were able to *elude* them. If a convict was able to escape and hide from police officers for 10 years, the convict was able to ____ . *Elude them*. If other players were not able to catch Jason during a game of hide and seek, he was able to ____ . *Elude them*.

Step 4: Check students' understanding.

Option 1. Have students distinguish between examples and non-examples.

Please get out your Yes and No cards. I will ask a question. When I say, "Show me," hold up a Yes or a No card.

    If a slave wanted to *elude* patrollers, would that slave protest slave practices in the marketplace? [Pause.] Show me. [Students hold up a No card.] Ones, tell your partner why runaway slaves would not protest slave practices in the marketplace. *If they protested slave practices in the marketplace, they would be noticed and caught.*

    If a slave wanted to *elude* patrollers, would that slave move only at night and then sleep undercover during the day? [Pause.] Show me. [Students hold up a Yes card.] Twos, tell your partner why a slave would move only at night and sleep undercover during the day. Use the word *elude* in your explanation. *If they moved only at night and slept during the day, they would be able to elude patrollers.*

Option 3. Ask questions that require deep processing of the word's meaning.

If you were a slave and you wanted to *elude* patrollers, would you want to leave in the morning or evening? *In the evening*. Twos, tell your partner why evening would be better. Start with: If you wanted to *elude* patrollers, it would be better to leave in the evening, because . . . *If you wanted to elude patrollers, it would be better to leave in the evening, because it would be dark and the patrollers would be at home sleeping.*

    If you were a slave and you wanted to *elude* patrollers, should you walk down a road or through the forest? *Through the forest*. Ones, tell your partner why walking through the forest would be better. Start with: If you wanted to *elude* patrollers, it would be better to walk through the forest because . . . *If you wanted to elude patrollers, it would be better to walk through the forest because you could hide behind tree trunks or under leaves. On the road, you could not hide.*

    Think about how the word *elude* might be used in a passage about Harriet Tubman. [Teacher provides thinking time.] Now talk it over with your partner. *When*

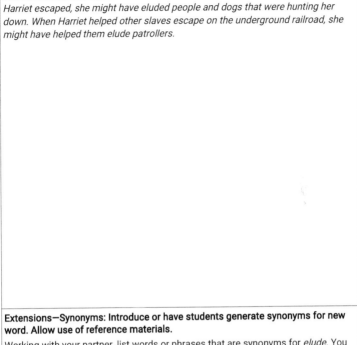

Harriet escaped, she might have eluded people and dogs that were hunting her down. When Harriet helped other slaves escape on the underground railroad, she might have helped them elude patrollers.

Extensions—Synonyms: Introduce or have students generate synonyms for new word. Allow use of reference materials.

Working with your partner, list words or phrases that are synonyms for *elude*. You are welcome to use a dictionary or thesaurus. [Teacher monitors and records words on an overhead transparency. The following synonyms are then shared with the class: *evade, avoid, escape from, run away from, dodge, shake off, break loose, get away.*]

77

FIGURE 3.2. Basic instructional routine for vocabulary: Intermediate grades.

Setting: Fifth-grade language arts
Situation: Introduction of new genre (autobiography)

Step 1: Introduce the word.

[Teacher displays the word.] This word is *autobiography*. What word? *Autobiography*.

Step 2: Introduce the meaning of the word.

Option 2. Guide students in analyzing the meaningful parts of the word.

[Teacher underlines biography in *autobiography*.] We have just finished reading a biography. Ones, tell your partner what a biography is. [Teacher monitors.] Yes, a biography is an account of someone's life that is written by another person. [Teacher circles *auto* in *autobiography*.] *Auto* means "self." What does *auto* mean? "Self." So an *autobiography* is an account of someone's life that is written by the person him- or herself.

Step 3: Illustrate with examples.

If I wrote about my life, it would be an . ~~Autobiography~~. If the leader of a country wrote about his or her life, he or she would write an   . *Autobiography*.

Step 4: Check students' understanding.

Option 1. Have students distinguish between examples and non-examples.

Please take out your Yes and No cards. Hold up Yes or No when I say, "Show me." Barbara Kramer wrote *Michael J. Fox: Courage for Life*. Think. Is this book an *autobiography*? Show me. [Students hold up a No card.] You are correct. This would not be an *autobiography* because another person wrote it. Michael J. Fox wrote about his own life in a number of books, including *Always Looking Up*. Is that book an *autobiography*? Show me. [Students hold up a Yes card.] Yes, Michael J. Fox wrote about his own life.

Barack Obama wrote about his life in a book called *Dreams from My Father*. Is the book an *autobiography*? Show me. [Students hold up a Yes card.] Ones, tell your partner how you know it was an *autobiography*. *It was about Obama and written by Obama*. Garen Thomas wrote *Yes We Can* about Barack Obama. Is that book an *autobiography*? Show me. [Students hold up a No card.] Twos, tell your partner how you knew it was not an *autobiography*. *It was about Obama but was written by someone else*.

Option 3. Ask questions that require deep processing of the word's meaning.

There are many reasons why someone might choose to write an *autobiography*. Think of some reasons.

[Teacher allows thinking time.] With your partner, come up with a number of reasons. [Teacher monitors.] Ones, I am going to call on a number of you to report for your partnership. [Teacher calls on students.]

Extensions—Word parts: Introduce other words containing the word part.

[Teacher writes *automobile* on the board.] Let's look at other words containing *auto*. This word is *automobile*. What word? *Automobile*. What is another word for automobile? *Car*. What does *auto* mean? "Self." *Mobile* means "to move." Why do you think cars were given the name *automobiles*? Ones, tell your partner your explanation. [Teacher calls on a student.] *You can use an automobile to move yourself from place to place, unlike a train, which requires someone else to drive it.*

[Teacher writes *autocrat* on the board.] This word is *autocrat*. What word? *Autocrat*. An autocrat is a leader of a government. Do you think an autocrat would head a dictatorship or a democracy? Twos, tell your partner. [Teacher monitors and calls on a student.] *"Auto" means "self," so I think an*
autocrat would head a dictatorship where one person had power.

(cont.)

FIGURE 3.2.

[Teacher writes *autograft* on the board.] This word is *autograft*. What word? *Autograft*. If a person was in a fire and some skin was burned, that person might need a *graft*, where new tissue would be placed over the burned area. If the person got an autograft, where would the skin come from? Tell your partner. [Teacher calls on a student.] *From another part of the person's own body. For example, if they had a burn on their arm, skin might be taken from their leg to form an autograft.*

[Teacher writes *autograph* on the board.] This word is *autograph*. Think about the meaning of *auto*. If I wrote down your name, would that be an autograph? Ones, tell your partner. [Teacher calls on a student.] *No, because "auto" means "self," I would have to write the name myself.* If you wrote down your name, would it be an autograph? Twos, tell your partner. [Teacher calls on a student.] *Yes, because "auto" means "self," I would write the signature myself.*

---

examples) and **You do it.** (check for understanding). However, when the concept is less familiar or difficult, it is useful to add a **We do it.** step, in which you guide students in examining examples and non-examples of the concept by asking questions about the critical attributes.

For the lesson in Figure 3.3, the geometry teacher introduces *chord* with more intensive instruction than you have seen in the previous example lessons. First, the meaning of the new word is introduced by having students break the glossary definition into parts or critical attributes. Next, the unknown concept is illustrated with both **examples and non-examples** to ensure

(cont.)

understanding **(I do it.)**. The teacher then guides students in examining examples and non-examples **(We do it.)**. Finally, students generated their own examples and non-examples of the concept to crystallize their conceptual knowledge **(You do it.)**. Because *chord* has more than one meaning, the teacher takes a moment at the beginning of the lesson to differentiate *chord* as it's used in math from its more common use as a musical term.

The lesson in Figure 3.4 represents the beginning of a 4-week unit of study. The high school teacher begins by introducing the term *genocide*, a concept that is central to understanding the unit. The teacher and students then employ a particular type of **graphic organizer** that can be used for introducing all major concepts. As the teacher proceeds through the lesson, students respond orally to questions and also fill in the graphic organizer.

Given the depth of understanding desired, this initial instruction is substantial and is followed by review of the term throughout the unit, as well as a culminating activity: **semantic mapping**, the use of another type of graphic organizer to connect other words and concepts to a basis concept (in this case, *genocide*). The purpose of semantic mapping (Heimlich & Pittelman, 1986) is to strengthen knowledge of the complex concept by relating it to other words. Students generate a list of related words, categorize the words, and determine labels for the categories. Notice how semantic mapping serves as an excellent review of the entire unit.

(text resumes on page 84)

FIGURE 3.3. Math concept: Use of examples and non-examples.

Setting: Eighth-grade geometry **Situation:** Vocabulary Instruction
Step 1: Introduce the word. (I do it.) [Teacher displays the word.] This word is *chord*. What word? *Chord*.

Extensions—Multiple-meaning words: Introduce other familiar uses of the word.
You probably have heard the word *chord* in the past. In music, it is a group of three or more notes that are sounded together. For example, if you were playing piano, you might play three notes with the same hand at the same time. The group of notes ~~would be a~~ —. *Chord*. On a guitar, the musician might press three fingers onto three different strings on the neck of the guitar to create a ——————— *Chord*. In geometry, *chord* has an entirely different meaning.

Step 2: Introduce the meaning of the word. (I do it.)

Option 3. Have students determine the critical attributes embedded in a glossary definition. Please locate the word *chord* in the glossary. [Teacher monitors.] Read the definition with me: *A chord is a line segment whose endpoints lie on a circle.* Record the word *chord* in your vocabulary log. [Teacher monitors.] Let's break the definition into the critical attributes. First, a *chord* is a ——————— ~~. Line~~-*segment*. We know that a line segment is straight. Next, the endpoints of the line segment lie on a . *Circle*. Please list the critical attributes under the word.
[Students' logs should be similar to this:] chord

     u   line   segment   u
     endpoints   lie   on
     circle

Step 3: Illustrate with examples and non-examples. (I do it.)

A〰B	The line segment AB is a chord. It is a line segment, a straight line with two endpoints, and the endpoints lie on a circle.
C D	The line segment CD is a chord. It is a line segment, and its two endpoints lie on a circle.
F E	The line segment EF is not a chord, because endpoint E is not on the circle.
G H	The line segment GH is not a chord, because only endpoint G lies on the circle.

**Step 4: Guide students in analyzing examples and non-examples, using the critical attributes.
(We do it.)**

B A	Is AB a line segment? *Yes*. Are the endpoints on the circle? *Yes*. Is AB a chord? *Yes*.
C D	Is CD a line segment? *Yes*. Are the endpoints on the circle? *No*. Is CD a chord? *No*. Yes, even though it is a line segment, the endpoints are

(cont.)

	not on the circle.

(cont.)

FIGURE 3.3.

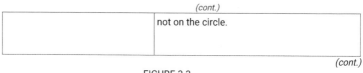

Is EF a line segment? *No.* No, it is not a line segment since it is not a straight. Is EF a chord? *No.* Correct. Remember, if either of the critical attributes are missing, it cannot be a chord.

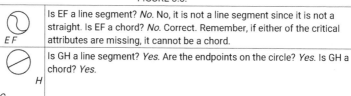

Is GH a line segment? *Yes.* Are the endpoints on the circle? *Yes.* Is GH a chord? *Yes.*

Step 5: Check students' understanding. (You do it.)

Option 2. Have students generate examples and non-examples.

Please take out your slates. Draw a circle on your slate. Add three chords. Label them AB, CD, and EF. [Teacher monitors as students draw a circle with three chords.] Please check your partner's drawing. Be sure that all three lines are chords. [Teacher continues to monitor.] Hold up your slates. [Teacher examines slates.] Erase.

Now draw a new circle on your slate. Draw three new lines that are not chords. Label the lines AB, CD, and EF. [Teacher monitors as students draw three lines that are not chords.] Everyone, hold up your slates. [Teacher examines slates.] Ones, explain to your partner why each of your lines is not a chord. Twos, explain to your partner why each of your lines is not a chord.

FIGURE 3.4. Complex concept instruction using a graphic organizer and semantic mapping.

Setting: Eleventh-grade global studies
Situation: Introduction to unit on genocide

Step 1: Introduce the word. (I do it)

[Teacher distributes the blank graphic organizer.] Today we are going to begin a unit on genocide. When the German government during World War II killed millions of Jews in an attempt to get rid of every Jew, the German government committed *genocide.* The "big concept" for this unit is *genocide.* [Teacher writes in the word *genocide* on the overhead transparency.] What word? *Genocide.* The word *genocide* is a noun.

Step 2: Introduce the meaning of the word. (I do it.)
Option 2. Guide students in analyzing the meaningful parts of the word.
Underline the two meaningful parts of the word *genocide*. [Teacher underlines geno and cide and writes genos and cide on the transparency.] *Genos* is a Greek word that means "race" or "tribe." *Cide* in Latin means "killing." [Teacher records these on transparency.] Thus *genocide* can mean the killing of a race. [Students fill in graphic organizer.]

Option 3. Have students determine the critical attributes embedded in a glossary definition. [Teacher fills in the graphic organizer as each attribute is introduced.] Let's explore the meaning of *genocide*. First, *genocide* is a deliberate act. The killing of the people is not random . . . it is intentional. It is deliberate. Next, it is systematic: The people who commit *genocide* have a plan that they carry out systematically. Next, *genocide* refers to the *destruction*, the killing, of a *group of people*. The destruction may be of the whole group or of part of the group. And finally, the destruction of the group is based on a *specific characteristic*, such as the ethnicity of the people, their race, their nationality, or their religion. Please be sure that you have filled in all of the critical attributes. [Teacher monitors.] Ones, pretend that your partner was not in class today. Explain *genocide*.

(cont.)

FIGURE 3.4. *(cont.)*

Step 3: Illustrate with examples and non-examples. (I do it.)

You are already familiar with the genocide of the Jews by the German government led by Adolf Hitler during World War II. Those actions are considered *genocide* because they were——.[Teacher points to attribute.] *Deliberate and systematic.* With the goal being the *– destruction* of a group of people based on a specific ——————— *characteristic*—in this case, religion. Please make a note of this example on your graphic organizer. [Teacher monitors.]

During the same war, many German and other Axis soldiers, and many American and other Allied soldiers, were killed in battle. Even though thousands were killed, this is not considered *genocide* because the purpose was to win a war, not to destroy a group of people based on some characteristic. Make a note of this non-example.

Step 4: Check students' understanding. (You do it.)

Option 1. Have students distinguish between examples and non-examples.

Get ready to tell me if this is an example of *genocide*. In 1994, the Hutus, an ethnic group in Rwanda in Africa, initiated a plan to kill all members of another ethnic group in Rwanda, the Tutsis. It is estimated that in a very short period of time, 800,000 Tutsis were killed. Would this be an example of *genocide?* Yes. Twos, tell your partner how you knew that this was genocide. [Teacher monitors.] You said that the killing of the Tutsis was both deliberate and   . *Systematic.* And that the destruction of the Tutsis was based on a specific   . *Characteristic.* In this case, ethnicity. Please add this example to your graphic organizer.

In 2004, a huge tsunami hit Indonesia, Sri Lanka, and other Pacific Rim nations. Approximately 230,000 people died. Would this be an example of *genocide? No.* Ones, tell your partner how you knew that this was not genocide. [Teacher monitors.] Excellent explanations. You said that there was no deliberate, systematic plan to kill a group of people. Here the tsunami was an act of nature. Add this non-example.

Extensions—Word parts: Introduce other words containing the word part.

One part of the word *genocide* is *cide*. Numerous words contain *cide* and refer to killing—for example, *suicide* and *insecticide*. With your partner, think of other words containing *cide* and add them to your graphic organizer. You may use reference materials. [Teacher monitors and then calls on students.] *Pesticide, infanticide, homicide, herbicide, bactericide, rodenticide.*

Extensions—Synonyms: Introduce or have students generate synonyms for new word. Allow use of reference materials.

Although there is not a perfect synonym for *genocide*, several words are fairly close. With your partner, generate a list of synonyms and record them on your graphic organizer. Again, reference materials can be used. [Teacher monitors and

FIGURE 3.4. *(cont.)*

then calls on students.] *Mass murder, massacre, annihilation, extermination, ethnic cleansing.*

Extensions—Word family: Using a connected story, introduce other words in the same "word family."
Find the cell on your graphic organizer labeled "Members of word family." The only other word in the family is *genocidal*, an adjective. When committing genocide, people carry out genocidal acts, such as starving or working others to death. Record *genocidal* on your graphic organizer.

(cont.)

Completed Graphic Organizer

Concept: genocide

Analysis of Word: genos = race or tribe
(Greek) cide = killing
(Latin)
Part of Speech: noun

Critical Attributes: u
deliberate
u
systematic
u destruction
u of a group of people (in whole or part)
u based on a specific characteristic (e.g., ethnicity, race, nationality, religion)

Examples	**Non-Examples**
Holocaust in WWII—killing of Jews	Killing of Axis and Allied troops in WWII
1994—Killing of Tutsis by Hutus in Rwanda (Africa)	2004—About 230,000 killed in Pacific tsunami

Associations:		**Synonyms:**
suicide	infanticide	Mass murder, massacre, annihilation,
homicide pesticide	insecticide	extermination, elimination, ethnic cleansing

FIGURE 3.4. *(cont.)*

Members of Word Family
genocidal (adj.)
Your Sentence
During World War II, <u>genocide</u> occurred when the German government under Hitler killed millions of Jews.

Extensions—Semantic mapping: Have students list, categorize, and label words that they associate with the target concept.

We have been studying *genocide* for the past 4 weeks. You are going to have 5 minutes to write down any words that come to mind when you hear the word *genocide*. For example, I immediately think of these words: *death, extermination, religion, Cambodia.* [Teacher lists these on overhead transparency.] Please begin. [Teacher moves around the room, writing down students' words and corresponding students' names on the transparency.] Read your list to your partner. Ones, then Twos. [Teacher continues to record students' ideas, with students' names next to the ideas, on the transparency.] Let's look at your classmates' ideas. [Teacher and students read the list of words on the transparency.]

  Now please join the members of your cooperative team. Select a recorder. [Pause.] Recorders, write the word *genocide* in the center of your group's poster. [Teacher models on overhead transparency.] Each of you has a list of words. You are going to group your words into categories. Your first team job is to come up with categories. My turn first. My first word was *death*. A category might be "Results of Genocide." [Teacher adds this category on overhead transparency.] Extermination could also go under that category. My next word was *religion*. I am going to have the category "Characteristics of Group."

  With your team, come up with your own categories. Don't record any of your words yet. [Teacher monitors, calls on recorders to report their categories, and adds categories to transparency.]

  Now you have your categories. Go around your team. Each person will say a word on their list and the corresponding category. Recorders, add to your team's poster. Continue until I say stop.

[Teacher monitors. Here is the semantic map created by one cooperative team.]

(cont.)

FIGURE 3.4. *(cont.)*

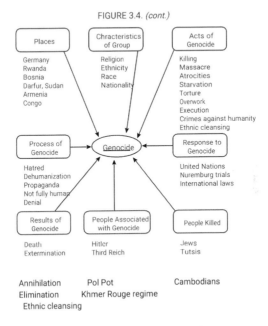

Annihilation   Pol Pot   Cambodians
Elimination   Khmer Rouge regime
Ethnic cleansing

VOCABULARY INSTRUCTION EXTENSIONS

We have provided a simple yet powerful instructional routine for teaching vocabulary. While reading the lessons, you may have noticed that we have frequently provided lesson extensions in order to deepen understanding of the target word and its underlying concept. The instructional routine can be thought of as the "cake" and the extensions as the "frosting." To determine the amount and nature of the lesson augmentation, we have considered each target word's importance, its difficulty, and the depth of learning desired. Below, we describe the extensions illustrated in the example lessons, as well as other possible extensions.

FIGURE 3.4. *(cont.)*

Synonyms (Same)

When you provide a well-chosen synonym—one that is very close in meaning to the vocabulary word and known to students—you ease acquisition of the new word for your students. You can also have students generate a list of synonyms drawn from their personal lexicon, a dictionary, or a thesaurus. When you are asking students to suggest synonyms, have them limit their choices to familiar words that they have heard and used, rather than listing all entries in a thesaurus. Discuss any subtle differences in meaning between the target word and synonym.

For example, when investigating synonyms for *genuine*, a cooperative team offered *honest*. The class then discussed the subtle differences between *genuine* and *honest*. When something is truly what it is said to be, it is *genuine* (a *genuine* piece of art rather than a fake; a *genuine* $100 bill rather than a counterfeit; a *genuine* person who appears kind and is kind). Thus *genuine* can be used to describe many things or actions, whereas *honest* usually refers to a person.

Antonyms (Opposite)

Antonyms, like synonyms, are often very helpful in clarifying the meaning of a word. An antonym shares all but one feature with the target word being taught, but is the opposite of the target word in that one feature. For example, *affluent* (target word) and *poor* (antonym) both refer to the amount of money one has, but *affluent* means having a good deal of money and *poor* means having little. Similarly, *reluctant* (target word) and *eager* (antonym) both refer to a manner of approaching a task, but one indicates no enthusiasm and the other indicates much enthusiasm.

When you present an antonym to students, it needs to be a word that they know, or the antonym will serve to confuse rather than clarify. For example, when you are teaching *optional*, the antonym *required* is likely to be more helpful than *compulsory* or *mandatory*, which are words that are probably unknown to students learning *optional*. Similarly, when you ask students to generate antonyms, the words should be familiar (words they have heard, read, spoken, and/or written).

Word Family

Nagy and Anderson (1984) and other researchers suggest expanding instruction beyond the target word to members of the so-called "word family," or words that are related morphologically and semantically (e.g., the word family for *stable* includes *unstable, stabilize, stabilized, stabilization, stability,* and *instability*). In their analysis of the 570 words in Coxhead's (2000) *Academic Word List,* Lubliner and Hiebert (2008) found that 76% had a morphological word family of three or more related words, making this practice very fruitful. When you are introducing a family of words, you can use the following procedure:

u Step 1: List the target word and "relatives" on the board, overhead, or SMART Board, so that the morphological similarities are obvious. For many words, the relationship is more easily "seen" than "heard" (e.g., *wild, wilderness; protest, Protestant, Catholic, Catholicism; declare, declaration; compile, compilation; acquire, acquisition*).

u Step 2: Model the pronunciation of each word, and have students repeat the words.

u Step 3: Introduce the meaning of the words by using a connected story. Ask students to add words to the oral story when you point to the missing words.

FIGURE 3.5. Introducing word families.

Word list	Story to introduce word "relatives"
apologize apologized apologizing apologetic apologetically apology	After lying to Jan, Gwen knew she needed to . *Apologize*. When she was wrong in the past, she always . *Apologized*. Gwen knew that *apologizing* was the best action. However, she was very angry at Jan and didn't feel very . *Apologetic*. Finally, Gwen did go to Jan and *apologetically* said that she was sorry. Jan graciously listened to the . *Apology*.

For example, in Figure 3.5, after teaching *apologize*, the teacher used a story to introduce students to other members of the "family."

Word Parts

When you introduce a word part (a prefix, suffix, or root) in the target word, you can also introduce other words with the same word part. Like the use of word families, this is a way to extend students' vocabulary and help them generalize their knowledge to other words.

Stahl and Nagy (2006) suggest introducing words with key word parts, using webs as shown in Figure 3.6. You can select words that contain the new word part, or you can have students suggest words.

Multiple-M eaning Words

Multiple-meaning words are very prevalent in English. Many high-frequency words have numerous meanings. Multiple-meaning words are likely to cause special difficulty when the meaning used in conversational English differs from a more specialized use in a content area. Misunderstanding is likely to occur when students in a music class are thinking of a baseball *pitch*, rather than the degree of highness or lowness of a *pitch*; when students in chemistry class are thinking of a *solution* to a problem, rather than a liquid *solution* in which a solid substance is dissolved; or when students responding to an item on a state test are thinking of *concrete* composed of cement, rocks, and water, rather than *concrete* evidence.

Graves (2006) suggests following these three steps when introducing multiplemeaning words: (1) Acknowledge the known meaning of a word, (2) teach the new meaning of the word, and (3) note any similarities between the meanings of the word.

Let's look back at Figure 3.3. At the beginning of the lesson on *chord*, the teacher acknowledges the musical meaning of *chord* and distinguishes that meaning from the mathematical term. After introducing *chord* as a geometry concept, the teacher notes that there is no semantic relationship between the two meanings of *chord.*

FIGURE 3.6. Word webs with prefixes and suffixes.

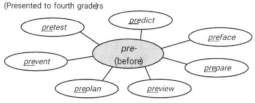

(Presented to fourth graders)

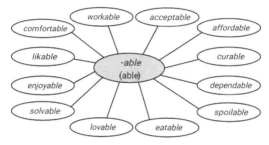

(Generated by sixth graders)

Graphic Organizers

Graphic organizers are powerful visual representations that help students organize and remember critical information. As shown in Figure 3.4, a teacher can use graphic organizers to introduce major concepts and have students make a record of the information presented by the teacher and/or generated by students. One of the most popular types of graphic organizers, **word maps** (Schwartz & Raphael, 1985), can be used at any grade level as evidenced by the two examples in Figure 3.7.

Logs of Vocabulary Words

Students in second grade and above should maintain logs of words introduced in reading, language arts, and content-area classes. A log can include each target word, its meaning (written in the student's own words), other useful information about the specific word (e.g., meanings of word parts, synonyms, antonyms, derivatives), and a response to the word that you designate (e.g., a representational drawing, an original sentence that includes the word and indicates its meaning, or examples and non-examples). Logs can be used for self-study, for peer partner study, for class review, and as a resource when writing. Often elementary teach-

FIGURE 3.7. Word maps.

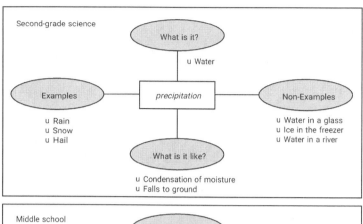

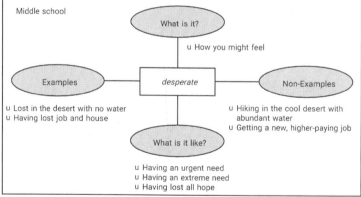

ers have students collapse vocabulary from all subjects into one alphabetized log, rather than have them keep separate logs or sections of logs by subject area. However, grouping semantically related words by subject is a better option, because it will facilitate initial learning, study, review, and retention.

Word Walls

In addition to having students keep vocabulary logs, you can post vocabulary words in the classroom. The benefits of this practice include (1) allowing you to provide quick review; (2) keeping the words in your own consciousness, which facilitates incorporating them into your oral language (e.g., after you teach *concentrate*, *educated*, and *impressed*, you might make these comments: "You are really *concentrating* on your math assignment," "Your papers reflect great effort—I was very *impressed*," and "You certainly are becoming *educated*"); and (3) making words available for students to integrate into discussions and written products.

As we have recommended for vocabulary logs, words should be displayed by subject rather than alphabetically, with some reminder of the context and domain. For example, a teacher might post a copy of a book's cover coupled with related vocabulary terms on a bulletin board labeled "Read-Alouds," or the major concepts and related vocabulary words (e.g., *natural resources*: *renewable resources*, *nonrenewable resources*, *energy sources*, *conservation*, *pollution*, *recycling*) under the label "Science Explorations."

Semantic Mapping

Semantic mapping (Heimlich & Pittelman, 1986), in which students generate words related to an important concept, categorize the words, and discuss relationships between words, is especially useful when the central concept is complex and associated with a rich reservoir of related terms. Many variations of the semantic mapping procedure have emerged over time, including the following.

Whole-Class Activity

The teacher writes the central concept on one side of the board. Students suggest words and phrases related to the central concept. The teacher explains concepts that are not universally known, suggests additional words, and records all words on the board. Next, students suggest categories and corresponding labels, which are recorded on the other side of the board. Finally, all words are placed under the category labels as the teacher and students discuss the relationships between the words.

Partner, Team, or Individual Project

A similar process is utilized: Students (1) begin with a central concept, (2) brainstorm related words and phrases, (3) determine categories and labels, and (4) categorize the words. After students have completed the mapping process, their maps can be shared and discussed with other class members. Revisit the semantic map on *genocide* (see Figure 3.4).

Generally, you would use semantic mapping to prepare students for reading a content-area chapter or studying a body of knowledge. When such maps are completed prior to reading, you can assess students' prior knowledge concerning the new topic. The activity will also activate the students' prior knowledge and increase their interest in the topic. After reading, you can assist students in adding categories and words to the concept map. As seen in Figure 3.4, semantic mapping is also an excellent culminating activity for summarizing the critical content of a chapter or unit of study.

Concept Map

Concept maps, also referred to as **mind maps**, are hierarchical, visual diagrams that show the relationships among concepts and convey even complex information at a glance (Novak, 1993). The concepts themselves are enclosed in circles, boxes, or other shapes, and the relationships between concepts are indicated with connecting lines or arrows that indicate the type of relationship (one-way, two-way, or nondirectional) and linking words that label the relationship (e.g., *like, produces, examples, including*). See Figure 3.8 for an example.

You can prepare concept maps to introduce or review critical concepts. Learners can also generate concept maps individually or with classmates, once they have had considerable experience in "reading" teacher-created concept maps. Learnerconstructed concept maps can be used to (1) assess students' understanding of the content, (2) summarize what has been taught/read, and (3) support study of the material.

FIGURE 3.8. Concept map for social studies class.

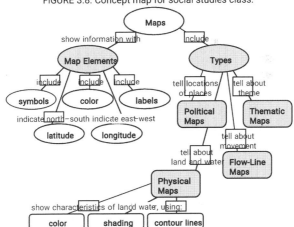

CHAPTER SUMMARY

Vocabulary instruction is central to all content areas at all grade levels. In this chapter, we have outlined explicit vocabulary instruction, from preparation to ongoing review. Preparation for vocabulary instruction begins with selecting terms that are unknown, critical to the content, useful in the future, and difficult to obtain independently. Next, the teacher determines how the meaning will be conveyed: by presenting a student-friendly explanation, analyzing a glossary definition, or exploring embedded word parts. Final preparation involves the development of examples and non-examples to illustrate the concept. When teaching a word's meaning to students, the teacher can use these instructional steps: (1) introduce the word, (2) introduce the meaning of the word, (3) illustrate with examples, and (4) check understanding. Depending on the depth of processing desired, the lesson can be augmented with carefully chosen extensions (synonyms, antonyms, word families, graphic organizers, vocabulary logs, word walls, semantic mapping, or concept maps). Consistent with teaching skills and strategies, review activities must be planned to ensure not only initial mastery but long-term retention.

In the next chapter, we present information on rule instruction. You will immediately see the similarities to vocabulary instruction, especially with regard to the use of examples and non-examples.

CHAPTER 4

Designing Lessons

Rules

A rule describes the relationship between a general principle or set of conditions and specific outcomes or behaviors. Rules are generally understood through **If–Then** statements: *If A occurs, then B will occur.* Examples of these lawful relationships are found in all content areas. (Note: In the examples, *when* is often substituted for *if;* the *then* may be either explicit or implied.)

Science: When heat is added, solids, liquids, and gases all expand.

Social studies: If the quantity produced increases, then usually the price is reduced, and vice versa.

Math: If the last digit is even, then the number is divisible by 2.

Reading (decoding): When the letter *c* is followed by *e, i,* or *y,* the letter *c* has the sound (phoneme) /s/.

Writing (spelling): When a noun ends in *ch, s, sh, x,* or *z,* and you want to make the noun plural, add *es*.

Writing (punctuation): If a sentence asks a question, then the end punctuation is a question mark.

Writing (grammar): If the subject is singular, then the verb must be singular. If the subject is plural, then the verb must be plural as well.

As with vocabulary terms, a teacher must do three things when introducing rules: (1) select appropriate rules that are useful not only currently, but also in the future; (2) develop examples and non-examples for introduction and practice; and (3) adapt the instructional routine to match the specific rule.

92

SELECT APPROPRIATE RULES FOR EXPLICIT INSTRUCTION

We have stressed in Chapter 3 that vocabulary words selected for expanded, explicit instruction should be words that are unknown, important to understanding a passage or unit, and useful in the future. Rules that deserve extended instruction should meet these same criteria. First, the rules should be unknown. For example, it will usually be more important to teach seventh graders the rule for using a comma to offset a phrase and/or the rule for using commas to separate items in a series than the rules for using a comma to separate dates and years or cities and states—rules that were probably mastered in earlier grades. Of course, prioritizing some rules above others will depend on the actual skills of the students being taught; some seventh graders will need to learn all of these rules.

Next, the rules should be important to understanding the content being taught. For example, during the teaching of a unit on energy, the first law of thermodynamics (*Energy can neither be created nor destroyed*) is an essential rule. When a math teacher is introducing exponents, the rule of exponents (*The exponent represents the number of times you multiply a number by itself*) is taught. Even in a subject such as art, critical rules can be identified as important to the content (e.g., *Objects are drawn smaller as the distance from their observer increases*).

Finally, as with all content that you choose to emphasize, rules should empower students in the future. This simply means that students should have many opportunities to use the rule in the future. For example, a fifth-grade teacher, having to limit the number of punctuation rules to teach, may emphasize the rules concerning end-of-sentence punctuation and commas over the rules governing the use of hyphens. A high school special education teacher may emphasize spelling rules concerning the addition of suffixes to words having different roots over the rules governing the selection of *ible* versus *able*. Similarly, a middle school English teacher may put more emphasis on rules concerning the use of quotation marks than on the rule for when to insert [*sic*] in a document. (For your own curiosity, [*sic*] is inserted when a writer is quoting material containing spelling or grammatical errors or confusing material, to indicate that the errors or confusion appeared in the original material.)

DEVELOP EXAMPLES AND NON- EXAMPLES

In Chapter 3, we have presented an instructional routine for introducing unknown vocabulary terms: (1) Introduce the word, (2) introduce the meaning of the word, (3) illustrate with examples, and (4) check students' understanding. The vocabulary routine consistently utilizes examples to illustrate new vocabulary terms, but uses non-examples only when a concept is more difficult. However, the careful creation of both examples and non-examples is essential to the teaching of rules. First, both examples and non-examples must be used in illustrating a rule, to ensure that students understand the boundaries of the concept: when the rule applies and when it does not apply. Next, although there are numerous ways to check students' understanding of a vocabulary term, distinguishing between examples and nonexamples is the most effective procedure for verifying understanding of a rule. The basic steps used to develop examples and non-examples for vocabulary terms are replicated for rules.

Step 1: Examine the Rule and Determine the Critical Attributes or Parts of the Rule

Remember that rules are **If–Then** relationships: One or more conditions (critical attributes) must be in place for the outcome or behavior to occur. In order to design examples and non-examples, you must begin by determining the critical attribute or attributes (**If**) that must be present for the outcome or behavior to occur (**Then**). This analysis is modeled and practiced in Application 4.1.

APPLICATION 4.1. DETERMINING CRITICAL ATTRIBUTES IN A RULE

Directions: Read the first three rules and corresponding critical attributes. Then determine the critical attributes for the last two rules. When you are finished, compare your responses to ours in *Feedback on Application Exercises*, page 260.

Rule: When a noun ends in *ch, s, sh, x,* or *z* and you want to make it plural, add *es* instead of *s*.

Critical attribute (If): Noun ends in *ch, s, sh, x,* or *z.*
Then: Add *es* (instead of *s*).

Rule: If the only divisors are 1 and the number itself, then the number is a prime number.

Critical attributes (If):
 u Divisor of 1. u
 Divisor of number
 itself.

u No other divisors.
Then: Number is prime number.

Rule: If you are showing a comparison, use *than*. If you are indicating time, use *then*.

Critical attribute (If): Showing a comparison. **Then:** Use *than*.

Critical attribute (If): Showing *when*.

Then: Use *then*.

Rule: Use commas to separate the words and/or word groups in a series of three or more.

Critical attributes (If):

Then: Separate with commas.

Rule: When a word ends in a vowel–consonant–final *e* and you want to add a suffix that begins with a vowel, drop the *e*.

Critical attributes (If):

Then: Drop the *e*.

Step 2: Design Examples in Which All Critical Attributes Are Present

When you are designing exemplars for vocabulary or rule instruction, all of the critical attributes must be present in each example. In addition, for both vocabulary terms and rules, a range of examples is necessary in order to promote clarity and understanding. When you are teaching the spelling rule that involves dropping the final *e*, if the only examples used are *hating, shining, timing*, and *requiring*, students may conclude that this rule only applies when the ending is *ing*. Similarly, if you introduce the use of the question mark with sentences beginning only with the words *What, Where, When*, and *Why*, students may conclude that a question mark should be placed at the end of any sentence beginning with the letter *W*. Soon students may be punctuating sentences in this manner: *We went to the piano concert? Wayne road his bike to school?*

Let's revisit the rules presented in Application 4.1 and see how examples for rule instruction would be designed (see Application 4.2).

APPLICATION 4.2. CREATING EXAMPLES TO ILLUSTRATE A RULE

Directions: Read each set of examples. Notice that several different examples are provided in each set. Create your own examples for the last two rules, and then compare your suggested examples to ours in *Feedback on Application Exercises*, page 261.

Rule: When a noun ends in *ch, s, sh, x*, or *z* and you want to make it plural, add *es* instead of *s*.

Critical attribute (If): Noun ends in *ch, s, sh, x*, or *z*.

Then: Add *es* (instead of *s*).

Examples: *waltzes, boxes, watches, sandwiches, flashes*.

Comment: The examples all end with *ch, s, sh, x*, or *z*, requiring the use of *es* rather than *s*. In addition, the words represent a range of examples, in that they vary in length and final letters.

Rule: If the only divisors are 1 and the number itself, then the number is a prime number.

Critical attributes (If):
u Divisor of 1. u
Divisor of number
itself.
u No other divisors.
Then: Number is prime number.

Examples: 7, 13, 29, and 89.

Comment: All examples are prime numbers having all of the critical attributes. The examples represent a range, in that they vary in value. However, very large prime numbers (e.g., 541) are not used as it would be time-consuming to determine whether there were any divisors other than 1 and the number itself.

Rule: If you are showing a comparison, use *than*. If you are indicating time, use *then*.

Critical attribute (If): Showing a comparison.

Then: Use *than*.

Critical attribute (If): Showing *when*.

Then: Use *then*.

Examples for *than*:

The new rose garden is even more beautiful *than* the old garden.

Many commuter trains travel two times faster *than* most freight trains.

The hybrid produces corn that is much larger *than* the original corn variety.

Examples for *then*:

The new rose garden bloomed earlier; *then* the old garden bloomed.

The commuter trains arrived, and *then* the freight trains pulled into the station.

The hybrid corn was harvested first, and *then* the original corn variety.

Comment: Often rules will come in pairs. When one rule doesn't apply, the other does. In this case, the examples for one rule (e.g., the use of *than*) can serve as the non-examples for the other rule (e.g., the use of *then*). The sentence examples have similar content, requiring that students really think. They can't simply say, "Oh, this sentence is also talking about a garden. I guess I will use *than* again."

Rule: Use commas to separate the words and/or word groups in a series of three or more.

Critical attributes (If): u
Words and/or word
groups.
u Series of three or more.

Then: Separate with commas.

Examples:

Rule: When a word ends in a vowel–consonant–final *e* and you want to add a suffix that begins with a vowel, drop the *e*.

Critical attributes (If):
u Word ends in
vowel–consonant–final *e*. u Suffix
begins with a vowel.
Then: Drop the *e*.
Your examples:

Step 3: Design Non-E xamples in Which One of the Critical Attributes Is Missing

When you are introducing a rule, both examples *and* non-examples are essential, because both help define the conditions under which the rule is and is not applied. In Chapter 3, we have presented a number of options for checking student understanding of vocabulary terms. However, when you check understanding of a rule, having students distinguish between examples and non-examples is indispensable.

To develop non-examples, you alter one of the critical attributes of the academic rule. For instance, if a rule has two critical attributes, you alter only *one* of the attributes. Consider the case of dropping the final *e* when adding a suffix: *If the* word ends in a consonant–vowel–consonant–final *e* (CVCe), and the suffix begins with a vowel, *then* drop the final *e*. *See + ing* is a non-example, because the first attribute has been altered: The root word does not end in a CVCe. However, the second attribute is in place: The suffix begins with a vowel. On the other hand, *time + less* is a non-example because the root word ends in a CVCe, but the suffix does not begin with a vowel. In both cases, only one attribute has been changed. The creation of effective non-examples will require you to think carefully about the critical attributes, but the outcome is that your students will also have to consider the rule attributes thoughtfully, which is the goal for this instruction.

Another procedure that encourages students to be thoughtful is to use **minimal pairs**. A minimal pair consists of an example and a non-example that differ on one critical attribute, with all other features remaining the same. When minimal pairs are used, students' attention is directed to the critical attributes of the rule, not the irrelevant features. For example, when you are teaching the spelling rule concerning dropping the final *e*, you might utilize this minimal pair:

Example: *hate + ing = hating*
Non-example: *hate + ful = hateful*

The word *hate* is used in both the example and the non-example. Because the root word remains the same, whether or not the root word ends in CVCe has for now become irrelevant, leaving students to concentrate on the suffix and whether it begins with a vowel. In the minimal pair just given, the relevant information for the example is that the suffix *ing* begins with a vowel. So students should drop the final *e*. The relevant information for the non-example is that the suffix *ful* does not begin with a vowel. Therefore, students should not drop the final *e*. In simple terms, the students can't simply guess and conclude, "There is *hate* again. I will drop the *e*." They will quickly learn that they must think, not guess.

Once again, let's return to the rules you have analyzed in Applications 4.1 and 4.2. As you examine the non-examples in Application 4.3, determine the critical attribute that has been deleted and any minimal pairs.

APPLICATION 4.3. CREATING NON-EXAMPLES TO ILLUSTRATE A RULE

Directions: Read each set of examples and non-examples. Create your own non-examples for the last two rules, and then compare your responses to ours in Application Exercises, pages 261–262.

Rule: When a noun ends in *ch, s, sh, x,* or *z* and you want to make it plural, add *es* instead of *s.*

Examples: *waltzes, boxes, watches, sandwiches, flashes.*
Non-examples: *walls, books, fathers, sandpipers, flashbacks.*
Comment: Both the example and non-example words end with different letters and vary in length. The non-examples end with a variety of consonants, but not *ch, s, sh, x,* or *z. Sandwiches–sandpipers* and *flashes–flashbacks would be considered minimal pairs; each pair consists of an example and a nonexample that are similar, except that in one case es must be added.*

Rule: If the only divisors are 1 and the number itself, then the number is a prime number.

Examples: 7, 13, 29, and 89.
Non-examples: 9, 15, 27, and 90.
Comment: The non-examples, like the examples, vary in number of digits. The non-examples have small enough divisors (2, 3, 5, 9, 10) that students can easily determine there are other divisors besides 1 and the number itself. Minimal pairs are not possible here.

Rule: If you are showing a comparison, use *than.* If you are indicating time, use *then.*
Examples for *than*:
The new rose garden is even more beautiful *than* the old garden.
Many commuter trains travel two times faster *than* most freight trains.
The hybrid produces corn that is much larger *than* the original corn variety.
Examples for *then*:
The new rose garden bloomed earlier; *then* the old garden bloomed.
The commuter trains arrived, and *then* the freight trains pulled into the station.
The hybrid corn was harvested first, and *then* the original corn variety.
Comment: Often rules will come in pairs. When one rule doesn't apply, the other does.

In this case, the examples for one rule (e.g., the use of *than*) serve as the non-examples for the other rule (e.g., the use of *then*). To ensure that students will really have to think, the content of the sentences is similar.

Rule: Use commas to separate the words and/or word groups in a series of three or more.

Examples: u Cameron, Cecilia, Jamie, and Cedric all take the bus to school. u Jasmine purchased notebook paper, pens, and a ruler for school.
u The children's favorite activities included playing dodge ball, reading library books, painting, working in the garden, and writing stories.
u Brianna was described as being extraordinarily energetic, hard-working, independent, humorous, and kind.

Non-examples:

Rule: When a word ends in a vowel–consonant–final *e* and you want to add a suffix that begins with a vowel, drop the *e*.

Examples: **Non-examples:** *hate + ing = hating shine + ing = shining time + ed = timed debate + able = debatable require + ed = required*

INSTRUCTIONAL ROUTINE FOR TEACHING A RULE

Throughout this book, we emphasize the utility of mastering efficient and effective instructional routines that you can use again and again. As you would expect, the instructional routine for teaching rules is analogous to the routine for teaching vocabulary, with a few subtle differences.

Step 1: Introduce the Rule

Care must be taken in the wording of the rule. As with definitions for unknown vocabulary words, students must understand the wording of the rule. This requires using terminology that is known and making the rule as simple as possible (as long as it is accurate). Generally, it is most useful to use the **If–Then** construction when presenting the rule, but other constructions can be used. In Application 4.4, select the best rule wording out of each set provided.

APPLICATION 4.4. WORDING OF RULES

Directions: Read each set of rule statements and select the wording that will best communicate the rule to students. Check to be sure that the rule is **accurate**, that the words will be **understood**, and that the rule statement is as **brief** as possible. When you have selected a rule statement from each set, compare your choices with ours in *Feedback on Application Exercises*, page 262.

SET 1

1. When a word ends in the letter *y*, you must change the *y* to an *i* before adding any suffix. (If you're adding *ist*, you usually keep only one *i*.)
2. When a word ends in a consonant and *y*, change the *y* to *i* before adding any suffix other than *ing*. (If you're adding *ist*, you usually keep only one *i*.)
3. If a word ends in a *y* and a consonant letter precedes the *y*, be sure to change the *y* to an *i* before adding a suffix, except in the situation where the suffix is *ing*. (If you're adding *ist*, you usually keep only one *i*.)

Examples: **Non-examples:**

reply + ed = replied   *reply + ing = replying*

beauty + ful = beautiful   *play + ful = playful*

pacify + ist = pacifist   *pacify + ing = pacifying*

accompany + ment = accompaniment   *accompany + ing =*

accompany + ist = accompanist   *accompanying*

SET 2

1. If you have two subjects in a sentence and both of the subjects are singular, and you connect them with *or* or *nor* (not *and*), then it will be necessary to use a matching singular verb.
2. If you use *or* or *nor* as a conjunction, use a singular verb.
3. When you have two singular subjects connected by *or* or *nor*, use a singular verb.

Examples:

My sister *or* my brother *is* fixing dinner tonight.
Neither my sister *nor* my brother *is* fixing dinner tonight.

Step 2: Illustrate the Rule with Examples and Non-Examples

In the vocabulary lessons in Chapter 3, the vocabulary terms are illustrated with examples unless a definition contains many critical attributes or represents a complex concept; then both examples and non-examples are used. In contrast, when teaching rules, it is always wise to illustrate the rule by using both examples and non-examples, in order to clarify the boundaries of the rule. Generally, you will first use examples to explain the rule, and then clarify the rule with non-examples.

Step 3: Guide Students in Analyzing Examples and Non- Examples, Using the Critical Attributes

In most vocabulary lessons, you will introduce the word and its meaning (**I do it.**) and then check understanding (**You do it.**). Only with more difficult or unfamiliar vocabulary terms such as *chord* is it necessary to use all three instructional steps: **I do it. We do it. You do it.** However, with rules, you will need to scaffold and support students' initial examination of the examples and non-examples by asking questions about the presence or absence of the critical attributes. Thus prompted/guided practice (**We do it.**) must be part of the instructional routine.

Step 4: Check Students' Understanding, Using Examples and Non- Examples

Checking students' understanding of rules involves having them distinguish between examples and non-examples (does the rule apply or not?) or generate examples and non-examples.

Because understanding is being ascertained, you must not guide or lead students; they must work independently. Of course, they are still under your watchful eye so that errors are not practiced.

Examine the model elementary, middle school, and high school lessons provided in Figures 4.1, 4.2, and 4.3, respectively, to see how this instructional routine applies to the teaching of rules. Again, the model lessons will be most valuable if read out loud or taught to a classmate, friend, or colleague.

(text resumes on page 107)

FIGURE 4.1. Model lesson 1: Spelling rule.

Setting: Fourth-grade classroom	
Step 1: Introduce the rule. We are going to learn a spelling rule about adding suffixes when the root word ends in *y*. Listen to the rule: When a word ends in a consonant and *y*, change the *y* to *i* before adding any suffix other than *ing*.	
Step 2: Illustrate the rule with examples and non-examples.	
Example: *cry + ed* =	I have the word *cry*, and I want to add the suffix *ed. Cry* ends in a consonant and *y*. [Teacher points to the letters *r* and *y*.] and I'm adding a suffix other than *ing*. [Teacher points to *ed*.] So I change the *y* to *i*. (Teacher crosses out the letter *y* and writes an *i* above it, and then writes *cried*.) Everyone, spell *cried*. C-r-i-e-d.
Example: *copy + ed* =	I have the word *copy*, and I want to add the suffix *ed. Copy* ends in a consonant and *y*. [Teacher points to the letters *p* and *y*.] And I'm adding a suffix other than *ing*. [Teacher points to *ed*.] So I change the *y* to *i*. [Teacher crosses out the letter *y* and writes an *i* above it, and then writes *copied*.] Everyone, spell *copied*. C-o-p-i-e-d.
Non-example: *copy + ing* =	I have the word *copy*, and I want to add the suffix *ing. Copy* ends in a consonant and *y*. [Teacher points to the letters *p* and *y*.] But I'm adding the suffix *ing*. [Teacher points to *ing*.] So I do not change the *y* to *i*. [Teacher writes *copying*.] Everyone, spell *copying*. C-o-p-y-i-n-g.

(cont.)

(cont.)
FIGURE 4.1.

Non-example: cry + ing =	I have the word *cry*, and I want to add the suffix *ing*. *Cry* ends in a consonant-y. [Teacher points to the letters *r* and *y*.] But I'm adding the suffix *ing*. [Teacher points to *ing*]. So I do not change the *y* to *i*. [Teacher writes *crying*.] Everyone, spell *crying*. C-r-y-i-n-g.
Example: pacify + ist =	Here is the word *pacify*, and I want to add the suffix *ist*. *Pacify* ends in a consonant and *y*. [Teacher points to the letters *f* and *y*.] And I'm adding a suffix other than *ing*. [Teacher points to *ist*.] So I change the *y* to an *i*. [Teacher crosses out the letter *y* and writes an *i* above it, and then writes *pacifist* with two *i*s.] Before you spell *pacifist*, look. When I'm left with two *i*s, I just keep one of them. [Teacher crosses off one *i*.] Everyone, spell *pacifist*. P-a-c-i-f-i-s-t.
Non-example: play + er =	Here is the word *play*, and I want to add the suffix *er*. *Play* ends in a vowel and *y*. [Teacher points to the letters *a* and *y*.] Play does *not* end with a consonant and *y*, so I don't change the *y* to an *i*. [Teacher writes *player*.] Everyone, spell *player*. P-l-a-y-e-r.

Step 3: Guide students in analyzing examples and non-examples, using the critical attributes.

Example: study + ed =	Let's spell some words together. We have the word *study*, and we want to add the suffix *ed*. Does *study* end in a consonant and *y*? Yes. Am I adding a suffix other than *ing*? Yes. Do we change the *y* to *i*? Yes. Write *studied*. Put your pencil down to show me that you are done. [Teacher monitors. When students are done, the teacher writes *studied* on the board.] Check your spelling. If you missed the word, cross it out and rewrite it. [Pause.] Spell *studied*. S-t-u-d-i-e-d.
Non-example: stay + ed =	We have the word *stay*, and we want to add the suffix *ed*. Does *stay* end in a consonant and *y*? No. Do we change the *y* to *i*? No. Write *stayed*. Put your pencil down to show me that you are done. [Teacher monitors. When students are done, the teacher writes *stayed* on the board.] Check your spelling. If you missed the word, cross it out and rewrite it. [Pause.] Spell *stayed*. S-t-a-y-e-d.
Example: funny + est =	We have the word ~~funny~~. And we want to add the suffix ~~est~~. Does *funny* end with a consonant and *y*? Yes. Are we adding a suffix other than *ing*? Yes. Do we change the *y* to *i*? Yes. Write *funniest*. Put your pencil down to show me that you are done. [Teacher monitors. When students are done, teacher writes *funniest* on the board.] Check your spelling. If you missed the word, cross it out and rewrite it. [Pause.] Spell *funniest*. F-u-n-n-i-e-s-t.

(cont.)

Example: *happy* + *ness =*	[Teacher guides students in the analysis of these words, using the same wording.]
Example: *accompany* *+ ment =*	
Non- example: *accompany* *+ ing =*	
Example: *accompany* *+* *ist =*	
Example: *vary + ance* *=*	
Non- example: *vary +ing =*	

(cont.)

FIGURE 4.1.

Step 4: Check students' understanding, using examples and non-examples.	
Example: *mighty + er* *=*	Now it is your turn. Here is the ~~word~~ *Mighty.* and we want to add the suffix ~~er.~~ Write *mightier.* [Teacher monitors.] When students are done, teacher provides feedback.] Does *mighty* end with a consonant and *y*? *Yes.* Are we adding a suffix other than *ing*? *Yes.* Do we change the *y* to *I*? *Yes.* [Teacher writes *mightier* on the board.] Check the spelling of *mightier.* [Pause.] Everyone, spell *mightier.* M-i-g-h-t-i-e-r.
Non- example: *replay + ed* *=*	This word ~~is~~ *Replay.* And we want to add the suffix ~~Ed.~~ Write *replayed.* [Teacher monitors. When students are done, teacher provides feedback.] Does *replay* end with a consonant and *y*? *No.* Do we change the *y* to *I*? *No.* [Teacher writes *replayed* on the board.] Check the spelling of *replayed.* [Pause.] Everyone, spell *replayed.* R-e-p-l-a-y-e-d.
Example: *envy + ous =*	[Teacher continues with additional examples and non-examples, providing instructional feedback. Notice that teacher provides

150 EXPLICIT INSTRUCTION

(cont.)

Non-example: *envy + ing =*	feedback after each item rather than after all six, to promote accuracy.]
Non-example: *enjoy + ed =*	
Example: *apply + ed =*	
Non-example: *apply + ing =*	
Example: *apply + ance =*	

FIGURE 4.2. Model lesson 2: Punctuation rule. Adapted from Archer, Gleason, and Isaacson (2008). Copyright 2008 by Sopris West Educational Services. Adapted by permission.

Setting: Eighth-grade resource room

Step 1: Introduce the rule.
We are going to learn how to separate adjectives using commas. Here is the rule: Use a comma to separate two or more adjectives, except when the last adjective is considered part of the noun. Use this test: If *and* makes sense between the two adjectives, add a comma.

Step 2: Illustrate the rule with examples and non-examples.

Example: *mysterious, twinkling star*	Read the words with me: *mysterious, twinkling star. Mysterious* and *twinkling* are adjectives that tell about *star. Twinkling* is not part of the noun. We don't often say "twinkling star." We need to separate *mysterious* and *twinkling* with a comma. To be sure, we use the *and* test. *Mysterious and twinkling star* does make sense, so we use a comma to separate the two adjectives.
Non-example: *famous movie star*	Read the words with me: *famous movie star. Famous* and *movie* are adjectives that tell about *star.* However, *movie* is part of the noun. We often say "movie star." We do not separate *famous* and *movie* with a comma. To be sure, we use the *and* test. *Famous and movie star* does not make sense, so we do not use a comma.

(cont.)

Example: *small, dark bedroom*	Read the words: *small dark bedroom. Small* and *dark* are adjectives that tell about *bedroom. Dark* is not part of the noun. We need to separate *small* and *dark* with a comma. To be sure, we use the *and* test. *Small and dark bedroom* does make sense, so we use a comma to separate the two adjectives.

(cont.)

FIGURE 4.2.

Non-example: *small living room*	Read the words: *small living room. Small* and *living* are adjectives that tell about the room. *Living* is part of the noun. We often say "living room." We do not separate *small* and *living* with a comma. To be sure, we use the *and* test. *Small and living room* does not make sense, so we do not use a comma.

Step 3: Guide students in analyzing examples and non-examples, using the critical attributes.

Non-example: *yellow school bus*	Read the words with me: *yellow school bus.* What adjectives tell about the bus? *Yellow and school.* Is *school* part of the noun? *Yes.* That's right, we often say "school bus." Should we separate *yellow* and *school* with a comma? *No.* Let's use the *and* test. Does *yellow and school bus* make sense? *No.* So we do not use a comma.
Example: *dirty, brokendown bus*	Read the words with me: *dirty broken-down bus.* What adjectives tell about the bus? *Dirty and broken down.* Is *broken-down* part of the noun? *No.* Right, we don't often say "broken-down bus." Should we separate *dirty* and *broken-down* with a comma? *Yes.* Let's use the *and* test. Does *dirty and broken-down bus* make sense? *Yes.* So we use a comma to separate the two adjectives.
courteous store clerk	[Teacher continues with guided practice, using parallel wording for all examples and non-examples. To clarify the examples and non-examples, we have added the punctuation. However, the items are presented to students with no commas.]
powerful back legs	
powerful, muscular legs	
hot, steaming cocoa	
steaming hot chocolate	
loud rock music	

(cont.)

loud, energetic music	
Step 4: Check students' understanding using examples and non-examples.	
delicious sweet cream	Read the words with me: *delicious sweet cream.* Think about whether to add a comma. [Pause.] Should we add a comma? *Yes.* Ones, explain your answer to your partner. [Teacher calls on a student.] *"Sweet" is not a part of the noun. Thus, you need to separate "delicious" and "sweet" with a comma. Also, it makes sense to say "delicious and sweet cream," so a comma is needed.*
delicious ice cream	Read the words with me: *delicious ice cream.* Think about whether to add a comma. [Pause.] Should we add a comma? *No.* Twos, explain your answer to your partner. [Teacher calls on a student.] *"Ice" is part of the noun. We often say "ice cream." We should not separate "delicious" and "ice" with a comma. It doesn't make sense to say "delicious and ice cream."*
long fur coat	[Teacher continues checking understanding with remaining items. Again, to clarify the examples and non-examples, we have added the punctuation. However, the items are presented to students with no commas.]
long, black coat	
tiny log cabin	
tiny, brown cabin	
marvelous, blue opal	
helpful flight attendant	

FIGURE 4.3. Model lesson 3: Grammar rule.

Setting; High school writing class	
Step 1: Introduce the rule. A number of you have asked about the use of *what* and *which* in questions, so today we are going to consider their preferred use. *What* is used when the number of choices is unlimited—when there are many, many choices. *Which* is preferred when the number of choices is limited—usually when someone is thinking of two or three items or a small number of known items.	
Step 2: Illustrate the rule with examples and non-examples. (Note: The examples for the use of *what* serve as non-examples for the use of *which*, and vice versa.)	
What is your favorite dessert?	Let's look at some examples. Read the sentence with me: *What is your favorite dessert?* There are unlimited choices for dessert, so the author has used *what.*
Which dessert do you prefer, apple pie or chocolate cake?	Read the sentence with me: *Which dessert do you prefer, apple pie or chocolate cake?* There are limited choices, so the author has used *which.*
What is your email address?	Read the sentence with me: *What is your email address?* Ones, tell your partner why the author has used *what.* [Teacher calls on a student.] *There are unlimited choices for email addresses.*
Which of your email addresses should I use?	Read the sentence with me: *Which of your email addresses should I use?* Twos, tell your partner why the author has used *which.* [Teacher calls on a student.] *The person probably has only two or three email addresses. Thus there would be a limited number of known choices.*
Step 3: Guide students in analyzing examples and non-examples using the critical attributes.	
—————airline do you normally fly?	Read the next sentence to yourself. [Pause.] Would there be limited or unlimited choices for airlines? *Unlimited.* Ones, tell your partner if *which* or *what* would be preferred. [Teacher calls on a student.] *"What" would be the preferred word, because there are many different airlines.*

—————flight are you taking to New York City from Lansing on Thursday afternoon?	Read the next sentence to yourself. [Pause.] Would there be limited or unlimited choices for a flight from Lansing to New York on Thursday afternoon? *Limited.* Twos, tell your partner if *which* or *what* would be preferred. [Teacher calls on a student.] *"Which" would be preferred, because there would be a limited number of known flights leaving for New York from Lansing on Thursday afternoon.*
—————would you like for your birthday?	Read the next sentence to yourself. [Pause.] Would there be limited or unlimited choices for a birthday gift? *Unlimited.* Ones, tell your partner if *which* or *what* would be preferred. [Teacher calls on a student.] *"What" would be the preferred word, because there are endless choices for a possible birthday gift.*
—————would you like for your birthday: a new iPod, a DVD player, a Nintendo system, or a watch?	Read the sentence to yourself. [Pause.] Are there limited or unlimited choices for a birthday gift? *Limited.* Twos, tell your partner if *which* or *what* would be preferred. [Teacher calls on a student.] *"Which" would be preferred, because the number of known choices is limited.*

(cont.)

FIGURE 4.3. *(cont.)*

Step 4: Check students' understanding, using examples and non-examples.

—————sandwich sounds better: tuna, baloney, or peanut butter?	Read the next sentence to yourself. Write down the best word: *which* or *what.* [Pause.] Ones, tell your partner the word you selected and why. [Teacher monitors.] *I selected "which," because there are only three choices.*
—————do you want in your sandwich?	Read the next sentence to yourself. Write down the best word: *which* or *what.* [Pause.] Twos, tell your partner the word you selected and why. [Teacher monitors.] *I selected "what," because you could ask for almost anything for your sandwich filling.*
—————kind of car does the family drive?	Read the next sentence to yourself. Write down the best word: *which* or *what.* [Pause.] Ones, tell your partner the word you selected and why. (Teacher monitors.) *I selected "what," because there are many, many kinds of cars.*

———————bus will you take to school?	Read the next sentence to yourself. Write down the best word: *which* or *what*. [Pause.] Twos, tell your partner the word you selected and why. [Teacher monitors.] *I selected "which," because there are only a few buses that you could take to school.*
———————is better: hot tea or iced tea?	Read the next sentence to yourself. Write down the best word: *which* or *what*. [Pause.] Ones, tell your partner the word you selected and why. [Teacher monitors.] *I selected "which," because there are only two choices.*

Now it's your turn. Use Application 4.5 to design a rule lesson on your own.

APPLICATION 4.5. DESIGN OF RULE LESSONS

Directions: Select one of the following rules or a rule that you are currently teaching, and design a lesson plan that follows the four instructional steps illustrated in the model lessons. Create your examples and non-examples carefully by following the guidelines introduced in this chapter. When you have finished, compare you work with our suggestions in *Feedback on Application Exercises*, pages 262–265.

Rule A. When a word ends in a vowel–consonant–final *e* and you want to add a suffix that begins with a vowel, drop the *e*.

Rule B. Separate three or more items in a series by adding a comma after each item except the last one.

CHAPTER SUMMARY

In this chapter, we have focused on how to teach **rules**, which are lawful relationships represented by **If–Then** statements. Although we teach skills, strategies, concepts, and vocabulary terms more often than rules, rules must be taught carefully with explicit instruction when they are taught, because many of these lawful relationships will not be discovered otherwise. Rule instruction begins with the selection of a rule that is unknown, important to the content being taught, and useful in the future. Preparation for instruction involves analyzing the rule, determining the critical attributes (**If**) that must be in place in order for the rule to be applied (**Then**), followed by the development of examples containing all of the critical attributes and non-examples devoid of one critical attribute. When rules are taught explicitly, these four steps are followed: (1) Introduce the rule; (2) illustrate the rule with examples and non-examples; (3) guide students in analyzing examples and non-examples; and (4) check students' understanding, using examples and non-examples. When these steps are used, the resulting explicit instruction is both effective and efficient.

CHAPTER 5

Organizing for Instruction

In Chapters 2, 3, and 4, we have discussed lesson design, and in Chapters 6 and 7, we focus on the type of lesson delivery that optimizes student participation and attention. The design and delivery of lessons are analogous to the development and delivery of a play: First the script is created, and then the play is performed, bringing life to the script. However, between the penning of the script and the performance of the play, the stage must be set. Similarly, you must set the stage in your classroom so you can deliver lessons in a way that promotes learning. Setting the classroom stage involves (1) organizing the physical space, (2) establishing classroom rules, and (3) determining and introducing routines and procedures that guide both teacher and student behavior throughout lessons. Let's examine each of these in turn.

ORGANIZING THE PHYSICAL SPACE

Have you noticed that when you step into certain classrooms, you get a feel for the "climate" of the room that is mirrored in the teacher's enthusiasm and students' engagement? The "climate" doesn't occur automatically. The teacher has set up certain conditions and organized the environment so that life in the classroom is positive and orderly. Interesting bulletin boards that reflect the content of the class; wall posters that announce the strategies emphasized in the class; posters communicating classroom expectations; displays of student work; technology for the

109

teacher (e.g., overhead projector, document camera, liquid crystal display (LCD) projector, SMART Board); technology for the students (e.g., computers, listening posts); bookcases filled with instructional materials and supplementary materials; and a general sense of order and care all come together to create a positive climate where teacher and students alike can thrive.

To begin establishing this positive climate for yourself and your students, you must consider the physical organization required for successful instruction. Although the requirements vary by subject and grade level, some general principles apply to organizing all environments for instruction. First, you should designate areas for specific activities. In the elementary classroom or self-contained special education classroom, these activities may include whole-group instruction, small-group instruction, gatherings on the rug, free-choice games and activities, quiet reading, and computer use. In addition, you must communicate behavioral expectations for each area. For example, you could teach students that access to the free-choice area depends on complete, accurate, neat independent work, and that students must be quiet and use materials appropriately in order to continue using the free-choice area.

Second, whether you are teaching small or large groups, you should be in close proximity to your students. When students are "up close and personal," it is much easier for you to connect with them, to monitor their behavior, to maintain their attention, and to engage them in instruction. Close proximity is not a challenge when you are teaching a small group gathered around a rectangle table or a kidney-shaped table in the primary grades. However, it is not possible to have proximity to all students at once when you are teaching larger groups. Often students widen the gap even more. Both of us have observed classrooms, particularly in high schools, where students choose to sit at desks on the periphery of the classroom that are as far removed from the teacher and class activities as possible. Frequently the students who sit furthest away are the students who most need the teacher's proximity to gain and hold their attention. In addition, we've seen many secondary students, while self-selecting seats, engage in seating disputes and/or take too much time to figure out the best seat, both of which could result in lost instructional time. Assigning seats usually prevents all of these problems. In the primary grades, you can place students' names on the desks. In secondary schools, placing names on desks is often not feasible, but an alternative procedure works well: Place a number on each desk. Make a seating chart that shows the desk numbers and the name of the students assigned to each seat. As students enter, hand them copies of the seating chart and ask them to locate their seats. Students can quickly locate their assigned seats with the seating chart, and they have a ready reference for learning the names of classmates. Assigning seats allows you to choose which students sit closest to where you will be standing when you are not moving around. As we discuss in Chapter 6, assigning seats also allows you to orchestrate optimum response partners and cooperative learning teams that take into consideration students' current functioning levels.

Third, students should face you during instruction. This seems like an obvious requirement, but we have both been in classrooms in which students are organized in clusters of four, with half of the students facing their tablemates rather than the teacher. Obviously, students will be less attentive when it is difficult for them to make eye contact with the teacher and for the teacher to monitor their behavior. In addition, a recent review of studies on room arrangement concluded that rows were more conducive than clusters to on-task behavior during independent work (Wannarka & Ruhl, 2008).

Fourth, you should arrange the seats so that students can easily share answers with a partner—one of the most effective active participation procedures. In classrooms with desks, place two desks together to facilitate partner work during teacher-directed instruction. When students are at a table, the students sitting next to each other can be partners. In Chapter 6, procedures for selecting partners are outlined.

Fifth, you should organize both teacher and student materials for easy access. You will want to have instructional materials at your fingertips—perhaps arranged on a table along with an overhead projector, document camera, or computer attached to an LCD projector or a SMART Board. As we have all experienced, in the time that it takes you to retrieve a missing teacher's guide, blank transparency, or marker from your desk or a closet at the back of the room, management problems can erupt even in the best of settings. One motto that we teachers cannot afford to forget is "Avoid the void, for they will fill it!" Similarly, student materials should be close to students, either in their desks or in containers on their tables. Again, if students have to get up to retrieve instructional materials, management challenges are likely to emerge.

You should also teach students organization skills and routines that permit easy retrieval and storage of materials. In third grade and above, you can require students to have a binder with dividers for each subject, a pen-and-pencil pouch at the front of the binder for writing tools, and paper at the back of the binder. In addition, a calendar for recording assignments, tests, and projects can be placed at the front of the binder. In kindergarten through second grade, students can have a pocket take-home folder with one side labeled "Take Home" and the other pocket labeled "Bring Back to School" for parent notices and homework.

Sixth, you should organize the room so that you can easily monitor the responses of students and be able to provide valuable feedback. As noted earlier, when you are teaching a small group with students gathered around you at a kidney-shaped table, being close enough to monitor responses and provide feedback is easy. However, when you are teaching a large group of 28 students, monitoring is more of a challenge. In this case, you want to be sure that no barriers impede movement around the room. You must be able to listen to students as they share answers with their partners, as well as to examine the students' written responses carefully. If a bookcase, a small-group table, equipment, or even a narrow aisle is a barrier to movement, your effectiveness will be reduced.

Seventh, you must be able to see all parts of the room and all students. Although this seems obvious, we often see students hidden behind bookcases, screens, walls of work stations, and free-standing blackboards. When a teacher cannot see some students and some students cannot see the teacher, management challenges emerge. Just think about the change in your own behavior when you spot a state patrol car next to the freeway.

Finally, you should post materials on classroom walls that support instructional efforts. A must in every classroom is a posted assignment calendar (or, at the secondary level, one calendar for each period). Either you or a designated student can record assignments, tests, and performances on the corresponding due dates on the class calendar. This calendar also serves as an effective communication tool for a student who has been absent, a student who is not sure of the spoken directions, the parent of a child who has been absent, or individuals who provide support to students (e.g., special education teachers or tutors). Next, materials posted in the classroom remind students of the critical content being stressed in the class and the strategies you want them to apply.

This informative material can include (1) **word walls** listing the vocabulary terms introduced paired with a reminder of the context, such as a copy of the first page in the story; (2) **strategy posters** outlining the steps in a writing strategy, the order of operations in algebra, the steps in scientific inquiry, or the steps in a learning strategy; (3) **rubrics** conveying expectations for written products or projects; (4) **content/reference information**, such as maps, the periodic table of elements, a poster showing the branches of the federal government, or a list of strong verbs for writing, a list of overused words and their alternatives; (5) **rule/guideline posters** conveying desired school behavior; and (6) **notices**, such as lunch menus, announcements of performances, or a schedule of upcoming events. Many teachers also post sayings or adages that communicate attitudes for students to adopt. Here are a few we have spotted in elementary classrooms:

u "Attitude = 100%." (Have children associate numbers with letters of the alphabet and add the numbers—for example, A = 1; T = 20.) u "Don't REST until you do your BEST." u "The dictionary is the only place where *success* comes before *work*."

We have also spotted various mottos in secondary classrooms—often with a touch of humor:

u "Boring is a choice."
u "Teachers open the door, but you must choose to enter." u "Floating is easy. That's how all dead fish end up downstream." u "Time is passing. Are you?" (Posted next to a clock.)

In addition to posting informative material, you should exhibit your students' work in the classroom. Displays of student work communicate to students, parents, support staff, and visitors that the focus of the class is academic attainment. At the elementary level, consider displaying the best work of each student. At one school, every room contains a "Personal Best" bulletin board. At the end of the week, students go through returned work and select the assignment for their space that represents their "Personal Best," post it on the bulletin board, and explain to their partner or the class why they selected the assignment. Though all of the posted work will not be perfect, this practice encourages students to reflect on their own progress and quality of work.

In summary, the physical organization of your classroom creates a positive climate for you and your students and supports you in delivering high-quality instruction. Use Application 5.1 to evaluate the organization of your own classroom. Then analyze the examples and non-examples of classroom arrangements provided in Application 5.2.

APPLICATION 5.1. Evaluating the Physical Organization of the Classroom: Setting the Stage

Directions: Use the guidelines listed in the following table to evaluate the organization of your classroom.

1. Have you designated areas for specific activities (e.g., whole-group instruction, small-group instruction, class gatherings on rug, free-choice area, quiet reading area, computer lab)?	Yes No
2. In instructional areas, are students in close proximity to you?	Yes No
3. Have you created seating charts and assigned seats?	Yes No
4. In instructional areas, are students facing you?	Yes No
5. During instruction, can students easily share answers with partners or team members?	Yes No
6. Have you arranged your instructional materials for easy retrieval?	Yes No
7. Are the student materials needed during instruction or independent work easily retrievable?	Yes No
8. Have students been taught organization skills (e.g., binders, folders, assignment calendar)?	Yes No

9. Can you move quickly and easily around the room, monitoring students without interference of physical barriers?	Yes No
10. Can you see all parts of the room and all students?	Yes No
11. Have you displayed material on the classroom walls that supports instruction (e.g., class calendar, vocabulary words, strategy posters, rubrics, reference material, rule/ guideline poster, notices)?	Yes No
12. Have you displayed student work?	Yes No
13. Is your classroom orderly?	Yes No

APPLICATION 5.2. ANALYSES OF CLASSROOM ARRANGEMENTS

Directions: Examine the following three sets of classroom arrangements. Each set includes an example that illustrates a desirable classroom organization and a non-example that presents a number of challenges. For each set, inspect the example and note the desirable qualities of the classroom, and then compare your observations to ours (see pages 266–270). Next, examine the corresponding non-example, record any suggestions that you would make, and compare your observations to ours (again, see pages 266–270).

Primary Classroom—Example

Primary Classroom—Non-Example

Special Education Classroom—Example

Special Education Classroom—Non-Example

Secondary Language Arts Classroom—Example

Secondary Language Arts Classroom—Non-Example

ESTABLISHING CLASSROOM RULES

Students profit greatly from completely clear expectations—whether in terms of the classroom rules, routines and procedures; directives for responding within the lesson; or requirements for independent work, projects, or homework. Before the beginning of the school year, you must give careful attention to the rules, routines, and procedures to be utilized in your classroom.

Well-designed **classroom rules** (frequently also referred to as **classroom guidelines**) promote safety, create a positive learning environment in which teachers can teach and students can learn, and support teachers' sanity. When you are establishing classroom rules, take into account the following suggestions. First, it is desirable to have few rules rather than many. Three to six rules will be adequate. As the number increases, the rules become more difficult to enforce and more difficult for students and the teacher to remember. Next, the guidelines should be positive in nature—that is, stated in terms of desired behavior rather than unwanted behavior. For example, "Listen to your teacher and classmates" is better wording than "Don't talk while others are talking." Why? A rule stated in terms of desired behavior adds to the positive environment that you wish to establish and is less likely to promote resistance. (Consider this: How do you respond when you are told not to do something?) Also, only when it is stated as desired behavior does it cover all behavioral infractions. For example, if the rule is "Don't talk while others are talking," does that leave the door open for singing, chanting, rapping, tapping, and snapping? If the rule is "No food in class," then what about gum, cell phones, or iPods? Stating rules in terms of desired behavior takes a little thoughtfulness, but it can happen. "No food, no gum, no iPods . . . " is transformed into the inclusive "Bring *only* school materials to class." "Don't hit others; don't throw things; don't touch people's things" is transformed into "Keep your hands and body to yourself."

When you are formulating written rules, keep them short and simple, preferably beginning with a verb. A rule such as "Respect others" is more to the point than "In order to have a community of learners, it is important in this classroom that everyone show respect for others through their words and actions." Although you might use this wording to explain the rule, it simply is not optimum "poster wording." Figure 5.1 provides various lists of rules we have seen in classrooms.

It is also critical that you define certain desired behaviors. A rule such as "Respect others" may be very differently interpreted by you and your students. To clarify rules, present examples and non-examples during initial introduction of the rules. For example, when presenting the rule "Keep your hands and body to yourself," you can share the examples and non-examples seen in Figure 5.2.

Now that the characteristics of effective classroom rules have been described, use Application 5.3 to evaluate your rules for your own classroom, if you have already developed a set.

FIGURE 5.1. Possible classroom rules.

Third-grade class	Fifth-grade class
The Be's u **Be** on time. u **Be** on task. u **Be** prepared. u **Be** respectful. u **Be** cooperative.	**Code of Conduct** 1. We will be respectful to our teachers and classmates. 2. We will come to class prepared with necessary materials and completed assignments. 3. We will always do our best. 4. We will follow directions immediately.
Middle school resource room	**High school language arts class**
1. Arrive on time. 2. Bring your notebook and your calendar. 3. Follow directions immediately. 4. Stay on task. 5. Be respectful of your teachers and	1. Come to class on time. 2. Bring *only* necessary school materials to class. 3. Be prepared. 4. Participate in all activities. 5. Listen to your teacher and

classmates. 6. Keep your hands and body to yourself.	classmates. 6. Be polite in words and actions.

FIGURE 5.2. Examples and non-examples for teaching a rule.

Keep your hands and body to yourself.	
Examples	**Non-examples**
u Folding your hands while listening to the teacher. u Walking down the hall with your hands to your side. u Writing your name on your paper. u Asking a classmate if you can borrow a piece of paper. u Holding the item that you have brought for "show and tell."	u Hitting someone during the lesson. u Poking the person who is ahead of you in line. u Writing on someone else's paper. u Grabbing paper out of someone's hands. u Touching a "show and tell" object that is sitting on a neighbor's desk.

APPLICATION 5.3. ANALYSES OF CLASSROOM RULES

Directions: Use the following guidelines to evaluate your classroom rules.

1. Are the rules few in number (i.e., three to six)?	Yes No
2. Are the rules stated in terms of desired behavior?	Yes No
3. Are the rules short and simple?	Yes No
4. Does each rule begin with a verb?	Yes No
5. Are the behaviors well defined in the rule (or through the presentation of examples and non-examples)?	Yes No

Many teachers prefer developing rules with their students to promote ownership of the rules and responsibility for their implementation. This is an acceptable practice if the outcome is a list of a few important rules that are positive in nature, fairly simple, and well defined. Another option for involving students is for the teacher to establish the rules but to have students generate examples and nonexamples of the rule, as will be seen in the next example lesson.

Effective implementation of classroom rules requires more than making a poster. On the first day of school, rules should be presented in every classroom. What happens in the following weeks is dependent on the age and behavior of your students. If your students are young or have difficulty making good behavioral choices, formal and informal lessons should be provided on each of the rules, followed by review. In some cases, you may even wish to break a rule down into a number of lessons. For example, if one of your rules is "Respect others," you can design one lesson on showing respect to teachers, another lesson on showing respect to classmates, and a separate lesson on showing respect to visitors. Regardless of the intensity of the initial instruction, rules should be briefly reviewed every day for a few weeks, coupled with feedback letting students know when they are following the rules or reminding them of the rules when they are not following them. Consistent expectations contribute to the climate you are trying to establish. In addition, you can have students participate in simple activities such as telling their partners the rules, writing down the rules, thinking of examples and non-examples for a rule, copying the rules and placing them in their binders, or answering questions on the rules. Remember, what we expect and clearly communicate through words and actions is what we will receive: **What we expect = What we get**.

In Chapter 4, you have seen examples of how to teach an academic rule. Now let's look at an example of how to teach a behavioral rule (see Figure 5.3).

FIGURE 5.3. Example lesson on classroom behavioral rule.

Background Information
Group being taught: Middle school students in a resource room.
Prior instruction: Students have been introduced to classroom rules on the first day of class.
Rule to be taught: Be respectful of your teachers and classmates (second part).
Goal of this lesson: Students will learn to show respect to classmates and exhibit respectful behavior in class.
Larger goal: Students will learn the classroom rules and exhibit behaviors that allow

the teacher to teach and the students to learn.

(cont.)

FIGURE 5.3. *(cont.)*

Opening of the Lesson

Gain students' attention. Look up here.

State the goal of the lesson. Yesterday we discussed classroom rules. In the next few weeks, we'll explore each rule, beginning with "Be respectful of your teachers and classmates." Today we'll discuss the part of the rule about showing respect for classmates.

Discuss the relevance of the target skill. When we show respect for other people, we consider their feelings and their well-being. We do not want to harm them. We also show respect when we consider the rights of others and treat them as we would wish to be treated.

Think for a moment. If every person in this class were respectful of their classmates, what would be some of the benefits? Please discuss this with your partner. Ones, you are the scribe. Write down the benefits that you and your partner generate. [Teacher moves around the room, recording students' ideas and their names on an overhead transparency. Teacher then uses the transparency for sharing with the class.]

Body of the Lesson

1.   Introduce the rule. [Teacher points to the rule poster.] Everyone, read Rule 5 with me: *Be respectful of your teachers and classmates.* We are going to discuss how you show respect to your classmates. Please write *Rule 5* on the top of your paper. [Teacher monitors.]

Remember, when we are respectful of others, we consider their feelings and their rights, and we avoid harming them. Everyone, when we consider another person's feelings and rights, and when we avoid harming them, we are being . *Respectful.*

2.   Illustrate with examples and non-examples. For example, to show respect during a discussion, you should turn toward the class member who is speaking, listen to what this person is saying, and not interrupt him or her. This shows regard for the person's feelings and honors his or her right to participate in the class. It is not respectful to interrupt classmates during a discussion, to make comments such as "That's stupid," or to talk while they are sharing ideas. These actions show no regard for the feelings and rights of the other class members, and certainly could harm them by hurting their feelings.

3.   Guide students in analyzing examples and non-examples using the critical attributes. Let's decide if this behavior shows respect. A student cuts in the line ahead of classmates. Did she show regard for the feelings and rights of her classmates? *No.* Did she show respect? *No.* A student offers assistance to a classmate trying unsuccessfully to open a bottle of paste. Did he consider the feelings and rights of his classmate? *Yes.* Did he show respect? *Yes.*

4.   Check students' understanding, using examples and non-examples. [Teacher places a blank T-chart with columns labeled *Respectful* and *Not respectful* on the overhead.] On your paper, draw a T-chart such as this one. Label the left column *Respectful* and the right column *Not respectful.* [Teacher monitors.]

We are going to start by listing behaviors that show respect to your classmates. My turn first. It would be respectful to listen when a classmate is speaking. [Teacher writes on the overhead transparency: *Listen to classmates.*] It would be respectful to ask a classmate if you could borrow a pencil rather than simply grabbing it. [Teacher writes: *Ask to borrow a pencil.*] Your turn. Write down behaviors that would show respect for your classmates. Continue writing until I say stop. [Teacher moves around the room, writing the best ideas on an overhead transparency.]

(cont.)

FIGURE 5.3. *(cont.)*

Ones, then Twos, share your ideas with your partner. If your partner has a good idea, add it to your list. [Teacher continues to move around the room, noting down ideas and names on the transparency. Teacher then uses the transparency to provide feedback to the class.]

Now we are going to add non-examples to our T-chart. Across from each idea on your T-chart, you are going to write a behavior that would not be respectful. For example, next to *Listen to classmates*, I might write *Interrupt classmates*. Next to *Ask to borrow a pencil*, I might write *Grab pencil*. Fill in your chart. [Teacher moves around the room, adding parallel non-examples to the chart on the transparency.] First Twos, then Ones, read your example and non-example pairs to your partner. [Teacher continues to move around, noting ideas and names on the transparency. Teacher then uses the transparency to give feedback to the class.]

Closing of the Lesson

I am so very impressed with your responses. All of you know how to show deep respect to your classmates. I am going to make a poster of your best examples and non-examples. I'll post it next to our rules to remind us how to be respectful of class members.

Tell your partner one thing that you plan to do in your other classes to show respect to your classmates. [Teacher monitors.]

If all of us are respectful—that is, and we consider the feelings and rights of others, and we avoid harming them—we will have the best school year ever!

ESTABLISHING ROUTINES AND PROCEDURES

In classes where routines and procedures (e.g., use of the bathroom, movement from activity to activity, falling silent when signaled, turning in papers) are clearly delineated, taught, reviewed, and used during the initial weeks of school, appropriate behavior is much more likely to occur, and the class is more likely to run smoothly. Literally, "Predictability predicts ability."

You must consider classroom routines carefully before the beginning of the school year, and even write them down, rather than fabricate them on the fly. If you wait until the need arises to create a routine, the off-the-cuff routine may spell disaster. Consider the possible results of the following: "Sure, you can sharpen your pencil whenever you need to," "Whenever you have a question of any kind, just raise your hand," "Yes, you can turn in assignments late."

Begin establishing your routines by considering the situations where the class needs a routine or a procedure. In Application 5.4, you will find a list of situations that call for a specified routine or procedure. Some of these will be more important in elementary classes than in secondary classes, or more important in classes serving students with learning and behavioral challenges.

APPLICATION 5.4. SITUATIONS REQUIRING A CLASSROOM ROUTINE OR PROCEDURE

Directions: Examine the following list, and check those situations that are relevant to your current or future teaching situation.

Type of situation	Check
Movement:	
u Into classroom	
u Out of classroom	
u Transition to a new activity	
u To another area in the school	
Use of:	
u Bathroom	
u Drinking fountain	
u Pencil sharpener	
u Lockers	
u Recess equipment	
u Computers	
u Specialized equipment (e.g., microscopes, Bunsen burners, tape	

recorders)	
Materials/assignments:	
u Bringing materials to class	
u Using binder or folder	
u Having no paper	
u Having no pencil/pen	
u Distributing materials	
u Communicating assignments	
u Determining assignments after being absent or not in class	
u Correcting work in class by using keys	
u Correcting work with teacher	
u Turning in work	
u Returning corrected work	
u Determining grades	
u Late work	
Cues for:	
u Attention	
u Stop!	
u Different voice levels	
Silence	
Quiet voice (only heard by partners or teammates)	

Discussion voice (easily heard by all classmates)	
Presentation voice (heard in all corners of the room)	
Outside voice (okay only at recess)	
Gaining assistance:	
u During a lesson	
u During independent work when the teacher is available	
u During independent work when the teacher is working with a small group	
u During cooperative team activities	
u During computer time	
How to act:	
u During whole-group instruction	
u During small-group instruction	
u During rug activities	
u During independent seatwork	
u During time at stations	
u During "specials" such as music, library, or PE	
u During silent sustained reading	
u At the beginning of the period	
u At the end of the period	
u When a visitor comes to class	

u When the principal observes	
u When a guest teacher is in class	
What to do when:	
u You are tardy	
u You have been absent	
u You need additional tutoring or help	
u You don't understand class material	
u You are feeling ill	
u You don't have lunch or lunch money	
u It's snack time	
u It's passing period/transition period between classes	
u There is a rainy-day recess	
u There is a fire, earthquake, or hurricane drill	
u There is a school lockdown	
u There is an assembly	

In all cases, routines should be ones that students have no difficulty following consistently; more important they should require little if any teacher involvement. If all routines flow through you as the teacher (e.g., "If you don't have a piece of paper, ask the teacher," "If you need to sharpen your pencil, ask the teacher," "If you want a drink of water, ask the teacher," "If you forgot your book, get one from the teacher"), your teaching will be interrupted frequently, and this will significantly reduce the amount of engaged instructional time. Study the chart of possible routines found in Figure 5.4. Perhaps you can use some of them in your classroom now. Then, revisit routines every year as you prepare for another great school year.

FIGURE 5.4. Examples of routines and procedures.

Situation: Movement into elementary class

1. Students assemble in designated area.
2. Teacher greets students.
3. Students and teacher walk to classroom door.
4. *Outside* of classroom, teacher gains students' attention and gives directions for next activity.
5. Teacher opens door, and students enter.
6. Students put away coats and other materials, and begin engaging in activity.

Situation: Movement into secondary class

1. Before bell rings, teacher opens door and stands at door.
2. Teacher greets students as they arrive.
3. When bell rings, teacher closes door.
4. Upon arrival to class, students put materials away and put homework in corner of desk.
5. Students begin warm-up activity when bell rings.
6. Teacher quickly scans class and takes attendance.
7. Teacher immediately begins new lesson.

Situation: Movement out of elementary class

1. Line leader goes to door.
2. Teacher dismisses rows, tables, or groups when materials are organized.
3. When excused, students stand up and push in chairs.
4. Students walk quietly to the door and line up, with an arm's length of space between one student and the next.
5. Students stand in line quietly and keep their hands and bodies to themselves.
6. When all students are lined up, line ender goes to end of line.
7. If necessary, teacher reviews guidelines for walking to new location (e.g., "Stay with the group; keep your hands and body to yourself; use 'whisper' voice").
8. Teacher walks in middle of group.

Situation: Movement out of secondary class

1. Students *do not pack up materials until teacher indicates that class is over.* Teacher, *not* bell, dismisses students.
2. Teacher moves to door and dismisses students.

Situation: Use of bathroom

1. Students should use bathroom before school, before class, during recess, or during passing period/between-class period.
2. If there is an emergency, students should go to bathroom during independent work time.
3. Students must sign out, turn over sign, or take pass.
4. If privilege is abused, teacher meets with student.

Situation: Correcting work in class

1. Students take out correcting pen (pen, red pen, or crayon).
2. Teacher gives each answer.
3. Students indicate whether answer is correct or incorrect on their papers.
4. Teacher reteaches difficult items.
5. Students use remaining time to correct any items they missed.

(cont.)

FIGURE 5.4. *(cont.)*

Situation: Tardy to secondary class

1. Student arrives late.
2. Teacher continues teaching.
3. Student signs tardy notebook and checks "excused" or "unexcused." Student attaches excuse.
4. Partner assists late-arriving student.
5. When free, teacher talks to tardy student.
6. When appropriate, teacher uses "payback" time as consequence.

Situation: Absent from elementary class

1. Partner collects assignments, homework, or notices handed out, and puts these in folder on desk of absent student.
2. Student returns to school and examines work in folder.
3. Student checks class calendar and notes work that needs to be completed.
4. Student has same number of days to make up work as he/she missed.
5. Completed work is placed in special box labeled "Make-Up for Absence."

Situation: Absent from secondary class

1. When partner enters classroom and notices that partner is absent, partner picks up folder and puts name of absent student on it.
2. Partner collects assignments, homework, or notices handed out, and puts these in folder. Partner may also fill out form with class information, including reading assignments, test dates, homework assignments, or long-term assignments.
3. At end of period, folder is placed in box labeled "Work for Students Who Are Absent."4. Student returns to school and examines work in folder.
5. Student checks class calendar and notes work that needs to be completed.
6. Student has same number of days to make up work as he or she missed.
7. Completed work is placed in special box labeled "Make-Up for Absence."

Situation: Turning in or collecting work

1. Students put number on paper with heading.
2. Students pass work forward.
3. Monitor collects all papers from front-row seats.
4. Monitor puts in numerical order.
5. Monitor places papers in box labeled by subject or period.
Or, if more accountability is necessary:
1. Students are given assignment.
2. Homework is placed on corner of desk.
3. Teacher circulates and personally collects homework.

Situation: Asking question during a lesson in elementary class

1. Students *do not* raise hands when teacher asks question.
2. Students raise hands when:
   u Teacher gives directive to raise hands.
   u Student has a *public* question (one for which answer will be useful to all students).
   u Student wishes to contribute to discussion.
3. When student has a *private* question, he or she does not interrupt lesson. Instead, student places hand on heart. When teacher has natural break, teacher goes to student.

(cont.)

FIGURE 5.4. *(cont.)*

Situation: Asking for assistance during independent work session in elementary or middle school

Red and Green Card
1. Student attempts task, consulting with examples in text or notes from instruction.
2. When student has question, red side of card is placed up. (Other signals may be used instead, such as "Help Wanted" sign or book standing up on desk.)
3. Student must continue working. Student skips item and works on next problem.
4. Teacher moves around room monitoring. (**Walk around. Look around. Talk around.**)
5. When teacher sees red card, he or she provides assistance.

Situation: Asking for assistance during middle school work session

Only When Near
1. When student has question and teacher is *not* near, student may consult with partner or use rule **Three before me**. (That is, student must consult with three classmates before asking teacher for assistance).
2. If assistance is not adequate, student circles item and continues working.
3. Teacher moves around room monitoring. (**Walk around. Look around. Talk around.**)
4. When teacher is *near*, student may raise hand and request assistance. This reduces amount of time that students are off task.

Situation: Signals for Voice Level
0—Silence. (Teacher raises closed fist.)
1—Whisper. (Teacher puts up one finger.)
2—Quiet conversation. (Teacher puts up two fingers.)
3—Speaking voice. (Teacher puts up three fingers.)
4—Outside voice. (Teacher puts up four fingers.)

Although rules should be introduced on the first day of school in all classes, specific routines should be introduced the first time they are needed. Thus, instruction on routines will be spread out over the first 2 weeks of school, so that students will not be overwhelmed. We recommend that you teach behavioral routines and procedures in the same manner that you introduce strategies and skills, as outlined in Chapter 2. Of course, the amount of instruction, subsequent review, and corrective feedback will differ by the type of classroom you are teaching and the age of your students. However, we would suggest that you don't commit "assumicide"—in this case, assuming, hoping, or even praying that students will exhibit the behaviors you desire. Remember, teaching is the most powerful of interventions.

Let's look at how a routine or part of a routine may be taught. The lesson in Figure 5.5 is designed to introduce transitions to primary students. Transitions— whether these are movements from area to area, group to group, or activity to activity—constitute a major source of off-task behavior (e.g., excessive talk, out-ofseat behavior, and horseplay). Therefore, you should give special attention to teaching, practicing, reviewing, and reinforcing appropriate transition behaviors, especially in elementary and special education classes (Colvin & Sugai, 1988; McIntosh, Herman, Sanford, McGraw, & Florence, 2004; Sprick, Garrison, & Howard, 1998).

FIGURE 5.5. Example lesson on classroom routines.

Background Information

Group being taught: Second graders on the second day of school.

Prior instruction: On the first day of school, students have been introduced to classroom rules and routines as the needs have emerged, including routines for using the restroom and the drinking fountain, saying choral answers, and saying answers to a partner.

Routine to be taught: Lining up and moving to a new location (first part).

Goal of this lesson: Students will line up quickly when excused, stand in line without touching, and be very quiet.

Larger goal: Students will line up and move to new locations in an orderly manner.

Opening of the Lesson

Gain students' attention. Eyes and ears on me. [Pause.]

State the goal of the lesson. There are many things that we do again and again in this class. These are called *routines*. Today we are going to being learning the routine for lining up and moving to a new location in the school. We will start with learning how to line up in an orderly way.

Discuss the relevance of the target skill. It is important to line up quickly and in an orderly way with no touching or talking, so that we can get to the new location on time. It is important that we line up without touching, so that all of us are safe in class. Tell your partner some places that you went in the building last year. [Teacher monitors and calls on individuals.]

Body of the Lesson

1. Introduce routine. [Teacher displays list using an overhead transparency.]

Routine for Lining Up

1. Get out materials for the next activity.
2. When the teacher excuses your group, stand up and push in your chair.
3. Walk quietly to the door.
4. Line up single file, with an arm's length between one person and the next.
5. Stand in line quietly. Keep your hands and your body to yourself.

Let's learn the routine for lining up. Read number 1 with me: *Get out materials for the next activity.* While you are sitting at your desk, you prepare for the next activity by getting out any necessary materials. Ones, tell your partner what we will carry to the library. [Teacher pauses and then calls on an individual. Teacher then continues with other locations, such as gym, lunchroom, music room, etc.] Read number 2 with me: *When the ~~teacher excuses~~ your group, stand up and push in your chair.* Should you stand up before your group is excused? *No.* To make the room safe for others, you need to push in your ____. *Chair.* Read number 3 with me: *Walk quietly to the door.* Lining up can be a confusing time, so you need to walk to ~~the door.~~ *Quietly.* Read number 4 with me: *Line up single file, with an arm's length between one person and the next.* Line up in a single line, so that you are right behind the person in front of you. Everyone likes to have space, so be sure to leave an arm's length of space between yourself and the person in front of you. Everyone, hold out your arm in front of you. [Teacher holds out his or her arm.] This is the amount of space that should be between you and the person in front of you. Read number 5 with me: *Stand in line quietly. Keep your hands and your body to yourself.* When you stand in line, you need to be quiet, and you need to keep your hands and your body to yourself. Let's review. First, get ready by getting out necessary ____. *Materials.*

(cont.)

FIGURE 5.5. *(cont.)*

When the teacher excuses you, stand up and ~~push in your~~ . *Chair.* Then walk to the ~~door~~ . *Quietly.* Line up single file, with how much space between one person and the next? *An arm's length.* Then stand in line . *Quietly.* And keep your hands and your body to . *Yourself.*

2. Model the routine. (I do it.) My turn to show you how to line up. But first, Colleen, Frank, and Luke, will you help me out? Please line up at the door. Be sure that you have an arm's length of space between you. [Pause.] Now pretend that I am a second grader sitting at my desk. [While describing the behaviors, teacher also performs the behaviors.] I know that we are going to the library, so I take my library book out. The teacher excuses my group, so I get up, push my chair in, and walk quietly to the door. I stand right behind Luke, with an arm's length of space between us. I stand in line quietly. I keep my hands and my body to myself. I am careful not to touch Luke or his things.

This time you are going to help me. [Teacher sits down in a student's desk. As teacher and students discuss the routine, teacher again models the behavior.] First I need to get out necessary . *Materials.* We are going to reading groups, so I take out my reading book.
[Teacher gets out reading book.] The teacher excuses my group, so I should stand up and push in
my . *Chair.* [Teacher stands and pushes in chair.] Next, I walk to the ~~door~~ . *Quietly.* I line up behind Luke, leaving how much space? *An arm's length.* I stand in line . *Quietly.* I should keep my hands and my body to myself.

Now watch me again. This time I'm going to make some mistakes. Be ready to tell me what I am doing wrong. We are going to the library, and the teacher excuses my group. [Teacher acts out the non-example by moving to the door without a library book, leaving his or her chair out, and standing very close to Luke. Teacher has students tell their partners the mistakes made, and then calls on individuals to report their observations. Teacher then presents additional non-examples and has students analyze them.]

3.   Provide prompted practice. (We do it.) Let's practice together. Pretend that we are going to the music room. So we don't need to take any materials. Group A, you are excused, so stand up and push in your chairs. [Pause.] Great. Now walk quietly to the door. [Teacher waits.] Line up single file with one arm's length between people. [Teacher waits.] Now hold out your arm so we can check the length.
Now stand in line quietly and keep your hands and your body to yourself. Group A, that was perfect. [Teacher guides each group in the lining-up procedure. If errors are made, teacher has the group return to their desks and repeat the process.]

4.   Check understanding. (You do it.) Let's practice again. Pretend that we are going to another room for reading group. Get out your reading book. I will watch each group and tell you how you did. [Teacher excuses each group, observes students' behavior, and gives feedback. Teacher repeats the practice a number of times, changing the location that students are moving to.]

Closing of the Lesson

Review. Ones, pretend that your partner was not here today. Explain the routine for lining up. [Teacher monitors.] Twos, your turn. Explain the lining up routine to your partner.

Preview. Later today, we will practice lining up *and* walking down the hall.

You may also wish to teach routines or procedures by using "Looks like/ Sounds like" charts that delineate desired behavior for a specific activity (see Figure 5.6). These charts were originally developed to convey desirable behaviors during cooperative learning groups. However, you could use them to effectively convey expected behaviors for repeated activities (e.g., small-group instruction, wholegroup instruction, transitions from setting to setting, independent work time, cooperative work time) or for special or rarely occurring events (e.g., oral presentations, science experiments, assemblies). As you may do with rules, you may choose to develop all or part of the "Looks like/Sounds like" charts with your students.

FIGURE 5.6. Examples of "Looks like/Sounds like" charts.

Lining Up and Walking to Another Location (transitions)	
Looks like	**Sounds like**
When we line up, it looks like you are: u Lining up quickly when excused. u Standing and pushing in your chair. u Carrying necessary materials. u Standing directly behind the person in front of you with an arm's length of space. u Keeping your hands and body to yourself.	**When we line up, it sounds like you are:** u Not talking at all *or* u Whispering quietly.
When we are walking, it looks like you are: u Moving quickly without running. u Walking right behind the person in front of you. u Keeping your hands and body to yourself. u Walking on the right side of the hallway.	**When we are walking, it sounds like you are:** u Not talking at all *or* u Whispering quietly.
Completing Independent Work (while the teacher teaches small reading groups)	
Looks like	**Sounds like**

You are:	You are:
u Working at your desk or designated area.	u Not talking as you work. u Quietly asking your neighbor for help.
u Doing assignments:	
Comprehension exercises.	u Quietly asking the "Expert" for help.
Handwriting practice.	(The "Expert" will be sitting at the
Spelling practice.	"Advice" desk and will have reviewed
Summary writing. u	the assignments with the teacher.)
Correcting your work with keys.	
u Reading a book when your assignments are complete, accurate, and neat.	

Oral Presentations: The Speaker	
Looks like	**Sounds like**
You are:	You are:
u Standing in front of class. u Facing your classmates. u Smiling (pleasant face).	u Presenting information with clarity. u Talking with expression and enthusiasm.
u Not fidgeting.	u Using a voice that is easy
u Prepared. (You have support materials such as overhead transparencies, charts, and notes ready.)	to hear. u Answering questions.

CHAPTER SUMMARY

Perhaps the Boy Scouts were thinking of teachers when they chose as their motto "Be prepared." In addition to selecting the content and designing lessons, you must set the stage for instruction by organizing the physical space and establishing classroom rules and routines. But, just as with a play, setting the stage is only the backdrop. The real test comes during the performance. Never forget that *you are the one who enhances the climate in your classroom every day—through your smile, your body language, your polite words, your kind acts, your enthusiasm for teaching, and your dedication to your students. In all these ways, you make your classroom climate both orderly and positive.*

We recommend the following books for in-depth study of

behavior management: *Winning Strategies for Classroom Management* (Cummings, 2000); *How to Survive and Thrive in the First Three Weeks of School* (McEwan, 2006); *Tools for Teaching: Discipline, Instruction, Motivation* (Jones, 2007); *CHAMPs: A Proactive and Positive Approach to Classroom Management* (Sprick et al., 1998); *Discipline in the Secondary Classroom: A Positive Approach to Behavior Management* (Sprick, 2006); and *The First Days of School: How to Be an Effective Teacher* (Wong & Wong, 2009).

CHAPTER 6

Delivering Instruction

Eliciting Responses

In Chapter 2, we have introduced a lesson design that includes an opening, a body, and a closing. However, even when you have crafted an exquisite, well-structured lesson or adopted a curriculum material with explicit lessons of high quality, it is still possible that some students may not be totally riveted to your every word or deeply processing the lesson content. Student attention and subsequent learning depend not only on the design of lessons, but also on the delivery of those lessons. Analogously, if a wonderful movie script is not delivered by talented actors, the resulting movie is likely to bomb at the box office.

In Chapter 1, four essential delivery skills have been introduced as part of the 16 elements of explicit instruction (see Figure 1.1):

1. Require frequent responses.
2. Monitor student performance carefully.
3. Provide immediate affirmative and corrective feedback.
4. Deliver the lesson at a brisk pace.

Whether you are teaching a large or small group, you must elicit **frequent responses** by requiring students to say, write, and/or do things. If instruction is truly interactive and students are constantly responding, then attention, on-task behavior, and learning increase, and behavioral challenges decrease. Similarly, you should maximize the amount of reading practice students engage in during instructional time, particularly when you are working with beginning readers or older struggling readers. Achieving maximum amounts of reading necessitates using alternative procedures to round-robin reading, especially in large-group settings. Effective instruction also requires constant **monitoring** of student responses, so that you

can give high-quality **feedback** (including corrections and affirmations) and can modify the lesson based on student performance. Finally, throughout the lesson, you need to maintain a **pace** of instruction that engages students and optimizes the amount of content covered without sacrificing adequate thinking time. The following diagram illustrates the relationship of these delivery skills.

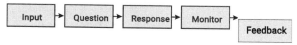

As you read this chapter, you may wish to stop and teach the example lessons. This "virtual teaching" will bring the chapter alive and help you transfer the delivery skills to your own teaching. If you incorporate the suggested practices into your current teaching, student teaching, or tutoring, these skills will soon be a part of your own repertoire. You probably already possess many of these skills, so be sure to acknowledge their existence as you read.

REQUIRE FREQUENT RESPONSES

The delivery skill most fundamental to explicit instruction is the eliciting of frequent student responses. Because of its importance, we focus in the remainder of this chapter on how to elicit frequent responses and how to use reading procedures that will maximize student engagement. The remaining delivery skills are covered in Chapter 7.

When eliciting frequent responses, a teacher presents a little information and then stops to ask for a response from students. Then the teacher repeats this pattern again and again, thus giving the students many opportunities to respond: **Input I Question I Response. Input I Question I Response. Input I Question I Response. Input I Question I Response**. Like good conversation, good instruction is interactive; it is not **Input I Input I Input I Input I Input I See you tomorrow**. In this latter condition, even the most motivated student would be tempted to "check out" and go into deep cognitive "floating." Giving students many opportunities to respond during a lesson has many proven benefits (e.g., Brophy & Good, 1986; Cavanaugh, Heward, & Donelson, 1996; Greenwood, Hart, Walker, & Risley, 1994; Skinner, Fletcher, & Henington, 1996). Students, of course, are more attentive and on task. More importantly, in the act of responding, students are retrieving, rehearsing, and practicing the information, concepts, skills, or strategies being taught, thereby increasing the probability of retention. In addition, through monitoring of student responses, you can check the clarity of your teaching and adjust the lesson as needed: reteaching critical information, clearing up any misconceptions, or moving ahead in the lesson. You can also provide corrective feedback to the group or individual when errors occur, thus reducing the discrepancy between current understanding or performance and the desired outcome. Increasing opportunities to respond also increases the opportunities for acknowledging correct responses and for task-focused praise, which are particularly beneficial to students with learning or emotional challenges (Gunter, Denny, Jack, Shores, & Nelson, 1993). Finally, if students are actively engaged and successful, behavioral challenges will be reduced. As Sutherland and Wehby (2001) concluded in their review of related research, higher opportunities to respond result in higher task engagement, higher academic achievement, and lower rates of inappropriate behavior.

Although there are many ways to request responses during a lesson, we outline a number of procedures that we have found particularly effective and easy to implement across settings and content areas. We emphasize **unison responding**, in which all students respond, rather than the traditional procedure in which the teacher asks a question, students raise their hands, and the teacher calls on a volunteer. Unison responding (e.g., saying an answer together, writing an answer on a response slate and holding it up, or holding up a response card) has been shown to increase not only the number of responses given by each student, but on-task behavior and academic attainment (Hamlin, Lee, & Ruhl, 2008; Heward, 1997). We have organized the responses according to the behaviors of the students: (1) oral responses, (2) written responses, and (3) action responses. As you read through these procedures, identify the ones that you already use and ones that you could add to your repertoire.

Oral Responses

The most common responses requested in lessons at any grade level are oral. There are a number of practices for eliciting oral responses that have particular promise: choral responses, partner responses, team responses, and carefully designed individual responses.

Choral Responses

Whether you are teaching math, reading, science, or social

studies, there are times when the oral answers you request are short and the wording is the same across learners. In special or general education, or in elementary or secondary classes, when the answer is short and there is only one correct answer, all students can be asked to say the answer together. **Choral responding** has proven to be a flexible procedure that is adaptable across grades and content for increasing the frequency of student responses and subsequent learning (e.g., Hamlin et al., 2008; Heward, Courson, & Narayan, 1989; Wood & Heward, 2005). Choral responses can be interspersed throughout lessons, but are particularly powerful when used to practice or review factual information. Examine the lesson segments in Figure 6.1 to see how choral responses can be elicited in different settings. Read the lesson from left to right to see the flow of **Input | Question | Response | Monitor | Feedback**. As you read all of the lessons in this chapter, give special attention to the **feedback** provided after student responses. Desirable attributes of feedback are discussed in Chapter 7.

FIGURE 6.1. Lesson segments: Choral responses.

Lesson segment 1: Beginning reading

Input ⟶	Question	Response →	Monitor ⟶	Feedback
On the board: *s, a, m, t*				
Let's review some sounds. When I touch under a letter, say its sound.	[Teacher touches under *s*.] What sound? [Teacher signals for response.]	/s/.	[Teacher listens carefully. All students say the correct sound.]	[Teacher moves on with no comment.]
	[Teacher touches under *a*.] What sound? [Teacher signals for response.]	/ ˘a/.	[Teacher listens carefully. Two students say /o˘/.]	[Teacher points to *a*.] This sound is /a˘/. What sound? [Teacher signals.] / ˘a/. [Teacher points to *s*.] What sound? [Teacher signals.] /s/. [Teacher points to *a*.] What sound? [Teacher signals.] / ˘a/.
[Teacher continues with remaining letters and then reviews them in random order.]			[Teacher listens carefully. All students say all sounds correctly.]	Great.

Lesson segment 2: Fifth-grade math

Input	Question	Response	Monitor	Feedback
On the board: x + 5 = 15 Look at this equation.	What is the unknown variable? [Pause.] Everyone? [Teacher signals for response.]	x.	[Teacher listens carefully. All students respond correctly.]	[Teacher moves on, indicating a correct response.]
	To isolate x, should we add or subtract 5 from each side? [Pause.] Everyone? [Teacher signals for response.]	Subtract 5.	[Teacher listens carefully.]	Yes, in order to isolate x, we must subtract 5 from each side.
	[Teacher writes x + 5 − 5 =]. If we subtract 5 from this side of the equation, what is left? [Pause.] Everyone? [Teacher signals for response.]	x.	[Teacher listens carefully.]	[Teacher writes x below x + 5 − 5.]
	[Teacher writes 15 − 5.] If we subtract 5 from this side of the equation, what is left? [Pause.] Everyone? [Teacher signals.]	10.	[Teacher listens carefully.]	[Teacher writes 10 below 15 − 5.]
	Everyone, what is the value of x? [Teacher signals.]	10.	[Teacher listens carefully.]	Let's check the answer by replacing x with 10. What is 10 plus 5? [Teacher signals.] 15. Both sides are equal to 15. So x does equal 10.

Lesson segment 3: Seventh-grade science

Input	Question	Response	Monitor	Feedback
On an overhead transparency: *shield volcano, composite volcano, cinder cone volcano*				
We have been studying three types of volcanoes. I will tell you about one type of volcano. You tell me which one I am thinking about.	This type of volcano has very steep sides. [Pause.] Everyone? [Teacher signals.]	*Composite volcano.*	[Teacher listens carefully. All students respond correctly.]	Yes, composite volcanoes have steep sides.
	This type of volcano has low-sloping sides. [Pause.] Everyone? [Teacher signals.]	*Shield volcano.*	[Teacher listens carefully. All students respond correctly.]	True, shield volcanoes, like the volcanoes of Hawaii that we looked at yesterday, have low-sloping sides.
	This type of volcano has layers of lava and ash. [Pause.] Everyone? [Teacher signals.]	*Composite volcano.*	[Teacher listens carefully. Many students don't respond correctly.]	Remember, *composite* means "made from more than one material." Composite volcanoes have layers of lava and ash. Everyone, volcanoes with layers of lava and ash are _____? [Teacher signals.] *Composite volcanoes.*

This type of volcano is built from shattered pieces of rock and cinders. [Pause.] Everyone? [Teacher signals.]

Cinder cone volcano.

[Teacher listens carefully. All students respond correctly.]

Great. And what type has layers of lava and ash? [Pause.] Everyone? [Teacher signals.] *Composite volcano.* Yes, now you've got all fthree types.

Researchers have identified numerous benefits of choral responses (Heward, 1997; Kamps, Dugan, Leonard, & Daost, 1994). The foremost benefit is that *all* students are involved, not just one. Thus the opportunities for each child to respond are increased. Because of the efficiency of choral responses, the number of responses requested can also be increased. Next, using choral responses is a very safe procedure for shy students, reluctant students, students with learning challenges, or students initially learning English (or any second language). Similarly, many of us feel more comfortable singing in a choir than singing a solo. Next, there is built-in support (scaffolding) for struggling students: They hear the answer and can join in, and also receive immediate feedback on the accuracy of their responses. Finally, you receive instant feedback on your students' knowledge as you listen to their responses.

Like an orchestra director creating beautiful music, you must direct your students so that they will say answers together. Some type of signal—either an **auditory signal** (e.g., a vocal command ["Everyone?"], a tap, a clap, or a snap) or a **visual hand signal**—must be adopted, taught to students, and consistently used. You can use any signal you choose, as long as it allows you to regulate the amount of thinking time given to students and cues them when to say the answer. You might find the signals outlined in Figure 6.2 helpful.

Teachers often identify a number of challenges with choral responses, including the student who mouths the words or does not respond at all, or the student who disregards the signal and "blurts out" the answer, therefore robbing classmates of the chance to formulate an answer (Hunter, 1982). The teacher's response is the same in each case: "Let's say that again." This gives the reluctant student a chance to say the answer the second time and can put peer pressure on the blurter to cease and desist.

A challenge with all responses is gauging the amount of thinking time that students need. If adequate time is not provided, students may be rushed into guessing, and errors will occur. One way to predict the amount of thinking time needed is to process the answer as students are processing it. Perhaps you are asking whether 5 is a prime number. In your head, you might say: "Okay, 5 is divisible by 5 and 1 but isn't divisible by any other number, so 5 is a prime number." By processing the answer yourself, you will find yourself giving students more thinking time. Another way to judge the amount of thinking time needed is to have students indicate when they have determined the answer. In elementary classes, you might have students put up a thumb to indicate that they have formulated an answer. In secondary classes, you can have students make eye contact with you to indicate that they have processed the answer. We do *not* recommend that students raise their hands to indicate having an answer, because this practice has a number of negative consequences. Some students who have not thought of the answer will raise their hands upon seeing the first hand go up, to save face with their peers.

FIGURE 6.2. Suggested signals for choral responses.

Situation	Signal/cue for choral response
Students are looking at the teacher.	1. The teacher asks a question and raises his or her hands. 2. The teacher gives students thinking time. 3. The teacher then lowers his or her hands and says, "Everyone?" 4. Students say the answer together.
Students are looking at a common stimulus, such as a word on the board, a location on a map, a step on a strategy poster, a picture in the big book, or a number on the overhead transparency.	1. The teacher points at the stimulus. 2. The teacher asks a question. 3. The teacher provides thinking time. 4. The teacher then taps next to the stimulus and says, "Everyone?" 5. Students say the answer together.

Students are looking at a worksheet, a page in a textbook, or a handout.	1. The teacher asks a question or gives a directive. 2. The teacher provides thinking time. 3. The teacher then invites students to say an answer, using a vocal command such as "Everyone?" 4. Students say the answer together.

Other students, upon seeing the first hand go up, give a sigh of relief and don't even try to think of an answer, thus totally abdicating to the hand-waving student. When the majority of students have indicated that they have an answer, the teacher signals for a response.

Some general guidelines can be followed for thinking time, no matter what type of response is requested. When you are asking a lower-cognitive-demand question, in which students must recall material recently read or taught, 3 seconds are generally adequate for thinking time. When you are asking a higher-cognitivedemand question, in which students must manipulate several logical arguments or information previously learned in order to create an answer, longer thinking time leads to more engagement, higher-quality answers, longer responses, and more variety in responses (Cotton, 2001). If students are repeating a short response you have modeled, an immediate signal for a response can be given—for example,
"This word is *was*. What word? [Immediate signal] *Was*."

Another challenge in using choral responses is the difficulty of discerning individual errors embedded within the choral response (Heward et al., 1989). When a student within the group makes an error, it may be difficult to implement individual correction procedures. Two practices can alleviate this difficulty. First, when an error occurs, instead of delivering a correction to the individual, you can implement the correction procedure with the entire group, thereby strengthening the learning of all students. Second, at the end of a choral response sequence, you can check the understanding of individuals by calling on a number of students. In fact, one study found that interspersing individual questions during choral responding led to increased responding, increased accuracy, and decreased disruptive behavior of those students most reluctant to participate, thus strengthening the effects of the choral responding procedure (Armendariz, 2005).

Partner Responses

Perhaps, one of the most effective ways to engage students is to have them share answers with their partners. Whether the answer is short or long, but particularly when the wording is long and the answers vary, students can turn to their partners and share their answers. Like choral responses, partner responses benefit both teachers and students. Once again, *all* children are involved as they either say the answer or listen to their partners' responses. Students also benefit from the richness of their partners' ideas, which often spark new ideas and perspectives in turn. Students receive feedback from their partners as well: If any answers are incorrect or incomplete, their partners can gently correct them or add to the answers. If they are not certain what the question is, partners can inform them. Partner work is also a fertile venue for building language proficiency, social skills, and cooperation skills, as well as for developing a community of learners in the classroom. Finally, students have an opportunity to interact socially, which is a major goal of intermediate and secondary students. This social interaction makes the lesson more pleasurable and fun for students.

Partner responses have great benefits for you, the teacher. As students are sharing answers, you can move around the room and listen to numerous responses, receiving information on your teaching not just from one student but from many. Consequently, you are able to provide feedback—whether it is acknowledgment, encouragement, or corrections—to numerous students. Partner time also gives you an opportunity to coach lower-performing students. As soon as you direct students to share with their partners, you can move around the room and coach struggling students, helping them formulate answers that are accurate and complete.

You can make the use of partner responses more effective by following a few guidelines. First, it is best if you select the partners. Children will tend to pick a partner like themselves, not always the best classroom match. When you are selecting partners, place the lowest-performing students with middle-performing students rather than with the highest-performing students. The middle-performing students will tend to be more supportive, allowing the lower-performing students more opportunities to respond. Next, have the partners sit next to each other (rather than across from each other at a table) and assign a designation to each partner, such as "One" or "Two." Once you have assigned numbers, you can request one student in each pair to say the answer ("Ones, tell your partner . . . " or "Twos, tell your partner . . . "), thus distributing opportunities to respond across classmates. It is often useful to give the higher-performing student in each partnership the "One" designation, so that this student can model for the other partner (e.g., "Ones, using your graphic organizer, teach your partner what we learned about the branches of the federal government," then "Twos, teach your partner").

One procedure for selecting partners for literacy instruction involves these steps (Fuchs, Mathes, & Fuchs, 1996):

1. Determine the oral reading fluency (correct oral words per minute) of each child. Have each child orally read a passage to you for 1 minute, and then calculate the number of words read correctly in a minute.

2. Rank the children from lowest to highest in fluency.
3. Cut the list in half and line up the two halves. The result is that the lowestperforming students will be paired with middle-performing students.
4. Use your knowledge of your students to adjust the partnerships so that students will work well together.

A few other practices can help you to make optimal use of partners. Perhaps students are taught in three different locations in your classroom: at their desks for whole-group instruction, at the "rug area" for whole-group instruction, and at a table for small-group instruction. In this case, assign students partners at their desks and the numbers One and Two. When they come to the rug, have them sit next to their partners and use the same numbers. But because small-group instruction generally involves homogeneous grouping, different partners will be needed. To facilitate assigning partners at the small-group table, tape index cards on the table announcing each student's number with an arrow pointing to the partner. It is also important to change the partnerships—not on a daily basis, but perhaps every 3–6 weeks. Also, teaching students how to be partners is essential. Teach a strategy such as **Look, lean, and whisper** ("Look at your partner, lean toward your partner, and whisper the answer to your partner"), or teach desired partnership behaviors by using a "Looks like/Sounds like" chart (see Chapter 5, Figure 5.6).

Finally, when you are asking students to share answers with their partners, it is helpful to give them a **sentence starter.** For example, after the reading of a paragraph in a content area book, this directive might be given:

> Review the paragraph and determine the main idea. [Teacher pauses and provides thinking time.] Ones, tell your partner the main idea of the paragraph. Begin by saying, "The main idea is . . . '"

There are several benefits of providing a sentence starter: The students will initiate their responses more quickly, utilize full sentences to express their answers, and be more likely to stay on topic. In addition, stating the sentence starter often helps in the cognitive retrieval and formulation of the answer.

Although there are many ways that partners can be used in classes, we are going to share a few practices that we have found particularly successful: (1) **Think– Pair–Share**, (2) **Think and Write–Pair and Write–Share**, (3) the **Pause** procedure, and (4) **Study–Tell–Help–Check**.

THINK–PAIR–SHARE

One of the simplest ways to utilize partners is to use a procedure developed by Frank T. Lyman, Jr. (Lyman, 1981; McTighe & Lyman, 1988): **Think–Pair–Share**. The procedure has two emphases: (1) giving students time to think before responding, and (2) directing students to say answers to their partners instead of calling on one student (e.g., "Think: What will happen next in the story? Twos, tell your partner"). Having students share answers with partners is particularly useful when the answers are long and the wording varies, making choral responses impossible. When you are using **Think–Pair–Share**, follow these steps:

1. **Think**. Ask a question and provide thinking time.
2. **Pair**. Ask students to pair up and communicate their ideas to their partners.
3. **Share**. Call on a number of students to share with the class. Or, if the answer is short and the wording is the same, have all students say the answer, or tell students the answers you have heard while circulating and monitoring.

The lesson segments in Figure 6.3 illustrate the varied uses of **Think–Pair– Share**. As you examine these lesson segments, attend to the use of partner responses and the feedback given to students.

THINK AND WRITE–PAIR AND WRITE–SHARE

In many situations, students need to brainstorm ideas related to a topic. For example, students may brainstorm ideas for an essay, uses of perimeter measures, benefits of a particular learning strategy, common causes of war, examples of renewable and nonrenewable resources, or additional words with the base *auto*. Just a few modifications to **Think–Pair–Share** can make it a viable brainstorming procedure. First, have students **think and write** down their ideas, thus increasing accountability and allowing you to monitor their responses, which is impossible if they are only "thinking." Next, when students **pair** up to communicate their ideas, have each student **write** down the partner's best ideas. If you occasionally ask students to share their partners' best ideas, they will feel more accountable for listening to their partners. While students complete the **Think and Write** and **Pair and Write** steps, move around the room and record their ideas and their names on an overhead transparency (or piece of paper, if a document camera is used). Then use this list of ideas during the **Share** step, which makes the sharing more efficient than the usual time-consuming practice of calling on individual students.

THE PAUSE PROCEDURE

The **Pause** procedure is perfect for illustrating the power of active participation at any grade level. This procedure was researched with learning-disabled and non-learning-disabled students in college classes with a traditional lecture format (Ruhl, Hughes, & Gajar, 1990; Ruhl, Hughes, & Schloss, 1987). As all of us have experienced, it is difficult to listen to any lecturer for a sustained period of time. In these studies, the instructor lectured for 12–18 minutes and then paused for 2 minutes, during which students worked in pairs to discuss the lecture and rework their notes. This simple procedure resulted in significantly higher retention of lecture content (as measured by free-recall quizzes and comprehension tests) for these college students, including those with learning disabilities. Johnson, Johnson, and Smith (1991) have suggested a reflective pause of 3–4 minutes, during which students can summarize the lecture segment, answer a focus question, predict what will be covered next in the lecture, and share their own experiences.

STUDY–TELL–HELP–CHECK

We suggest using an active participation procedure that is similar to the **Pause** procedure. **Study–Tell–Help–Check** can be used at the beginning of a class to review previously taught content, at the end of class to review the day's lesson, or intermittently during the lesson. Using this procedure, the teacher gives students an opportunity to **study** their notes, handout, or textbook for a short period of time (e.g., 1–2 minutes). The teacher then directs one member of each partnership to **tell** the other partner all they remember about the topic without consulting any reference materials. Their partners **help** them out by asking them questions, giving them hints, or telling them any missing information. When both partners in each pair have exhausted their recall of the information, they look back at their handouts or textbooks to **check** their responses and to locate any missing information. Like the **Pause** procedure, the use of **Study–Tell–Help–Check** throughout a lesson helps students feel more accountable for their learning, and the rehearsal and retrieval also help them retain more information. Examine the lesson segments in

Figure 6.4 to see the use of these procedures in varying situations.

You can use partners in many other ways as well. Partners can read to each other, explain a process by using an example, teach the content of a graphic organizer to each other, dictate spelling words and provide feedback on spelling accuracy, edit each other's work, help each other stay on task, collect materials for an absent partner, assist during independent work time, and study material together. The uses are endless, and the benefits are great. In the lesson provided in Figure 6.5, identify how the teacher uses partner responses.

(text resumes on page 149)

FIGURE 6.3. Lesson segments: **Think–Pair–Share.**

Lesson segment 1: Kindergarten reading

Input ⟶	Question ⟶	Response ⟶	Monitor ⟶	Feedback
[Teacher has read aloud *Wolf* by Becky Bloom (1999).]	Think. . . . "What surprised you the most in *Wolf?* [Pause for 5 seconds.]	[Students think about answer.]		
	First Ones, then Twos, tell your partner what surprised you the most.	[Students tell their partners what surprised them in the story.]	[Teacher moves around the room, monitoring and coaching.]	
	Adam, what surprised you the most?	*Well, on the first page of the story the wolf was very hungry, but it didn't eat until the last page.*	[Teacher listens to Adam's answer.]	Everyone, raise your hand if that surprised you, too. I agree. It surprised me that the starving wolf didn't eat until the picnic.
	Bethany, what surprised you? [Teacher calls on two other students.]			Wow, what good thinkers you are!

Lesson segment 2: Fifth-grade math

Input ⟶	Question ⟶	Response ⟶	Monitor ⟶	Feedback
[Students have been studying decimals for 2 weeks.]				

On the board: .4 .40 .400	Read these numbers with me. Everyone?	*Four tenths, forty hundredths, four hundred thousandths*	[	]	Great.
	Think. Are these decimals equivalent or not? Be ready to explain your thinking to your partner. Write down information that you can use in your explanation. [Teacher gives students abundant thinking time.]	[Students think about the fractions, recording notes as needed.]	[Teacher moves around the room, watching to see that each student is recording ideas.]		
	Ones, tell your partner if the decimals are equivalent or not, and explain your answer.	[Students pair up and explain their answers to their partners.]	[Teacher moves around the room, listening to explanations and ready to reteach the concept if students are inaccurate or confused.]	[Teacher provides affirmative feedback to partnerships.]	
	Everyone, are the decimals equivalent? [Teacher signals.]	*Yes*	[Teacher listens carefully		Yes, these are equivalent
	Elizabeth, please share your explanation.	*I changed the decimals into fractions: 4/10, 40/100, and 400/1000 I could reduce both 40/100 and 400/1000 to 4/10 so I knew the decimals were equivalent.*	[Teacher listens carefully.		Excellent. You really used what we have learned about the relationship between fractions and decimals.
	Drew, share your explanation.	*I know that you can remove zeros at the end of a decimal without changing its value. So I crossed off the zeros, and all of the decimals were four-tenths.*	[Teacher listens carefully.		Yes, you can remove the zeros at the *end* of a decimal and not change the value. Class, look at this decimal: .400. If I cross out the zeros, have I changed the value? *No* Look at this decimal: .004 If I cross out the zeros, will I change the value? .

FIGURE 6.4. Lesson segments: Partner procedures.

Lesson segment 1: Fourth-grade writing lesson using Think and Write–Pair and Write–Share

Input ─────────→	Question	Response	Monitor	Feedback
[Yesterday, the students each selected a holiday to write a report about.] In preparation for researching your holiday, we have to determine the topics that might be covered. We need to narrow down the topics so you can cover a few in depth.	First, tell your partner the holiday that you are going to write about.	[Students tell partners the name of their chosen holiday.]		
	Now we are going to brainstorm general topics that all of you might address in your report. For example, we could all determine the history of our holiday. We could also investigate any special foods associated with our holiday. [Teacher writes *history* and *foods* on overhead transparency.] I could write a paragraph or more about either of these topics. Now, on your paper, write some other general topics that could be explored for any given holiday.	[Students write down possible topics.]	[Teacher moves around the room, writing down topics and corresponding student names on a overhead transparency.]	[Teacher gives corrective feedback if the topic could not generate at least a paragraph or is unrelated to the study of holidays.]

Ones, then Twos, read your list to your partner. If your partner has a topic that you might cover in your report, add it to your list.

[Students read their lists to their partners and record excellent ideas from their partners' lists.]

[Teacher continues to move around the room, recording topics on the overhead transparency.]

[Teacher continues to provide acknowledgment, praise, and corrective feedback.]

Look up here. Let's read the list of topics that you generated: *History*

Foods
Special decorations (Sylvia)
Presents or prizes (Sean)
Significance (Pedro)
Special clothing (Freda)
Where observed (Jason)

Lesson segment 2: Eighth-grade science using Study–Tell–Help–Check

Input	Question	Response	Monitor	Feedback
[Students have just begun a unit on electricity and are viewing page 55 is their textbooks.]	**Study** Students, you will have 2 minutes to study page 55. Be ready to tell your partner about sources of electricity.	**Study** [Students study page 55.]	[Teacher moves around the classroom and observes.]	[Teacher reinforces on-task behavior with private praise.]
	Tell Twos, tell your partner what you remember about sources of electricity. Ones, help them out	**Tell** Partner Two: *This section was talking about producing energy in power plants. It said that burning coal could be transformed into electricity.* **Help** Partner One: *What other fuels can be used to generate electricity?* Partner Two: *Oh, yeah, fossil fuels . . . and nuclear energy.* Partner One: *Don't forget about the force of moving water. Let's check the book.* **Check** [Students look over page 55.] Partner One: *We forgot about the alternative sources, like solar energy and energy from the wind or tidal waves that can be used to generate electricity.*	[During the **Tell**, **Help**, and **Check** steps, teacher moves from partnership to partnership, listening carefully to students' responses.]	[Teacher reinforces on-task behavior, cooperative behavior, and correct information.]

FIGURE 6.5. Partner responses in a lesson.

Sixth-grade writing

Input ⟶	Question ⟶	Response ⟶	Monitor ⟶	Feedback
We have been learning how to expand sentences to make them more interesting and informative. Today we are going to add words and phrases to our sentences to tell *when* something happens.				
Shown on overhead: *Charles arrived at the office. From this first sentence, we have no idea when Charles arrived.*	*Read this sentence with me. Charles arrived at the office.*	*Charles arrived at the office.*	[Teacher listens carefully.]	
Shown on overhead: *Before dawn, Charles arrived at the office.*	Now, read the new sentence with me. *Before dawn, Charles arrived at the office.*	*Before dawn, Charles arrived at the office.*	[Teacher listens carefully.]	
	Ones, tell your partner the phrase that tells *when* Charles arrived at the office.	*Before dawn.*	[Teacher moves around room and listens to partners.]	

	Everyone, when did Charles arrive at the office?	*Before dawn.*	[Teacher listens carefully.]	Yes, before dawn. Now we know when Charles arrived. Notice that the phrase at the beginning of the sentence is followed by a comma.
Shown on overhead: *Charles arrived at the office just after lunch.*	Read the new sentence with me. *Charles arrived at the office just after lunch.*	*Charles arrived at the office just after lunch.*	[Teacher listens carefully.]	
	Twos, tell your partner the phrase that tells *when* Charles arrived at the office.	*Just after lunch.*	[Teacher moves around room and listens to partners.]	The phrase that tells when is *just after lunch.* Notice that at the end of the sentence, a comma is not used to separate the phrase from rest of the sentence.
Shown on overhead: Yesterday, Charles arrived at the office. Read the new sentence with me. *Yesterday, Charles arrived at the*	*office.* Everyone, what word tells *when* Charles arrived at the office? [Teacher signals.]	*Yesterday, Charles arrived at the office.* *Yesterday.* [Teacher listens	carefully.] [Teacher listens carefully to answers. All students	respond correctly.] *Yesterday.* Here a word that tells when, rather than a phrase, was added to make the

me. *The train pulled into the station.*

On your paper, write down words or phrases that could tell *when* the train pulled into the station. For example, you might write *this morning* or *one winter afternoon.* [Teacher writes these phrases on the overhead.] Continue writing words or phrases until I tell you to stop.

First Ones, then Twos, read your list to your partner. If your partner has a great idea, add it to your list.
The train pulled into the station.

[Students write down possible words or phrases that would tell when the train might pull into the station.]

[Students read lists to
partners and add new
ideas
to their lists.]
[Teacher listens carefully.]

[Teacher moves around
the room, examining
papers, providing verbal
feedback to students, and
writing down accurate
words or phrases and
corresponding student
names on the overhead
transparency.]

[Teacher continues to
move around the room,
writing down ideas and
names on the overhead
transparency.] sentence
more interesting and
informative.

You had many words
and phrases that would
really add to the
sentence. Let's read
some of your
classmates' ideas.
[Teacher and students
read the following
list:] *One
morning
(Tracy)
At dusk (Sean)
Before the scheduled*

*time
(Grace)
Right at noon (Kendal)
Yesterday (Marcus)
At 6:03 as scheduled
(Diego)
Three days late (Mary
Lee)
After being gone 2
weeks
(Nash)*

(cont.)

FIGURE 6.5. *(cont.)*

Input	Question	Response	Monitor	Feedback
				In the late afternoon (Jenn) *Before the whistle sounded (Marta)*
	Now circle your best *when* word or phrase. [Pause.]	[Students circle the best *when* word or phrase.]	[Teacher circulates and monitors choices.]	
	Now write your sentence. If you put your phrase at the beginning of the sentence, remember to put a comma after the phrase.	[Students write sentences.]	[Teacher moves around the room and writes a number of sentences on a transparency.]	
	Read your sentence to your partner.	[Students read sentences to their partners.]	[Teacher moves from partnership to partnership, listening to answers and writing down sentences.]	Let's read some of your classmates' sentences. *At 7:30, the train pulled into the station. (Kevin)* *As the clock struck 6:00, the train pulled into the station. (Anne Maria)* *The train pulled into the station before we arrived at the gate. (Troy)*

Notice that the *when* phrases make the sentences much more interesting.

Shown on overhead: *Chad entered the city library.*	Read this sentence with me. *Chad entered the city library.*	*Chad entered the city library.*		
	Write this sentence, adding a *when* word or phrase.	[Students write edited sentence.]	[Teacher circulates and writes down sentences.]	
	Read your sentence to your partner.	[Students read their sentences to their partners.]	[Teacher moves around the room and listens to sentences.]	Let's listen to some of your classmates' sentences. [Teacher Calls on individuals.]

Team Responses

In some cases, you may wish two partnerships to join together to form a cooperative team, or you may wish to use teams of four exclusively for responding in your classroom. Partner and team responses are both elements of **cooperative learning**, which is described by Johnson, Johnson, and Holubec (1993) as "the instructional use of small groups so that students work together to maximize their own and each other's learning" (p. 6). When you are forming teams, select students of different abilities, ethnicity, and gender, and give each member a number. If you are using both pairs and teams in a class, give students the number One or Two in their partnerships and the designation A, B, C, or D on their teams. Many activity structures (e.g., Kagan, 1989, 1992) have been developed for use by cooperative teams, but one, Numbered Heads Together, has a particularly strong research base (e.g., Maheady, Mallette, Harper, & Sacca, 1991; Maheady, Michielli-Pendl, Harper, & Mallette, 2006).

NUMBERED HEADS TOGETHER

When you are using **Numbered Heads Together** (Kagan, 1989, 1992), place students on teams and give each person in a team either a number or a letter designation. Then pose a question and ask students to "put their heads together" to come up with an answer. Have students continue their discussion until all team members are confident of the answer and feel prepared to share it with the whole class. Then randomly call out a number or a letter; the student in each group with that number or letter becomes the spokesperson for the group. To randomize the number you call out, and to increase student motivation, you can use a spinner or roll a die.

Over time, cooperative learning with its many activity structures has grown in popularity, often resulting in less direct instruction being provided to students. As a result, numerous researchers caution that cooperative learning must always be integrated with explicit instruction and not used as the sole method of instruction (Andersen, Nelson, Fox, & Gruber, 1988; Slavin, Madden, & Leavey, 1984). If students are asked to engage in cooperative learning activities before adequate information has been provided and strategy modeling has occurred, error rates will be high, and students will experience failure and frustration.

Individual Oral Responses

Although choral, partner, and team oral responses are excellent procedures for engaging all students, sometimes you want to call on an individual student to verify his or her learning. Before we examine best practices for calling on individual students, let's discuss some very common procedures that need to be minimized in teaching.

The most common form of teacher questioning is to call on volunteers (Brophy & Good, 1986). That is, the teacher asks a question; requests students to raise their

150   EXPLICIT INSTRUCTION

hands and volunteer; and then calls on one of the eager, hand-waving students. When this practice is used, the highest-performing, most assertive, and most
English-proficient students are most likely to be called on (Maheady et al., 1991). As a result, the teacher ends up "teaching the best and leaving the rest." The practice of calling on volunteers should be limited, so that *all* students can be engaged in the lesson. A simple guideline can be applied: When the answer comes from information that you have presented or from material that students have read, don't invite students to volunteer, because all students should be expected to have an answer. However, if the answer has its genesis in students' own experiential backgrounds, request that students volunteer for responding. This practice of only calling on volunteers when the

answer comes from students' personal background knowledge or experiences significantly reduces the number of volunteer responses requested in a lesson.

Another practice that should be minimized (if not avoided altogether) is calling on students when they are inattentive. The time to call on a student is not when the student is rummaging through a backpack or lunging for a purse. In this case, there is little likelihood of getting a sterling answer that adds to the class discourse. Most often teachers call on inattentive students in order to guide them back to the lesson. However, there are better ways to bring them back into the fold without calling on them, including (1) moving closer to an inattentive student; (2) giving a directive to the whole group (e.g., "I need everyone looking up here"); or (3) giving students something physical to do (e.g., "Put your finger on the heading," "Write a heading on your paper," "Draw a T-chart on your paper").

If you are not going to ask for volunteers or call on inattentive students, what are your alternatives? Let's examine three alternatives: **Partners First, Question First,** and **Whip Around or Pass.**

PARTNERS FIRST

One procedure for calling on individuals is first to have students share the answer with their partners, and then to call on students randomly to share an answer. You might notice that this takes us right back to **Think–Pair–Share.** When sharing with partners occurs before an individual is called on, the answer will often be of higher quality: Students have had a chance to think, to rehearse their answers, and to receive feedback from their partners (and perhaps from the teacher), all of which will help them develop and refine their answers.

QUESTION FIRST

In some cases, you may choose not to have students share with their partners first. Another possibility is to ask a question, give everyone thinking time, and then randomly call on a student. It is important to note that you ask the question, provide thinking time, and **then** call on the student, rather than saying the student's name first and then conveying the question. If the name is mentioned first, the remaining students in the class are less likely to listen to the question, think of an answer, or attend to their classmate's answer.

One challenge when calling on individual students is that you may tend to favor some students, calling on them often and other students seldom or never. To ensure that all students are involved in lessons, you need to have a plan for distributing the individual responses. One possibility is to write each student's name on a card and place the cards in a container. During the lesson, draw a name and call on that student. Another possible practice is to divide the room into sections (in your own mind) and call on students in different sections of the room. Using either of these practices will broaden the distribution of responses in the classroom.

Another challenge when calling on individuals occurs when a student responds, "I don't know," or "I don't remember." When a teacher receives these responses, the teacher often calls on other students until finding someone with a correct answer. Unfortunately, the teacher may be inadvertently teaching students that it is perfectly acceptable not to have an answer, resulting in a viral epidemic of "I don't knows" rushing through the classroom. Instead of going on a "fishing expedition," you need viable alternatives that go beyond the fruitless action of repeating the question in a louder voice. When a student cannot give an answer, you can support the student and scaffold the response through a number of practices, which include (1) breaking the task down into easier segments and guiding the student in its completion by asking questions; (2) allowing the student to confer with a partner while you call on other students, but then returning to the first student for the newly generated answer; (3) guiding the student in referring back to the textbook, handout, assignment, or notes to locate the answer; (4) asking the student to comment on the answers that have been given by peers; or (5) simply telling the student the answer and having him or her repeat it.

In some situations, it is appropriate for you to have students take turns responding. For example, in **Whip Around or Pass** (Harmin, 1994), you can go up and down rows rapidly and have students contribute with no intervening comments by you or their classmates. Tell students to say "Pass" when they don't have a response or their answer has already been suggested. This method for calling on individuals is particularly useful when there are many possible answers and the answers are derived from students' personal background knowledge. For example, **Whip Around or Pass** works well with directives such as these:

1. "Tell your favorite food. **Whip Around or Pass**."
2. "We are making a pie graph concerning favorite pets. Be ready to tell your favorite pet. **Whip Around or Pass**."
3. "We have just learned the vocabulary term *compulsory*. Get ready to tell something that is *compulsory* at this school. **Whip Around or Pass**."

152   EXPLICIT INSTRUCTION

As with all active participation practices, providing thinking time before you ask for responses will increase your students' confidence and the quality of their answers. You might have students write their ideas down before beginning **Whip Around or Pass.**

Written Responses

In many subjects, students are asked to produce written responses during lessons. For example, teachers dictate spelling words for students to write. In math classes, teachers display problems on a blackboard or SMART Board and have students solve them. In writing lessons, students brainstorm and record possible arguments to be used in persuasive essays.

Though requesting written responses in a lesson appears to be a simple procedure, problems can emerge. First, some students write answers very quickly, whereas others take an inordinate amount of time to write the same response. As a result, early finishers are left waiting for their classmates to finish—and, as we have all experienced, when there is a void, students will fill it. To avoid unproductive waiting time, it is helpful to construct lesson activities so that students are engaged in written responses for a brief amount of time. (This is not necessary during independent work sessions.) For example, when you are teaching a math lesson, it is better to have students complete one problem with immediate feedback than six items before receiving corrective feedback. The amount of student waiting time and the number of emergent behavioral challenges will be reduced; simultaneously, student success will be increased because of the immediacy of feedback and additional instructional input.

Another challenge with written responses occurs when students have a worksheet or textbook assignment in front of them. Often a few students will proceed ahead of the others; instead of doing Item 1 as directed and waiting for feedback, these students do Items 2, 3, and 4. Unfortunately, the "sneakers" may make errors because they are not attending to the teacher's input or feedback. These early finishers may also create a disturbance by boasting about their item completion. Simple procedures can reduce the challenge of the "sneakers." Give a directive: "When you are done, put your pencil down and look up," or "When you are done, turn your paper over." One of these practices, along with careful monitoring, is usually all that is needed to encourage students to stay with you during the lesson.

Response Cards and Response Slates

When we think of written responses, we generally envision students writing on paper, but many other options are available for reviewing and practicing information. These include the use of **response cards** and **response slates**.

When **response cards** are used, teachers give students a limited set of preprinted cards or have students prepare their own set of cards by writing possible answers on the cards (under the teachers' guidance). Possible answers include true or false; yes or no; A, B, C, or D; agree or disagree; or content-specific answers. For example, primary students may have letter cards on their desks. The teacher says a sound, and students display the matching letter. In English class, students may have cards with various literary terms (*theme, mood, moral, foreshadowing,* etc.). The teacher asks a question, and students hold up the correct card. In science, students can be given cards with terms for three types of volcanoes (*shield volcanoes, composite volcanoes, cinder cone volcanoes*). The teacher describes a volcano or asks a question about it, and students display the corresponding card. Similarly, the librarian may use response cards labeled *title page, copyright page, glossary, table of contents,* and *index* to review reference materials found within an expository textbook.

When **response slates** are used, teachers ask questions, and students record their responses on a small whiteboard or slate or plastic sleeve protector (with cardboard insert). Reading teachers can dictate sounds or words and have students record the corresponding letter or written word. Math teachers can have students complete a problem on their slates and display the completed problem. A social studies or science teacher can pose a question and scan the written answers of all students.

For both response cards and response slates, you ask a question and provide thinking time, and then the students hold up their answers (on either cards or slates) for your inspection. You can then monitor all student responses and respond as needed: correct errors, clarify misperceptions, reteach information, or move forward in the lesson. The use of response cards and slates has been proven to benefit students and teachers across a variety of age groups and subject areas by (1) increasing for each student the opportunities to respond, (2) increasing the number of students participating in the lesson, (3) increasing the academic achievement of students, and (4) decreasing off-task and disruptive behavior (e.g., Armendariz & Umbreit, 1997; Cavanaugh et al., 1996; Christle & Schuster, 2003; Heward et al., 1996; Lambert, Cartledge, Heward, & Lo, 2006; Maheady, Michielli-Pendl, Mallette, & Harper, 2002; Narayan, Heward, Gardner, Courson, & Omness, 1990; Randolph, 2007; Skinner et al., 1996).

Whether you use response cards or response slates will depend upon what you are trying to accomplish during a particular lesson. With response cards, students have a limited field of answers to select from rather than all possible responses, and many quick responses can be requested until students have a very firm grasp of the concepts or information. Response cards are an excellent choice when the number of potential answers is limited. On the other hand, you may choose response slates when answers are longer, more divergent, or more dependent upon personal preferences or experiences.

After examining the lesson segments in Figure 6.6, think of other situations where the use of response cards or response slates could enrich the lesson.

(text resumes on page 158)

FIGURE 6.6. Lesson segments: Response slate and response card usage.

Lesson segment 1: Spelling lesson in resource room using response slates				
Input ➝	Question ➝	Response ➝	Monitor ➝	Feedback
[This is the second day of instruction on dropping the e when adding a suffix that begins with a vowel.]				
On the board: ride + ing excite + ment excite + ed fame + ous refuse + al use + ing use + ful race + ist	Get your slates out. [Pause.] Yesterday, we learned that when a word ends in vowel–consonant–final e and you want to add a suffix that begins with a vowel, you should _____. Everyone? [Teacher signals.]	Drop the e.	[Teacher listens to responses. All are correct.]	Yes, when the word ends in an e and we want to add an ending that begins with a vowel, we drop the e.
	Let's do one together. Everyone, does ride end in a vowel–consonant–final e? [Teacher signals.]	Yes.	[Teacher listens to responses.]	[Teacher moves on.]
	Everyone, does the suffix begin with a vowel? [Teacher signals.]	Yes.	[Teacher listens to responses.]	[Teacher moves on.]
	So do we need to drop the e? [Teacher signals.]	Yes.		
	Write the word riding on your slate. [Pause.]	[Students write riding on slates.]	[Teacher walks around and monitors.]	
	Hold up your slates.	[Students hold up slates.]	[Teacher glances at the slates. All students are correct.]	Good. You dropped the e before adding ing. [Teacher writes riding on the board.]
	Next, we have excite + ment. Write excitement on your slates. [Pause.]	[Students write excitement on slates.]	[Teacher walks around and monitors.]	

Question	Response	Monitor	Feedback
Hold up your slates.	[Students hold up slates.]	[Teacher glances at slates. Numerous students have written the word incorrectly as *excitment*.]	Let's look at this one together. [Teacher guides students in applying the rule.] Does *excite* end in a vowel–consonant–*e*? *Yes*. Does the suffix begin with a vowel? *No*. So do we drop the *e*? *No*. [Teacher writes *excitement* on the board.] If you made an error, erase and write *excitement*. Show me your slates. [Later in the lesson, students are again asked to write *excitement*.]

Lesson segment 2: Third-grade math using response slates

Input ⟶	Question ⟶	Response ⟶	Monitor ⟶	Feedback
[Students have been taught six shapes: circle, square, rectangle, triangle, hexagon, pentagon.]	Let's review shapes. Get out your slates. [Pause.] Write down the number of sides in a rectangle. [Pause.] Hold up your slates.	[Students write 4 on their slates.]	[Teacher examines responses on slates. All students are correct.]	Yes, a rectangle has four sides.
	Ones, tell your partner what else we know about rectangles.	*They are closed figures. The sides are straight lines.*	[Teacher walks around and listens to a number of partnerships.]	Great. I heard that rectangles are closed figures with straight lines and four sides.
	Now draw rectangles on your slates. Keep drawing rectangles until I tell you to stop. Make them different sizes. [Pause.]	[Students draw rectangles on their slates.]	[Teacher walks around the room and looks at rectangles.]	

| | Hold up your slates. | [Students hold them up.] | [Teacher examines slates. All shapes are rectangles.] | All of your rectangles are closed figures with four sides. Good. Let's try some more difficult shapes. |
| [Teacher continues in the same way with the remaining shapes.] | | [Students continue to show appropriate shapes.] | | |

(cont.)

FIGURE 6.6. *(cont.)*

Lesson segment 3: Seventh-grade language arts using response cards

Input ———▶	Question	Response	Monitor	Feedback
Sentence on the board: *Jeff cryed out, stop! The table will brake under the wait of that box.*	Look over the sentence and count the number of errors. [Pause.] Show me the number with your fingers.	[Students hold up between three and seven fingers.]	[Teacher looks carefully at number of fingers.]	There are six errors in this sentence. Let's find the errors.

Class members review the sentence, holding up the corresponding response card: *no error* spelling error capital period (.) question mark (?) exclamation mark (!) comma (,) quotation marks (" ")	[Teacher points to *Jeff* in the sentence.] Get ready to hold up the card or cards. [Pause.] Hold up your card.	[Students hold up *no error*.]	[Teacher examines response cards.]	Excellent. There are no errors here. Tell your partner why *Jeff* is capitalized. [Teacher listens to a number of partner responses.] Yes, *Jeff* is a proper name, and it is also the first word in the sentence.
	[Teacher points to *cryed* and pauses for a few seconds.] *Hold up your card.*	*[Most students hold up spelling error.* However, a number of students hold up *no error.*]	[Teacher looks carefully at response cards.]	*Cryed is not spelled correctly. Let's review the spelling rule. When a word ends in a consonant and a y, and we add a suffix that begins with any vowel except i, what should we do?* [Teacher signals.] *Change the y to an i.* Spell *cried* as I rewrite the word. *c-r-i-e-d.* [Teacher crosses out *cryed* on the board and writes *cried.*]
	[Teacher continues in the same manner through the remainder of the sentence.]		[Teacher looks carefully at response cards.]	[For errors, teacher leads students to the correct answer, as above.]

Lesson segment 4: High school chemistry using response cards

Input ▸	Question ▸	Response ▸	Monitor ▸	Feedback
On the SMART Board: 1. *An element's atomic number is the same as its* a. *number of electrons* b. *number of protons* c. *number of neutrons*	Let's review what we learned yesterday. Read Item 1 on the SMART Board. Pick the best answer and select the best card, a, b, or c.	[Students read Item 1 and select response card.]	[Teacher walks around and monitors responses.]	
	Please compare your answer with your partner's answer. [Pause.] Show me your answers	[Students compare answers with partners, and then hold up their response cards.]	[Teacher walks around and listens to partners, then looks at response cards.]	Yes. The atomic number is the same as the number of protons. Remember that the periodic chart is organized by the atomic number.
2 *The most abundant element in the universe is* a. *helium* b. *carbon* c. *hydrogen.*	Read Item 2. Select the best answer.	[Students read Item 2 and select response card.]		
	Compare your answer with your partner's. If your answers are different, check in your book. [Pause.]	[Students compare answers with partners and start looking in books.]		
	Hold up your cards	[Students hold up their cards.]	[Teacher examines cards. A number of students have selected a. *helium*.]	The correct answer is c. *hydrogen*. Look at the chart in your book and find out how abundant hydrogen is, then find out how abundant helium is. [Pause.] What did you find for hydrogen? [Teacher calls on an individual to read the number of nuclei per million.] What did you find for helium? [Teacher calls on an individual to read the number of nuclei per million.] Which number is higher? [Teacher calls on an individual to say which number.] So, everyone, which one is the most abundant? [Teacher signals.] *Hydrogen*. Yes, hydrogen is the most abundant element in the universe. Helium is also very abundant but not as abundant, as hydrogen.

Action Responses

We have introduced a number of ways in which students can give both oral and written responses. Of course, students can also respond with a designated action, such as touching or pointing at a stimulus, responding with gestures, giving hand signals, or acting out an answer. Often this type of action response can increase students' interest, attention, and pleasure. Let's examine each of these action responses.

Touching/Pointing

Teachers of primary students and struggling students should constantly ask their students to touch specific items. This request should ring throughout the lesson: "Put your finger on the letter," "Put your finger on the word," "Put your finger on the picture," "Put your finger on the heading." This simple response is designed to bring students' attention to the stimulus and to allow the teacher to monitor students to see whether they are at the right place in the text. With struggling students or young students, teachers may also wish to direct partners to verify that their partners are in the right place. A simple directive, such as "put your finger on the first word in the paragraph" followed by "Now check your partner," will increase the number of students who are at the correct place.

Acting Out/Responding with Gestures or Facial Expressions

We recognize that students may act out of their own accord, but we are not referring to that type of "acting out" here. We are referring to *orchestrated* "acting out." Scenery, parts, scripts, and costumes are not necessary. Rather, you can incorporate acting out into a lesson to make it more memorable and interesting to students, regardless of age or grade. For example, as you read a story in kindergarten, you can ask a few members of the class to become the major characters and act out the story events to support all students' comprehension. In a high school English class, you can ask partners to act out vocabulary terms to enhance their memory of the terms. When students are learning the differences among solids, liquids, and gases in a science class, you can have students stand close together with no movement to demonstrate a solid, stand slightly separated with slight movement to illustrate a liquid, and disperse around the room to illustrate a gas. In all cases, the acting out will make the concepts easier to remember.

Similarly, students can respond with simple gestures or facial expressions that will also make the lesson content more vivid. For example, when learning the characteristics of composite volcanoes, you can have students form the base of the volcano with their hands and show the steep sides as they bring their hands to a peak. In math, students can signal which type of operation to perform by forming a plus

(+) sign, minus (−) sign, or multiplication (r) sign with their arms. When learning the word *furious*, students can demonstrate their knowledge of *furious* versus *not furious* by altering their facial expressions. When learning a specific sound, kindergarten students can put their hands on their heads when they hear the sound. Obviously, the uses of acting out, gestures, and facial expressions are as varied as the settings in which you teach. All that is required is a little creativity to add to the richness of a lesson.

Hand Signals

Another effective unison response procedure is for students to show answers via hand signals (Pratton & Hales, 1986). At the simplest level, students can indicate "yes" with a thumb up, "no" with a thumb down, or "I don't know" with a sideways thumb placement. In addition, any time there are a number of possible answers, students can indicate the answer by holding up a corresponding number of fingers. For example, a social studies teacher writes this on the board:

1. Legislative
2. Executive
3. Judicial

The teacher then asks questions, and students put up the number of fingers that correspond with the answer. Hand signals of this type are particularly useful in reviewing factual information, such as types of rocks (1, igneous; 2, sedimentary; 3, metamorphic), states of matter (1, solid; 2, liquid; 3, gas), types of volcanoes (1, shield; 2, composite; 3, cinder cone); measurements (1, perimeter; 2, area), final punctuation marks (1, period; 2, question mark; 3, exclamation mark), or vocabulary taught for a selection (e.g., 1, *enemy;* 2, *disgusting;* 3, *relieved;* 4, *concentrate*).

The benefits of hand signals are similar to those of response cards and slates: All students are involved, the number of responses requested can be increased, and the teacher can monitor the responses of all students. Although the use of hand signals can be very effective, there is one potential challenge: the hand signal "blurter" who immediately displays an answer, followed by classmates' copying the response, regardless of its accuracy. To reduce this challenge, students can be asked to form the hand signal on their desks or under their chins and then to hold up their hands when requested to do so.

In the lesson segments in Figure 6.7, note how action responses are incorporated into the lessons, and reflect on how you can use these techniques in your teaching.

(text resumes on page 162)

FIGURE 6.7. Lesson segments: Action responses.

	Lesson segment 1: Fifth-grade social studies using hand signals			
Input →	**Question** →	**Response** →	**Monitor** →	**Feedback**
[Students have been studying the branches of the U.S. government, with a recent focus on the Senate and the House of Representatives.]				
On the board: *1. Senate* *2. House of Representatives* *3. Both*	We have been studying the legislative branch of our federal government. Let's review what we know. I am going to give you some information. If I am referring to the Senate, hold up one finger when I request an answer. If I am referring to the House of Representatives, hold up two fingers. In some cases, I will be referring to both the House and the Senate, and you will hold up three fingers. Form your answer under your chin so I can see it, and then hold it up when I ask.			
	First fact. The number of members is based on the population of the state. [Pause.] Show me.	[Students hold up two fingers to indicate House of Representatives.]	[Teacher carefully examines students' hand signals.]	Yes, the number of representatives from each state serving in the House of Representatives varies, because the number is based on the population of the state.

Next fact. The Vice President can break a tied vote.	[Most students hold up one finger, but other students hold up two or look confused.]	[Teacher examines hand signals and notes that not all students have a firm grasp of this information.]	The Vice President can only vote when necessary to break a tied vote in the Senate. Remember, the Vice President is the ex officio President of the Senate. Although the Vice President seldom actually presides over the Senate, as that role can be given to others, the Vice President can break tied votes in the Senate.
[Teacher continues with facts such as these:] Two from every state. (Senate) Two-year term. (House of Representatives) Six-year term. (Senate) Initiates revenue bills. (House) Consents to treaties. (Senate) Elects President if there is a deadlock in the Electoral College. (House) Representatives from states. (Both) Passes laws. (Both) Confirms cabinet secretaries. (Senate) Impeaches officials. (House) Confirms federal judges. (Senate) Presiding officer—Speaker. (House) Members must be U.S. citizens who reside in state. (Both)			[Each time students have errors, teacher tells answer and has them repeat it.]
			[At the end, teacher repeats all the questions student had errors on.]

SUCCESSFUL RESPONDING

Despite the importance of opportunities to respond, they should not be used to "dress up" poorly designed or inadequately prepared lessons. As discussed in Chapter 1, high success rates are correlated with increased learning, and low success rates are correlated with decreased learning. The goal is not to increase the number of responses but the number of *successful* responses. During initial instruction, students should respond with at least 80% accuracy. During drill or independent work, a 90% or higher accuracy rate is desired (Council for Exceptional Children, 1987). If students experience continued failure, motivation quickly dissipates. Also, when teachers request responses without providing the information that will lead to accurate answers, students engage in higher rates of undesirable behavior (Gunter, Shores, Jack, Denny, & DePaepe, 1994).

As emphasized throughout this book, many practices can promote accurate responding, including teaching prerequisite skills before introducing a new strategy, skill, or rule; providing well-organized explicit instruction; carefully modeling the strategy, skill, or rule; and guiding students step by step in performance of the strategy, skill, or rule. Two additional procedures can increase student success during a lesson: (1) Ensure that the question and the desired response are clear and easy to understand, so that any errors are not due to lack of clarity; and (2) anticipate errors that students may commit, and provide **precorrections** to encourage accuracy. Let's examine these additional methods for increasing student success.

Students can make an error for two reasons. First, they may not have a firm grasp of the information that has been taught; therefore, they make a "performance error." For example, the teacher asks for the sound of a grapheme (letter or letter combination), and students say the wrong sound, or the teacher asks, "Do members of the Senate or the House have terms of 6 years?" and students wrongly respond "House." On the other hand, students may respond inaccurately because they don't understand the question or the type of response requested. For example, students respond with a letter name when a sound is requested, or they convey important details from a paragraph rather than a main-idea statement to their partner. Teachers need to eliminate the second cause of errors through clear communication. Then student errors will only be made for the first reason—not having a firm grasp of information—and appropriate corrections can be provided.

Many times, we can anticipate the errors that students might make. When we can anticipate the error with confidence, it is useful to provide a **precorrection** that increases the likelihood of correct student responses. A precorrection involves the artful use of reminders and prompts *before* students respond, for the purpose of maximizing success (Colvin, Sugai, & Patching, 1993; Miao, Darch, & Rabren, 2002). For example, a teacher may note in math that the failure to line up the columns in column addition has been contributing to student errors, so the teacher gives the following directive: "Copy this problem onto your slate and solve it. Be sure that you line up the ones, tens, and hundreds columns." Or perhaps

a teacher has noticed that students frequently mispronounce the vowels within words, so the teacher asks students to say the sound for each vowel before asking them to sound out a word. Or, in a spelling lesson, students are writing words for the following items: *take + ing* = —————— , *see + ing* = —————— , *age + less* = —————— . The teacher anticipates that students may spell *seeing* as *seing*, so he or she provides this precorrection: "Be careful. Remember, you only drop the *e* when adding a suffix that begins with a vowel if the root word ends in a vowel— consonant—Final *e*." Precorrections not only promote accurate responding, but also reduce time spent on corrections, set up a situation for positive affirmation, and help to create a positive classroom environment.

As we conclude this discussion of active participation, use what you have learned to analyze the non-example and example provided in Application 6.1.

(Application 6.1 begins on page 164)

APPLICATION 6.1. ANALYSES OF ACTIVE PARTICIPATION LESSONS

Directions: Read the following non-example lesson. Write down any concerns you have about this lesson. Also, make notes about how you would revise the lesson. Next, read the parallel example lesson, and note the improvements that have been made over the non-example lesson. After you have examined both lessons, compare your observations to our comments (see *Feedback on Application Exercises*, pages 270–271).

NON-EXAMPLE LESSON: COMPOUND WORD MEANINGS

Input →	Question →	Response →	Monitor →	Feedback
Today we are going to learn a strategy for figuring out the meaning of compound words. Let's review compound words. A compound word is made up of two real words. [Teacher points to *mailman* on the overhead.] For example, *mailman* is made up of the words *mail* and *man*. [Teacher points to *daydream* on the overhead.] *Daydream* is made up of the words *day* and *dream*.				
When we read compound words, we read left to right. [Teacher points to each remaining word in the list.] Listen as I read these compound words: *armchair backstroke barnyard bedtime cornerstone courthouse daylight dogcatcher paperback lifeboat dressmaker evergreen farmhouse fingerprint gravestone hairbrush*				
When we read compound words, we read left to right. However, when we want to figure out the meaning of the compound word, it is useful to look at the second word and ask how it relates to the first word. [Teacher points to the second word, then the first word in each compound word.] For example, *a mailman is a man* who delivers the mail. *A daydream is a dream* you have during the day. *An armchair is a chair* with arms. The *backstroke is a swimming stroke* that is done on your back. *A barnyard is a yard* around a barn. *Bedtime is the time* that you should go to bed.				
A *cornerstone is a stone* put in the *corner* of a building.				
	Your turn. Raise your hand if you can explain the meaning of *courthouse*.	*It is a house or building where courts meet.*	[Teacher listens.]	Good.

Input	Question	Response	Monitor	Feedback
	[Teacher calls on student with raised hand.] Jason?			
	Raise your hand if you can explain the meaning of *daylight* [Teacher calls on Melissa.]. Melissa?	*Daylight is light that we see during the day.*	[Teacher listens.]	Great!
	Who can explain the meaning of *dogcatcher* [Teacher calls on Jason.] Jason?	*That's a person who catches dogs.*	[Teacher listens.]	Right again, Jason.
	[Teacher continues through the list, calling on individual students.]			
Tomorrow we will practice this strategy with more difficult words.				

EXAMPLE LESSON: COMPOUND WORD MEANINGS

Input	→ Question	→ Response	→ Monitor	→ Feedback
[Before the lesson, the teacher hands out the following worksheet:] 1. *mailman* 11. *paperback* 2. *daydream* 12. *lifeboat* 3. *armchair* 13. *dressmaker* 4. *backstroke* 14. *earmuff* 5. *barnyard* 15. *evergreen* 6. *bedtime* 16. *farmhouse*				

7. *cornerstone*   17. *fingerprint*
8. *courthouse*   18. *gravestone*
9. *daylight* 19. *hairbrush*
10. *dogcatcher*   20. *handshake*

Input ──────────────────────────────────────→	Question ────→	Response →→	Monitor →→	Feedback
Today we are going to learn a strategy for figuring out the meaning of compound words.	What kind of words? [Teacher signals for a response.]	*Compound words.*	[Teacher listens carefully.]	
Let's review compound words.	Is a compound word made up of one or two real words? [Pause, then teacher signals for a response.]	*Two real words.*	[Teacher listens carefully.]	Yes, compound words are composed of two real words.
For example, *mailman* is made up of the words *mail* and *man.* [Teacher points to *mailman* on the overhead, and underlines *mail* and *man.*)	Underline the two words in *mailman* on your paper.	[Students underline *mail* and *man.*]	[Teacher looks at a number of papers.]	
Daydream is made up of the words *day* and *dream.* [Teacher points to *daydream* on overhead and underlines *day* and *dream.*]	Underline the two words in daydream.	[Students underline *day* and *dream.*]	[Teacher looks at a number of papers.]	

When we read compound words, we read left to right. However, when we want to figure out the meaning of the compound word, it is useful to look at the second word and ask how it relates to the first word. [Teacher points to the second word and then the first word in each compound word.] For example, a *mailman* is a *man* who delivers the *mail*. A *daydream* is a *dream* you have during the *day*.

Now read the rest of the compound words to yourself. Underline the two words that make up each compound word.

[Students underline the two words in each compound word.]

[Teacher moves around the room and gives feedback to individual students.]

[Teacher uncovers the remaining words on the overhead.] Check your underlining.

Your turn. An *armchair* is a *chair* with ————. [Teacher signals.]	*Arms.*	[Teacher listens carefully to the choral responses. Answers are strong and accurate.]	[Teacher moves quickly to the next item.]
[Teacher continues the process with several more sentences, such as: The *backstroke* is a swimming stroke done on your ————.]		[Teacher continues to listen carefully to the choral responses.]	[Teacher affirms students' firm and accurate responses by nodding, smiling, and moving on.]
Read Item 9. Everyone?	*Daylight.*		
Ones, explain the meaning of *daylight* to your partner.	*"Daylight" is light that we see during the day.*	[Teacher listens to a number of partner responses.]	
Maddie, explain the meaning of *daylight*. [Teacher continues in the same manner with the remaining words.]	*Well, that is light that occurs during the day.*	[Teacher listens.]	Great. You told how the second word related to the first word.

So, when we want to figure out the meaning of a compound word, we ask how the second word relates to the first word. Tomorrow we will practice this strategy with more difficult words. For homework this evening, see if you can find a number of compound words that we can analyze.

ALTERNATIVE PASSAGE- READING PROCEDURES

In many classes, students are asked to read text of various lengths, from assignment directions to pages of discourse. You often have a range of readers in your classroom, however, which makes passage reading more challenging. When a class consists of students with disparate reading skills, teachers often accommodate the lower-performing readers by reading the materials to students. But reading the material to students has two disadvantages: Students may not follow along, and only the teacher is gaining reading practice. The second procedure that teachers often select is round-robin reading, in which the teacher calls on a student and asks him or her to read orally to the class. Unfortunately, round-robin reading in a large class situation has many disadvantages. Because the reading practice is dispersed across members of the class, individual practice is limited; the larger the group, the smaller the amount of reading practice each individual engages in. When the lowest -performing students are asked to read, the text is often above their current reading level; thus they read haltingly, with many errors, and may be embarrassed by their performance. In addition, many students are not following along, lose their place, or are otherwise off task. Also, because the activity is often slow-moving, students become bored, and management problems emerge. Although round-robin reading is an acceptable procedure in a small group, alternatives are needed when the group grows beyond six students. Following are some alternative passage-reading procedures for groups of that size.

Echo Reading

Echo reading is a rereading strategy designed to help beginning readers develop accurate fluent reading with appropriate expression. In echo reading, the teacher reads a short segment of text, and a student echoes back the same sentence or phrase (or all students do this) while following along in the text.

Although echo reading has been shown to contribute to the reading growth of low-achieving students (Mathes, Torgesen, & Allor, 2001), it should be faded as reading skills are developed, so as to shift more responsibility to students.

Choral Reading

During **choral reading**, the teacher and students read the material out loud, thus engaging all students in reading practice. To optimize choral reading, you can do a number of things. First, you should read the material at a moderate rate—not too fast, as students may not be able to read at the same rate, or too slow, as the gist may be lost. Next, you should have students silently read the text before choral reading; this allows them to preview the material, to grow in confidence, and to

Delivering Instruction: Eliciting Responses   169

employ their decoding skills in attacking unknown words. As you read the material, model appropriate reading rate and expression. Finally, in anticipation of a student's rushing ahead of the group, provide a precorrection, such as "Keep your voice with mine."

Choral reading has a number of benefits over round-robin reading. First, more students are on task and gaining reading practice. Second, because you are reading with your students, you are modeling appropriate fluency and prosody (expression). Finally, you provide support (scaffolding) for the lowest-performing readers, because they immediately hear any words they don't know.

Cloze Reading

Another practice that you may be less familiar with is called **cloze reading**. Using this procedure, you read the text and pause at certain words that you want students to read. For example, if you were using the cloze procedure with the following paragraph, you would pause at the words in boldface, and students would say those words. Notice that you would have students read the words that help them to create meaning.

CANOES

A canoe is a long, narrow boat that does not have a motor or a sail. Several people can sit in most canoes. These people face the front of the boat, or the bow. They use paddles to move the canoe through the water and to make the canoe change directions.

The cloze procedure is very useful when you want all students to be attentive and you wish to read the material quickly. For example, cloze reading can be used in these situations: (1) reading the directions to an assignment, (2) reading an explanation of a process in a textbook, (3) reading the initial pages of a chapter, (4) reading an example or non-example essay in a writing lesson, (5) rereading a passage one more time to increase students' decoding fluency, or (6) reading a problem in math story. In this last situation, you can have students say specific words in the story problem to bring students' attention to the needed operation— for example, "There were **four** birds sitting on the fence. Eight **more** birds joined them. How **many** birds were there **altogether**?"

When you are using cloze reading, it is important to have students say the words that enhance comprehension. Occasionally, teachers will pause on words that students can all read, but that are not important to comprehension. Imagine the impact on comprehension if a teacher were to pause at the following boldfaced words:

CANOES

A canoe is a long, narrow boat that does not have a motor or a sail. Several people can sit in most canoes. These people face the front of the boat, or the bow. They use paddles to move the canoe through the water and to make the canoe change directions.

Augmented Silent Reading

It is often appropriate and desirable to have students read a

section of a contentarea textbook or a narrative passage silently. Unfortunately, at every grade level, you are likely to have "silent reader fakers"—that is, students who are merely looking at the words and not reading, *or* students who are engaging in an activity other than reading. A number of practices will increase the probability that students are actually reading the material. First, pose a question before students read and ask the question after they have read the material. When a question is posed before and after passage reading, students will feel more accountable for actually reading the material. One of the challenges with silent reading involves early finishers who have to wait for the other students and may fill the time with disruptive behavior. To reduce this challenge, simply give students a directive: "When you finish reading the section, please go back and reread the material to verify your answer." Also, as students are reading, you can move from student to student, listening to a number of students "whisper-read" to you. With this procedure, you can hear many students read and will have continuous feedback on their current reading skills, which, when combined with curriculum-based measures, can give you a complete view of student progress.

Partner Reading

One of the best alternatives to round-robin reading is **partner reading**. With younger students or with struggling readers, partner reading is best used to provide additional reading practice after a passage has been read chorally, silently, and/or with individual turns. In the upper grades, after introduction of a narrative or expository passage, you can have students read it to their partners. The benefits of partner reading are many. First, students get a great deal of reading practice. Second, as with silent reading, you can move around the room and listen to many students read. Third, you can ensure that students are actually reading— something that is not always possible with silent reading.

Before partner reading is initiated, a few preparations are necessary. As in pairing partners for responses (discussed earlier), you should select the partners carefully, placing the lowest-performing students with middle-performing peers. It is useful to make the better reader in each partnership the "One" and the lowerperforming reader the "Two," which will allow the better reader to model for the

poorer reader in some situations. Next, you will need to tell students the amount of text to read (a word, a sentence, a paragraph, or a page) or the amount of time (e.g., 5 minutes) they will read before alternating with a partner. With young students or students with beginning reading skills, alternating by word or sentence generally works well, affording much reading practice while keeping the students on task. When expository materials are used at any grade level, students should alternate by paragraph, stopping after each paragraph to respond to the content by retelling the passage, summarizing the content in a main idea statement, recording notes on the important content, or filling in a graphic organizer. When longer narrative passages are read in the upper grades, a partner can read for a 5-minute interval before the teacher indicates that the other partner should commence reading.

The partners will also need to be taught how to correct any errors they hear. We generally use an **Ask, then tell** correction procedure. When a partner hears an incorrect word, he or she immediately touches the word and inquires, "Can you figure out this word?" If the word has not been pronounced correctly after about 4 seconds, the partner says "This word is . What word? Now reread the sentence." Even young children have successfully learned how to correct their partners' errors.

Another reality must be addressed before partners are used in your class. Inevitably, there will be a student in the group who is unable to read the material to his or her partner; thus you will need to have an established plan to accommodate that student.

We have seen four different procedures used to support the lowest-performing readers:

1. Students read the material *together.*
2. The highest-performing reader reads a designated amount, and the lowerperforming reader then reads the *same* material.
3. A low-performing reader is placed in a triad and sits between two other students. One of the peers is designated the "One," and the low-performing reader and the other peer are designated "Twos." When the teacher says, "Ones, read to your partner," the One reads to both peers. When the teacher directs Twos to read to their partners, the Twos in the triad read together.
4. Another possibility is to introduce the **Me or We** option. When it is a partner's turn to read, he or she can say, "Me," indicating that he or she will read the material, or "We," inviting the other partner to read chorally with him or her.

CHAPTER SUMMARY

Throughout every lesson, regardless of lesson content or grade level of your students, you can elicit oral responses (choral, partner, team, or individual oral responses); written responses (especially use of response cards or slates); and/or action responses to promote rehearsal of information, to check understanding, and to determine any necessary adjustments to the current lesson.

In the end, which of these active participation or passage-reading procedures you select is less important than offering a large number of opportunities to respond and keeping *all* students involved. To be truly effective, instruction must be interactive. This constant involvement not only improves learning, but also reduces management problems and makes instruction more enjoyable for both the students and the teacher.

CHAPTER 7

Delivering Instruction
Other Critical Delivery Skills

Chapter 6 has reminded you of four essential delivery skills: eliciting frequent responses, monitoring performance, providing feedback, and brisk pacing. In Chapter 6, we have concentrated on how to make instruction interactive by requiring frequent responses during a lesson. In this chapter, we focus on the other three delivery skills.

MONITOR STUDENT PERFORMANCE CAREFULLY

Besides eliciting frequent student responses, teachers must carefully attend to student responses in order to gain information on student performance, provide corrections and affirmations, and adjust the instruction within the lesson or in future lessons. How to monitor student performance during a lesson differs, depending on the type of response requested and the number of people responding at one time. When you request an oral response from one individual, monitoring simply requires carefully listening to that student so that you can identify and correct errors. On the other hand, when you are calling for an oral response from several individuals, listening becomes more complex. When students are saying choral responses or reading chorally, you will want to intentionally listen to everyone. At the same time, you will want to direct more of your attention to the lowerperforming students, because they are the students most likely to make errors. Similarly, when you ask students to respond by holding up their slates or response cards or by showing answers with hand signals, monitoring involves carefully

scanning multiple responses, with attention going to everyone but more attention going to the lower-performing students.

In some cases, monitoring requires that you add the behavior of circulating around the room. For example, as students share answers with partners or team members, you will want to move around the room and listen to numerous responses, again with more attention to the lower-performers. When you ask students to respond by writing something on their papers or by touching items on their papers or in their books, monitoring also requires you to move around the room, carefully examining responses, looking for details that define responses as correct or incorrect. Sometimes this requires you to stop and examine individual words, letters, problems, or numerals. Although we focus in this chapter on monitoring during teacher-directed lessons, you will also need to circulate around the room when students are completing independent work and examine their responses (see Chapter 8).

As you carefully listen to and look at student responses, ask yourself these questions:

1. Is each response correct or incorrect?
2. If the response is incorrect, what type of correction procedure should be used?
3. If the response is correct, what type of affirmation/praise would be appropriate?

4. What adaptations, if any, should be made in the current lesson?
   a. Can the lesson go forward?
   b. Should confusing facts, concepts, skills, or strategies be retaught imme-diately?
   c. Should additional practice be provided within the lesson?
5. What adaptations, if any, should be made in future lessons?
   a. Should facts, concepts, skills, or strategies be retaught?
   b. Should additional practice be provided?

We describe effective monitoring and giving of feedback this way: **Walk around. Look around. Talk around.** This teaching procedure reminds us that it is not enough to meander through the room or scan the room without focusing on student responses. These monitoring behaviors must be coupled with careful observation of all students' responses and with communication to the students, affirming correct responses, correcting any errors, and encouraging effort.

PROVIDE IMMEDIATE AFFIRMATIVE AND CORRECTIVE FEEDBACK

One of the most powerful instructional acts is to provide feedback to students on their performance. Feedback has the goal of closing the gap between students' current performance and the desired performance by informing students whether an answer is correct or incorrect, whether their understanding is correct or flawed, and what can be done to improve future performance (Hattie & Timperley, 2007; Lenz, Ellis, & Scanlon, 1996). Appropriate feedback is a powerful tool for promoting student learning (Kluger & DeNisi, 1996; Stronge, 2002). The operative term here is *appropriate*; feedback can be helpful to students or harmful, depending on what and how it is conveyed. In this section, we focus on feedback given during explicit, teacher-directed lessons. In Chapter 8, feedback on independent work, an equally important topic, is explored. For additional information concerning the research on feedback and the application of research to daily practice during lessons and in response to independent work, we refer you to the writings of Hattie and Timperley (2007), Marchand-Martella et al. (2004), and Thalheimer (2008a, 2008b).

As stated previously, the goal of feedback, whether it is given on responses during instruction or on products produced during independent work or homework, is to close the gap between the student's current response and the desired response. Thus the feedback must be crafted to reach that goal and will be dependent on whether the response is correct or incorrect; hesitant or quick; or related to a fact, concept, strategy, or rule. Rosenshine and Stevens (1986) considered all of these factors when outlining types of feedback provided during an explicit lesson. Their schema has been expanded here to include not only feedback given for individual responses, but also for unison responses, and not only for fact or strategy errors, but also for reading errors.

Types of Responses and Corresponding Feedback

In Figure 7.1, you will see various types of responses that students might give. Then you will see a specific type of

EXPLICIT INSTRUCTION

feedback correlated to each type of response. For example, in the first two cells, you will read about two types of correct responses. If students are confident, quick, and firm when responding correctly, the teacher gives affirmative feedback and move right on in the lesson. If students are hesitant or lacking in confidence when responding correctly, the teacher gives affirmative feedback but reteaches rather than moving on. Similarly, the Figure shows four types of incorrect responses and the corresponding types of feedback. As you examine the contents of Figure 7.1, attend carefully to all the examples; these provide models for you to use in giving a particular type of feedback to your students.

Once you have determined what type of response your students have given, and you have chosen the corresponding type of feedback, you will want to follow some additional guidelines for how to convey the feedback. We address the implementation of feedback in two sections: (1) guidelines for corrections for incorrect responses; and (2) guidelines for affirmations (or praise) for correct responses, appropriate behavior, and effort.

FIGURE 7.1. Types of feedback.

Type of response	Type of feedback
Correct response that is confident, quick, and firm	**Affirm and move on.** When the answer given by the individual or all group members is correct, quick, and confident, it is appropriate to provide a brief affirmation ("Great," "True," "Yes") and then move on. A nod, thumbs up, or smile coupled with moving on is adequate to communicate that the answer is correct. **Example:** Let's review these "tricky" words. [Teacher points to *there*.] What word? *There*. [Teacher moves on and points to *again*.] What word? *Again*. [Teacher smiles, moves on, and points to *said*.] What word? *Said*. Excellent, all correct.

Correct response that is hesitant, reflecting that the student or students are not firm on the material	**Affirm and reteach.** When an individual response is correct but hesitant, *or* when a unison response is requested and a number of students are hesitant in their responses, *or* students are correct but the information has just been introduced, it is appropriate to affirm or acknowledge that the answer is correct but repeat the fact or review the concept, strategy, or rule. **Example:** Let's review the three branches of the U.S. government. Get ready to hold up the correct response card. Which branch carries out the laws? [Pause.] Show me. [All students hold up the *executive branch* card, but teacher notices that many students are looking around the room, verifying their answers by looking at other students' cards.] Yes, while the legislative branch makes the laws, the departments of the executive branch carry them out. For example, when an education law is passed, the Department of Education writes and communicates regulations for carrying out the law. So what branch carries out the laws? *The executive branch.* [Teacher asks additional questions about the branches of the government, returning to this question later in the session.] **Example:** Write this on your $\frac{1}{2}$ slate: $=\frac{}{4}$. Please determine an equivalent fraction. [Teacher moves around the room, examining slates. Although the answers are correct, teacher notices that there is a good deal of erasing and that the "work" is not always shown.] Hold up your slates. Yes, one-half and two-fourths are equivalent. Let's do it together. What number times 2 is equal to 4? *2.* [Teacher writes: $\frac{1}{2}$ u = .]. I want to multiply by a fraction equal to 1. $\frac{2}{2}$ $\frac{}{4}$ How many halves equal one? *Two.* Yes, two halves equal one. [Teacher writes: $\frac{1}{2}$ u = .] Next, we multiply 1 times 2. What is 1 times 2? *Two.* [Teacher writes 2 in $\frac{2}{2}$ $\frac{}{4}$ the numerator.] So, to determine an equivalent fraction, we multiply by a fraction equal to 1 in which the numerator and the denominator are the same. Let's try another example.

Type of response	Type of feedback
Incorrect response due to lack of knowledge (declarative knowledge) or understanding	**Restate fact or knowledge. Check understanding. (I do it. You do it.)** When an individual responds with the wrong factual information, *or* on a unison response a number of students give the wrong answer, state the fact and have students repeat the information. Immediate and delayed practice should also be provided.
	Example: [The word *brain* is written on the board. Teacher points to the underlined letters.] What sound? [Teacher signals. A number of students say /aˉ/ instead of /a/.] The sound is /a/. What sound? /a/. Sound out the word. Put your thumb up when you know the word. [Pause.] What word? *Brain.* [Teacher continues with the following words: *ran, train, rain, frail, and tan.* Teacher then returns to *brain.*]
	Example: [34.84 is written on the board.] Look at this number. How many tenths? [A number of students say *3.* Teacher points to the 8.] This column represents the tenths. How many tenths? *8.* [Teacher continues the review, using the following numbers: 201.45, 60.2, 98.54, and 53.02. Teacher then returns to 34.84.]

(cont.)

FIGURE 7.1. *(cont.)*

Type of response	Type of feedback

Incorrect response on strategy or rule (procedural knowledge)	**Guide students in applying the strategy or rule. (We do it. You do it.)** When an individual student or a number of students are incorrect in utilizing a strategy or rule, guide them in applying the strategy or rule. Then check their understanding again, using a new item. Delayed practice can also be provided later in the lesson.
	
	  Example: Write *trading* on your slate. [Pause.] Hold up your slate. [Many students write *tradeing*.] Let's look at this together. [Teacher writes *trade + ing* on the board.] Does *trade* end with a vowel–consonant–final *e*? *Yes.* Does the suffix begin with a vowel? *Yes.* So do we drop the *e* when we add the ending *ing*? *Yes.* Write *trading*. [Pause.] Hold up your slate. [Answers are correct. Teacher writes *trading* on the board.] Check your word. [Teacher dictates additional words, including *settlement*, *settling*, *safer*, and *safely*. Later in the day, teacher returns to a word similar to *trading* and one or two others that help students apply the rule again.]
	
	  Example: [This sentence is on the board: *The famous movie star sipped coffee.*] Write this sentence on your paper. Let's review what you have learned about commas. Add the necessary punctuation to this sentence. [Teacher circulates around the room. Students make numerous errors on commas.] Let's do this one together. Here we have *famous movie star*. What two adjectives tell about *star*? "Famous" and "movie." Do we often say *movie star*? *Yes.* So the noun is *movie star*. So do we put a comma between *famous* and *movie*? *No.* Fix up your answer if it is incorrect. Now explain to your partner why we don't place a comma between *famous* and *movie*. [Students are given several more sentences to punctuate. Below, the punctuation has been added. Right before lunch, the teacher puts a sentence parallel to the first couple of sentences on the board and has students apply the rule again.]
	
	  [Items used during the lesson:]
	    The famous movie star sipped coffee.
	    He looked at the bright, twinkling star.
	    They watched TV in the small living room.
	    They watched TV in the small, dark kitchen.
	
	  [Items used later in the day:]
	    Students climbed onto the yellow school bus.
	    She pushed open the rickety, rotting gate.

| Incorrect word when reading orally | **Say the word. Have students repeat the word and reread the sentence. (I do it. You do it.)** When a student mispronounces a word, say the correct word, have the student repeat the word, and then have the student reread the sentence (Nelson, Alber, & Gordy, 2004).
Example: Text students are reading.

The lead dogs and their teams lined up for the running of the Iditarod race in Alaska. Big Blue, a 9-year-old husky, who had won a third- and sixth-place trophy in past years, guided his team into Position 15. As he waited anxiously for the beginning of the race, Big Blue knew it was his last chance.

[In a small group, the teacher asks Jason to begin reading.] *The lead dogs and their teams lighted up* . . . [Teacher touches under the word *lined* in Jason's book.] Jason, the word is *lined.* What word? *Lined.* Please read the sentence again. *The lead dogs and their teams lined up for the running of the Iditarod race in Alaska . . .* |

(cont.)

FIGURE 7.1. *(cont.)*

Type of response	Type of feedback
Incorrect answer to reading comprehension question	**Guide students to the correct answer. (We do it.)** When students answer a higherorder comprehension question incorrectly or say "I don't know," guide them to the correct answer by asking them lower-order (literal) questions to provide a foundation for answering the higher-order question. **Example:** Why did Big Blue know it was his last chance? [Pause for 5 seconds.] Ones, tell your partner. [Pause.] Merry, why did Big Blue know it was his last chance? *I don't know.* Class, has Big Blue ever won first place? *No.* Is Big Blue a young or an old dog? *Old.* Will Big Blue be more athletic next year? *No.* Think, everyone. Why did Big Blue know it was his last chance? [Pause.] Merry? *Well, Big Blue has never won first place, and he is an old dog, so his chances won't be any better next year. If he doesn't win this year, he will never win.* Excellent. You really thought through your answer. **Note:** When you are teaching lower-performing students, it is useful to adopt a "success-based" rather than a "failure-based" practice for higher-order questions. When you can anticipate that students will have difficulty answering a higher-order question, build up their foundation knowledge during the story reading by asking literal questions before posing the higher-order question.)

More on Corrective Feedback

Although basic correction procedures have been introduced in Figure 7.1, you should consider a number of other practices when orally correcting errors during a lesson or when providing written comments on students' written products.

Provide Corrections

When new material is being learned, errors are inevitable. Often teachers are reluctant to correct student errors, because they believe that corrections will harm students' self-esteem. However, students' view of themselves as learners is much more likely to be negatively affected if errors are not corrected and learning does not occur. Teachers must notice every error, determine the type of error that has occurred, and provide a correction that leads to a correct answer (Watkins & Slocum, 2004).

Provide Immediate Corrections

Within a lesson, errors should be immediately corrected before additional retrieval opportunities are provided, so as to reduce practice errors. If students make repeated errors, the error pattern may become habitual, making it more difficult to eradicate from the students' repertoire.

Provide Specific, Informative Corrections

The purpose of all corrections is to reduce the distance between the current response and the desired response. A correction such as "No" or "That's not how it is done" contains no information that can assist a student in changing future performance. Even telling students the correct answer is often not adequate. For example, if a student reads the word *tape* as "tap," and the teacher says, "No, the word is *tape*," the student gains no information that will help reduce this type of error in the future. Corrective feedback such as this is preferable:

> The word ends in an *e*. So we say the name of this letter. [Teacher points to the letter *a* in the word.] What is the name? *a*. Sound out the word. [Pause.] What word?

Tape.

Planned, specific information is more likely to influence student performance than haphazard, general feedback (Herschell, Greco, Filcheck, & McNeil, 2002).

Focus on the Correct Answer versus the Incorrect Answer

When you are providing corrective information, it is essential to focus on the correct response rather than the incorrect response. Focusing on the incorrect answer is not only negative but may confuse students. For example, if a student adds the tens column and then the ones column, this correction would be confusing: "You added the tens first. You moved from left to right. We do that in reading, but not in math." This would be a much better correction:

> First, add the ones column. [Teacher points to the ones column.] Which column do we add first? *The ones column.* What is 5 plus 2? *7.* Yes, 7. Write 7 in the ones column. Next, we add the tens column. [Teacher points to the tens column.] What is 3 plus 5? *8.* Write 8 in the tens column. What is the sum? *87.* Let's review. Which column do we add first? *The ones.* Which column do we add next? *The tens.* Great. [Teacher provides additional practice.]

Utilize an Appropriate Tone When Correcting Errors

It is not just the wording of a correction that can cause harm, but also the affect used in delivering it. Students need to understand that the goal in any lesson is learning, and that making mistakes is a natural part of learning. When corrections are informative and delivered without anger, irritation, or disgust, students will feel safer in the learning environment and will become more willing to take risks. Thus corrections should be positive, not punitive; constructive; not destructive; respectful, not insulting; and encouraging, not demoralizing.

End Every Correction by Having Students
Give the Correct Response

We have often observed teachers telling students the correct answer but requesting no subsequent response. Failing to have students repeat or review the information or strategy is unfortunate, because it is in the retrieval and responding that performance is strengthened. If students are not required to produce the correct response after a correction procedure, less learning will occur (Barbetta & Heward, 1993). Besides the fact that learning is enhanced if the correction procedure includes requiring a response, the outcome is much more positive for students when their final performance is correct. In addition, it is often effective to provide a "delayed test," in which you return to the item or a similar item later in the lesson to check understanding (Watkins & Slocum, 2004).

In summary, good corrections are consistently and immediately provided, match the type of error made by the student, are specific in the information they convey, and focus on the correct response. In addition, corrections are delivered in an encouraging tone and end with the correct response.

Now it is your turn. In Application 7.1, use the attributes discussed above to analyze non-examples and examples of corrections.

APPLICATION 7.1. EXAMPLES AND NON-EXAMPLES OF
CORRECTIONS

Directions: As you examine the non-examples, note any changes that should be made in the correction procedure, and compare your observations to ours (see *Feedback on Application Exercises*, pages 271–274). For the final three vignettes (Items D, E, and F), analyze the non-example correction and then write a more appropriate correction and compare your suggestions to ours.

Correction procedure	Analysis

Item A. Non-example	The correction is:
[Listed on the board: 4, 8, 19, 20, 21, 25, 34.] These numbers represent the number of students on each bus that arrived this morning. Are the numbers listed in ascending or descending order? [Pause.] Everyone? [Many students say *descending order*.] It is obvious that you are still not carefully looking at the numbers. That is not correct. *Descending* means going from largest number to smallest number. These are in ascending order. What order? *Ascending*.	▯ a. Provided. ▯ b. Immediate. c. The appropriate type of correction (see Figure 7.1). d. Specific and informative. e. Focused on the correct (vs. incorrect) response. f. Delivered with appropriate tone. ▯ g. Ended with students' giving the correct response. **Comments:** This correction is negative and disrespectful. In addition, it is unlikely to close the gap between current understanding and desired understanding, because the teacher focuses on the incorrect response and gives no specific information that will improve future performance.

Correction procedure	Analysis
Item A. Example [Listed on the board: 4, 8, 19, 20, 21, 25, 34.] These numbers represent the number of students on each bus that arrived this morning. Are the numbers listed in ascending or descending order? [Pause.] Everyone? [Many students say *descending order*.] Let's look at these numbers again. Do the numbers go up or down in value? *Up.* The word *ascending* means going up. Here the numbers are going up in value. So, when the numbers go up in value, the numbers are in what order? *Ascending.* [Teacher presents additional lists of numbers, and the students determine whether the numbers are ordered in ascending or descending order.]	**The correction is:** ▯ a. Provided. __b. Immediate. ▯ c. The appropriate type of correction (see Figure 7.1). ▯ d. Specific and informative. ▯ e. Focused on the correct (vs. incorrect) response. ▯ f. Delivered with appropriate tone. ▯ g. Ended with students' giving the correct response. **Comments:** First, this correction is much more positive. The teacher simply treats the incorrect response as an opportunity to reteach the concept. In addition, specific information is given that can really strengthen the students' understanding of the concept. The teacher also focuses on the correct

	rather than the incorrect response, and verifies understanding at the end of the correction and with additional practice items.

Item B. Non-example
[Students have five response cards for science vocabulary in front of them: *melting, freezing, evaporation, condensation, precipitation*.] I am going to tell you about one of your vocabulary terms. I am thinking of the process in which water turns from a vapor into a liquid. [Teacher pauses for 3 seconds.] Show me. [Students hold up vocabulary card. Many of them hold up the card labeled *precipitation*.] The answer is *condensation*. Many of you held up *precipitation*. Remember, *precipitation* refers to the liquid that falls to the earth in the form of rain, snow, or hail. Everyone, hold up *condensation*.
	The correction is:
	☐ a. Provided.
	☐ b. Immediate.
	       c̲. The appropriate type of correction (see Figure 7.1).
	       d̲. Specific and informative.
	       e̲. Focused on the correct (vs. incorrect) response.
	☐ f. Delivered with appropriate tone.
	___g. Ended with students' giving the correct response.
	Comments: The main problem with this correction is that the teacher focuses on the incorrect response (*precipitation*) rather than the correct response (*condensation*). The teacher does not convey any information to assist students' understanding of *condensation*. In addition, there is no checking of understanding. Though the students give the correct response at the end, they merely repeat what the teacher has said, which does not confirm their understanding.

Correction procedure	**Analysis**

Item B. Example	The correction is:
[Students have five response cards for science vocabulary in front of them: *melting, freezing, evaporation, condensation, precipitation.*] I am going to tell you about one of your vocabulary terms. I am thinking of the process in which water turns from a vapor into a liquid. [Teacher pauses for 3 seconds.] Show me. [Students hold up vocabulary card. Many of them hold up the card labeled *precipitation.*] The answer is condensation. When water turns from a vapor (which is a gas like steam) into a liquid, the process is called *condensation.* When vapor turns into a liquid, the process is called ___. *Condensation.* In the water cycle, condensation occurs when water vapor in the clouds collects into droplets of water. Ones, explain to your partner the meaning of condensation. [Teacher monitors and then continues with other vocabulary terms, returning to *condensation* a number of times.]	☐ a. Provided. ☐ b. Immediate. ☐ c. The appropriate type of correction (see Figure 7.1). ☐ d. Specific and informative. ☐ e. Focused on the correct (vs. incorrect) response. ☐ f. Delivered with appropriate tone. ☐ g. Ended with students' giving the correct response. **Comments:** In this correction, the teacher does present information that will strengthen students' understanding of condensation. In addition, the teacher focuses on the correct response, thus reducing student confusion. In the end, the students give the correct answer and demonstrate understanding by sharing with their partners. The teacher also checks understanding later in the lesson.
Item C. Non-example	**The correction is:**
We have been learning a difficult spelling rule . . . how to spell the suffix /uˉbl/ as *a-b-l-e* or *i-b-l-e.* The pronunciation of the suffix doesn't help, but knowing the spelling of other related words does. Write the word *application* on your paper. [Teacher circulates around the room and then writes *application* on the overhead transparency.] Check the spelling. If you made an error, cross it out and write *application.* [Pause.] Now write the word *applicable.* [Teacher circulates around the room and notices that many students have written *applicible* instead. Teacher then writes *applicable* on the transparency.] If you	☐ a. Provided. ☐ b. Immediate. <u>c.</u> The appropriate type of correction (see Figure 7.1). <u>d.</u> Specific and informative. ☐ e. Focused on the correct (vs. incorrect) response. ☐ f. Delivered with appropriate tone. ☐ g. Ended with students' giving the correct response. **Comments:** This correction is given with an appropriate tone and is focused on the spelling of *applicable.* But the teacher provides information that only helps students spell *applicable;* the information does not reinforce the rule so that

made an error, cross it out and write *applicable*. Let's try some more words. [Teacher dictates additional words.]	students can generalize the rule to other words. Thus the correction will have a limited impact on students' future spelling.

Correction procedure	Analysis
Item C. Example We have been learning a difficult spelling rule . . . how to spell the suffix /uˉbl/ as *a -b-l-e* or *i-b-l-e*. The pronunciation of the suffix doesn't help, but knowing the spelling of other related words does. Write the word *application* on your paper. [Teacher circulates around the room and then writes *application* on the overhead transparency.] Check the spelling. If you made an error, cross it out and write *application*. [Pause.] Now write the word *applicable*. [Teacher circulates around the room and notices that many students have written *applicible* instead.] Let's use our rule to figure out the spelling of *applicable*. Look at *application*. Does it end in *ation*? *Yes.* Use *a-b-l-e* when there is a corresponding *ation* word. So should we use the suffix *a-b-l-e* or *i-b-l-e*? *A-b-l-e.* [Teacher writes *applicable* on the transparency.] Check the spelling of *applicable*. If you missed it, cross it out and rewrite it. [Pause.] Let's try some	**The correction is:** ☐ a. Provided. ☐ b. Immediate. ☐ c. The appropriate type of correction (see Figure 7.1). ☐ d. Specific and informative. ☐ e. Focused on the correct (vs. incorrect) response. ☐ f. Delivered with appropriate tone. ☐ g. Ended with students' giving the correct response. **Comments:** In this example, the teacher guides students in using the spelling rule to determine the spelling of *applicable*. As a result, the teacher provides information that is specific as well as generalizable to other words.

more words. [Teacher dictates additional words containing both spellings of /u˘bl/.]

Item D. Non-example

[Text students are reading.]

Bry and Grace, the best artists in fifth grade, raced to Ms. Pateros's room. Ms. Pateros was to announce the winner of the "Rural Youth Painting Contest." While most of the students had only spent a few minutes on their entries, the girls had worked for weeks on their watercolor paintings of the rolling fields of Kansas, being careful to meet all the requirements for the contest and to create a painting full of detail and beauty. Each was sure that *she* was the winner.

[After students read this passage, teacher asks this question.] Why did both Bry and Grace believe that they had won the contest? [Teacher provides thinking time.] Stephen? *Because they entered paintings in the contest.* No, Stephen, they both thought they were winners because they were the best

The correction is: _____ a. Provided.

b. Immediate.

c. The appropriate type of correction (see Figure 7.1).

d. Specific and informative.

e. Focused on the correct (vs. incorrect) response.

f. Delivered with appropriate tone.

g. Ended with students' giving the correct response.

Comments:

artists in fifth grade, had put a good deal of time into the paintings, and had worked to ensure that their paintings were detailed and beautiful and exactly what the contest wanted.	

Correction procedure	Analysis

Item D. Example	The correction
[After students read this passage, teacher asks this question.] Why did both Bry and Grace believe that they had won the contest? [Teacher provides thinking time.] Stephen? *Because they entered paintings in the contest.* **Your correction:**	**is:** _____a. Provided. b. Immediate. c. The appropriate type of correction (see Figure 7.1). d. Specific and informative. e. Focused on the correct (vs. incorrect) response. f. Delivered with appropriate tone. g. Ended with students' giving the correct response. **Comments:**
Item E. Non-example [Definitions on the board:] Longitude u Imaginary lines u Divide earth east and west u Meet at poles Latitude u Imaginary lines u Divide earth north and south u Never meet Let's review longitude and latitude. Is the equator an example of longitude or latitude? Discuss this with your partner. [Pause.] Amy, so which is it, longitude or latitude? *Longitude.* Amy . . . don't you remember? We talked about this yesterday. The equator is an example of latitude.	**The correction is:** _____a. Provided. b. Immediate. c. The appropriate type of correction (see Figure 7.1). d. Specific and informative. e. Focused on the correct (vs. incorrect) response. f. Delivered with appropriate tone. g. Ended with students' giving the correct response. **Comments:**

Correction procedure	Analysis
Item E. Example [Definitions on the board:] Longitude u Imaginary lines u Divides earth east and west u Meet at poles Latitude u Imaginary lines u Divides earth north and south u Never meet Let's review longitude and latitude. Is the equator an example of longitude or latitude? Discuss this with your partner. [Pause.] Amy, longitude or latitude? *Longitude.* **Your correction:**	**The correction is:** _____a. Provided. b. Immediate. c. The appropriate type of correction (see Figure 7.1). d. Specific and informative. e. Focused on the correct (vs. incorrect) response. f. Delivered with appropriate tone. g. Ended with students' giving the correct response. **Comments:**
Item F. Non-example The side of each square represents 1 foot. Determine the perimeter of this figure. [Pause.] Compare your answer with that of your partners. [Pause.] Johnathan, what is your answer? *20 square feet.* Johnathan, that would be the area of the figure. The area is the number of square units covered in a figure. The perimeter, on the other hand, will be 22 feet. So, Johnathan, what is the perimeter? *22 feet.*	**The correction is:** _____a. Provided. b. Immediate. c. The appropriate type of correction (see Figure 7.1). d. Specific and informative. e. Focused on the correct (vs. incorrect) response. f. Delivered with appropriate tone. g. Ended with students' giving the correct response. **Comments:**

Correction procedure	Analysis
Item F. Example The side of each square represents 1 foot. Determine the perimeter of this figure. [Pause.] Compare your answer with that of your partners. [Pause.] Johnathan, what was your answer? *20 square feet.* **Your correction:**	**The correction is:** _____a. Provided. b. Immediate. c. The appropriate type of correction (see Figure 7.1). d. Specific and informative. e. Focused on the correct (vs. incorrect) response. f. Delivered with appropriate tone. g. Ended with students' giving the correct response. **Comments:**

More on Praise

In our introduction of feedback and description of ways to respond to students' answers in a lesson, we have suggested that correct responses can be affirmed with a nod, a smile, a brief comment, or simply moving on. In addition, throughout the lesson, when students consistently respond correctly, meet behavioral expectations, or demonstrate exemplary academic or behavioral performance, more elaborated praise can be offered. This praise can enhance academic learning, increase on-task behavior, shape future actions, improve teacher–student relationships, and help create a more positive learning climate (Good & Brophy, 1997; Lampi, Fenty, & Beaunae, 2005).

To praise or not to praise . . . that has been the question. For example, Alfie Kohn (1993) has suggested that any attempt to encourage learning behavior, including use of incentives and praise, will harm students' intrinsic motivation—the desire to do something for its own sake and the pleasure gained from the action. However, Kohn's viewpoint is not consistent with the conclusions drawn from two comprehensive meta-analyses on this question (Cameron, Banko, & Pierce, 2001; Cameron & Pierce, 1994; Pierce & Cameron, 2002). These researchers found little evidence that rewards such as praise (extrinsic motivation) decrease or extinguish intrinsic motivation. Instead, they found that praise enhances intrinsic motivation if the praise is *appropriately* administered. So, like corrections, praise can be helpful or harmful, depending on its content and manner of delivery. A number of authors have outlined the characteristics of effective praise (e.g., Brophy, 1981; Lampi et al., 2005; Marzano, 2000).

Provide Praise Contingent on Behavior That Meets Requirements

Cameron et al. (2001, p. 21) concluded that "The most important requirement is to closely tie rewards to meeting attainable behavioral criteria and performance standards." A teacher needs to apply the "If–Then rule" in delivering praise: "*If* students consistently compute the math problems accurately, *then* I will praise them. *If* students include all of the required elements in their story, *then* I will praise them. *If* students write a heading on the paper [a behavior that is seldom exhibited], *then* I will gleefully praise them." On the other hand, if praise comments are given in a random, unplanned manner with no connection to desired behavior, the praise will have little positive effect on behavior.

Provide Specific Praise Rather Than Global Reactions

Remember, the purpose of all feedback is to strengthen future performance. Like corrections, elaborated praise statements should explicitly state what positive behavior the student has performed, so that it can be duplicated in the future. For example, a teacher is circulating the room as students write sentences and comments to Maria, "Nice sentence, Maria." What exactly is "nice" about the sentence? Does it have the desired punctuation? Does it have a subject and predicate? Has the student written the sentence legibly? Is the sentence content interesting? Compare that comment to the following: "Maria, you really put effort into your sentence. Your sentence has a subject and a predicate and makes sense." Now Maria can say to herself, "Ahhh. A good sentence must have a subject and a predicate and make sense. I can do that in the future." Following this guideline does not mean that you should abandon all short, quick affirming statements, such as "Yes," "Good," or "That's right." You will still want to use these statements when you have requested a one-dimensional answer that is either right or wrong (e.g., "What is 3 times 5?" *15*), and you want to affirm correctness of the response and also move quickly from one response to the next. You have seen the use of this type of feedback in the first cell of Figure 7.1.

Provide Praise for Noteworthy Effort or Success on Difficult Tasks

In order for students to feel that the praise is genuine, it must recognize performance that *really* is exemplary for a particular class or student. In a high school chemistry class, independently filling in all the elements on the periodic chart is certainly more praiseworthy then writing names on a test paper. If students in a sixth-grade math class take extra care to line up the columns to reduce careless errors, praise is appropriate. However, if they have consistently done this for weeks, praise is less appropriate or necessary. It is often helpful to ask yourself whether the class or student would believe that their performance is an accomplishment before you lavish praise on them.

Provide Praise That Focuses on Effort and Achievements

Researcher Carol Dweck (2008) and her colleagues have identified two mindsets that people may use to view the world. Some individuals may have what Dweck termed a *fixed mindset*, in which they believe that performance is primarily due to a fixed, inherent attribute. Such individuals believe that doing well is evidence that they are inherently smart or talented or athletically endowed, and doing poorly is evidence that they are inherently "stupid" or lack talent in the performance area. Having a fixed mindset has numerous consequences for learners. Because they believe that good or poor performance is a product of an inherent quality rather than effort and learning, such students' desired outcome is to do well and to look good to validate their intelligence. They are unwilling to take risks that might lead to failure, and they have difficulty handling failure. Also, since they believe that being smart is an inherent quality, they feel that excellent performance should not require effort; if a task does take a great deal of sustained effort, they use this as evidence of lack of intelligence or talent. As you can see, having a "fixed mindset" definitely puts a ceiling on learning.

Other individuals may have what Dweck and colleagues term a *growth mindset*. These individuals believe that success is related to effort and learning. As a result, their approach to learning is significantly different. They are willing to take risks and readily accept challenges. When faced with a mistake, rather than retreating, they are eager to learn and apply the necessary effort to improve. For them, learning itself is the desired outcome. So whether it is learning how to solve equations, to play the cello, to research a topic, or to do a back flip off the diving board, these individuals are willing to learn and exert effort.

It is obvious that having a *growth mindset* is useful to learners of any age. The question then becomes this: How can we as teachers promote this way of viewing experience? One of the major ways is in the wording of our praise, in which we honor achievement, effort, and learning rather than inherent qualities of intelligence or talent. Praise that helps to promote a growth mindset focuses on strategy use, task performance, and study strategies, as well as on attributes that the student can manage and control, such as effort, persistence, practice, concentration, and making good choices. It does not highlight such inherent qualities as talent, intelligence, or inherited athletic ability; effective praise should help students make a connection between effort and success. As a result, comments such as "You are so smart," "You are a born athlete," or "Your talent as an artist is amazing," can be replaced with more effective comments such as "You really must have worked hard on these problems," "Your daily practice really paid off at the swim meet," or "You have learned so many watercolor techniques. They are more and more evident in your paintings."

Provide Praise That Uses Students' Own Past Performance for Comparisons

In addition to focusing on achievement and effort rather than inherent attributes, effective praise establishes the student's own prior performance rather than the accomplishments of peers as the context for describing present accomplishments (Corpus, Love, & Ogle, 2005). As a result, comments such as

"That's the best performance of anyone in sixth grade," or "Most first graders don't do as well as you," will be replaced with comments such as "You've really learned how to solve these problems," or "You have learned how to decode words you couldn't read 2 months ago."

Provide Praise That Is Positive, Credible, and Genuine

As with corrections, the tone of the praise will predict how students receive it. When hearing a praise comment, the students must believe that the teacher *really* means what he or she is saying. Many variables can add to the credibility of the comments. First, the words must actually be positive. For example, this would hardly be interpreted as positive by a class of seventh graders: "Amazing. You actually got the answer correct . . . and to think it only took 5 weeks of the semester. Well, let's hope you remember it tomorrow."

To ensure that praise will be viewed as genuine, praise comments should vary and should demonstrate that the teacher has recognized and is attending to excellent performance. Students will tune out to rote, bland comments that sound and feel as if they have nothing to do with them.

Communication is so much more than the words that we say. We communicate through our stance, the movements of our arms, the expressions on our faces, our tone of voice, the furrowing of our brows. All of these variables need to be positive if the praise is to feel honoring to students. If praise is delivered in a harsh tone coupled with a grim expression, its power is dissipated.

Finally, it is useful to determine whether individual praise should be given publicly or privately. Some students really appreciate being praised publicly and thus acknowledged in front of their peers, while other students much prefer quiet, private acknowledgment.

Provide Praise That Flows with the Lesson

Effective praise adds to the lesson. It doesn't interfere with the pace of the lesson or draw students' attention away from the critical content being introduced. Thus it is unobtrusive.

In summary, praise statements, like corrections, need to be thoughtfully given if they are to support our learners. Praise that is contingent, specific, informative, and genuine not only can honor students and inform them about their growth, but can help establish a positive climate where learning is encouraged and can strengthen the relationship between students and the teacher. The principles of effective praise discussed above are illustrated in Application 7.2.

APPLICATION 7.2. Examples and Non-Examples of Praise

Directions: Carefully read the first two non-example and example sets. For the remaining two sets, evaluate the non-examples and suggest alternative wording for the verbal praise. Then compare your suggestions with ours (see *Feedback on Application Exercises*, pages 274–276).

Praise statement	Analysis

Item A. Non-example
[These words are written on the board for the kindergarten students: *sad, fan, cap, tan, dad.*] [Teacher points to *fan.*] Sound out this word. Put your thumb up when you know it. [Pause.] What word? *Sad.* Great. Sound out the next word. [Pause. Teacher waits for thumbs up.] What word? *Fan.* [Teacher smiles and moves on. Teacher points at *cap* and pauses.] What word? *Cap.* Yes. [Teacher points at *tan* and provides thinking time.] What word? *Tan.* Final word. [Teacher points to *dad* and gives thinking time.] What word? *Dad.* Let's go back to the top and reread these words. *Sad, fan, cap, tan, dad.* Wow . . . you are so much better than my morning class! You are
	Praise is:
	◻ a. Contingent **(If–Then)**.
	___b. Specific.
	◻ c. Provided for noteworthy
	   performance.
	d. Focused on achievement and effort
	   rather than personality attributes.
	e. Comparing students to themselves
	   rather than to others.
	f. Positive, credible, and genuine.
	g. Unobtrusive.
	Comments On the positive side, the teacher provides quick affirmations after correct responses. However, there are several problems with the elaborated praise statement. First, no specific information is contained in the statement that can be duplicated in the

really smart.	future. Second, the praise focuses on an inherent attribute, intelligence, rather than task performance. Finally, the students are compared to another class rather than to themselves in the past.
Item A. Example [These words are written on the board for the kindergarten students: *sad, fan, cap, tan, dad*.] [Teacher points to *fan*.] Sound out this word. Put your thumb up when you know it. [Pause.] What word? *Sad*. Great. Sound out the next word. [Pause. Teacher waits for thumbs up.] What word? *Fan*. [Teacher smiles and moves on. Teacher points at cap and pauses.] What word? *Cap*. Yes. [Teacher points at *tan* and provides thinking time.] What word? *Tan*. Final word. [Teacher points to *dad* and provides thinking time.] What word? *Dad*. Let's go back to the top and reread these words. *sad, fan, cap, tan, dad*. Wow . . . all correct. You really looked at the letters!	Praise is: ☐ a. Contingent **(If–Then)**. ☐ b. Specific. ☐ c. Provided for noteworthy performance. ☐ d. Focused on achievement and effort rather than personality attributes. ☐ e. Comparing students to themselves rather than to others. ☐ f. Positive, credible, and genuine. ☐ g. Unobtrusive. **Comments** Here the teacher focuses the praise on the students' performance rather than personality attributes, and gives the students specific information that they can use to strengthen and maintain future performance.

Praise statement	Analysis

Item B. Non-example	Praise is:
[The fifth graders have read a paragraph and have been asked to list at least three important details under the topic *canoes.*] [Teacher moves around the room, examining each student's work. Paul has written one detail under the topic *canoes.* The teacher quietly provides this praise statement.] Super. Paul, that is a great answer. That is a critical detail because it tells something important about canoes. You did a really good job.	___a. Contingent **(If–Then)**. ☐ b. Specific. ___c. Provided for noteworthy performance. ☐ d. Focused on achievement and effort rather than personality attributes. ☐ e. Comparing students to themselves rather than to others. ☐ f. Positive, credible, and genuine. ☐ g. Unobtrusive. **Comments** The teacher has established an expectation of three details, but praises Paul rather profusely for one detail–not a noteworthy accomplishment unless the student is very lowperforming. It would be better to encourage Paul and then to praise him when the response is complete. However, the praise is positive and specific.
Item B. Example [The fifth graders have read a paragraph and have been asked to list at least three important details under the topic *canoes.*] [Teacher moves around the room, examining each student's work. Paul has written one detail under the topic *canoes.*] Paul, that is a critical detail about canoes. Add two more. I will be back. [Teacher continues to circulate around the room and then returns to Paul's desk.] Wonderful. Three details that all give critical information about canoes. You really searched through the paragraph.	Praise is: ☐ a. Contingent **(If–Then)**. ☐ b. Specific. ☐ c. Provided for noteworthy performance. ☐ d. Focused on achievement and effort rather than personality attributes. ☐ e. Comparing students to themselves rather than to others. ☐ f. Positive, credible, and genuine. ☐ g. Unobtrusive. **Comments** Here the teacher encourages Paul to complete the task. When his response matches the expectation of three critical details, the teacher praises Paul for his effort, making the praise specific.

Item C. Non-example	Praise is:
This week we have been studying the rule about *i* before *e* except after *c*. I am going to dictate a word. Write it on your slate. The first word is *chief*. Write it. Show me. [All students get the word correct.] Yeah . . . you did it. You all got it right. You remembered to put the *i* before the *e* when spelling the word *chief*. So many people don't know this rule, but you weren't fooled. I just got a letter from my son . . . you know, the one at college . . . and he spelled *receive r-e-c -i-e-v-e*. But not my third-period class. You would never make that error. You are so smart. Let's try another word . . .	a. Contingent **(If–Then)**. b. Specific. c. Provided for noteworthy performance. d. Focused on achievement and effort rather than personality attributes. e. Comparing students to themselves rather than to others. f. Positive, credible, and genuine. g. Unobtrusive. **Comments**

Praise statement	Analysis
Item C. Example This week we have been studying the rule about *i* before *e* except after *c*. I am going to dictate a word. Write it on your slate. The first word is *chief*. Write it. Show me. [All students get the word correct. Teacher continues with the words *niece, priest, receive, deceive, relief*, and *ceiling*, giving brief affirmations such as "Great," "Correct," "Perfect," or a smile. Of the 24 students in the class, only 2 make any errors . . . one apiece.] **Your praise statement:**	Praise is: a. Contingent **(If–Then)**. b. Specific. c. Provided for noteworthy performance. d. Focused on achievement and effort rather than personality attributes. e. Comparing students to themselves rather than to others. f. Positive, credible, and genuine. g. Unobtrusive. **Comments**

Item D. Non-example [Written on the board: 5.42, 5.46, 5.15, 5.5, 5.51.] We have been studying ascending and descending order. Please write the numbers on the board in descending order vertically . . . down the page. [Teacher moves around the room and examines students' papers. Then teacher writes the numbers in descending order on the board.] Please check your numbers with mine. [Pause.] Raise your hand if yours is the same as mine. [All students raise their hands.] Great job. You are *so* brilliant!	Praise is: a. Contingent **(If–Then)**. b. Specific. c. Provided for noteworthy performance. d. Focused on achievement and effort rather than personality attributes. e. Comparing students to themselves rather than to others. f. Positive, credible, and genuine. g. Unobtrusive. **Comments**
Praise statement	**Analysis**
Item D. Example [Written on the board: 5.42, 5.46, 5.15, 5.5, 5.51.] We have been studying ascending and descending order. Please write the numbers on the board in descending order vertically . . . down the page. [Teacher moves around the room and examines students' papers. Then teacher writes the numbers in descending order on the board.] Please check your numbers with mine. [Pause.] Raise your hand if yours is the same as mine. [All the students raise their hands.] **Your praise statement:**	Praise is: a. Contingent **(If–Then)**. b. Specific. c. Provided for noteworthy performance. d. Focused on achievement and effort rather than personality attributes. e. Comparing students to themselves rather than to others. f. Positive, credible, and genuine. g. Unobtrusive. **Comments**

As we conclude this section on feedback, it is very important to remember the primary importance of explicit instruction. We have discussed the importance of providing *appropriate* corrections and praise to strengthen students' academic and behavioral performance—but, as Hattie and Timperley (2007) have suggested, "Instruction is more effective than feedback. Feedback can only build on something; it is of little value when there is no initial learning or surface information" (p. 104).

DELIVER THE LESSON AT A BRISK PACE

In our exploration of the delivery of lessons, we have considered three critical skills: providing students opportunities to respond, carefully monitoring those responses, and providing appropriate feedback (including both corrections and affirmations). Effective delivery requires one more skill. Not surprisingly, students are more likely to be engaged and on task when the lesson is presented at a lively pace, in which the lesson moves smoothly and quickly from input to response to feedback and back again to input, response, and feedback. Maintaining a perky rather than a pokey pace also allows you to cover more content and to give your students more opportunities to respond, which increases their learning (Brophy & Good, 1986). Let's explore the teaching practices that you can use to increase the pace of a lesson.

Be Prepared

Of course, the pace of an explicit instructional lesson is very dependent on your level of preparation. When you can articulate the goal of the lesson; know what you are going to do during the opening, body, and closing of the lesson; have examples and non-examples designed in advance; and are thus confident about the quality of the lesson, flow will occur. Similarly, if you have carefully previewed the lessons provided in your curriculum materials and have done any necessary additional preparation, you will be able to present the material fluidly to your students.

Provide *Just* Enough Thinking Time

Although it is important not to rush frenetically through material by minimizing thinking time and forcing students to guess, it is also important that you don't provide too much thinking time. Generally, 3–5 seconds of thinking time is adequate for most responses. For some types of short responses (saying sounds that correspond with letters, answering factual questions, etc.), you may be able to shorten the thinking time once students have become confident of their responses.

Provide *Just* Enough Time for Oral, Written, or Action Responses

If students are given too much time to make a response, the pace of the lesson will stall. Also, you will have early finishers—and, as we have discussed in earlier chapters, when students have a void, they will fill it. This may result in management problems. As you monitor, observe how students are responding; when the majority of students complete a response, move on.

After Providing Feedback on a Response, Move On

Many teachers will ask for a response, give feedback, and then feel it is necessary to expound on the response when it would be more appropriate to move forward in the lesson. In some cases, a teacher will pause rather than going forward. Carnine (1976) demonstrated that moving quickly to the next response during drill-andpractice activities not only increased opportunities to respond, but also increased accuracy. He attributed these increases to improved attentiveness as a result of the brisk pace.

Avoid Digressions

Verbosity is the enemy of perky pace. If a memory of a personal adventure or past instructional incident pops into your mind, do not feel compelled to share it. Often these digressions, rather than inspiring attention, promote inattention or prompt the students to share digressions of their own.

Utilize Instructional Routines

An **instructional routine** is a set of teaching behaviors that can be used again and again in presenting new information or providing practice on information. For example, the following instructional routine can be used when students are asked to sound out a word.

Stimulus on board:	Instructional routine
Teacher writes: *s*	What sound? */s/*
Teacher adds *a*: *sa*	What sound? */a˘/* Blend the sounds. */sa˘/*
Teacher adds *t*: *sat*	What sound? */t/* Blend the sounds. */sa˘t/* What word? *sat*
Teacher writes: *m*	What sound? */m/*
Teacher adds *a*: *ma*	What sound? */a˘/* Blend the sounds. */ma˘/*
Teacher adds *p*: *map*	What sound? */p/* Blend the sounds. */ma˘p/* What word? *map*

Because the teacher is using the same instructional routine for each consecutive word, the pace of the instruction is brisk. While instructional routines benefit us as teachers, they are also very helpful to students. When we are guiding students in performing a task such as sounding out a word, spelling a dictated word, or solving a story problem, students' cognitive energy must be divided between the task and the content. However, if an instructional routine is used, students can place their attention solely on the content, which is exactly where we want them to focus.

Now examine the lessons in Application 7.3, which illustrate a slow and a brisk pace for a reading lesson. Note especially the value of an instructional routine for moving things along at a brisk pace.

APPLICATION 7.3. Lessons Illustrating Slow and Brisk Pace

Directions: As you read through the non-example lesson below, identify the practices that are making the lesson's pace pokey versus perky. Make notes on what you would do to improve the lesson's pace. Then compare your observations with the changes made in the example lesson illustrating a brisk pace, and with our comments following each lesson.

NON-EXAMPLE: FIRST-GRADE READING LESSON ILLUSTRATING SLOW PACE

[These words are written on the board: *made, late, slate, fad, fade, tap, tape.*] Yesterday we learned how to read words with a final *e*. Let's practice with new words. [Teacher points to *made.*] Does this word end with an *e*? *Yes.* [Teacher points to the letter *a.*] So do we say the name of this letter? *Yes.* What is the name of the letter? *A.* Sound out the word and put your thumb up when you know the word. [Teacher pauses for 20 seconds.] What word? *Made.* Yes, we *made* holiday cookies yesterday. I can't wait for our party . . . I particularly want to try the orange puffs. Yummmmmm. Well, let's try another word. [Teacher points to *late.*] Does this word end with that tricky *e*? *Yes.* [Teacher points to the letter
a.] So we say the name for this letter. Whisper the word to your partner. [Teacher pauses for 2 minutes.] Everyone, what word? *Late.* Wow! Wow! You got two words correct. Let's give ourselves a round of applause. [Teacher and students clap with their fingers in a circle.) Yes, that word is *late.* We can't be *late* to library today. Ms. Johnson will be reading holiday stories. I wonder which one? What story do you hope she reads? [Teacher calls on a number of students.]

Okay, let's try a really difficult word. Let's go sound by sound. Follow my magic finger and say each sound. [Teacher moves her finger under each of the letters. Some students say the short sound instead of the name.] Oops . . . we had better look at this one again. It has the silent *e* at the end. That tricky *e* fooled us. We have to say the name of this letter. [Teacher points to the letter *a*.] Now sound out the word and look at me when you know it. [Teacher pauses for 15 seconds.] Everyone, what word? *Slate.* Yes, it is like the slates we use in math. In fact, I was thinking we should use our *slates* more often maybe for our spelling words. [Jenn raises her hand.] *Can we draw on our slates during story time?* Interesting idea, Jenn . . . Oops, we had better hurry . . . it's almost library time. The next word is an easy one. Notice there is no *e* at the end. What word? [Teacher pauses for 8 seconds.] *Fad.* That time I didn't fool you. Yes, the word is *fad.* You know . . . a fad is something that is around for only a little time. Here today, gone tomorrow. Last month, all of you wanted to wear sweatshirts for baseball teams . . . but that fad ended right after Halloween. I bet you can think of some other fads that came and went quickly. [Mark raises his hand.] *You mean something like a Mohawk haircut.* You are right, Mark . . . lots of boys last year had Mohawk haircuts, but only a few this year. That haircut was a fad . . . popular for a moment and then gone. Oops . . . look at the clock. Time for library. We will read the rest of these words tomorrow. You are such smart readers.

Comments: Although this teacher has done a little preparation (the words are listed on the board), this lesson perfectly illustrates the hazards that can damage the pace of a lesson. First, the teacher changes the instructional routine on every word, slowing the pace of the lesson and confusing students. The thinking times provided are much longer than necessary. Equally damaging are the lengthy comments after gaining a response. These comments not only slow the pace of the lesson, but direct students' attention away from the content of the lesson. (Aren't you curious about the taste of the "orange puffs" and the holiday story to be read in the library?) As a result of this very slow pace, the teacher and students have only read four words. It is unlikely that the students will have advanced reading skills by the end of the year.

EXAMPLE: FIRST-GRADE READING LESSON ILLUSTRATING BRISK PACE

[These words are written on the board: *made, late, slate, fad, fade, tap, tape.*) Yesterday we learned how to read words with a final *e.* Let's practice with new words. [Teacher points to *made.*] Does this word end in an *e*? *Yes.* [Teacher points to *a*.] So do we say the name of this letter? *Yes.* What is the name?
A. Sound out the word. Put your thumb up when you know the word. [Teacher pauses for 4 seconds.] What word? *Made.* [Teacher smiles and moves on. Teacher points to *late.*] Does this word end in an *e*? *Yes.* [Teacher points to *a*.] So do we say the name of this letter? *Yes.* What is the name? *A.* Sound out the word. Put your thumb up when you know the word. [Teacher pauses for 3 seconds.] What word? *Late.* Yes, *late.* [Teacher points at *slate.*] Does this word end in an *e*? *Yes.* [Teacher points to *a*.] So do we say the name of this letter? *Yes.* What is the name? *A.* Sound out the word. Put your thumb up when you know the word. [Teacher pauses for 4 seconds.] What word?

Slate. This is like the slates we use in math. What is the word again? *Slate.*
[Teacher points at *fad.*] Does this word end in an *e*? *No.* So do we say the name of
this letter? [Teacher points to *a.*] *No.* What is the sound of this letter? /˘*a*/. Sound out
the word. Put your thumb up when you know the word. [Teacher pauses for 5 seconds.]
What word? *Fad.* A fad is something that is popular . . . everyone wants it or does it for
a short time. For example, last year many boys had Mohawk haircuts, but very few boys
chose that type of haircut this year. It was a   . *Fad.*

[Teacher points to *fade.*] Does this word end in an *e*? *Yes.* [Teacher points to *a.*]
So do we say the name of this letter? *Yes.* What is the name? *A.* Sound out the word.
Put your thumb up when you know the word. [Teacher pauses for 4 seconds.] What
word? *Fade.* When you wash a T-shirt again and again and again, the colors begin to .
Fade. [Teacher points to *tap.*] Sound this word out to yourself. Put your thumb up
when you know the word. [Teacher pauses for 5 seconds.] What word? *Tap.* Yes.
[Teacher points to *tape.*] Sound this word out to yourself. [Teacher pauses for 5
seconds.] What word? *Tape.* Yes. Excellent. You really noticed the *e* at the end of the
word. Let's read these words again. [Teacher points, and students read the words
chorally.] Ones, read the list to your partner. [Teacher monitors.] Twos, read the list to
your partner. [Teacher monitors.] Excellent reading. Please line up for library.

Comments: The first thing that is evident is that the students receive more practice
under the "perky" conditions, reading 21 words versus 4 words. The teacher
increases the amount of content covered by using a consistent instructional routine,
giving enough but not too much thinking time, moving on once a response is elicited,
and significantly reducing the digressions. Instructionally, when the students
demonstrate success, the teacher also gradually fades the support or scaffolding,
shifting more and more responsibility to the students. Students are more motivated
to participate in this lesson because they are learning.

In summary, the pace of a lesson must be brisk if we wish to
capture and maintain students' attention and to maximize
content coverage and learning. Preparation and avoiding major
digressions are the primary keys to a pace that students will
appreciate.

CHAPTER SUMMARY

Whether you are teaching in preschool, elementary school,
middle school, high school, or even college, you will want to
elicit responses during instruction, carefully monitor students'
responses, provide both corrective and affirmative feedback,

and maintain a brisk pace. Although these delivery skills are researchvalidated teaching practices, they also represent the "art of teaching." Over the course of your career, these practices can become automatic, though initially they will take conscious application. However, working to enhance your delivery skills will result in lessons that are more rewarding to you and your students.

As you are working on delivery skills, especially active participation, observational feedback is useful. Perhaps a supervisor or trusted colleague can observe a portion of a lesson you give, and fill in the observation form found in Application 7.4.

APPLICATION 7.4. OBSERVATION OF A LESSON

Teacher   **Observer**
_____

Date ——————————   **Beginning time**
_____

————————— **Ending time**————————

(In the following box, make a sketch of the classroom. Include the desks or tables and the teaching area.)

———
———
———
———
———

All students respond: **Oral responses—Choral** (Tally
responses under category.) **Oral responses—Partner**

Written responses Action responses

One **student responds: Individual responses**

(Record I on the "desk" of a student to indicate an individual response.) (After the lesson, determine the total number of responses.)

Total number of responses   ——

Monitoring:

(Record M on a student's "desk" if the teacher stops and looks at the student's work or in any other way interacts with the student.)

Affirmative feedback and praise: ——

(Tally affirmations and elaborated praise given to class or individuals.)

Using the data above, answer the following questions. (Note: This analysis can be done by either the teacher being observed or the observer.)

1. Were many responses elicited during the lesson?

2. Were all students given opportunities to respond?

3. Were the individual responses distributed across students?

4. Did the teacher move around the room and monitor?

5. During monitoring, did the teacher connect with many students?

6. Did the teacher affirm, honor, and praise students?

Other observations:

CHAPTER 8

Providing Appropriate Independent Practice

Once students can perform a target skill at a high rate of success within the context of a lesson (i.e., the "check for understanding" step of an explicit instruction lesson), they need opportunities to practice the skill independently without teacher prompting. Appropriate independent practice along with feedback is a critical part of the learning process. Without it, students—especially those with learning problems—have difficulty retaining or becoming fluent in the skill. In the common vernacular, they need to "use it or lose it."

As noted in Chapter 1, Swanson and Sachse-Lee (2000) found large effect sizes associated with instruction that included drill-and-practice activities and systematic review. In addition, Brophy (1986) concluded:

> Development of basic knowledge and skill to the necessary levels of automatic and errorless performance requires a great deal of drill and practice. . . . Drill and practice activities should not be slighted as "low level."

Carried out properly, they appear to be just as essential to complex and creative intellectual performance as they are to the performance of a virtuoso violinist. (p. 1076)

Two major purposes of practice are building skill proficiency and maintaining it. When students are proficient in a skill, they use it both accurately and quickly, with little or no conscious thought (Binder, 1996; Bloom, 1986; Ericsson, Krampe, & Tesch-Römer, 1993). Once proficiency has been reached, additional practice over time is needed to maintain that proficiency. Skill fluency has been shown to be a

201

useful goal of instruction (Binder, 1996), and practice is the primary method of obtaining that goal. If students can perform component skills (e.g., saying math facts, reading words, reading passages, spelling words, reciting steps of a strategy) fluently, it decreases working memory load for situations when they have to use these skills in the context of problem-solving or comprehension tasks (Beck & Clement, 1991; Binder, 1996). For example, if students can read words fluently within a text passage, they can focus more of their attention and working memory on comprehending what they read. Fluent reading at the word level has been shown to result in increased reading comprehension for many students, including those with learning disabilities (Chard et al., 2002; Kubina & Hughes, 2007). In addition, there is a strong empirical relationship between students' passage-reading fluency (correct oral words per minute) and reading comprehension (Fuchs, Fuchs, Hosp, & Jenkins, 2001). In math, if a student does not have fluent basic computation skills (e.g., adding, subtracting, multiplying), complex operations will be interrupted as the student attempts to recall basic facts (Woodward, 2006). Likewise, when handwriting and spelling are not automatic processes, these deficits can conflict with generating and structuring content (Torrance & Galbraith, 2006). If a student must stop and contemplate the spelling of a word (e.g., "Is *receive* spelled with an *ie* or *ei*?") or the formation of a letter, the writing process is impeded.

Although some educators decry the use of extended practice of skills as an instructional tool (see Chapter 1), research on how people become experts or elite performers indicates that even the most gifted among us reach their pinnacles through practice—and lots of it (Ericsson & Charness, 1994). It appears that worldlevel expertise in an area (e.g., sports, chess, music, academics) is not due simply to innate capacity or ability, but to a large degree depends on frequent (i.e., every day), deliberate (i.e., to achieve a specific goal) practice over a long period of time (i.e., about 10 years), along with supervision (i.e., feedback on performance) of that practice. We are not suggesting that the typical learner needs to practice academic skills that long and that often; however, this research stresses that in order to achieve proficiency, both practice and feedback on the quality of that practice are necessary. It behooves us to remember the old adage: "How do you get to Carnegie Hall? Practice, practice, practice."

The research on how a person becomes an expert also raises an interesting point about motivation. Obviously, being motivated to devote that much time and effort to practice is key. Typically, practice in and of itself is not inherently motivating and only infrequently leads to immediate rewards. Thus we all often find ourselves in the situation of knowing that doing something—in this case, practice— results in long-term benefits, but nonetheless being disinclined to do it because of the lack of perceived short-term benefits. Therefore, not only will you need to provide your students with practice opportunities; you will also need to incorporate methods and procedures that increase the likelihood that your students can and will practice something. To that end, Kame'enui, Carnine, Dixon, Simmons, and Coyne (2002) present the concept of **judicious review** when referring to independent practice. They define this as "the process of repeatedly considering material in sensible and well-advised ways" (p. 14). This means that you need not only to provide practice, but also to ensure that what is being practiced is meaningful and linked to effective instruction. This chapter focuses on the development of meaningful, motivating, and effective practice opportunities that allow students to become proficient in applying and generalizing acquired skills, knowledge, and strategies. Before we proceed, however, three important and related types of practice need to be described: **initial practice**, **distributed practice**, and **cumulative practice/review**.

INITIAL PRACTICE

As discussed in Chapter 2, **initial practice** of a skill, strategy, concept, or rule should occur under the watchful eye of a teacher as a part of a teacher-directed lesson. After you have modeled a skill and guided students in performance of the skill, you should check their understanding. When students demonstrate accuracy on a number of items within the group setting, independent practice can begin.

In many cases, it is appropriate to provide one or two massed practice sessions, in which students independently practice a single skill with many examples of the skill immediately after it has been taught. This type of practice helps students quickly strengthen their acquisition of the skill. It should be noted that even though initial independent practice may focus on a single skill that has been introduced, often discrimination items must be inserted to ensure that the students are carefully thinking about the application of the skill, strategy, concept, or rule. For example, when you provide initial practice on subtraction with regrouping from the tens column, you must also give students problems that require no regrouping, in order to guarantee that students don't simply regroup from the tens without careful consideration. Similarly, if students have been introduced to the sound of the grapheme *ai*, initial practice exercises should include words containing the graphemes *a* (*trap*) and *i* (*slip*) in addition to words with *ai* (*train*), to ensure careful examination of the vowel letters. Though initial massed practice is often needed to crystallize performance of the new skill, distributed practice (practice spaced over time) should follow in order to maintain the skill and to build fluency.

DISTRIBUTED PRACTICE

Distributed practice refers to studying or practicing a skill or skill set in sessions that are of relatively short duration and spaced over time. The effectiveness of spreading out practice for long-term retention of information was acknowledged as early as the late 1800s by Hermann Ebbinghaus and has been shown over the years to be the most effective method for scheduling practice sessions (Dempster & Farris, 1990; Willingham, 2002). Because retention of information is a problem for many students, providing distributed practice is essential.

From the research that compares massed to distributed practice, we can conclude with confidence that distributing practice over time aids retention in a variety of academic areas (e.g., math facts, vocabulary, problem solving) and for a variety of students (e.g., elementary, secondary, and college) (Bahrick & Phelps, 1987; Donovan & Radosevich, 1999; Hattie, 2009). However, one logistical issue arises: How can we provide practice sessions for the seemingly overwhelming number of skills we teach? For example, if you teach 20–30 skills or concepts in a month, will your students need to practice each one, over time, in isolation? If so, this will require development of numerous distinct practice sessions. One way to address this pragmatic issue is to provide cumulative practice.

CUMULATIVE PRACTICE AND CUMULATIVE REVIEW

Cumulative practice involves adding related skills to skills that were previously acquired and practiced, in such a way that all of the skills are practiced together in one practice activity (set) or session. Mayfield and Chase (2002) describe this procedure as follows:

> Cumulative practice begins by independently training two skills to criterion and then practicing them together, usually by mixing tasks for both skills within the same practice set. After a criterion is met on the cumulative practice set, a third skill is trained to criterion. Next, the new skill is added to the two previously trained skills in a cumulative set involving all three skills. This procedure is continued until all the skills in a sequence or hierarchy have been trained, with the mastered skills accumulating across the cumulative sets. (p. 106)

For example, if you are using this procedure when you are presenting a unit on several spelling rules related to adding endings to root words, you will provide distributed practice for the first rule taught. Once your students learn the second spelling rule in the unit, you will provide a practice task requiring application of *both* rules, and so on until all rules taught are included in a practice set. Alternatively, if you are teaching basic math facts, you will develop practice activities that include solving problems in *all* basic math fact groupings taught to date as these are acquired, including addition, subtraction, multiplication, and division facts. Cumulative practice of component skills has *even* been shown to result in higher performance on application and problem-solving items in college algebra classes (Mayfield & Chase, 2002).

Whereas cumulative practice involves the ongoing incorporation of previously taught items into daily practice activities, less frequent **cumulative review** activities can also be intentionally provided to increase long term retention of facts, skills, strategies, rules, and concepts (Dempster, 1991). For example, all previously taught vocabulary may be reviewed on Friday, math review homework assignments may be given every Tuesday and Thursday, or a warm-up exercise consisting of three previously taught items may be given at the beginning of each algebra class.

Many curriculum materials do not reflect our best knowledge of initial, distributed, and cumulative practice/review. Thus teachers must augment the materials to maximize student learning and retention. In Figure 8.1, numerous examples are provided to illustrate different ways that teachers can strengthen the initial, distributed, and cumulative practice/review provided in curriculum materials. Carefully examine each of these examples and the teacher's rationale. Then design practice plans for the examples found in Application 8.1 or for curriculum materials that you are currently utilizing.

FIGURE 8.1. Analysis of initial, distributed, and cumulative practice/review.

Example 1: Ms. Dion's 90-minute core reading program—Vocabulary strand
Population: Fifth-grade students

Description of adopted curriculum: The core reading program provides five 90-minute lessons on each passage in the text. On the first day, students are provided explicit instruction on critical passage vocabulary terms and complete one independent assignment that involves using the vocabulary words to fill in blanks in sentences.

Teacher's analysis of practice activities: Although the core program provides initial practice of the vocabulary terms, there is no distributed practice or cumulative review. As a result, the probability of retention is very low.

Teacher's plan: At the beginning of the second, third, and fourth days of instruction on a passage, Ms. Dion will provide practice on the passage vocabulary, using the following response card activity:
Students will place vocabulary cards on their desks with words facing up (definitions are on the back). The teacher will tell about one of the words, and students will hold up the corresponding response card. On the fifth day of instruction, students will sort all previously taught words into categories announced by Ms. Dion (e.g., nouns vs. other parts of speech; words that tell about people vs. words unrelated to people; descriptive vs. nondescriptive words; positive vs. negative words). Students will share their responses with their partners, followed by a class discussion of suggested words for each category and the reason for the decision. As a result of this plan, Ms. Dion's students will have distributed and cumulative practice on vocabulary terms.

Example 2: Mrs. Epley's general math class
Population: Seventh-grade students

Description of adopted curriculum: The math text provides 15 units. The individual lessons in each unit include 2–3 examples of a new skill/strategy for use during explicit instruction, 10–25 practice items on the new skill/strategy to be completed independently, and 5–10 problem-solving items using the target skill. At the end of each unit, practice exercises provide review of all skills taught in the unit.

Teacher's analysis of practice activities: The students need more guided practice on easy, then difficult, items during the teacher-directed lesson, to promote accuracy in independent practice. All practice on a new skill occurs in one lesson, with no distributed practice. The only review occurs at the end of the unit, with no cumulative review of skills and strategies taught in previous units. There is also no cumulative review of mathematical vocabulary.

(cont.)

FIGURE 8.1. *(cont.)*

Teacher's plan: Mrs. Epley decides to adopt the following structure for each lesson:

1. **Warm-up activity.** Begin class with a warm-up activity containing 2 items from each of the past three lessons and 3 items from previous units. This warm-up activity will allow Mrs. Epley to infuse distributive and cumulative practice into her math program with a minimum of additional preparation.
2. **Vocabulary.** Provide explicit instruction on math vocabulary and have students maintain a vocabulary log. Post vocabulary under unit title on a bulletin board.
3. **Modeling (I do it.).** Utilize the examples provided in the text to model the new skill/strategy.
4. **Guided/scaffolded practice (We do it.).** Guide students in solving easy, then difficult, items selected from the text's practice items.
5. **Unprompted practice (You do it.).** Have students complete selected practice items ranging in difficulty from easy to complex. After each item has been completed, provide feedback. Continue until students are consistently demonstrating accuracy.
6. **Assign homework.** Have students complete the remaining practice and

application items.

7. **Exit task.** End class with a quick vocabulary review. Students are directed to look at the vocabulary bulletin board. Tell students the meaning of a word, have them discuss which word Mrs. Epley is referring to with their partners, and then have students say the vocabulary term. This review will continue until the bell rings, with at least five terms reviewed.

Example 3: Mr. Kirsch's spelling lessons
Population: Second-grade students

Description of adopted curriculum: The spelling book introduces a list of 20 words that represent a specific spelling pattern or rule with discrimination items (e.g., the rule about doubling the final consonant, with examples such as *running* and non-examples such as *listing*). In addition, 4 irregular words (not spelled as expected, given their sounds) are also in the list. On Monday, a pretest is given, and the teacher introduces the spelling pattern or rule via explicit instruction. On Tuesday to Thursday, practice activities focused on the 24 words are provided. The activities vary from week to week, but include looking the words up in the dictionary, completing a word search or crossword puzzle, writing sentences that contain the spelling words, alphabetizing the spelling words, and filling in the blanks in sentences with the words. On Friday, a posttest is given. At the end of the unit (every 10 weeks), review is provided on the unit spelling words.

Teacher's analysis of practice activities: One major challenge with this curriculum material is that the practice activities do not require spelling from memory, but rather involve simple copying of the spelling words. Although the students may get better at looking words up in the dictionary, completing word searches or crossword puzzles, alphabetizing words, or using context clues, these activities will not boost spelling of the words. (Note: Matching the practice task to the desired skill is discussed later in this chapter.) Another challenge is the lack of meaningful distributed or cumulative practice/review. Given that there is a 10-week delay before spelling patterns or rules are revisited, students are likely to make many errors.

Teacher's plan: Mr. Kirsch devises a plan that dramatically alters the spelling program. While keeping the word lists (a district requirement), the pretest, and explicit instruction, Mr. Kirsch revamps the 3 days of practice and the posttest.

1. **Preparation.** First, he develops three practice lists for midweek practice: Tuesday, half of word list *plus* 6 review words; Wednesday, half of word list *plus* 6 review words; Thursday, 10 difficult words from the list *plus* 6 review words.
2. **Introduction.** On Monday, a pretest is given, and explicit instruction is provided on the pattern or rule emphasized in the word list.

(cont.)

FIGURE 8.1. *(cont.)*

3. **Daily practice.** Mr. Kirsch dictates a word, and students repeat the word. If the word is a "regular word," students and Mr. Kirsch says the sounds (for a single-syllable word) or the parts (for a multisyllabic word) in the word, and then the students say the sounds or parts to themselves as they write the word on their slates. When asked, students display their slates so the teacher can see the word. Next, Mr. Kirsch displays the word on the screen; students orally spell the word and check their word. If an error is made, students cross off the word and rewrite it. If errors occur, Mr. Kirsch provides corrective feedback (e.g., "*See* ends in a consonant–vowel–vowel. We only drop the *e* if the word ends in a consonant–vowel–consonant"). Students are thus receiving both distributed and cumulative practice.
4. **Posttest.** On Friday, a posttest is given on the new words and review words studied during the week. Immediate feedback is provided via self-corrections.

Example 4: Ms. Doyle's geography class
Population: Eighth-grade students

Description of adopted curriculum: Students are introduced to major countries on each continent through the following activities: (1) reading chapter in text concerning the country; (2) exploring websites; (3) watching related films; (4) listening to lectures provided by the teacher, visitors, and fellow students; (5) responding to information by answering questions; (6) writing country summaries; and (7) completing map activities.

Teacher's analysis of practice activities: Ms. Doyle, an experienced teacher, realizes that:

1. Students are introduced to one country after the next, but their retention of basic country information is limited by the lack of cumulative review.
2. Students' knowledge of country location remains limited again because of no cumulative review of map knowledge.

Teacher's plan: Ms. Doyle decides to add two cumulative review activities to her program.

1. **Country information review.** Ms. Doyle has developed a one-page country form that includes the following information: name of country, continent, capital, language(s), type of government, ethnic group(s)/race(s) of people, and important things to remember about the country. After studying a country, students will complete the country form in cooperation with team members and place it in their binders. Three times a week, students will engage in an activity with the following steps: (a) take out the designated country form, (b) study the form for 1 minute, (c) list facts for 2 minutes without referring to the form, (d) count the number of facts listed, and (e) record the number of listed facts on the back of the country form. Over the course of the two-semester class, each country will be reviewed at least five times.

2. **Country location review.** Ms. Doyle has a set of 10 specialized globes in her classroom. On Friday, 15 minutes will be dedicated to playing a game called "Globe." Students will be divided into groups of four. In the game, each student in the group hears the name of a country and then must touch it with a "magic pen." If the student's response is correct, another country is named. This continues until the game time expires. The winner of the game is the player that identifies the most countries. This game not only inspires students to study countries around the world but provides entertaining practice.

APPLICATION 8.1. Designing Initial, Distributed, and Cumulative Practice

Directions: For each example, read the description of the teacher's curriculum and the analysis of the embedded practice activities. Then outline a plan for improving the initial, distributed, and/or cumulative practice/review. Our suggestions are found in *Feedback on Application Exercises, page* 276.

Example 1: Mrs. Bishop's reading class
Population: First-grade students

Description of adopted curriculum: The core reading program has a major decoding strand involving the following activities: introduction of letter–sound associations, review of previously introduced letter–sound associations, word-reading practice, passage reading of decodable passages containing new and previously introduced letter–sound associations, and independent assignments requiring word and passage reading.

Teacher's analysis of practice activities: The core program provides adequate initial, distributed, and cumulative practice for the majority of students. However, five students have very high error rates on word reading, passage reading, and independent assignments, and are showing no growth on reading fluency measures.

Teacher's plan:

Example 2: Ms. Carley's math class
Population: Fourth-grade students

Description of adopted curriculum: The adopted math text is divided into units. Each lesson provides 4–6 items on the new math skill, 15–20 review items, and 4–5 application items. Students have very high error rates on new and review items.

Teacher's analysis of practice activities: The math program provides excellent distributed and cumulative practice. However, not enough initial practice of the new skill is provided. As a result, the students do not develop accuracy or automaticity.

Teacher's plan:

From Figure 8.1 and Application 8.1, it should be clear that initial, distributed, and cumulative practice/review are powerful tools that enhance students' short- and long-term performance on a variety of academic measures, including basic skills, problem solving, and rule application. This independent practice is provided in two ways: through in-class activities or assignments, and through homework. These two types of independent practice share common considerations, including (1) what will be practiced; (2) how the assignment will be designed; (3) what practice format (paper–pencil, group, peer-focused, or computer activity) will be used; (4) how the assignment will be presented to students; (5) how the assignment will be evaluated and feedback provided; and (6) what routines will be put in place to facilitate independent practice. Because homework presents additional challenges for students, particularly for secondary students with learning challenges, teacher and student homework strategies are presented at the end of this chapter.

WHAT WILL BE PRACTICED?

Determining what students should practice begins with two questions. First, what skills have been taught that merit independent practice? And, second, can students perform the skill at a high level of success without teacher support or scaffolding? In regard to the first question, careful selection of *what to teach* leads directly to *what students should practice.* Although this book does not cover what to teach in all subject areas, in Chapters 1 through 4 we have emphasized focusing on skills, strategies, concepts, and rules that are (1) unknown, (2) critical to students' current academic performance, (3) useful to students in the future, and (4) consistent with their prior knowledge or prerequisite skills. When these targeted skills have been taught and proficiency has been verified in an instructional group, initial independent practice, distributed practice, and cumulative practice/review can proceed. Of course, the most important consideration for deciding what students should practice independently is this: Can they perform the skill at a high level of success without teacher support or scaffolding? If they can, this increases the likelihood that students will attempt and complete the task with a high degree (i.e., 90–95%) of accuracy.

Every instructional activity associated with explicit instruction—from the selection of skills to introduce, to the development of examples and non-examples, to the careful design of lessons (**I do it. We do it. You do it.**)—*is purposeful.* Similarly, independent practice activities should be assigned for a specific purpose: (1) strengthening initial accuracy; (2) building fluency; (3) increasing skill retention; (4) preparing students for a test; or (5) helping students extend and generalize acquired skills (e.g., practicing newly learned writing skills by writing a short essay or journal entry; practicing a previously learned reading comprehension strategy in actual textbooks vs. with short passages). Practice activities must be intentional and purposeful to have a positive impact on student achievement. Regardless of the purpose, you should keep in mind the principles of distributed and cumulative practice, especially for building skill fluency and retention.

Another part of this determination process is deciding when to provide practice in the coordinated application of related skills. As mentioned earlier, explicit instruction often requires that more complex skills be broken into subskills that are taught separately. A potential problem of teaching this way is that students may learn "splinter" skills without learning to combine them as a whole. Thus, when your students have acquired all skills in a unit or process, the purpose of independent practice should be to use *all* of the skills in concert in a meaningful context. Perhaps you have taught a number of lessons on the use of commas (e.g., comma rules for separating three or more items in a series, beginning a sentence with a dependent clause, or using a coordinating conjunction when combining two independent clauses). You can then give students an assignment requiring application of these rules in the context of their own writing. For example, they may be given the following writing prompt, which will naturally generate use of commas: *Pretend that you are filling a box with items that best represent your life as a sixth grader. Describe what you are putting in the box and your reason for including each item.* Another way to move knowledge of comma rules to integrated use in generating written products is to add the use of commas to the list of mechanics in the rubric used to edit and evaluate classroom compositions.

HOW WILL THE ASSIGNMENT BE DESIGNED?

Once you have established what to practice and the purpose of that practice, the next step is to **design, select,** or **adapt** the activity itself. Often you will not actually create practice activities, but will use preexisting activities found within curriculum materials. This, however, requires careful evaluation of the appropriateness of the task. The fact that a worksheet or activity is part of a published curriculum does not guarantee that it is well designed or meets the specific needs of students and the goals of instruction. Whether you are designing, selecting, or adapting a practice activity, consider the following in order to promote successful performance and ensure that the goal of the practice activity is met: (1) Match the task to the skill; (2) control for other skill demands; (3) provide clear, concise directions; (4) provide prompts as needed to promote success; (5) determine an appropriate length for the assignment; and (6) use various practice structures (paper–pencil, group, peer, or computer activities).

Match Task to Skill

One of the first considerations in designing or selecting practice activities is to ensure that the task matches the skill you have taught. The **skill** is *what* you have taught your students to do (e.g., how to add two-digit multiplication problems, how and when to end a sentence with a question mark, describing what an adjective is, how to add an ending to a root word, carrying out the steps of a paragraph-writing strategy). The **task** is the *way* students will practice the skill (e.g., completing a worksheet with multiplication problems to solve, adding necessary punctuation to a series of sentences with no end punctuation, circling words that are adjectives within sentences, writing spelling words with endings when dictated by a partner, writing a descriptive paragraph when given a prompt). It is essential that the task require students to perform the target skill. For example, if the instructional objective is that students can write specific manuscript letters, the task should require that they actually write the letters; a task that asks students to circle words beginning with a particular letter is not an appropriate match between skill and task.

Similarly, consider this scenario: A spelling book offers four practice activities for learning a list of spelling words:

1. Alphabetize the words.
2. Complete a word search of the spelling words.
3. Solve a crossword puzzle with the words.
4. Study the words, using **Read–Cover–Write–Check:** *Read* and spell the word (say the letter names orally); *Cover* up the word; *Write* the word from memory; *Check* the spelling of the word (compare with original word).

Although the students' skills at alphabetizing, doing word searches, and solving crossword puzzles may improve as they participate in the first three activities— the fourth activity, direct studying of the spelling words—is the only activity that requires students to spell words from memory. Thus it has the highest probability of increasing students' spelling proficiency in the least amount of time.

The importance of matching the task to the skill may seem obvious; however, worksheets and other practice activities provided in commercial curricula often don't entail use of the actual target skill. As a result, due diligence is required of teachers.

In addition to matching the task to the skill, it is typically better to develop a task that requires a production response versus a selection response. Although production responses take a little more time for the students to complete and the teacher to grade or evaluate, they usually align more closely with most instructional goals that require students to *do* something. For example, the first task below requires a selection response, whereas the second requires a production response. If the instructional goal is for the student to *read* words with a consonant–vowel– consonant pattern aloud, the second task matches the goal more closely.

1. Circle the word that matches the picture.

big   bag   bug

2. Read these words out loud to your partner or parent.

big   bag   bug

Both tasks require students to apply knowledge of letter–sound associations; however, the second task more closely matches the skill of actually reading an entire word out loud. There may be certain times when selection responses are appropriate. For instance, if there is no opportunity to read aloud to someone who can verify accuracy, the first task may be an acceptable alternative.

Control for Other Skill Demands

Often, developing a practice activity involves skills other than the target skill. For example, when students are presented with math word problems to solve (the target skill), they must first read the problem in order to solve it. If the reading level of the problem is too high, it will hinder their ability to solve it. Because the goal of the practice activity is solving math word problems and not reading per se, it is best to write the problem at the students' reading level. For example, the two word problems below require the same sequence of computation but are written at different reading levels.

1. John participated in an Arbor Day activity in which students in his fifth-grade class planted trees in a neighboring park. John planted one third of all the Serbian spruce saplings planted by his class. His class planted a total of 36 saplings. How many saplings did John plant?
2. John's class planted 36 trees in the park. John planted one-third of them. How many trees did John plant?

Certainly the first problem is more interesting to read, and for some students it may be an appropriate practice item. But for poorer readers and/or those who are distracted by extraneous information, the complexity of the text will probably hinder their ability to actually practice the target skill of problem solving.

If you are not creating an assignment but rather selecting an existing one from curriculum material, and the task requires skills that your students don't possess, you will need to scaffold/support them in other ways. For example, before they leave the instructional group, you can read the story problems to them and have them highlight the critical words, making it feasible for them to work independently. Another possibility is to allow the struggling students to read the story problems with their partners before completing the items. In other words, as teachers we must be alert to variables in the materials that may hinder independent performance, and we must find ways to support students in such cases.

Provide Clear, Concise Directions

Directions must be clear, concise, and unambiguous, whether they are presented orally or in writing. In particular, written instructions should be written as simply as possible. Examine the following two sets of directions for the same practice assignment.

Skill being practiced: Correctly adding suffixes to root words.

Task: A series of sentences that are missing a word. Three choices are provided for each sentence, and the student selects the correct spelling of the missing word.

Sample item: John is _____ into his uniform.

a. *changeing*   b. *changing*   c. *changeeing*

Direction 1: Circle the correct spelling of the missing word, and write it in the blank.

Direction 2: Read each sentence. Keeping in mind the spelling rule, read each of the choices, and decide which is the word that fits best. Once you have decided, draw a circle around the appropriate word. Then write the word on the blank line that has been provided for you.

The first set of directions is more concise, and so there is less opportunity for students to misunderstand what to do. This is an especially important concern for students with reading and/or attention problems. The length and complexity of directions are often increased, especially in commercial instructional materials, by the addition of explanatory material about the target skill. Consider this example:

Directions: Read each sentence. Keeping in mind the spelling rule in question, read each of the choices and decide which is the word that fits best. Once you have decided, draw a circle around the appropriate word. Remember the spelling rule: When a root word ends in a vowel, a consonant, and final *e* (VCe), and you want to add an ending that begins with a vowel, you drop the *e* before adding the ending. For example, think about *give + ing*. Because *give* ends in *Vce* and *ing* begins with a vowel, you drop the *e* in *give*.

What makes this set of directions so lengthy is the embedded reteaching of the spelling rule. Also, given the presence of the additional information, if a student completes the assignment accurately, the teacher cannot conclude that the student can perform the skill *independently*—the primary purpose of providing independent practice.

Provide Prompts as Needed

In certain circumstances, however (e.g., initial practice of a complex skill in which the practice purpose is to strengthen accuracy), prompts may be needed to promote success. In such instances, teachers may provide **completed or worked examples** of the skill performance—a procedure that has proven very successful in improving students' accuracy (Crissman, 2006). For example, a completed example of twodigit multiplication can be written on the assignment sheet or displayed on the overhead projector or computer screen to remind students of the algorithm:

$$
\begin{array}{r}
2\,5 \\
37 \\
\underline{r\,48} \\
296 \\
\underline{1480} \\
1776
\end{array}
$$

When the purpose of the initial practice is to crystallize performance of the skill while limiting errors, other prompts may be necessary, such as listing the strategy steps on the worksheet; providing the rule that is to be applied, coupled with examples; providing "dotted letters" for tracing manuscript letters; or having students write their numbers on graph paper to promote proper alignment when completing math problems. However, when students' performance is accurate and the purpose shifts to fluent practice, these prompts need to be faded.

Let's stop and apply these principles to the design of practice activities for each of the objectives listed in Application 8.2.

APPLICATION 8.2. Selecting Practice Activities

Situation 1: Vocabulary for Chapter 1 of *The Family Under the Bridge* (Carlson, 1958/1986) has been introduced to fifth graders on the previous day.

Objective: Students will understand the meaning of targeted vocabulary terms.

Your directions: The teacher has three possible practice activities that could be used for distributed practice. Rank the assignments 1 (best choice), 2 (middle choice), or 3 (worst choice). Justify your rankings. Then compare your ratings to our ratings in *Feedback on Application Exercises*, page 277.

Assignment A.   **Ranking:** ————————

Directions: Circle yes or no for each statement.

1. If a vase is *fragile*, it

a. will hold many flowers.	Yes	No
b. would break into many pieces if it fell on the floor.	Yes	No
c. should be washed by hand, not put in the dishwasher.	Yes	No
d. is made from many different fragments (pieces).	Yes	No

2. If a young boy *cowered* when a dog entered the room, the child might
   a. pat the dog's head.   Yes   No
   b. cover up his toys so the dog would not chew them.   Yes   No
   c. hide under a table and cry.   Yes   No
   d. put a leash on the dog and take him for a walk.   Yes   No
3. If a house cleaner was *fastidious*, the house cleaner would
   a. wipe spots off glasses.   Yes   No
   b. work very quickly. Yes   No
   c. finish cleaning the house before lunch.   Yes   No
   d. line up the cups in the cabinet.   Yes   No

Assignment B.   **Ranking:** ————————

Directions: These words are in the first chapter of *The Family under the Bridge*. Think of how the word is used in the chapter. Draw a line from the word to the correct definition.

1. *cowered*   a. very careful about small details
2. *fragile*   b. to bend low and move back when afraid
3. *gratitude*   c. standing around in a public place for no reason
4. *loitering*   d. a feeling of thanks
5. *roguish*   e. showing in a playful manner that you have done something wrong
6. *fastidious*   f. easily broken

Assignment C.   **Ranking:** ─────

Directions: Rewrite the sentence by removing the underlined word and replacing it with the meaning of the word. Be sure that your new sentence makes sense.

1. The *fragile* amphora is encased in a transparent vessel.

2. Overwhelmed by the benevolence and cordiality of the aide workers, Iona's heart swelled in *gratitude.*

3. Filled with apprehension at the sound of gunfire, Jacob *cower*ed behind the divan.

Situation 2: The students in this middle school language arts class have been taught two spelling rules in the past 2 weeks for adding endings/suffixes: (a) dropping the final *e* and (b) doubling the final consonant.

Objective: Students will correctly apply spelling rules for adding endings/suffixes to words.

Your directions: The teacher has three possible practice activities that could be used for cumulative practice of the spelling rules. Rank the activities 1 (best choice), 2, or 3 (worst choice). Justify your rankings. Then compare your ratings to our ratings in *Feedback on Application Exercises*, page 277.

Assignment A.   **Ranking:** ─────

Directions: Dictate each word to your partner. Then show him or her the correctly spelled word. If the word is misspelled, have your partner cross out the word and rewrite it.

1. *referral*   5. *creating*
2. *reddish*   6. *hoping*
3. *admitted*   7. *cutest*
4. *flapping*   8. *shaking*

Assignment B.   **Ranking:** ─────

Directions: Write the correct spelling of the word. Don't forget the rules. If a word ends in a VCe and the ending begins with a vowel, drop the *e*. If a word ends in a consonant–vowel–consonant and the ending begins with a vowel, double the consonant. (Reader's note: The answer is in italics.)

1. stop + ing = *stopping*   6. shift + ing = *shifting*
2. work + er = *worker* 7. vote + er = *voter*
3. agree + able = *agreeable*   8. remake + ing = *remaking*
4. hope + ing = *hoping*9. trap + ing = *trapping*
5. hope + less = *hopeless*   10. stoop + ing = *stooping*

Assignment C.   Ranking: ————————

Directions: Read each sentence. Circle the correctly spelled word that makes sense in the sentence.

1. (*Lately, Latly*) the Camera Club members have been (shooting, shootting) photos in the desert.

2. They are (*working, workking*) on (*takeing, taking*) photos of the (redish, reddish) sands at sunset.

3. (*Unfortunately, Unfortunatly*) their (*shakeing, shaking*) hands make this a (*hopless, hopeless*) task.

Consider How Long the Assignment Will Take to Complete

Another consideration when you are designing practice opportunities is assignment length (i.e., how many items/problems to assign). An important factor in deciding on length is the amount of time available for students to complete the practice activity. For example, seatwork activities are often assigned before or after group instruction. In either case, there is a relatively fixed block of time available for independent practice (e.g., 15 minutes). If the assignment is too short, then it's highly likely that students will not be engaged throughout the period. If the assignment is too long, students may not finish and may become frustrated. The question then becomes how to estimate the length of time it will take students to finish the task. One method is for you to complete the task yourself and then multiply the time to complete it by two or three, depending on the age and instructional level of your students.

Decisions about how long an assignment should be and how long it will take to complete can also be framed in the context of individualization. That is, consider the interaction between the requirements (i.e., type and complexity) of the task and the characteristics of your students (e.g., fluency, processing speed, attention problems, fine motor skills), and then individualize the practice activity as necessary (by reducing the number of problems/items required, providing more space to write answers, etc.). Teachers or students may perceive this process as "unfair." However, we would respond with the oft-used phrase, "Fairness does not always mean treating people equally." For practice activities, it may be advisable for you to differentiate or individualize the amount of homework or seatwork you give, based on the fact that it takes some students longer to do it (in some cases, much longer). A not uncommon scenario related to assigning different amounts of homework to students with different characteristics is provided in Application 8.3.

APPLICATION 8.3. CASE STUDY: INDIVIDUALIZING SAMUEL'S ASSIGNMENTS

Directions: Read this case study, and then answer the questions at the end. Compare your answers with our comments in *Feedback on Application Exercises*, page 278.

Samuel is a fourth-grade student with an identified learning disability. He receives math instruction in a general education classroom. His class has been learning to compute long-division problems. Although he is capable of solving this type of problem, Samuel is still dysfluent. Part of his difficulty is that he is not fluent in using the computation skills needed for long-division (subtraction and multiplication), and this dysfluency hinders his use of the procedural knowledge needed to perform the operations in the correct order.

Recently, Samuel's teacher assigned the class 25 long-division problems from the textbook. It took Samuel 2 hours to complete the homework, despite the fact that he was on task almost the entire time (and this was not his only homework assignment). There were several reasons why it took him so long to complete the homework. First, he had to copy the problems from the book onto paper. The process of near-point copying is very difficult for Samuel, given some of his processing difficulties. Most students were able to look at the textbook and hold the problem in memory while writing it on paper. Samuel can only hold two or three numbers in his short-term memory. In addition, like many students with learning disabilities, Samuel has some problems with motor skills and does not write as quickly or legibly as most students. Thus copying the problems took him two or three times longer than his peers. When Samuel finished this laborious task, he then began to solve the problems. Given his low level of fluency in basic computational skills, solving the problems took him much longer than it did other students (who could mentally compute addition, subtraction, and multiplication facts accurately and quickly).

Knowing that Samuel would probably be assigned similar homework over the next few weeks, his distraught parents wrote a note to the teacher explaining the information above. They asked the teacher to assign Samuel fewer problems and, if possible, to provide him with the problems on paper, so he would not have to spend so much time copying problems.

If you were Samuel's teacher, would you agree to do this? Why or why not?

Use Various Practice Formats

There are a number of ways that distributed and cumulative practice can be provided: by (1) assigning paper–pencil tasks as seatwork or homework, (2) embedding distributed and cumulative practice activities within group instruction, (3) utilizing partner or team activities, or (4) using computer programs.

Paper–Pencil Tasks

Paper–pencil tasks are the most common practice assignments provided in school settings; they are often given to students as seatwork while the teacher instructs another group, or as independently completed homework. Given the tandem goals of student success and independence, it is particularly critical that teachers (1) have students demonstrate proficiency in the skill before assigning the paper– pencil assignments as seatwork or homework; (2) carefully control the other skills demanded by the assignment; (3) use clear, concise directions; and (4) repeat assignment formats, so that students recognize what to do without the need for extended input.

Not all distributed or cumulative practice or review needs to involve worksheets or other paper–pencil tasks. This is not to say that you should never use worksheets; often they are the best vehicle for a particular purpose (e.g., building fluency in basic skills and facts). However, varying the practice tasks can help motivate students to complete the tasks and can also address other purposes of practice.

Practice Activities during Instructional Group

Distributed and cumulative practice/review can often be embedded in teacherdirected lessons, as seen in these examples: a kindergarten teacher who reviews all letter sounds taught to date at the beginning of small-group instruction; a third-grade math teacher who has students complete an individualized 1-minute timing on math facts every day; a sixth-grade reading teacher who reviews vocabulary terms listed on a word wall at the end of each class; an eighth-grade language arts teacher who has students proofread two example sentences daily to maintain punctuation rules; a ninth-grade math teacher who has students complete five warm-up review problems at the beginning of the period; and a tenthgrade social studies teacher who provides vocabulary review every Friday. These activities provide students with necessary practice on previously taught content, and they afford teachers an opportunity to provide immediate performance feedback.

Repeating the same practice activities with different items is especially beneficial, because class time can be dedicated to practice rather than task explanation. In Figure 8.2, we have taken one area needing cumulative review, vocabulary instruction, and listed three practice activities that can be used again and again.

Peer-Focused Practice Activities

Alternatives to students' completing worksheets at their desk include practicing in pairs or cooperative groups. Hughes and Macy (2010) and Hughes, Maccini, and Gagnon (2003) reviewed **peer-focused practice activities** and found several approaches to have positive impacts on student learning in both resource and general education classrooms:

FIGURE 8.2. Examples of practice activities for vocabulary.

WORD PAIRS (Stahl & Kapinus, 2001). This activity promotes deep processing and lively classroom discussion. Pairs of previously introduced words are presented on a chart. Students read each word pair and check a category that they deem the best match (though not necessarily a perfect match): *Same, Opposite, Go together,* or *No relationship.* Students then share and defend their choices with their partners, followed by a class discussion. Although this activity affords excellent word review, it requires minimal preparation.

Word pair	Same	Opposite	Go together	No relationship
1. *scarce–abundant*		||		
2. *stoic–reckless*		||		
3. *dispute–rancor*	||		||	
4. *catastrophic–tempest*			||	
5. *anonymity–regulations*			||	||
6. *melancholy–frenzied*		||		

COMPLETION ACTIVITY (Curtis & Longo, 1997). In this activity, remind students of the definition of a review word, and then give students a sentence stem that they must complete either orally or in writing. When responses are written, have students use the brainstorming strategy **Think–Pair–Share**. As students **think** and write down their ideas, move around the room and write down their ideas and names. When students **pair** up with their partners, continue to write down ideas and names. Then **share** students' responses with the class.

How would you complete these sentence stems?

I was *tenacious* when_____ .

Some things that should not be *conspicuous* include_____.

YES/NO/WHY (Beck et al., 1982; Curtis & Longo, 1997). In this practice activity, you prepare questions that contain two or three target words. Students determine whether the best answer would be *yes* or *no,* and *why.* Then, have students share answers with partners. Finally, lead students in a class discussion. Would you select *yes* or *no* for the following questions? How would you defend your choice?

Social studies: Do *territories* that are *possessions* have *autonomy*? Yes/No Why?

Math: Can a *whole number* be a *fraction*? Yes/No Why?

Literature: Would an author *foreshadow* a *flashback*? Yes/No Why?

1. **Peer-Assisted Learning Strategies** (e.g., Fuchs, Fuchs, & Kazdan, 1999; Fuchs, Fuchs, Mathes, & Simmons, 1997;

Fuchs, Fuchs, Yazdian, & Powell, 2002), which incorporate structured peer interactions to address the development of reading and math skills at the elementary level for all students in a classroom, including those with learning difficulties.

2. **Classwide Peer Tutoring** (e.g., Maheady, Sacca, & Harper, 1988), in which students form teams after the teacher provides instruction on a specific topic and then quiz each other about the content.

3. **Team-Assisted Individualization** (Slavin, 1984; Slavin, Madden, & Stevens, 1989/1990), in which students work on math units in cooperative groups subsequent to teacher-led, skill group instruction on the math topic.

What is clear from research on various peer-focused practice activities, whether designed for partners or cooperative groups, is that these methods should not be implemented haphazardly. All of these effective approaches have several characteristics in common:

1. Teachers spend time explicitly teaching new skills prior to having students practice them. Peer-focused activities do not replace initial instruction by teachers.

2. Teachers assign specific procedures, including how to present information and provide positive and corrective feedback.

3. Students receive structured training in delivering the activity, responding to errors, and recording student responses.

4. After training, the peer-focused activities are consistently used within the classroom. They are not seen as "one-time-only" events.

5. For group activities, members are assigned specific roles, to avoid having only one or two students do most or all of the actual work.

6. Careful consideration is given to matching peers and assigning group membership. Most often, students with disabilities are matched with middleperforming or higher-performing peers; groups are either homogeneous or heterogeneous, depending on the purpose of the activity.
7. Teachers monitor peer and group activities to ensure that students are engaged appropriately and to provide support and feedback.
8. For group activities, individuals are held accountable for their own performance as well as the performance of the entire group.

Although we highly recommend that you investigate the peer-focused approaches listed above, in Figures 8.3–8.6 we present some simple partner practice activities that can be implemented with ease in your classrooms. In each case, provide skill instruction before students engage in the practice activity; teach the procedures to your students using explicit instructional steps (**I do it. We do it. You do it.**); consistently use the practice activity; and monitor your students as they engage in the activity.

(text resumes on page 223)

FIGURE 8.3. Partner spelling practice. Following explicit instruction on a spelling pattern or rule, students can study the spelling words with their partners during a number of practice sessions.

Tutor (one of the partners)	**Tutee** (one of the partners)
Takes out list of spelling words.	
Says the word. Asks tutee to repeat the word. Says the word in a sentence if one is provided on the spelling list.	Listens. Repeats the word.
Asks tutee to write the word.	Writes the word.
Shows the word on the list.	Looks at the word; checks the spelling of the word.

	If the word is incorrect, crosses out the word and rewrites it.

Note: On the following day, partners reverse roles as the tutor and tutee.

FIGURE 8.4. Partner reading: Content-area textbooks. Before reading a section of a content-area textbook, students receive instruction on difficult-to-pronounce words, unknown vocabulary terms, and background knowledge for the passage. The teacher then guides students in reading the initial portion of the selection (generally one or two pages). Students read the remainder with their partners using the procedure outlined below.

Partner 1	Partner 2
Decides to read the paragraph alone ("Me") or with his or her partner ("We").	
Says either "Me" or "We." If "Me," reads a paragraph to Partner 2. If "We," reads with Partner 2.	If "Me," follows along and corrects any reading errors. If "We," reads with Partner 1.
Answers the questions, referring back to the chapter as necessary.	Asks Partner 1 the following questions, based on the **Paragraph-Shrinking Strategy** (Fuchs, Fuchs, Mathes, & Simmons, 1996, 1997): 1. Name the *who* or *what* (the main person, animal, or thing). 2. Tell the most important thing about the *who* or *what*. 3. Say the main idea in 10 words or less.

Note: For the next paragraph, the partners switch roles.

FIGURE 8.5. Partner vocabulary study. When vocabulary terms are introduced, students write the word on one side of an index card and the part of speech and meaning on the other side. The new vocabulary cards are placed in an envelope labeled *Study*. Each student also has an envelope labeled *Mastered*.

Tutor (one of the partners)	Tutee (one of the partners)
	Hands tutor his or her two envelopes.
Removes an index card from tutee's *Study* envelope, shows and reads the word to the tutee, and asks the following questions: 1. What is the part of speech? 2. What does the word mean? 3. Say a sentence using the word.	Answers the questions.
If tutee answers all the questions about a vocabulary term correctly, puts a plus (+) sign on the back of the card.	

If tutee misses any of the answers, tutor puts a minus (−) sign on the back of the card.	
When the card has three consecutive plusses, it is placed in the *Mastered* envelope.	
This process continues with additional words until the end of the study period (generally 10–15 minutes).	

Notes: The roles of tutor and tutee are reversed for the next practice period. A review test can be given, and all items missed can be returned to the *Study* envelope. Other content can be studied by using this same procedure; for example, partners can study math facts, information on countries, sight vocabulary, or science terms.

FIGURE 8.6. Partner repeated reading. This procedure, in which students read a short passage a number of times, is valuable procedure for increasing students' oral reading fluency. Adapted from Adams and Brown (2007). Copyright 2007 by Sopris West Educational Services. Adapted by permission.

Partner 1	Partner 2
Partners take out necessary materials: two copies of a passage at their independent or instructional reading level and two graphs. The passage has the cumulative number of words written in the left margin, to facilitate determining the number of words read in 1 minute.	
Reads for 1 minute. Stops reading when the teacher says, "Stop."	Follows along as Partner 1 reads, underlining any word errors and circling the last word read.
	Provides feedback to Partner 1, saying the number of words read correctly in a minute and going over any word errors.
Partner 1 follows along as his/her partner reads, underlining any word errors and circling the last word read.	Reads for 1 minute. Stops reading when the teacher says, "Stop."
Provides feedback to Partner 1, saying the number of words read correctly in a minute and going over any word errors.	
Both partners record the number of correct oral words read on their own graphs.	
Note: This procedure is usually repeated five times, using the same passage. Thus students can visually track reading rate growth on their graphs.	

Computer-Assisted Instruction

Another method for providing practice is through the use of computer-assisted instruction (CAI) programs. Drill-and-practice CAIs are used to build proficiency in previously taught skills. These programs are also a method for increasing academic learning time with minimal effort on the teacher's part.

Hall et al. (2000) and Hughes and Maccini (1997) reviewed studies of CAIs designed to address reading and math skills for students with learning disabilities. Although a number of these studies used CAIs for the purpose of initial instruction, many focused on drill and practice. Overall, these studies indicated that drilland-practice formats were highly effective in building proficiency in the following skills: (1) math facts in all four basic operations, (2) math problem-solving, (3) reading comprehension, (4) reading fluency, (5) word recognition, (6) spelling, and (7) concepts/vocabulary. The CAIs that provided effective practice had a number of common design features, including provision of multiple opportunities to practice; immediate and elaborative (i.e., beyond indicating "right" or "wrong") feedback; and recycling problems until accuracy criterion was reached.

HOW WILL THE ASSIGNMENT BE PRESENTED TO STUDENTS?

When you assign practice activities to be completed at home or in class, you must ensure that students understand the directions and task expectations. Too often, especially for homework, students are confused about how to complete a task; this results in their practicing errors or avoiding assignment completion altogether. Some task formats are used frequently, so they require little additional explanation. However, when you use a new task format, it is advisable to **clarify** and **verify** students' understanding of what to do.

Clarify

You can clarify an assignment by (1) reading the directions with students, (2) having students highlight critical action words in the directions, and (3) modeling completion of an item. You can also write the assignment on the board or on a class calendar for additional clarification. Requiring students to record assignments, especially homework assignments, on a calendar or assignment record will further increase the probability that the assignment will be completed. Finally, you should also communicate any other additional information needed, such as the due date and evaluation criteria.

Verify

Have the students been listening? Do they actually understand the assignment? You must not only clarify but also verify their understanding. You can verify understanding by (1) having students explain the assignment to their partners; (2) asking students assignment-related questions (e.g., "How many paragraphs should you write? *Two* What must each paragraph have? *A topic sentence.* When are the paragraphs due? *Thursday*"); (3) having students complete an item under your watchful eye; and (4) checking their calendars or assignment records to verify accurate assignment recording.

HOW WILL THE ASSIGNMENT BE EVALUATED AND FEEDBACK PROVIDED?

In Chapter 7, we have discussed the importance of giving feedback during explicit instruction lessons, with the goal of closing the gap between students' current performance and desired performance. Feedback has consistently been shown to have a powerful impact on student learning (Hattie, 2009), whether it is given during lessons or in response to in-class or homework assignments. We have addressed giving feedback during lessons in Chapter 7; we now discuss in-class and homework assignment feedback. For these types of assignments, you will need first to determine the **criterion** that you wish students to meet, and then to decide how **feedback** will be provided.

Establishing a Performance Criterion

Students will gain much more if a specific performance goal is established (Fuchs & Fuchs, 1986; Hattie, 2009; Locke & Latham, 1990). The power of having goals is often seen in the athletic world as a marathon runner sets a goal time for the race, a quarterback attempts to gain more yards during games, or a swimmer tries to trim seconds from past trials. The performance criterion for an assignment can be framed in terms of participation, completion, accuracy, fluency, or performance on specific criteria.

Participation or Completion

For some practice activities, your goal for students will be **participation** in or **completion** of the activity. Your goal may be participation for in-class practice activities that do not specify a particular number of items for each person, such as review of vocabulary terms listed on the word wall, a vocabulary review game, or a flash card review of letter–sound associations. On the other hand, you may choose completion as your goal when you expect each student to finish a specified number of items or amount of work. Completion would be the criterion for such activities as 30 minutes of independent reading (verified by a parent's signature), rehearsal of 10 lines of Spanish dialogue for class the following day, or 30 minutes of daily practice on a stringed instrument for orchestra. Of course, when students play a stringed instrument, they receive immediate feedback:

Does it sound harmonious or not?

Accuracy

When you give students an assignment with a number of items, you may convey a particular percentage as the performance goal. Given that independent assignments are given *after* students have demonstrated that they can perform the skill accurately, the desired performance criterion should be 90–95% accuracy. When students' performance is significantly off this mark, reteaching (with greater clarity and expanded examples) for either the entire group or a small group is called for.

Fluency

Fluency is the goal of practice in cases where accuracy alone is an inadequate indication of mastery. For example, fluency would be the goal for reading words, reading words in passages, writing manuscript or cursive letters, and saying basic math facts. Long-term goals for performance of these skills generally begin with established benchmarks that reflect desired performance at a grade level. Obtainable short-term goals are then established for individual students, especially when their current performance is significantly below a benchmark. For example, in the Six-Minute Solution reading fluency program (Adams & Brown, 2007), desired benchmarks are based on the reading fluency data collected by Hasbrouck and Tindal (2006). An appropriate benchmark for a sixth grader would be 150 correct oral words per minute in the spring, representing the performance at the 50th percentile. If a student currently reads only 40 correct words per minute, a goal of 150 will frustrate rather than motivate. On the other hand, adding 30–40 words to current performance will establish an attainable goal of 70 correct words per minute.

Specific Criteria (Rubrics)

In many cases, performance cannot be quantified by using accuracy or fluency measures. When more subjective judgments are needed, you can use a **rubric** to indicate "what counts." (See the example in Figure 8.7.) A rubric is a scoring tool that delineates (1) one or more **dimensions/criteria** on which performance is rated (e.g., "The selected dimensions for an oral presentation were clarity, volume, posture and eye contact, content, and focus on the topic"); (2) a **rating scale** with different levels indicating the degree to which the standard is met; and (3) **definitions** and **examples** to clarify the meaning of each rating. Rubrics can be used to communicate gradations of quality for a persuasive essay, a class presentation, an instrumental performance, a video production, a lab report, an art creation, a science project, or the like. For a rubric to be effective, you should introduce it to students before using it as a feedback/evaluation tool. Present the rubric by using an instructional routine similar to the procedures presented in Chapter 4 for teaching vocabulary and concepts: (1) Introduce each dimension and the rating descriptions; (2) illustrate the rubric with an example product; and (3) if possible, guide students in evaluating non-example products with the rubric.

Rubrics serve many purposes in addition to enabling teachers to assess students' projects, products, compositions, or performances. Rubrics give direction to students as they complete a product or prepare for a performance. Rubrics also assist students in evaluating and refining their own work, as well as allowing them to give productive feedback to peers.

FIGURE 8.7. Example rubric: Oral presentation. This rubric was designed by using the tools provided on the federally funded (free) website *rubistar.4teachers.org*.

Category	4	3	2	1

Speaks clearly	Speaks clearly and distinctly all (95–100%) of the time, and mispronounces no words.	Speaks clearly and distinctly all (95–100%) of the time, but mispronounces a few difficult or unfamiliar words.	Speaks clearly and distinctly most (85–94%) of the time. Mispronounces a few difficult or unfamiliar words.	Often mumbles or cannot be understood, *or* mispronounces many words.
Volume	Volume is loud enough to be heard by all audience members throughout the presentation.	Volume is loud enough to be heard by all audience members at least 90% of the time.	Volume is loud enough to be heard by all audience members at least 80% of the time.	Volume is often too soft to be heard by all audience members.
Posture and eye contact	Stands up straight; looks relaxed and confident; establishes eye contact with everyone in the room during the presentation.	Stands up straight and establishes eye contact with everyone in the room during the presentation.	Sometimes stands up straight and establishes eye contact.	Slouches and/or does not look at people during the presentation.
Content	Shows a full understanding of the topic.	Shows a good understanding of the topic.	Shows a good understanding of parts of the topic.	Does not seem to understand the topic very well.
Stays on topic	Stays on topic all (100%) of the time.	Stays on topic most (90–99%) of the time.	Stays on topic some (75–89%) of the time.	It is hard to tell what the topic is.

Providing Feedback on Independent Assignments

As articulated in Chapter 7, feedback on performance must go beyond simply indicating correct and incorrect responses; it must provide **corrective feedback** on what can be done to improve future performance, and **praise** when performance standards are met. The guidelines for providing corrective feedback and praise during teacher-directed lessons can also be followed for providing oral or written feedback on independent assignments. When you are responding to incorrect answers, provide specific information on how performance can be improved, focus on the correct versus the incorrect response, and deliver the feedback in an appropriate tone (if you are giving it orally). If you want your feedback to make a difference in subsequent performance, be sure to have students correct their errors or redo selected items. When you praise students for their performance, make your praise contingent on noteworthy performance, and focus on effort and meeting the established criterion rather than on the learners' inherent attributes. In addition, construct your praise so that it is positive and genuine.

There are many ways that you can check assignments (e.g., self-corrections against a key, self-corrections during an instructional group, self-evaluation using a rubric, peer evaluation using a rubric, teacher grading) and mark assignments (e.g., checkmarks placed on incorrect items, errors circled, fluency rates graphed, ratings on rubric highlighted). Similarly, there are many ways to provide feedback. Oral feedback can include comments given to individual students while moving around the room and monitoring, conferences with individual students, comments to the entire group, or reteaching of difficult items to class. Written feedback can include written comments, circled or checked items, corrected answers, or additional completed examples. We have provided a wide variety of both oral and written examples in Figure 8.8. Read these carefully and see whether you could apply any of these teachers' feedback procedures in your classes. Notice how the teachers manage the workload of evaluating, grading, and providing feedback on assignments.

WHAT ROUTINES WILL BE PUT
IN PLACE TO FACILITATE

INDEPENDENT PRACTICE?

As we have emphasized in Chapter 5, **routines** are the usual or unvarying ways that activities are carried out in the classroom. Routines save time because students know what they are supposed to do and how they are supposed to do it. When students have been taught routines, they are less likely to interrupt their teachers' instructional activities, and the opportunities for them to be academically engaged increase (Archer et al., 1987; Emmer & Stough, 2001). Classroom routines should be taught at the beginning of the year via modeling, practice, and feedback, just

(text resumes on page 231)

FIGURE 8.8. Examples of feedback on assignments.

Example 1: Correcting against a key
Situation: Ms. Watanabe's special education resource room serving fourth-, fifth-, and sixth-grade students

Ms. Watanabe's students come to the resource room for 60 minutes of reading intervention. Based on the intervention placement test, Ms. Watanabe has formed two instructional groups and provides 30 minutes of explicit instruction to each group. When not in an instructional group, students engage in three 10-minute activities: (1) fluency practice with the paraeducator, (2) partner reading of independent-level books, and (3) independent paper–pencil assignments that relate to the content of the instructional group. For each of these activities, Ms. Watanabe has developed different criteria and feedback procedures.

Fluency: (Criterion—meeting fluency goal.) Based on a student's current oral reading fluency (correct oral words per minute), a new goal is set. The paraeducator has the student read for 1 minute on a new passage ("cold" timing). The student then practices the passage at least three times. When they believe that the student can meet the goal, the paraeducator times the student again ("hot" timing). If the goal is met, the student graphs the cold- and hot-timing data. If the goal is not met, this procedure is repeated again the next day with a new passage but with the same goal.

Partner reading: (Criterion—participation, book completion.) The partners have selected an independent book to read. Each day they record the start page; read orally for 10 minutes, alternating with each other on each page; and then record the stop page.

Independent paper–pencil assignments: (Criterion—95% accuracy/100% on corrected assignments.) The independent assignments are introduced at the end of the instructional session. If the format is unfamiliar, Ms. Watanabe reads the directions with students, asks questions to verify their understanding, demonstrates an item if necessary, and has students do one item. Students complete assignments at their desks. Once a student has completed the assignment, the student goes to the "Check" table and compares his or her work to a key. If an item is incorrect, the student circles the number, indicating that he or she needs to redo that item. After correcting missed items and ensuring that the assignment meets all of the criteria (accurate, neat, complete, heading), the student places it in the "Done" box. At the end of the day, Ms. Watanabe reviews all the assignments and selects any items that were consistently missed to review in the instructional group on the following day.

Example 2: In-class corrections—Spelling
Situation: Mr. Johnson's third-grade classroom

(Criterion—95% accuracy on 20 words.) Mr. Johnson, aware that progress in spelling is facilitated by self-correction of spelling tests, utilizes the following correction routine. After all words have been dictated and recorded by students, students take out a correcting pen and put away all other writing tools. Mr. Johnson then provides feedback on each word by writing it on the overhead. If a student misses an item, he or she crosses out the word and rewrites the entire word. As students correct errors, Mr. Johnson moves around the room and examines their work. If numerous students miss a word, Mr. Johnson provides additional input on the correct spelling. He then asks students to turn their papers over and dictates the word again. Mr. Johnson repeats this procedure for each missed word. Students record their scores on the "Spelling Score Sheet" maintained in their binders and turn their papers in. Occasionally, Mr. Johnson will check the accuracy of students' self-corrections and give bonus points for accurate corrections.

Example 3: In-class corrections—Math
Situation: Mrs. Jacobson's tenth-grade math class

Mrs. Jacobson knows that having secondary math students complete a reasonable amount of homework increases achievement. However, with five classes of math involving three different preparations, she realizes that if she personally corrects every assignment, she will not have adequate time to prepare for explicit instruction. Mrs. Jacobson decides to base the class grade on homework completion and weekly tests.

(cont.)

FIGURE 8.8. *(cont.)*

Homework: (Criterion—completion of all items.) At the beginning of class, Mrs. Jacobson asks students to take out their homework assignments. She then provides feedback on four to six carefully selected items (difficult or "tricky" items). Students put checkmarks next to missed items. Students then redo any of the focus items that they missed. Homework is filed in their binders. On Friday, all homework assignments are turned in with the weekly math test. Ten points are awarded for each completed assignment, representing one-third of the weekly grade.

Weekly test: (Criterion—90–100% accuracy.) Each week students are given 10 items that parallel homework items. These tests are graded by the teacher and returned the following Monday, when Mrs. Jacobson provides oral feedback to the class with an emphasis on appropriate praise. If consistent errors are made, Mrs. Jacobson goes over those items with her students. Weekly tests are worth a maximum of 100 points (two-thirds of the weekly grade). Of course, if students consistently complete homework and attend when daily feedback is given, test performance will be facilitated.

Example 4: Correcting against a rubric

Situation: Mr. Cortez's eighth-grade language arts class for struggling writers

Mr. Cortez is teaching a unit on persuasive writing. He understands that students need to write numerous persuasive essays in order to master the genre, and that students benefit from ongoing feedback. However, he faces the same challenge as Mrs. Jacobson: many classes, many students, and many assignments to grade. In order to optimize the amount of student writing practice and to provide the feedback that will move students to the desired level of performance, Mr. Cortez has designed a plan involving a rubric.

Rubric: Mr. Cortez has adopted the following student-friendly rubric, to be used in numerous ways: to introduce the genre, to evaluate example and non-example persuasive essays with the class, to guide students in writing persuasive essays, to allow students to analyze their own essays and those of their partners, and to provide teacher feedback to the writers.

	Introduction
Yes No	Does the introduction state the author's opinion?
Yes No	Does the introduction state the author's major reasons for his or her opinion?

Yes No	Does the introduction capture the reader's interest?
	Body
Yes No	Does each paragraph present a reason to support the author's opinion?
Yes No	Do the remaining sentences in each paragraph present evidence and examples to support the reason?
Yes No	Has the author considered arguments on the other side of the issue?
Yes No	Are the reasons convincing?
	Conclusion
Yes No	Does the author restate his or her opinion?
Yes No	Does the author summarize his or her reasons for the opinion?
Yes No	Does the essay have a definite end?
	Conventions
Yes No	Do the sentences make sense?
Yes No	Are capitals used correctly?
Yes No	Are punctuation marks used correctly?
Yes No	Are the words spelled correctly?
Yes No	Are the paragraphs indented?
Yes No	Is the handwriting/typing neat and legible?

(cont.)

FIGURE 8.8. *(cont.)*

Assignments—Five essays: At the beginning of the 6-week unit on persuasive writing, Mr. Cortez presents the rubric and guides students in examining an example essay and two non-example essays. He then guides students in planning and writing essays, using the steps in the writing process: plan, draft, revise, edit. The amount of guidance is gradually faded until the students complete all of the steps independently.

Feedback on all five essays: Mr. Cortez gives feedback in a number of ways on the five essays:

1. As the students are writing, Mr. Cortez moves around the room, giving praise, encouragement, and corrective feedback,
2. Students evaluate their own essays against the rubric, revising as indicated,
3. Peer partners also use the rubric to provide feedback.
4. Mr. Cortez provides written feedback to each student on a limited part of the rubric (e.g., only the introduction, the conclusion, or the second paragraph of the body), followed by oral feedback to the entire class based on his overall evaluation. A maximum of 50 points can be awarded for each essay (10 points for completion, 10 points for self-evaluation, 10 points for peer evaluation, 20 points for teacher evaluation).

Final essay. At the end of the unit, the students select one of their essays for in-depth revising, editing, and publishing. Before a student can turn the assignment in, two peers have to give feedback on the essay, with subsequent revising and editing by the author. Mr. Cortez gives very complete feedback on the selected essay: specific written comments, a score using the rubric, and oral feedback to each student. This essay is worth a maximum of 250 points, half of the total points for the unit.

Example 5: Oral feedback

Situation: Ms. Valentine's writing class for special education students in ninth grade

Ms. Valentine has found that oral feedback is most effective with her struggling writers. After introducing a writing assignment to the class, Ms. Valentine confers with each of her five students concerning their homework. Notice that Ms. Valentine provides positive feedback and specific corrective feedback, and requires that students fix up any errors.

Assignment: Write two paragraphs describing your favorite television show and why you like it. Make sure you write a topic sentence for each paragraph. Try to use different types of sentences, and use correct punctuation and capitalization.

Criteria: Topic sentence for each paragraph, variety of sentence structures, correct punctuation and capitalization, correct spelling on high-frequency words and words that can be copied (e.g., title of TV show, names of characters).

Teacher's oral feedback: Let's go over last night's assignment. First, what do you think you've done well? *Both paragraphs had a topic sentence.* I agree. You've done a great job of using topic sentences. You have one for each paragraph, and each topic sentence lets the reader know what you are going to talk about in the paragraph.

I also like how you've used different types of sentences, especially compound sentences. They make your writing more interesting than if you just use simple sentences. I do notice that in some of your compound sentences, you've forgotten to use a comma before the coordinating conjunction, such as *but, and,* or *yet.* Remember, you do this when you join two independent clauses. Here's a reminder of the test: If the part of the sentence after the coordinating conjunction can be a stand-alone sentence, you use a comma. Now go ahead and read your two paragraphs from last night, and insert commas where you need them.

as you would teach any other skill. In the context of

independent work completed in class, routines include how to determine what to do, how to request assistance, and what to do when the work is finished. We have derived the following in-class practice routines from the work of Archer et al. (1987) and Meese (2001).

Routines for Determining What to Do

At various times during the school day, students are expected to engage in independent practice activities—completing a worksheet, writing in their journal, or working in pairs or groups. Thus they need to be able to determine what work they are expected to do and when they should begin. Rather than giving directions and passing out materials each time you assign a practice activity, you can teach routines for these. Which routines you use will depend on the **nature of the task** (e.g., novel or familiar, simple or complex), **student characteristics** (e.g., more or less need for structure), and **setting** (i.e., special or general education classroom). Some routines related to students' knowing what to do and when to do it include (1) writing daily in-class and homework assignments on the board for students to copy, (2) writing homework assignments on a class calendar visible to all students, or (3) placing in-class assignment sheets in student folders.

Another aspect of knowing what to do relates to obtaining materials needed to complete the assignment. Routines for this purpose can include having a designated student hand out materials, placing assignments in student work folders, placing assignments in an out-box, having materials ready at a work station, and so on.

Routines for Obtaining Needed Assistance

Often when some students are working on practice assignments at their desks, others are receiving small-group instruction from the teacher. In this situation, students having difficulty with their seatwork often raise their hands and ask for help, or interrupt the teacher's instruction by coming up to the group and asking for help. In either case, the student requesting help is not academically engaged, and the small-group instruction is disrupted. You can use several routines for requesting assistance to minimize these interruptions. First, rather than calling out that they need help, students can be taught to indicate the need for assistance by putting a "help sign" on their desks. You then acknowledge (orally or by making eye contact) that you have seen the sign and you know they need help. This way, your students know that they will get help as soon as possible, and that they don't have to sit there with hands raised. Other routines include having students go to a designated peer or paraprofessional to get help with their problems. Another option is for students to have a backup folder with assignments that require them to work on skills they are capable of completing, but with which they still need to build fluency. This way, they can remain engaged until you or someone else can get to them.

Routines for What to Do When the Assignment Is Completed

Ideally, you should take task length and allotted practice time into consideration, in order to minimize the amount of unoccupied time students have between task completion and initiation of the next activity. However, despite the best planning, students do complete their in-class assignments at varying rates and may find themselves with nothing to do (academically speaking). Because this type of "down time" can result in behaviors that are at best nonproductive and at worst disruptive, routines for what to do when work is completed are important. Frequently, teachers deal with this situation by having a routine requiring students to be involved in a "buffer" task. This type of task is usually more enjoyable than the recently completed assignment, but is still academically relevant. Buffer tasks do not result in interrupting other students or the teacher, do not require the involvement of other students, and are flexible in regard to length of time (because the time available will vary across students and from day to day). Buffer tasks can include completing other assignments, studying for tests, taking out a book and engaging in silent reading, working on puzzles, or going to the computer center.

Often teachers require that an assignment be corrected before a student can engage in buffer tasks. This is a good idea, given that some students may rush through assignments (possibly making errors) so that they can do the more enjoyable buffer activity. In addition, getting immediate feedback is helpful to learning. Routines for correcting completed assignments include peer correction, teacher correction, and self-correcting stations where students can compare their answers to a key. Regardless of the method, each student should be required to make any corrections before moving to the next task. A final consideration related to the use of buffer tasks when students finish in-class assignments involves fairness. Some students, who may be working hard but have motor or processing speed issues, may not complete the assignment before the end of the designated period and thus may only infrequently gain access to the more pleasurable buffer activities (e.g., computer time, reading a favorite book). Teachers should be aware of this potential problem and ensure that all students gain access to buffer tasks, possibly by shortening the practice activity.

All of the independent practice procedures that we have addressed to this point in this chapter are summarized in Figure 8.9. Up to now, we have discussed designing, presenting, and routinizing independent practice opportunities, with an emphasis on in-class assignments. In the next section, we examine effective teacher and student strategies to support students (especially those in secondary classes) in the completion of homework.

FIGURE 8.9. A checklist for independent practice. These statements can be used to analyze independent practice assignments.

1. Taught the skill to be practiced during group instruction.
2. Established that students are capable of completing the task independently.
3. Established a clear purpose for the assignment (e.g., increasing accuracy, building fluency).
4. Designed or selected a practice task/activity that matches the skill and is consistent with the learning objective.
5. Controlled for other skill demands.
6. Provided clear, concise directions.
7. Provided prompts when needed.
8. Considered the length of time needed to complete the activity and the amount of time available to complete it.
9. Clarified and verified students' understanding of the assignment.
10. Established evaluation criteria (participation, completion, accuracy, fluency, other).
11. Provided oral or written feedback on student performance.
12. Established routines to facilitate independent practice.

HOMEWORK

Ever since formal education began, homework has been a part of it. Often used (and often maligned) as an instructional tool, homework has the purposes of providing additional academic learning time, distributed practice, and additional opportunities to apply and generalize skills and knowledge outside of school. In addition to the frequent concern about whether students are required to do too much homework, a central question is whether completion of homework has educational benefits (e.g., increased achievement, generalization of skills). The answer to that question appears to be a qualified *yes*.

Although evidence of the effectiveness of homework is

sometimes conflicting, generally there appears to be convergent support for well-designed homework activities (Cooper, 1989; Cooper, Lindsay, Nye, & Greathouse, 1998; Cooper & Nye, 1994; Keith, 1992; Paschal, Weinstein, & Walberg, 1984). In a special issue on homework in the *Educational Psychologist*, Cooper and Valentine (2001) found that the sum of available research indicates that doing homework results in better student achievement than not doing it. They also noted that, overall, the more homework that is done (up to a certain point), the greater the impact on achievement. Finally, they concluded that the achievement effects of homework are larger for high school students than for middle school students, and for middle school students than for students at the elementary level. Some research actually indicates that homework has little or no impact on academic achievement for elementary school students (Cooper & Valentine, 2001). Thus age seems to be an important qualifier in answers to the question "Is homework effective?"

It is not our purpose to provide an extensive review of the literature on the topic of homework, or to take a particular stance on the issue; we realize that this can be an emotionally charged topic, and that no amount of empirical evidence about achievement will dissuade some people from their position on whether homework should be given. But we address it here because the reality is that homework is assigned in our schools and students are required to complete it. At the secondary level, homework may total 10–12 assignments requiring up to 8 hours a week, and it may account for up to one-third of a student's grade in a class (Bryan, Nelson, & Mathur, 1995; Epstein, Polloway, Foley, & Patton, 1993; Putnam, Deshler, & Schumaker, 1993). Given that homework is—and will probably continue to be—assigned frequently, and that it affects grades, it makes sense to maximize its advantages (e.g., increased learning) and minimize its disadvantages (e.g., frustration on the part of students and parents, reduction in leisure and community activities).

Thus, in this section, we describe procedures to make homework more effective and efficient, especially for students with special learning needs. These considerations are predicated on the premise that homework can be effective only if teachers assign appropriate tasks and if students complete those tasks successfully (Hughes, Ruhl, Schumaker, & Deshler, 2002). Although most research on homework has been conducted with general student populations (i.e., the studies did not differentiate results by students with and without disabilities), some research shows that students with learning disabilities make improvements if homework is short and focuses on building fluency and maintenance of basic skills, if performance is monitored and timely feedback provided, and if parental involvement is promoted (Cooper & Nye, 1994; Hughes et al., 2002). Below, we present techniques, procedures, and considerations for teachers as they design effective homework, as well as some skills and strategies students can use to complete these assignments.

What Teachers Can Do to Facilitate Accuracy and Completion of Homework

To return to a principle mentioned earlier in this chapter, an independent practice task needs to involve suitable content at appropriate instructional levels that match students' current functioning. Unfortunately, there is evidence that neither general nor special education teachers consistently design, assign, or evaluate homework appropriately (Rademacher, Schumaker, & Deshler, 1996; Salend & Gajria, 1995).

Designing Homework

The design considerations for developing independent practice activities described earlier in this chapter also apply to homework. However, because homework is completed outside of school with no teacher support and often involves tasks typically not given as in-class assignments (e.g., researching and writing a paper, studying for a test), planning and designing considerations are more complicated. To that end, Rademacher, Deshler, Schumaker, and Lenz (1998) have developed a homework routine called the Quality Assignment Routine (see Figure 8.10). This routine is designed to help teachers plan, deliver, and evaluate homework assignments, particularly more complex assignments that are completed over time. During the planning phase of this routine, teachers consider the purpose of the assignment, as well as students' needs and interests, develop clear and detailed directions; and decide how the assignment will be evaluated.

The Quality Assignment Routine consists of a series of steps, the first letters of which form the mnemonic PLAN. Step 1, *Plan the purposes of the assignment*, requires the teacher to indicate what students will accomplish, how they will do it, and what the benefits of completing the assignment are. The next step, *Link assignment to student needs and interests*, involves thinking about students' characteristics (e.g., level of current functioning, second-language issues) and interests in order to make the assignment more relevant to them. In addition, options related to how the task may be completed are explored. Some thought is also given to possible pitfalls (e.g., the students may not have some prerequisite knowledge for completing the task) and how they can be addressed (e.g., spend time teaching prerequisites). The third step, *Arrange clear student directions*, asks the teacher to think about the action steps students will take in order to complete the assignment, the materials and resources needed, and the grading criteria to be used. The teacher will keep this information in mind when developing directions for completing the assignment. The last step of PLAN, most of which occurs after the assignment has been turned in, is *Note evaluation date and results.* In this step, a date is established for evaluating the assignment: How effective was the assignment? Should the assignment be modified in the future?

One last consideration for planning and designing homework deals with the oft-expressed concern about the amount given (i.e., too much!). In addition to the potential negative impact that spending 2–3 hours or more per night on homework has on students' home and social life, there is some evidence that after a certain amount of time, there are diminishing academic returns. For example, in middle and high school, the benefits of homework level off after an hour to an 1–1½ hours on all subjects combined. And, again, doing more than a total of 20–30 minutes per night has few benefits for younger students. Thus some planning regarding the amount of homework assigned should occur. This planning can take place both individually and among teachers as a team. To ensure a reasonable amount of homework per night, teachers need to communicate with each other about what homework is given to students, when, and how long it will take. Otherwise, if all of a student's teachers give assignments on the same night, it creates an undue burden on the student and parents, and there is no defensible pedagogical rationale for doing so.

FIGURE 8.10. Planning worksheet for the Quality Assignment Routine. From Rademacher, Schumaker, and Deshler (1996). Reprinted with permission from Joyce Rademacher.

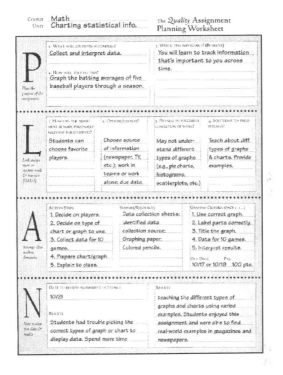

Assigning/Presenting Homework

Because many students, including those with learning disabilities, have difficulties recording assignments accurately and completely, teachers should consider methods for presenting homework assignments in ways that facilitate accurate recording. Having specific routines and guidelines for when and how homework is assigned, as well as for verifying understanding of the assignment, will go a long way toward helping you achieve this goal. The routines described below are based on the work of Ruhl and colleagues (Hughes et al., 2002; Ruhl & Hughes, 2005).

u *Allot enough time*. Often homework is given at the end of a class period, when students are getting ready to leave and there is little remaining time. Because many students with learning disabilities write slowly and have difficulty processing multistep directions, rushing through this process can result in incomplete and/ or inaccurate recording of assignments. Thus allotting sufficient time will accommodate these difficulties and allow for questions.

u *Ensure student attention*. Similar to starting a lesson, presenting information about an assignment when students are not listening or paying attention may result in students' missing information necessary for completing the homework assignment. If the homework assignment process is routinized, a simple cue (e.g., "It's homework assignment time!") is all that is necessary for your students to stop what they are doing and focus on recording homework.

u *Prompt the use of assignment books*. Assignment books have been shown to assist students in recording and keeping track of homework (Hughes et al., 2002). Thus you should prompt students to get them out when it is time to assign homework, as well as encourage their use outside of class. A sample assignment book and procedures for teaching students to use it effectively are presented later in this chapter.

u *Present the assignment both orally and in writing*. Students with learning problems often have listening comprehension and/or reading comprehension difficulties. Listening comprehension problems may be exacerbated if students are listening to spoken directions at the same time they are trying to quickly write assignments down. Providing assignments in writing as well as orally helps ensure accuracy and completion of recording.

u *Demonstrate how to complete the task if necessary*. If the task is novel to your students, or the target skill is complex and/or newly taught, it may be appropriate to model completion of an item/problem.

u *Verify student understanding of the assignment.* As we have noted earlier in this book, asking students "Does everybody understand [the assignment]?" does not verify that they understand what they are supposed to do—and many students will signify that they do understand even when they don't! If you ask your students specific questions about the requirements of the homework assignment, or in some instances require them to complete one problem/item in class and then check to see whether they have completed it accurately, you can get a much clearer picture of your students' levels of understanding.

u *Explain evaluation criteria.* In addition to giving directions for completing the assignment, you should explicitly state (and provide in writing) any special evaluation criteria, such as expectations for accuracy, length, and neatness, and verify the students' understanding of these.

Evaluating Homework

An often overlooked part of the homework process—evaluating and providing corrective feedback on student performance—is crucial to homework's effectiveness. Without timely feedback, the benefits of homework diminish significantly (Paschal et al., 1984). As discussed earlier, you can provide feedback orally and/or in written form to individual students or to your entire class. Remember to provide specific information on how performance can be improved, rather than merely assigning a grade or making general comments such as "Well done" or "Needs improvement." If improvement is needed, you should clearly communicate what students need to do in order to improve their performance. After the correction, students should be required to demonstrate that corrections have been successful by accurately performing all tasks in need of improvement.

To summarize, you can make homework more effective by using good practices involving selecting, designing, presenting, and evaluating homework, as well as keeping in mind that families need time together and that students have other activities and responsibilities apart from schoolwork. You can also teach students skills and strategies that will help them record, plan, complete, and turn in homework.

What Students Can Do to Increase Homework Accuracy and Completion

Many students, including those with learning disabilities, experience difficulties with various aspects of homework (Bryan, Burstein, & Bryan, 2001; Cooper & Nye, 1994; Hughes et al., 2002; Polloway, Foley, & Epstein, 1992). Some of these difficulties occur during assignment presentation:

1. Being unaware that an assignment is being given.
2. Recording assignments on whatever piece of paper is handy, and subsequently losing track of it.
3. Only partially recording an assignment because of slow writing.
4. Failing to ask for clarification when uncertain about assignment requirements for fear of appearing "stupid."

Other difficulties occur with planning and organizing homework:

1. Underestimating the amount of time it will take to complete a particular assignment.
2. Not scheduling a time to work on the assignment.
3. Forgetting to gather and take home needed materials/supplies.
4. Forgetting to take the completed assignment to school

and turn it in.

Although you can address some of these difficulties by how you develop, assign, and evaluate homework, it is also important to teach your students skills and strategies that will help them deal with these difficulties *independently.*

There have been a few studies in which students with learning disabilities have been taught to use procedures that helped them increase the amount and accuracy of homework completion. For example, Lenz, Erin, and Smiley (1991) used goal setting (i.e., setting a target goal for amount and quality of homework projects completed), and Trammel, Schloss, and Alper (1994) had students record whether or not they turned in homework, graph their completion data, and set goals for the future. Both studies resulted in improved performance on homework that resource room teachers assigned; however, neither study examined the impact of the techniques on homework assigned in general education classes that was to be completed at home (e.g., in one of the studies, homework was completed in the resource room).

Hughes, Ruhl, Schumaker, and Deshler (1995) developed a learning strategy to help struggling students independently address their difficulties related to recording, planning, and completing homework. This seven-step strategy (the first letters of the steps form the mnemonic PROJECT helped students double the rate of homework completion in their general education classes, as well as improve the grades they received on assignments. The steps of the strategy are presented in Figure 8.11 and are described below as they relate to aspects of homework completion (e.g., recording, planning).

Strategies and Skills for Recording Homework

Using a book to record homework helps students accurately record and keep track of their assignments. No research indicates that one type of assignment book, recording sheet, or calendar is better than another; however, some common-sense guidelines include providing (1) adequate room to record the assignment, (2) a place to indicate which class the assignment is for, and (3) a place to record due dates and completion. Hughes et al. (2002) used the PROJECT recording form, pre-

FIGURE 8.11. Steps of the Assignment Completion Strategy (PROJECT).

Step 1:	Prepare your forms (monthly, weekly, and daily).
Step 2:	Record and ask questions.

Step 3:	Organize your completion plan:
	    Break assignment into parts.
	    Estimate number of sessions.
	    Schedule the sessions.
	    Take materials home.

Step 4:	Jump to it.
Step 5:	Engage in the work.
Step 6:	Check the work.
Step 7:	Turn it in

sented in Figure 8.12. At the top of the form are places to record the subject (e.g., English, math), when the assignment was given, when it is due, and when it is completed and turned in. The form also contains a row of words—*Read, Answer, Write*, and *Other*—which are the common "action" words related to homework. In order to record assignments quickly, students can select to circle or underline the appropriate action words rather than write them. For example, if the assignment is to "Read Chapter 6 and answer the questions at the end of the chapter," students can underline *Read* and *Answer*.

Hughes and Suritsky (1994) and Hughes et al. (2002) noticed that many students with learning disabilities do not use abbreviations when recording information. Thus, in the PROJECT strategy, students are taught to use abbreviations when recording assignments. As part of this instruction, students develop cue cards with common abbreviations related to homework, including subject areas (e.g., *Eng., Rdg., Alg., Sci.*) and assignments (e.g., *Txt., Def., Chap., Pg., Para.*). They are also taught some general rules about personal abbreviations, such as "Use the first

FIGURE 8.12. PROJECT Assignment sheet.

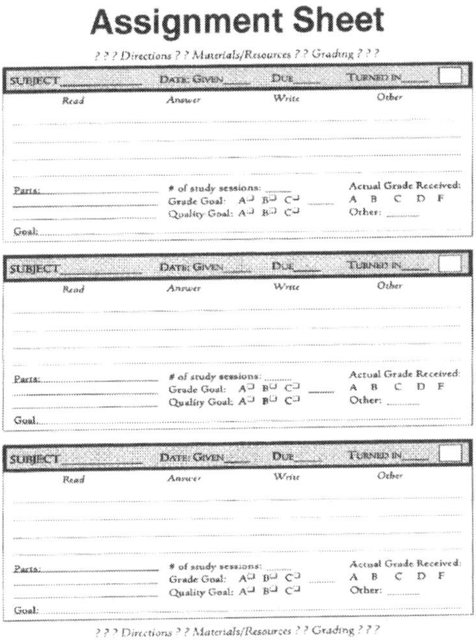

Assignment Sheet

? ? ? Directions ? ? Materials/Resources ? ? Grading ? ? ?

SUBJECT____ DATE GIVEN____ DUE____ TURNED IN____ ☐

Read *Answer* *Write* *Other*

Parts: ____ # of study sessions: ____ Actual Grade Received:
Grade Goal: A☐ B☐ C☐ ____ A B C D F
Quality Goal: A☐ B☐ C☐ Other: ____
Goal: ____

SUBJECT____ DATE GIVEN____ DUE____ TURNED IN____ ☐

Read *Answer* *Write* *Other*

Parts: ____ # of study sessions: ____ Actual Grade Received:
Grade Goal: A☐ B☐ C☐ ____ A B C D F
Quality Goal: A☐ B☐ C☐ Other: ____
Goal: ____

SUBJECT____ DATE GIVEN____ DUE____ TURNED IN____ ☐

Read *Answer* *Write* *Other*

Parts: ____ # of study sessions: ____ Actual Grade Received:
Grade Goal: A☐ B☐ C☐ ____ A B C D F
Quality Goal: A☐ B☐ C☐ Other: ____
Goal: ____

? ? ? Directions ? ? Materials/Resources ? ? Grading ? ? ?

two or three letters of the word," and "Use first letters for word pairs" (e.g., *social studies = SS, language arts = LA*).

The final part of the strategy related to recording homework prompts students to ask for clarification if they don't understand directions or think they have missed something. Because asking questions is difficult for some students, it is a good idea to explore options for asking questions that minimize such students' discomfort, such as waiting until the rest of the class leaves. In addition, role-playing asking assignment-related questions may increase your students' willingness and ability to ask clarification questions.

Strategies and Skills for Planning Homework Completion

The PROJECT strategy includes an *Organize* step, in which students perform several actions when planning how and when they will complete their assignments. The first of these actions, *Break the assignments into parts*, requires students to identify the major parts of an assignment. Some assignments, such as a worksheet of multiplication problems, have only one major activity (i.e., completing a worksheet). Other assignments are more complex. For example, completing a book report involves five major parts: locating a book, reading the book, creating an outline, writing the report, and editing the report. Referring to the assignment sheet in Figure 8.12, your students would record a brief description of the parts in the "Parts" section. Analyzing the parts of an assignment helps students estimate how long they will take.

Next, students *E*stimate the number of study sessions and *Schedule the sessions*. In the PROJECT strategy, study sessions consist of half-hour blocks of time (see Figure 8.13). Students estimate how many study sessions each part will take. For example, selecting a book may take a student one session, reading the book may take four sessions, writing an outline may take one, writing the report may take three sessions, and editing may take one. The student thus schedules 10 half-hour sessions and then records the number 10 on the assignment sheet where it says "# of study sessions." Once the number of sessions has been estimated, the student blocks out the study sessions on the weekly study schedule.

Other steps of the PROJECT strategy prompt students to *Jump to it* by gathering needed materials, finding a good spot to work, and looking over the assignment. Students then *Engage in the work* by getting started and recruiting help from parents or a "study buddy." After completion, they *Check the work* by evaluating the accuracy and quality of their product. They also place the completed work in a place where it won't get damaged (e.g., a folder) and put it where they won't forget it in the morning (e.g., in their backpack). The final step, *Turn it in,* cues them to remember to hand in the homework and to record completion on the assignment sheet.

FIGURE 8.13. A weekly study schedule.

Date: Time	Saturday	Sunday	Monday	Tuesday	Wednesday	Thursday	Friday
6:30							
7:00							
7:30							
8:00							
8:30							
9:00							
9:30							
10:00							
10:30							
11:00							
11:30							
12:00							
12:30							
1:00							
1:30							
2:00							
2:30							
3:00							
3:30							

4:00							
4:30							
5:00							
5:30							
6:00							
6:30							
7:00							
7:30							
8:00							
8:30							
9:00							
9:30							
10:00							

CHAPTER SUMMARY

Practice, practice, practice. This is not always the first choice of human beings. And yet if initial instruction is not yoked to judicious practice, skills will not be retained. Too often this is exactly what occurs: Initial instruction is not followed by well-designed distributed and cumulative practice, which results in exposure to content rather than mastery. Through thoughtful planning and intentional actions, teachers can provide effective practice activities, leading to mastery and retention of content.

Conclusion

As we reach the conclusion of this book, we hope that the information and the examples provided throughout this text have bolstered your knowledge and skill in designing and delivering effective and efficient explicit instruction lessons. As teachers, we constitute the most critical variable in student achievement. What we do on a daily basis has an enormous impact on students' learning, for the adage "How well you teach = How well they learn" is true for all students, especially those with special needs.

In keeping with the message of Chapter 8 (the power of cumulative review), five reproducible chapter summaries are included on the following pages to be copied and reviewed over time, so that you can keep the "big ideas" of this book alive in your daily instruction. We also invite you to visit our website (*www.explicitinstruction.org*) to watch videos illustrating explicit instruction.

Reproducible Materials

Exploring the Foundations of Explicit Instruction
(Chapter 1)

Sixteen Elements of Explicit Instruction

1. Focus instruction on critical content.

2. Sequence skills logically.

3. Break down complex skills and strategies into smaller instructional units.

4. Design organized and focused lessons.

5. Begin lessons with a clear statement of the lesson's goals and your expectations.

6. Review prior skills and knowledge before beginning instruction.

7. Provide step-by-step demonstrations.

8. Use clear and concise language.

9. Provide an adequate range of examples and non-examples.

10. Provide guided and supported practice.

11. Require frequent responses.

12. Monitor student performance closely.

13. Provide immediate affirmative and corrective feedback.

14. Deliver the lesson at a brisk pace.

15. Help students organize knowledge.

16. Provide distributed and cumulative practice.

Principles of Effective Instruction
1. Optimize engaged time/time on task.
2. Promote high levels of success.
3. Increase content coverage.
4. Have students spend more time in instructional groups.
5. Scaffold instruction.
6. Address different forms of knowledge.

247

Designing Lessons
(Chapters 2, 3, and 4)

Opening of the lesson	**Gain students' attention.**	**Review:** Review critical prerequisite skills.	**Preview:** State the goal of the lesson.
Body of the lesson	**Skill or strategy**	**Vocabulary or concept**	**Academic rule**
I do it.	u **Modeling:** Show and tell. Involve students.	u Introduce the word. Introduce the meaning of the word. Illustrate with examples and non-examples.	u Introduce the rule. Use **If–then** construction for the rule. Illustrate the rule with examples and nonexamples.

We do it.	u **Prompted or guided practice:** Guide students in performing the skill or strategy. Provide physical, verbal, or visual prompts. Gradually fade scaffolding. Guide students in analyzing examples and non-examples using the critical attributes.	u Guide students in analyzing examples and non-examples, using the critical attributes.	
You do it.	u **Unprompted practice:** Check students' understanding. Have students perform the skill/strategy without prompts.	u Check students' understanding. Have students distinguish between examples and nonexamples. Have students generate examples and nonexamples. Ask questions that require deep processing.	u Check students' understanding, using examples and nonexamples.
Closing of the lesson	**Review:** Review critical content.	**Preview:** Preview the content of the next lesson.	**Assign independent work.**

248

Organizing for Instruction
(Chapter 5)

Organizing the physical space

1. Have you designated areas for specific activities (e.g., whole-group instruction, small-group instruction, class gatherings on rug, free-choice area, quiet reading area, computer lab)?	Yes No

REPRODUCIBLE

2. In instructional areas, are students in close proximity to you?	Yes No
3. Have you created seating charts and assigned seats?	Yes No
4. In instructional areas, are students facing you?	Yes No
5. During instruction, can students easily share answers with partners or team members?	Yes No
6. Have you arranged your instructional materials for easy retrieval?	Yes No
7. Are the student materials needed during instruction or independent work easily retrievable?	Yes No
8. Have students been taught organization skills (e.g., notebooks, folders, assignment calendar)?	Yes No
9. Can you move quickly and easily around the room, monitoring students without the interference of physical barriers?	Yes No
10. Can you see all parts of the room and all students?	Yes No
11. Have you displayed material on the classroom walls that supports instruction (e.g., class calendar, vocabulary words, strategy posters, rubrics, reference material, rule/guideline poster, notices)?	Yes No
12. Have you displayed student work?	Yes No
13. Is your classroom orderly?	Yes No

Establishing classroom rules

1. Are the rules few in number (i.e., three to six)?	Yes No
2. Are the rules stated in terms of desired behavior?	Yes No
3. Are the rules short and simple?	Yes No
4. Does each rule begin with a verb?	Yes No
5. Are the behaviors well defined in the rule (or through the presentation of examples and nonexamples)?	Yes No

Establishing routines and procedures

1. Have situations needing classroom routines or procedures been identified? (See page——— to ———)	Yes No
2. Have effective and efficient routines been determined for each situation?	Yes No
3. Are routines taught and practiced at the beginning of the school year or semester?	Yes No
4. Are the routines reviewed and reinforced throughout the year?	Yes No

249

Delivering Instruction
(Chapters 6 and 7)

1. Require frequent responses.

Oral responses	Oral responses	Action responses
Choral responses	Individual oral responses	u Touching/pointing
Partner responses u Think–Pair–Share u Think and Write–Pair and Write–Share u Pause procedure u Study–Tell–Help–Check	u Partners First u Question First u Whip Around or Pass	u Acting out u Gestures and facial expressions u Hand signals
	Written responses	**Alternative passage-reading procedures**
	u Response slates u Response cards	u Echo reading u Choral reading u Cloze reading u Augmented silent reading u Partner reading
Team responses u Numbered Heads		

2. Monitor student performance carefully.
Are the responses correct or incorrect?

3. Provide immediate affirmative and corrective feedback.

Corrective feedback (correction) is:	Affirmative feedback (praise) is:
a. Provided.	a. Contingent (If–Then).
b. Immediate.	b. Specific.
c. The appropriate type of correction.	c. Provided for noteworthy performance.
d. Specific and informative.	d. Focused on achievement and effort.
e. Focused on the correct (vs. incorrect) response.	e. Comparing students to themselves.
f. Delivered with appropriate tone.	f. Positive, credible, and genuine.

g. Ended with students' giving the correct response.	g. Unobtrusive.

Deliver the lesson at a brisk pace.
a. Be prepared.
b. Provide *just* enough thinking time.
c. Provide *just enough response time.*
d. After providing feedback, move on.
e. Avoid digressions.
f. Utilize instructional routines.

4.

250

Providing Appropriate Independent Practice

(Chapter 8)

Initial practice
↓
Distributed practice
↓
Cumulative practice and cumulative review

Checklist for independent practice

1. Teach the skill to be practiced during group instruction.

2. Establish that students are capable of completing the task independer

3. Establish a clear purpose for the assignment (e.g., increasing accuracy
fluency).

4. Design or select a practice task/activity that matches the skill and is c
with the learning objective.

5. Control for other skill demands.

6. Provide clear, concise directions.

7. Provide prompts when needed.

8. Consider the length of time needed to complete the activity and the an
time available to complete it.

9. Clarify and verify students' understanding of the assignment.

10. Establish evaluation criteria (participation, completion, accuracy, fluen

11. Provide oral or written feedback on student performance.

12. Establish routines to facilitate independent practice.

Feedback on Application Exercises

CHAPTER 2

APPLICATION 2.1. EXAMPLE: OPENING OF AN EXPLICIT LESSON

What good practices do you note as you examine the lesson opening?

u Attention is gained at the beginning of the lesson.
u The teacher regains attention as
needed. u A clear goal is stated and
repeated in the opening.
u The teacher reviews prerequisite skills: topic sentence, detail sentence, and the term *sequential.* u All students participate in the review.
u The teacher moves around the room and listens to students' responses, to verify prerequisite skills.
u Definite tasks, not vague questions, are used to verify prerequisite skills. u The teacher discusses when sequential paragraphs may be written. u Students are involved in the discussion of relevance. APPLICATION 2.2. ANALYSES OF LESSON OPENING, MODELING, AND PROMPTED OR GUIDED PRACTICE

What good practices occur during the opening of the lesson?

u The teacher gains attention at the beginning of the lesson.
u The teacher discusses why the strategy is important and

when it can be used. u The teacher and the students discuss times when this strategy can be used.

253

u Students are actively involved in establishing the relevance of the strategy. The teacher involves students by using the brainstorm strategy of **Think– Pair–Share** (see Chapter 6). During the **Think** and **Pair** steps, the teacher records students' ideas and their names on an overhead transparency, and then uses the list for a more efficient sharing of ideas.

u The teacher reviews critical prerequisite skills by having students complete a task (turning a question into part of the answer and writing the partial answer).

What positive practices are used during the modeling?

u A strategy chart is used to introduce the study strategy.

u The students are immediately involved when they read the strategy steps during the first model.

u The teacher models the use of the strategy—proceeding step by step, showing students how to perform the strategy, and telling students what the teacher is doing and thinking.

u Consistent wording is used in each model.

How does the teacher prompt students during prompted or guided practice? u The teacher guides the students step by step in applying the strategy.

u Feedback is provided throughout this practice in a number of ways: (1) The teacher monitors and provides feedback, (2) peers give feedback to their partners, and (3) the teacher gives oral feedback to individuals and to the class.

u The scaffolding is gradually removed, requiring the students to perform the strategy with more and more independence.

APPLICATION 2.3. MODEL LESSON: ALGEBRA LESSON ON PARENTHESES

What exemplary practices are evidenced during the opening, the body, and the closing of the lesson?

OPENING OF THE LESSON

- u The teacher gains students' attention at the beginning of the lesson and every time that the students need to refocus on the teacher.
- u The goal of the lesson, and the relevance of the skill to solving algebraic equations, are briefly stated.
- u Well-organized review is provided. Students are given tasks to perform that demonstrated their understanding of the terms *variable* and *expression*. The teacher is able to verify that all of the students understand these terms.

BODY OF THE LESSON

Modeling (I do it.) u The teacher models the skill three times. u The teacher demonstrates and describes the skill performance.

- u During the first model, the teacher involves students by asking questions that tap what they already know.
- u In the second model, the teacher reduces the amount of teacher talk but retains the key words.
- u By presenting two expressions with the parentheses in different locations, the teacher dramatically shows the importance of doing the operations within the parentheses first.
- u During the third model, students answer additional questions as they help the teacher determine the value of the expression.

Prompted or guided practice (We do it.) and unprompted practice (You do it.) u To reduce the possibility of errors, the teacher asks students not to go forward until directed. To keep students from sneaking ahead, the teacher asks students to put their pencils down to indicate completion. u The teacher prompts the students orally on a number of problems.

u As students demonstrate proficiency, the teacher gradually fades the amount of scaffolding. u On the last item, the teacher provides only a brief reminder.

u Following guided practice, the teacher checks the students' understanding

before assigning independent work.

CLOSING OF THE LESSON u A brief
review and preview are provided.
u Independent work is assigned.

APPLICATION 2.4. MODEL LESSON: DETERMINING THE MAIN IDEA

How does the teacher involve the students during each segment of the lesson?

OPENING OF THE LESSON u The students answer questions concerning when and where the paraphrasing strategy may be used.

u When reviewing the topic sentence, the students are asked to write the number corresponding to the topic sentence on their response slates. Use of the slates allows the teacher to monitor all of the students' responses.

BODY OF THE LESSON

Modeling

u After the teacher models the procedure once, the students are invited to help the teacher by answering questions on the procedural steps. However, the teacher actually performs the behaviors.

Prompted or guided practice u Initially, the students are told what to do, and they complete each step in the procedure. Next, the teacher asks questions guiding students in completion of the procedure. Finally, following a reminder, the students complete the steps in the procedure.

Unprompted practice u During this segment of the lesson, students use the procedure for determining the main idea independently, while the teacher moves around the room monitoring their performance.

CLOSING OF THE LESSON u During the lesson review, the teacher asks students questions concerning the importance of determining the main idea and of asking questions that can direct them to the main idea.

APPLICATION 2.5. MODEL LESSONS: THREE CONSECUTIVE SENTENCECOMBINING LESSONS

How does the teacher alter the opening, the body, and the closing over the 3 days of instruction? Why do you believe these changes are made?

OPENING OF THE LESSON

State the goal of the lesson. The teacher states the goal in all three lessons, to ensure that the students know the focus of the lesson.

Discuss the relevance of the skill. Since the students are just beginning their work on sentence combining, in the first lesson the teacher tells them why the skill is important. However, in the second lesson, the students, having had some experience with sentence combining, are asked the relevance of the skill. Note that the teacher focuses on the relevance of the larger goal, sentence combining, rather than on combining sentences with adjectives.

Review critical prerequisite skills. In the first lesson, the teacher reviews the meaning of *adjective* and when to use the articles *a* and *an*. This is not repeated in the subsequent two lessons, due to the students' demonstrated proficiency in these skills.

BODY OF THE LESSON

Modeling. The teacher models the combining skill in the first lesson. However, because the students demonstrate proficiency during the prompted practice, modeling is not repeated on Days 2 and 3.

Prompted or guided practice. On Day 1, the teacher guides students in doing the first item by telling them what to do. On the next two items, the teacher asks students questions to promote their performance. On Day 2, the teacher guides students in the same manner as on Day 1, but with fewer items because of the students' demonstrated proficiency. On Day 3, the teacher only prompts students on one item.

Unprompted practice. Because students have not yet demonstrated proficiency in this new skill, no unprompted practice is provided in the first lesson. On the second day, the students do one item independently; on Day 3, the unprompted practice occurs on three items.

CLOSING OF THE LESSON

On the first day, the closing is a little longer and includes both a review of what had been taught and what will be introduced on the subsequent day. On Days 2 and 3, a very brief closing is used.

APPLICATION 2.6. IDENTIFYING POTENTIAL PROBLEMS AND GENERATING POSSIBLE SOLUTIONS

1. When reviewing a prerequisite skill during the opening of the lesson, the teacher has three of eight students go to the board and solve the problems.

   Potential problem: Because the teacher has only verified that three students can perform the prerequisite skill, it is possible that all or some of the remaining five cannot. If this is the case, the students may not be ready to learn the new material.

   Potential solution: Have *all* the students perform the prerequisite skill to verify that they are ready to learn the new target skill.

2. When discussing why the target skill for the lesson is important to know, the teacher tells them all the reasons.

   Potential problem: Because the purpose of this discussion is to promote motivation to learn the new skill, it is advisable to try to involve the students in this discussion, so that the purpose of learning it is more personalized.

   Potential solution: Ask the students why the skill is important to learn and where and when it may be useful. However, there are times when the target skill is so unfamiliar that the students will not initially be able to determine the relevance. In this case, the teacher can initially tell them the relevance and later have the students reiterate and expand on the relevance.

3. When modeling the new skill of solving two-digit addition problems, the teacher demonstrates once and then asks everyone if they understand.

   Potential problem: Asking students whether they understand the model does not verify that they do. Many students will answer "Yes" when they don't understand, to avoid appearing "stupid" to their classmates.

Potential solution: Involve the students in the model (after it is demonstrated by the teacher one or two times) by asking them questions. Their answers will tell the teacher whether they are truly understanding what the teacher is saying and doing.

4. When modeling the new skill of solving two-digit addition problems with regrouping, the teacher demonstrates once and then moves into guided practice.

Potential problem: Often one demonstration is insufficient, especially when the target skill is more complex. If the students are not involved in the model, the teacher does not have any idea of what the students can do or understand. Moving to guided practice after one model with no student involvement increases the opportunity for errors.

Potential solution: If the target skill is difficult, demonstrate at least twice and then involve students in further demonstrations.

5. During guided practice, the teacher begins with a high-level verbal prompt (i.e., "tells") and then says, "Great job, everybody. Do the next one on your own."

Potential problem: Given that the students have only completed one problem with a lot of teacher support, asking them to complete one on their own may result in errors and frustration.

Potential solution: Provide more opportunities for guided practice, and fade the level of prompting, before asking the students to complete the task or problem on their own.

CHAPTER 3

Note: Feedback on Applications 3.1, 3.2, and 3.3 is provided in

Chapter 3.

APPLICATION

3.4. CREATING STUDENT- FRIENDLY EXPLANATIONS

Setting and population	Vocabulary word: Dictionary or glossary definition	Student-friendly explanation
Second-grade read-aloud	*nervous* (adj.)—easily agitated, excited, or irritated; apprehensive	When you feel frightened or worried, you feel *nervous*. (Developed from definition provided in *Longman Dictionary of American English*, 2006)
Fifth-grade reading lesson	*cower* (v.)—to crouch from something that menaces or dominates	When you *cower*, you crouch down or curl up because you are afraid.
Seventh-grade language arts	*sublime* (adj.)—of such magnificence, grandeur, or exquisiteness as to inspire great veneration	If you describe something as *sublime*, you mean that it has a wonderful quality that affects you deeply. (Developed from definition provided in *Collins COBUILD Student's Dictionary*, 2005)
Eleventh-grade science lesson	*empirical* (adj.)—based on, related to, verifiable by experience, experiment, or observation	*Empirical* knowledge or evidence is based on observation, experiment, and experience rather than theories. (Developed from definition provided in *Collins COBUILD Student's Dictionary*, 2005)

APPLICATION 3.5. DETERMINING CRITICAL ATTRIBUTES FROM DEFINITIONS

Definition	Critical attribute or attributes
independent variable An *independent variable* is a variable in an experiment that is changed on purpose.	*independent variable* u variable in an experiment u changed on purpose
immigration *Immigration* is the process of people coming into a country with the intent to live and work there.	*immigration* u people coming into a country u with the intent to live and work there

APPLICATION

retaliate When you harm someone in return for an injury or wrong he or she has done, you *retaliate*.	*retaliate* u harm someone u in return for an injury or wrong he or she has done

3.6. DESIGNING EXAMPLES AND NON-EXAMPLES

Critical attribute or attributes	Examples	Non-examples
immigration u people coming into a country u with the intent to live and work there	If Brazilians came to the United States with the idea that they would find work and make a new permanent home, this would be an act of *immigration*.	If Brazilians came to the United States for a 2-week stay to visit their cousins, this would not be *immigration*, because they would have no intention to live or work in the United States. If a Brazilian family moved from southern Brazil to northern Brazil because of new job opportunities, this would not be considered *immigration*, since they did not go to a new country.
sufficient u enough	The painter had 5 gallons of paint. The paint easily covered the outside of the house. There was *sufficient* paint.	The painter had 5 gallons of paint. The paint covered only three of the four outside walls of the house. The amount of paint was not *sufficient*.
retaliate u harm someone u in return for an injury or wrong he or she has done	On his blog, James wrote a number of lies about Justin. These lies really hurt Justin, so he *retaliated* by writing even meaner things about James in his blog.	Bernard wrote lies about Justin on his blog. Though the lies really hurt Justin, he decided to ignore the comments because he realized that Bernard often lied. Justin did not *retaliate*. Bernard wrote lies about Justin on his blog. Justin had never harmed Bernard in any way. Bernard did not *retaliate*, as he was not responding to any harm done to him. He was just

cruel.

CHAPTER 4

APPLICATION 4.1. DETERMINING CRITICAL ATTRIBUTES IN A RULE

Rule: Use commas to separate the words and/or word groups in a series of three or more.

Critical attributes (If): u
Words and/or word
groups.
u Series of three or more.
Then: Separate with commas.

Rule: When a word ends in a vowel–consonant–final *e* and you want to add a suffix that begins with a vowel, drop the *e*.

Critical attributes (If):
u Word ends in vowel–consonant–final *e*.
u Suffix begins with a vowel.
Then: Drop the *e*.

4.2. CREATING EXAMPLES TO ILLUSTRATE A RULE

Rule: Use commas to separate the words and/or word groups in a series of three or more.

Critical attributes (If): u
Words and/or word
groups.
u Series of three or more.
Then: Separate with commas.

Examples: u Cameron, Cecilia, Jamie, and Cedric all
take the bus to school. u Jasmine purchased
notebook paper, pens, and a ruler for school.
u The children's favorite activities included playing dodge ball, reading library books,

APPLICATION

painting, working in the garden, and writing stories.

u Brianna was described as being extraordinarily energetic, hard-working, independent, humorous, and kind.

Note: A good deal of variety is provided in this set of examples. Some of the series contain three items, while others contain four or five. The items include single words or multiple words. Also, some of the items in the series are nouns, while others are adjectives or verbs.

Rule: When a word ends in a vowel–consonant–final *e* and you want to add a suffix that begins with a vowel, drop the *e*.

Critical attributes (If):

u Word ends in vowel–consonant–final *e*. u Suffix begins with a vowel.

Then: Drop the *e*.

Examples:

hate + ing = hating
shine + ing = shining
time + ed = timed
debate + able =
debatable require +
ed = required

APPLICATION 4.3. CREATING NON-EXAMPLES TO ILLUSTRATE A RULE

Rule: Use commas to separate the words and/or word groups in a series of three or more.

Critical attributes (If): u Words and/or word groups. u Series of three or more.

Then: Separate with commas.

Examples: u Cameron, Cecilia, Jamie, and Cedric all take the bus to school. u Jasmine purchased notebook paper, pens, and a ruler for school.

u The children's favorite activities included playing dodge ball, reading library books, painting, working in the garden, and writing stories.

u Brianna was described as being extraordinarily energetic, hard-working, independent, humorous, and kind.

APPLICATION

Non-examples:
u Cameron and Cedric take the bus to
school. u Jasmine purchased numerous
supplies for school.

u The children's favorite activities included reading library books and writing engaging stories. u Brianna was described as being extraordinarily energetic and passionately independent.

Note: Both the examples and non-examples have a good deal of variety in terms of word type (nouns, verbs, adjectives), placement in the sentence, and number of words in the phrases being separated. The content of the sentences is similar, so that students will have to focus on the critical attribute (three or more items in the series) to determine the use of commas.

Rule: When a word ends in a vowel–consonant–final *e* and you want to add a suffix that begins with a vowel, drop the *e*.

Critical attributes (If):
u Word ends in vowel–consonant–final *e*. u Suffix begins with a vowel.

Then: Drop the *e*.

Examples:	Non-examples:
hate + ing = hating	*hate + ful = hateful*
shine + ing = shining	*shoe + ing = shoeing*
time + ed = timed	*time + less = timeless*
debate + able = debatable	*agree + able = agreeable*
require + ed = required	*require + ment = requirement*

Note: In teaching this rule, it is particularly useful to use pairs of examples and non-examples that differ only on one critical attribute. For example, the use of the example *require + ed* and the non-example *require + ment* will force students to consider the importance of the first letter in the suffix. The use of the example *debate + able* and the non-example *agree + able* will force students to notice whether the root word ends in vowel–consonant–final *e*.

APPLICATION 4.4. WORDING OF RULES

SET 1

Feedback: Our choice would be Item 2. Item 1 is actually inaccurate, because the *y* is not changed to an *i* when the word ends in a vowel and *y* or when the suffix is *ing*.

SET 2

Feedback: Our choice would be Item 3. Item 1 is accurate but wordy; Item 2 is brief but inaccurate.

APPLICATION 4.5. DESIGN OF RULE LESSONS

RULE A: SPELLING LESSON

Setting: Fifth-grade classroom	
Step 1: Introduce the rule.	
	We are going to learn a spelling rule about adding suffixes when the word ends in *e*. Listen to the rule.
	When a word ends in a vowel–consonant–final *e* and you want to add a suffix that begins with a vowel, drop the *e*. When a word ends in a vowel–consonant–final *e* and you want to add a suffix that begins with a vowel, drop the . *E*.
Step 2: Illustrate the rule with examples and non-examples.	
Example: *ride* + *ing* =	Here I have the word *ride*, and I want to add the suffix *ing*. *Ride* ends in a vowel– consonant–final *e*. [Teacher points to the letters *i-d-e*.] And the suffix *ing* begins with a vowel. [Teacher points to the letter *i* in *ing*.] So I drop the *e*. [Teacher crosses out the letter *e* in *ride* and writes *riding*.] Everyone, spell *riding*. R-i-d-i-n-g.
Example: *fame* + *ous* =	I have the word *fame*, and I want to add the suffix *ous*. *Fame* ends in a vowel– consonant–final *e*. [Teacher points to the letters *a-m-e*.] And the suffix *ous* begins with a vowel. [Teacher points to the letter *o* in *ous*.] So I drop the *e*. [Teacher crosses out the letter *e* in *fame* and writes *famous*.] Everyone, spell *famous*. F-a-m-o-u-s.
Example: *excite* + *ing* =	I have the word~~————.~~ *Excite*. And I want to add the su~~ffix——. *Ing.*~~ *Excite* ends in a vowel–consonant–final *e*. [Teacher points to the letters *i-t-e*.] And the suffix *ing* begins with a vowel. [Teacher points to the letter *i* in *ing*.] So I drop the *e*. [Teacher crosses out the letter *e* in *excite* and writes *exciting*.] Everyone, spell *exciting*. E-x-c-i-t-i-n-g.
Non-example: *excite* + *ment* =	I have the word~~————.~~ *Excite*. And I want to add the su~~ffix——. *Ment.*~~ *Excite* ends in a vowel–consonant–final *e*. [Teacher points to *i-t-e*.] But the suffix *ment* does not begin with a vowel, so I do not drop the *e*. [Teacher writes *excitement*.] Everyone, spell *excitement*. E-x-c-i-t-e-m-e-n-t.
Step 3: Guide students in analyzing examples and non-examples using the critical attributes.	
Example: *use* + *ing* =	Let's do some together. We have the~~ word————.~~ *Use*. and we want to add the suffix~~ . *ing.*~~ Does *use* end with a vowel–consonant–final *e*? *Yes*. Does *ing* begin with a vowel? *Yes*. Do we drop the *e*? *Yes*. Write the word *using*. [Teacher writes *using* on the overhead.] Check the spelling of *using*. [Pause.] Everyone, spell *using*. U-s-i-n-g.

Non-example: use + ful =	We have the word~~————. Use~~. And we want to add the suffix~~———. Ful.~~ Does *use* end with a vowel–consonant–final *e*? *Yes.* Does the suffix *ful* begin with a vowel? *No.* Do we drop the *e*? *No.* Write *useful*. [Teacher writes *useful* on the overhead.] Check the spelling of *useful*. [Pause.] Everyone, spell *useful. U-s-e-f-u-l.*
Non-example: see + ing =	We have the word~~————. See~~. And we want to add the suffix~~————.~~ *Ing.* Does *see* end with a vowel–consonant–final *e*? *No.* Do we drop the *e*? *No.* Write *seeing*. [Teacher writes *seeing* on the overhead.] Check the spelling of *seeing.* [Pause.] Everyone, spell *seeing. S-e-e-i-n-g.*
Example: race + ist =	[Teacher guides students in the analysis of these words, using the same wording.]
Example: pure + ity =	
Step 4: Check students' understanding using examples and non-examples.	
Example: slice + ing =	Now it is your turn. Here is the ~~word. Slice~~. And we want to add the suffix *ing*. Write *slicing*. [Teacher monitors. When students are done, teacher provides feedback.] Does slice end with a vowel–consonant–final *e*? *Yes.* Does *ing* begin with a vowel? *Yes.* Do we drop the *e*? *Yes.* [Teacher writes *slicing* on the overhead.] Check the spelling of *slicing*. [Pause.] Everyone, spell *slicing. S-l-i-c-i-n-g.*
Non-example: shame + ful =	Here is the word_____. *Shame*. And we want to add the suffix~~———. Ful. Wri~~te *shameful*. [Teacher monitors. When students are done, teacher provides feedback.] Does *shame* end with a vowel–consonant–final *e*? *Yes.* Does *ful* begin with a vowel? *No.* Do we drop the *e*? *No.* [Teacher writes *shameful* on the overhead.] Check the spelling of *shameful*. [Pause.] Everyone, spell *shameful. S-h-a-m-e-f-u-l.*
Example: shame + ed =	[Teacher continues with additional examples and non-examples, providing instructional feedback. Notice that teacher provides feedback after each item rather than after all six, in order to promote accuracy.]
Non-example: free + ing =	
Non-example: shape + less =	
Example: shape + able	

=	

RULE B: PUNCTUATION LESSON

Setting: Sixth-grade writing class

Step 1: Introduce the rule.

We are going to learn when to add commas when we have a series of items in a sentence. Here's the rule: Separate three or more items in a series by adding a comma after each item except the last one.

Step 2: Illustrate the rule with examples and non-examples.

José, Jenny, and Marcus learned about different breeds of dogs.	Read the sentence with me: *José, Jenny, and Marcus learned about different breeds of dogs.* Here we have a series: *José, Jenny, and Marcus.* [Teacher underlines *José, Jenny,* and *Marcus.*] There are three items in the series. We separate the items by putting a comma after each item except the last one. [Teacher points to the commas after *José* and *Jenny.*]
Dachshunds, greyhounds, and beagles are hound breeds.	Read the sentence with me: *Dachshunds, greyhounds, and beagles are hound breeds.* Here we have a series: *dachshunds, greyhounds, and beagles.* [Teacher underlines *dachshunds, greyhounds,* and *beagles.*] There are three items in the series. We separate the items by putting a comma after each item except the last one. [Teacher points to the commas after *dachshunds* and *greyhounds.*]
Pekingese and toy poodles are types of toy dogs.	Read the sentence with me: *Pekingese and toy poodles are types of toy dogs.* Here we have a series: *Pekingese and toy poodles.* [Teacher underlines *Pekingese* and *toy poodles.*] However, there are only two items in the series, so we don't separate them with commas.
The children sat quietly listened to the story and laughed.	Read the sentence with me: *The children sat quietly listened to the story and laughed.* Here we have a series: *sat quietly, listened to the story, and laughed.* [Teacher underlines *sat quietly, listened to the story,* and *laughed.*] There are three items in the series. We separate the items by putting a comma after each item except the last one. [Teacher points to the commas after *sat quietly* and *listened to the story.*]

Step 3: Guide students in analyzing examples and non-examples using the critical attributes.

Megan Joshua and Andrew go to the same school.	Read the sentence with me: *Megan Joshua and Andrew go to the same school.* Is there a series of items? *Yes.* Ones, tell your partners the items in the series. [Teacher calls on a student.] What are the items in the series? *Megan, Joshua, and Andrew.* [Teacher underlines *Megan*, *Joshua*, and *Andrew*.) Are there three or more items in the series? *Yes.* Do we separate the items with commas? *Yes.* Do I put a comma after Megan? *Yes.* Do I put a comma after Joshua? *Yes.* Do I put a comma after Andrew? *No.* [Teacher adds commas as indicated.]
However, they take only English and social studies together.	Read the sentence with me: *However, they take only English and social studies together.* Is there a series of items? *Yes.* Twos, tell your partner the items in the series. [Teacher calls on a student.] What are the items in the series? *English and social studies.* [Teacher underlines *English* and *social studies*.] Are there three or more items in the series? *No.* Do we separate the items with commas? *No.*
Megan's favorite school activities are reading books painting pictures writing stories and completing science experiments.	Read the sentence with me: *Megan's favorite school activities are reading books painting pictures writing stories and completing science experiments.* Is there a series of items? *Yes.* Ones, tell your partners the items in the series. [Teacher calls on a student.] What are the items in the series? *Reading books, painting pictures, writing stories, and completing science experiments.* [Teacher underlines *reading books, painting pictures, writing stories,* and *completing science experiments*.] Are there three or more items in the series? *Yes.* Do we separate the items with commas? *Yes.* Do I put a comma after books? *Yes.* Do I put a comma after pictures? *Yes.* After stories? *Yes.* After experiments? *No.* [Teacher adds commas as indicated.]

Step 4: Check students' understanding using examples and non-examples.

Joshua enjoys investigating historical events and solving math problems.	Read the sentence with me: *Joshua enjoys investigating historical events and solving math problems.* Now underline the items in the series, and add commas if necessary. [Teacher monitors.] Ones, explain your answer to your partner. Twos, if you disagree, explain your answer. [Teacher monitors and then calls on a student.] *There is a series of two items: investigating historical events and solving math problems.* *There are only two items in the series, so no commas are needed.*

| Each student must have many school supplies including a notebook notebook paper two pencils two pens a yearly calendar a ruler and one art tablet. | Read the sentence with me: *Each student must have many school supplies including a notebook notebook paper two pencils two pens a yearly calendar a ruler and one art tablet.* Now underline the items in the series, and add commas if necessary. [Teacher monitors.] Twos, explain your answer to your partner. Ones, if you disagree, explain your answer. [Teacher monitors and calls on a student.] *There is a series of seven items: a notebook, notebook paper, two pencils, two pens, a yearly calendar, a ruler, and one art tablet. I put a comma after each item except after "tablet."* |

Note. The Rule B lesson is adapted from Archer, Gleason, and Isaacson (2008). Copyright 2008 by Sopris West Educational Services. Adapted by permission.

CHAPTER 5

APPLICATION 5.2. ANALYSES OF CLASSROOM ARRANGEMENTS

SPECIAL EDUCATION CLASSROOM—EXAMPLE

Desirable qualities u Specific areas have been designated for whole-class instruction, small-group

instruction, computer use, and listening to CDs and recorded books.

u **Whole-group instructional area**

ıThe teacher has a table for projector and instructional materials. Other instructional materials are nearby, allowing easy retrieval. When teaching in the front of the room, the teacher can see all areas of the classroom and can move around and monitor students.

ıWhen students are at their desks during whole-group instruction, they are facing the teacher and can easily share answers with a partner. Students can keep their supplies in their desks or can retrieve them with ease from the bookcase.

u **Small-group instructional area**

ıInstructional areas are designated for the teacher and

paraeducator. In both areas, the instructors have easy access to instructional materials and can write on a whiteboard.

Both the teacher and paraeducator are facing out into the classroom, so that they can monitor any students who are working independently. All parts of the room are visible from the small-group instructional areas.

Students are grouped around kidney-shaped tables in close proximity to the teacher or paraeducator.

u General climate

The teacher has posted information that will guide students' behavior (rules poster), support their academic endeavors (strategy posters, word walls, rubrics), facilitate classroom routines (assignment in-box, late box), and honor students' academic efforts (displays of student work).

The teacher's desk is at the back of the room, signaling that it will not be the teacher's main venue during instruction, but rather will be used before and after class.

SPECIAL EDUCATION CLASSROOM—NON-EXAMPLE

Suggestions u Whole-group

instructional area

The overhead projector is on a cart that does not have adequate room for necessary instructional materials, such as manuals, pens, and transparencies. Placing all instructional materials on a table would better support the teacher.

Students are sitting in clusters, with half of the children facing away from the teacher. Students would be more likely to stay on task if they were facing the teacher and sitting in desks.

The teacher's desk is at the front of the room, leading the

teacher to spend more time at his or her desk than if it were placed at the back of the room.

When standing in the front of the room, the teacher will have difficulty monitoring students working with the paraeducator or reading in the freereading area.

There is no indication that the teacher's instructional materials are organized in a nearby location.

u **Small-group instructional areas**

Although having small-group instructional areas designated for the teacher and the paraeducator is desirable, having the areas so close together may be distracting.

Using tables that promote close proximity of the teacher to the students is great. However, the paraeducator should be on the other side of the table to allow monitoring of the rest of the room, and the teacher should not have a major barrier (the free-standing bookcase) that curtails classroom visibility and monitoring.

u **General climate**

Some potential challenges are lurking in the computer area, because it appears that the students are facing each other and that the organization of their computer stations doesn't allow visual monitoring by the teacher.

Although the teacher has posted the rules and student work, and has added nature pictures to make the classroom more attractive, no materials that would support academic instruction (e.g., strategy posters, rubrics) are posted.

PRIMARY CLASSROOM—EXAMPLE

Desirable qualities u Specific areas have been designated for large-group instruction, small-group

instruction, rug activities, and computer use.

u **Rug activities**

This area appears to be used at the beginning of the day for calendar activities and for reading books to students. The teacher has wisely posted the vocabulary words from the read-aloud books that have been explicitly taught, to allow quick review.

This area also serves as a free-reading area, with books readily available to the students.

If the teacher is teaching in this area, all other areas of the room are visible.

u **Whole-group instructional area**

The teacher can teach the entire group, using either the whiteboard or the overhead projector.

The projector and other instructional materials are placed on a table in the front of the room. The teacher can access instructional materials from the nearby bookcase.

Although the students' desks are grouped together, they are not in clusters, and all of the students are facing the teacher.

When arranging the desks, the teacher has created an aisle to make monitoring easier.

u **Small-group instructional area**

The instructional table and the teacher's chair are situated so that the teacher can easily monitor all areas of the room while working with a small group.

The teacher has a whiteboard to write on during the lesson.

Students are close to the teacher and won't be distracted by children at their desks.

u Other desirable characteristics

Computer stations are visible from both the front of the room and the small-group table.

The students' storage cabinet is appropriately located next to the door, allowing easy storage of coats and boots.

The teacher's desk is at the back of the room, with file cabinets for ease of planning before and after school.

The things posted on the bulletin boards add to the educational environment by promoting desired behavior (rules poster), academic performance (word walls, strategy posters), and a community of learners (student work and pictures).

PRIMARY CLASSROOM—NON-EXAMPLE

Suggestions u Whole-group instructional area

The teacher has placed the overhead projector on a table and has the option of using the overhead or the whiteboard. However, this is where the kudos end.

The students are facing each other in clusters, with half of the class facing away from the teacher—two factors that will surely reduce attention and on-task behavior.

During whole-group instruction, monitoring will be stifled by the placement of the teacher's desk and the table with student materials.

When teaching in front of the room, the teacher will not be able to observe the students seated on the rugs in the front or back of the room.

u Small-group instructional area

Unfortunately, the teacher cannot observe all areas of the

room . . . but the students can. This error, coupled with those previously mentioned, will definitely lead to misbehavior among the troops.

Although the teacher has a whiteboard in the small-group area, it cannot be used, given the current furniture arrangement.

There is no indication of storage of instructional materials near the teacher.

u **Other suggestions**

The teacher has posted a number of things that are very desirable: children's art, word walls, and class calendar. However, it would be helpful to add a rules poster and student work (not just artwork).

It is good that the student storage area is near the door, but the project table makes lining up and general traffic flow difficult.

SECONDARY LANGUAGE ARTS CLASSROOM—EXAMPLE

Desirable qualities u The class set of books, the assignment in-box, and the late box are all located near the door, so that students can get organized before class.

u Student desks are organized in rows but also in pairs, to allow partner work. u The students are all facing the front of the room.

u Students have been given a seating chart that indicates their seats and corresponding numbers. Each student has also been assigned a partner (the student sitting at the next desk) and a larger "huddle group" that occasionally meets in the corners of the room for discussions.

u The teacher has organized all technology on a table at the front of the room, allowing the teacher to face the students during instruction. u Instructional materials are nearby for easy retrieval.

u The teacher can easily see all areas of the room, including students at the listening and computer stations.

u There are no barriers that would reduce the teacher's ability to move around and monitor.

u Materials have been posted that support appropriate behavior (rules), completion of assignments (class calendars, information on major projects, rubrics), instruction (writing process poster, word wall, map of England), and on-task behavior ("Time is passing—are you?"). The teacher has also displayed student work and made examples of former students' projects available.

u The teacher has established an "office" (desk, file cabinet, storage cabinet) at the back of the room, separate from the instructional area. This physical arrangement signifies that during class time the teacher is *not* at the desk, but rather interacting with students.

SECONDARY LANGUAGE ARTS CLASSROOM—NON-EXAMPLE

Suggestions u First, the teacher's desk should be moved to the back of the room, creating a planning area for before and after school. Its current location makes it a barrier to students entering and leaving the classroom. Also, the teacher is likely to spend too much instructional time sitting at the desk.

u The teacher has placed all of the instructional technology on a table. However, the teacher has effectively created a barrier between the teacher and the students with the placement of the tables, file cabinet, and teacher's desk at the front of the room. The teacher will have to negotiate around this barrier to monitor students as they work independently or respond during a lesson.

u Placing students in rows works well for independent work, but during instruction, the teacher may wish to have students move next to their partners for sharing. There is no indication that seats have been assigned.

u The teacher's instructional materials are at the back of the room and thus are not accessible during teaching. Similarly, the students' supplies are inaccessible, requiring that students leap tall file cabinets or desks to reach their supplies.

u The teacher has put up a number of informative and decorative items concerning England. However, the room lacks a rules poster, displays of student work, word walls, reference materials, rubrics, posters with learning strategies, and the like.

CHAPTER 6

APPLICATION 6.1. ANALYSES OF ACTIVE PARTICIPATION LESSONS

REFLECTIONS ON NON-EXAMPLE LESSON

Concerns about the non-example lesson:

u The opportunities to respond are very limited. Certainly this lesson does not represent interactive instruction.

u No unison responses are used, so very few children participate in the lesson.

u The only responses involve calling on volunteers, even though the questions request information that has been introduced to all students. Calling on volunteers should be limited to questions requiring answers based solely on students' personal background knowledge or experiences.

u The individual turns are not distributed across class members. As often happens, one child, Jason, is favored.

REFLECTIONS ON EXAMPLE LESSON

Improvements in the lesson:

u Many responses are requested during the lesson.

u The majority of responses involve *all* students, including choral responses (when the desired answer is short and the same), written responses (underlining two words in a compound word), and partner responses (explaining examples to partners).

u Before calling on individual students, the teacher has students share with their partners—a procedure that is likely to increase students' accuracy and confidence.

u Students are given *lots* of practice.

u When introducing the strategy for determining the meaning of the compound word, the teacher uses an instructional routine for each example, resulting in a perky pace.

CHAPTER 7

APPLICATION 7.1. EXAMPLE AND NON-EXAMPLE CORRECTIONS

Correction procedure	Analysis
Item D. Non-example [Text students are reading: Bry and Grace, the best artists in fifth grade, raced to Ms. Pateros's room. Ms. Pateros was to announce the winner of the "Rural Youth Painting Contest." While most of the students had only spent a few minutes on their entries, the girls had worked for weeks on their watercolor paintings of the rolling fields of Kansas, being careful to meet all the requirements for the contest and to create a painting full of detail and beauty. Each was sure that *she* was the winner. [After students read this passage, teacher asks this question.] Why did both Bry and Grace believe that they had won the contest? [Teacher provides thinking time.] Stephen?	**The correction is:** ⊔ a. Provided. ⊔ b. Immediate. c. The appropriate type of correction (see Figure 7.1). d. Specific and informative ⊔ e. Focused on the correct (vs. incorrect) response. ⊔ f. Delivered with appropriate tone. ___ g. Ended with students' giving the correct response. **Comments:** Although the teacher does give immediate feedback to Stephen that focuses on the correct response, it would be more appropriate to guide Stephen to the correct answer so that he can see how literal knowledge can support responding to a higher-order

Because they entered paintings in the contest. No, Stephen, they both thought they were winners because they were the best artists in fifth grade, had put a good deal of time into the paintings, and had worked to ensure that their paintings were detailed and beautiful and exactly what the contest wanted.	question. Also, Stephen makes no response after feedback is provided.

Correction procedure	Analysis
Item D. Example [After students read this passage, teacher asks this question.] Why did both Bry and Grace believe that they had won the contest? [Teacher provides thinking time.] Stephen? *Because they entered paintings in the contest.* **Our correction:** Stephen, let's review what we've learned about Bry and Grace that can help answer this question. Were Bry and Grace talented or poor artists? *Talented.* What does the author tell us about their watercolor paintings? *That they worked on them for weeks . . . and they put a lot of detail in the paintings and made them beautiful . . . Also, they tried to do everything the contest wanted.* Great. Now why do you think each girl believed that she was the one to win? *Well, both of them were good artists, and they really worked on making their paintings detailed and beautiful, spending a lot more time than the other*	**The correction is:** ⊔⊥ a. Provided. ⊔⊥ b. Immediate. ⊔⊥ c. The appropriate type of correction (see Figure 7.1). ⊔⊥ d. Specific and informative. ⊔⊥ e. Focused on the correct (vs. incorrect) response. ⊔⊥ f. Delivered with appropriate tone. ⊔⊥ g. Ended with students' giving the correct response. **Comments:** Here the teacher guides Stephen to an appropriate answer to the higher-order question by asking lower-order, literal questions. The teacher is demonstrating that answering higher-order questions requires putting together bits of literal information. In the end, Stephen gives the correct response.

kids. Also, they were careful that their paintings met all of the contest requirements.

Item E. Non-example [Definitions on the board:] Longitude Imaginary lines Divide earth east and west Meet at poles Latitude Imaginary lines Divide earth north and south Never meet Let's review longitude and latitude. Is the equator an example of longitude or latitude? Discuss this with your partner. [Pause.] Amy, so which is it, longitude or latitude? *Longitude.* Amy . . . don't you remember? We talked about this yesterday. The equator is an example of latitude.	**The correction is:** ⊔ a. Provided. ⊔ b. Immediate. <u>c.</u> The appropriate type of correction (see Figure 7.1). <u>d.</u> Specific and informative. ⊔ e. Focused on the correct (vs. incorrect) response. <u>f.</u> Delivered with appropriate tone. <u>g.</u> Ended with students' giving the correct response. **Comments:** This correction has no instructional value. Not only is the tone negative, but the teacher provides no information to assist Amy in understanding these concepts. Asking Amy whether she remembers what was discussed on the previous day is not a useful prompt, as it contains no helpful information.

Correction procedure	**Analysis**

Item E. Example	The correction is:
Let's review longitude and latitude. Is the equator an example of longitude or latitude? Discuss this with your partner. [Pause.] Amy, longitude or latitude? *Longitude.*	⊔_a. Provided. ⊔_b. Immediate. ⊔_c. The appropriate type of correction (see Figure 7.1).
Our correction: Class, let's examine this question together. [Teacher holds up a globe.] This line represents the equator. What does it represent? *The equator.* We know, of course, that the equator is an imaginary line on the earth, not a real line. Notice that the equator divides the earth north and south. [Teacher points north of the equator and then south.] Also, does the equator meet at the poles? *No.* So if the imaginary line divides the earth north and south and doesn't meet at the poles, is it latitude or longitude? [Pause. Teacher directs students' attention to the definitions.] Everyone? *Latitude.* Ones, explain to your partner why the imaginary line that represents the equator is an example of latitude. [Teacher circulates and listens to explanations. Later in the lesson, teacher poses this question again.]	⊔_d. Specific and informative. ⊔_e. Focused on the correct (vs. incorrect) response. ⊔_f. Delivered with appropriate tone. ⊔_g. Ended with students' giving the correct response. **Comments:** Often, one student's making an error indicates that many members of the class are unsure of the information. Thus it is often appropriate to involve all of the students in the correction procedure, to strengthen everyone's learning. In this correction procedure, the teacher provides specific information about latitude and focuses on the correct response. In addition, the correction ends with all students' giving the correct response. Later in the lesson, the teacher checks their understanding of the concept again.

Item F. Non-example	The correction is:
Item F. Non-example The side of each square represents 1 foot. Determine the perimeter of this figure. [Pause.] Compare your answer with that of your partners. [Pause.] Johnathan, what is your answer? *20 square feet.* Johnathan, that would be the area of the figure. The area is the number of square units covered in a figure. The perimeter, on the other hand, will be 22 feet. So, Johnathan, what is the perimeter? *22 feet.*	**The correction is:** ⎵⎵_a. Provided. ⎵⎵_b. Immediate. <u>c.</u> The appropriate type of correction (see Figure 7.1). <u>d.</u> Specific and informative. <u>e.</u> Focused on the correct (vs. incorrect) response. ⎵⎵f. Delivered with appropriate tone. ⎵⎵g. Ended with students' giving the correct response. **Comments:** Although the tone of the correction is respectful, the teacher focuses on the incorrect response and gives very little information to help Johnathan be more successful in the future in determining perimeters or distinguishing between measurements of area and perimeter.
Correction procedure	**Analysis**
Item F. Example The side of each square represents 1 foot. Determine the perimeter of this figure. [Pause.] Compare your answer with that of your partners. [Pause.] Johnathan, what was your answer? *20 square feet.* **Our correction:** The perimeter is the measurement of the distance around a figure or object. Everyone, the measurement of distance around a figure or object is the ? *Perimeter.* In this case, we can count the number of feet around the figure. Everyone, help me out.	**The correction is:** ⎵⎵_a. Provided. ⎵⎵_b. Immediate. ⎵⎵_c. The appropriate type of correction (see Figure 7.1). ⎵⎵_d. Specific and informative. ⎵⎵_e. Focused on the correct (vs. incorrect) response. ⎵⎵f. Delivered with appropriate tone. ⎵⎵g. Ended with students' giving the correct response. **Comments:** This correction procedure involves all of the students, clarifying the concept of perimeter and guiding students to a correct answer. This correction procedure will assist the class in determining perimeters in the future. In addition, the teacher checks understanding with further examples.

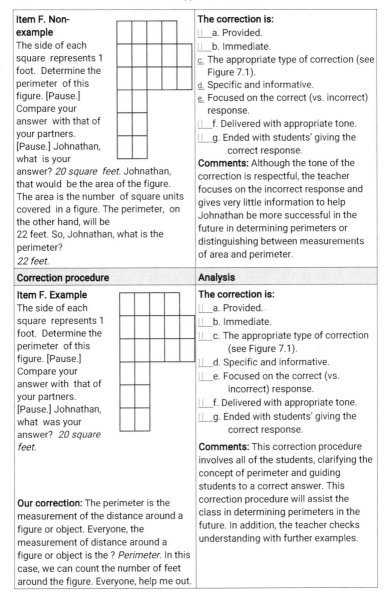

I will mark each foot that we count. [Teacher and students count out loud the number of feet in length around the figure.] So, everyone, what is the perimeter? *22 feet.* [Teacher then presents additional figures and asks students to determine the area or perimeter.]	

APPLICATION 7.2. EXAMPLES AND NON-EXAMPLES OF PRAISE

Praise statement	Analysis
Item C. Non-example This week we have been studying the rule about *i* before *e* except after *c.* I am going to dictate a word. Write it on your slate. The first word is *chief.* Write it. Show me. [All students get the word correct.] Yeah . . . you did it. You all got it right. You remembered to put the *i* before the *e* when spelling the word *chief.* So many people don't know this rule, but you weren't fooled. I just got a letter from my son . . . you know, the one at college . . . and he spelled *receive r-e-c -i-e-v-e.* But not my third-period class. You would never make that error. You are so smart. Let's try another word . . .	Praise is: ___a. Contingent (If–Then). || b. Specific. c. Provided for noteworthy performance. d. Focused on achievement and effort rather than personality attributes. e. Comparing students to themselves rather than to others. f. Positive, credible, and genuine. g. Unobtrusive. **Comments:** The major problem with this praise is that it is simply too much, too early, too overdone—and very disruptive to the flow of the lesson. Although the teacher gives specific praise, the teacher also includes a comparison with another person and a focus on a personal attribute. At this rate, the teacher will not finish the word dictation this period. The teacher needs

to read the next section of this chapter, on the brisk pacing.

Praise statement	Analysis
Item C. Example This week we have been studying the rule about *i* before *e* except after *c*. I am going to dictate a word. Write it on your slate. The first word is *chief*. Write it. Show me. [All students get the word correct. Teacher continues with the words *niece, priest, receive, deceive, relief,* and *ceiling,* giving brief affirmations such as "Great," "Correct," "Perfect," or a smile. Of the 24 students in the class, only 2 make any errors . . . one apiece.] **Our praise statement:** Class, you really studied these words. You have consistently followed the rule of *i* before *e* except after . . . Everyone? *C*. Terrific. Today we are going to learn the one other time when *i* is not placed before the *e* . . . another exception.	Praise is: ⊔ a. Contingent (If–Then). ⊔ b. Specific. ⊔ c. Provided for noteworthy performance. ⊔ d. Focused on achievement and effort rather than personality attributes. ⊔ e. Comparing students to themselves rather than to others. ⊔ f. Positive, credible, and genuine. ⊔ g. Unobtrusive. **Comments:** In this scenario, the teacher gives brief acknowledgments during the dictation, allowing the lesson to flow. At the end of the exercise, the teacher praises students in a manner that should feel genuine and sincere to the students. It occurs after all of the words have been dictated and spelled correctly (noteworthy performance), and it honors their effort and achievement. This praise statement does not interrupt the flow of the lesson, but is used as a natural transition into the next activity.

Item D. Non-Example	Praise is:
[Written on the board: 5.42, 5.46, 5.15, 5.5, 5.51.] We have been studying ascending and descending order. Please write the numbers on the board in descending order vertically . . . down the page. [Teacher moves around the room and examines students' papers. Then teacher writes the numbers in descending order on the board.] Please check your numbers with mine. [Pause.] Raise your hand if yours is the same as mine. [All the students raise their hands.] Great job. You are *so* brilliant.	⊔__a. Contingent (If–Then). ___b. Specific. ⊔__c. Provided for noteworthy performance. <u>d.</u> Focused on achievement and effort rather than personality attributes. <u>e.</u> Comparing students to themselves rather than to others. ⊔__f. Positive, credible, and genuine. ⊔__g. Unobtrusive. **Comments:** The teacher provides feedback on the task by showing students the correct answer on the board, a very efficient practice. Although the praise is positive, it focuses on personal attributes (intelligence) rather than effort, carefulness, or learning—qualities that students can manipulate.
Praise statement	**Analysis**
Item D. Example [Written on the board: 5.42, 5.46, 5.15, 5.5, 5.51.] We have been studying ascending and descending order. Please write the numbers on the board in descending order vertically . . . down the page. [Teacher moves around the room and examines students' papers. Then teacher writes the numbers in descending order on the board.] Please check your numbers with mine. [Pause.] Raise your hand if yours is the same as mine. [All students raise their hands.] **Our praise statement:** As I monitored, I noticed that you carefully lined up the whole numbers, the decimals, the tenths, and the hundredths. Because of your care, you all got this item correct. Nice work.	Praise is: ⊔__a. Contingent (If–Then). ⊔__b. Specific. ⊔__c. Provided for noteworthy performance. ⊔__d. Focused on achievement and effort rather than personality attributes. ⊔__e. Comparing students to themselves rather than to others. ⊔__f. Positive, credible, and genuine. ⊔__g. Unobtrusive. **Comments:** Here the teacher gives specific praise that will strengthen students' future performance. The praise is focused on achievement and effort, is positive, and fits easily into the flow of the lesson.

Note: Feedback on Application 7.3 is provided in Chapter 7.

CHAPTER 8

APPLICATION 8.1. DESIGNING INITIAL, DISTRIBUTED, AND CUMULATIVE PRACTICE

Example 1: Mrs. Bishop's reading class **Population:** First-grade students
Teacher's plan: Mrs. Bishop will need to provide small-group instruction to the five students. Two 15-minute instructional periods could be provided to increase the distribution of practice. These sessions should focus on the essential elements that will increase the reading proficiency of the students: (1) daily review of sounds, (2) daily review of irregular words, (3) practice in sounding out words with the letter–sound associations being taught, and (4) reading of decodable passages. Frequent (weekly) assessment of fluency on sounds, words, and pages should be obtained to allow adjusting of the program.
Example 2: Ms. Carley's math class **Population:** Fourth-grade students
Teacher's plan: Ms. Carley decides to develop 10 additional items that parallel the items provided in the program. These items will be used for modeling, prompted and unprompted practice, and initial skill practice.

APPLICATION 8.2. SELECTING PRACTICE ACTIVITIES

SITUATION 1

Assignment A.   **Ranking:** 1 (best choice) Assignment A requires that the students carefully consider the meaning of each word, which is the goal of the lesson. Other advantages of this assignment: (1) The directions are clear and concise, (2) the reading level of the items is appropriate, and (3) it can be easily corrected in class or quickly by the teacher. Although production items are generally desirable, it is also important to consider grading time. In this case, the teacher will receive good feedback on the students' understanding of the words, given that they must respond in a number of ways.

Assignment B.   **Ranking:** 2 (middle choice) The major challenge with Assignment B is that it is a simple recognition task, not requiring deep thoughtfulness. By the process of elimination, students might correctly match up words and definitions. Also, the directions are wordy, with unnecessary explanations.

Assignment C. **Ranking:** 3 (worst choice)

The actual task in Assignment C is actually our favorite, as it is a production task that requires students to carefully consider the meaning of the words. However, the reading level of the items is very high, and the nontargeted vocabulary is too difficult. If the students are learning *fragile, gratitude,* and *cowered,* they will not know *amphora, benevolence, cordiality,* and *apprehension.* This assignment cannot be done independently. Even if the teacher does the assignment with students, this will be of little benefit, as the students' attention will be directed at the nontargeted vocabulary rather than at the targeted words.

SITUATION 2

Assignment A. **Ranking:** 1 (best choice)

Did you have difficulty deciding on the best assignment? It was our intention to make this more challenging, and also to communicate that often you have to select from slightly imperfect assignments. In Situation 2, there are challenges with all three assignments, but we believe that Assignment A is the best choice. Students must produce words representing the two spelling rules without any scaffolding, and they receive immediate feedback from their partners. The students probably also appreciate an opportunity to work with a partner as a break from paper–pencil tasks. This assignment would be greatly improved with the addition of non-examples (e.g., words in which the consonant is not doubled or the final *e* is not dropped)—a modification that could be easily made.

Assignment B. **Ranking:** 2 (middle choice)

Perhaps you selected this assignment as it involves a production task, though with scaffolding (the words and endings are provided). The strength of this assignment is the use of examples and nonexamples, including minimally different pairs (e.g., *hope + ing, hope + less*) that force the students to consider the rules being reviewed. Unfortunately, the directions are unnecessarily long, due to the embedded reteaching of the rule.

Assignment C. **Ranking:** 3 (worst choice)

Perhaps you ranked this assignment 1, given that the directions are clear and concise, and the task does require careful consideration of the spelling rules. The major challenge is that the task doesn't match the objective, as it is a proofreading rather than a spelling task. Students may be able to select the correctly spelled word, but may be unable to produce the word.

APPLICATION 8.3. CASE STUDY: INDIVIDUALIZING SAMUEL'S ASSIGNMENTS

In this application, we have asked whether you would agree to assign Samuel fewer math problems for his homework, given his difficulties (i.e., dysfluency in basic math skills and facts, motor problems, processing speed and capacity) that resulted in his taking 2 hours to complete an assignment that probably took most of his peers 30 minutes to complete. As in many instructional decisions, there are various issues to consider.

One of the first issues is that of fairness: If most students have to do the work, it is not fair that some students don't have to. One response to the fairness issue is brought up in the chapter text: Being fair is not always synonymous with treating everyone the same. With regard to this scenario, you could view the "work" in terms of time spent versus the number of problems completed. For example, is it "fair" that Samuel has to works two or three times longer to complete the same number of problems?

Another issue to consider is pedagogical in nature. That is, if Samuel's teacher reduces the number of problems that he must complete, he will lose some opportunity to practice long division—and, given his problems in this area, he could use as much practice as possible! Although this may be a legitimate concern in some situations, one variable to consider is how much practice on a particular skill is sufficient. In Samuel's case, it could be argued that 25 problems (especially long division) are not necessary and can be reduced if sufficient distributed practice is provided. It is likely that 10 problems will be sufficient for one homework assignment if Samuel has multiple opportunities to practice the skill over an extended period of time (as all students should).

A final issue relates to the impact on the family of a child's taking 2–3 hours per night to do homework. We note later in Chapter 8 that although homework is an effective teaching tool, there are points of diminishing academic returns associated with the amount of time spent doing homework. Add the limited benefit of doing more than an hour or so of homework per night (depending on grade level) to the impact of Samuel's spending the majority of evenings doing homework on the quality of family interactions, and a case can be made for reducing the amount of homework given to him.

Of course, the problem of taking 2 hours to complete this type of homework assignment can be ameliorated to some extent by providing Samuel (and all students?) with a copy of the problems that he can write directly on. This eliminates the laborious process of copying them and allows him to spend his time solving the problems—which is the purpose of the assignment to begin with!

References

Adams, G., & Brown, S. (2007). *Six-minute solution.* Longmont, CO: Sopris West.

Adams, G. L., & Engelmann, S. (1996). *Research on direct instruction: 25 years beyond DISTAR.* Seattle, WA: Educational Achievement Systems.

Andersen, M., Nelson, L. R., Fox, R. G., & Gruber, S. E. (1988). Integrating cooperative learning and structured learning: Effective approaches to teaching social skills. *Focus on Exceptional Children, 20*(9), 1–8.

Anderson, L. W. (1976). An empirical investigation of individual differences in time to learn. *Journal of Educational Psychology, 68*(2), 226–233.

Anderson, L. W., & Walberg, H. J. (Eds.). (1994). *Timepiece: Extending and enhancing learning time.* Reston, VA: National Association of Secondary School Principals.

Archer, A., L., Gleason, M. M., & Isaacson, S. L. (2008). *REWARDS writing: Sentence refinement.* Longmont, CO: Sopris West.

Archer, A. L., Gleason, M. M., & Vachon, V. (2005). *REWARDS Plus: Reading strategies applied to social studies passages.* Longmont, CO: Sopris West.

Archer, A. L., Isaacson, S., Adams, A., Ellis, E. S., Morehead, M. K., & Schiller, E. P. (1987). *Academy for Effective Instruction: Working with mildly handicapped students* [Training notebook and video]. Reston, VA:
Council for Exceptional Children.

Armendariz, F. R. (2005). Improving participation during choral responding. *Dissertation Abstracts International, 66*(09), 5073B. (UMI No. 3190130) (Available online at *gradworks.umi. com/31/90/3190130.html*)

Armendariz, F. R., & Umbreit, J. (1999). Using active responding to reduce disruptive behavior in a general education classroom. *Journal of Positive Behavior Interventions, 1*(3), 152–158.

Bahrick, H. P., & Phelps, E. (1987). Retention of Spanish vocabulary over 8 years. *Journal of Experimental Psychology: Learning, Memory, and Cognition, 13*(2), 344–349.

Baker, S. K., Simmons, D. C., & Kame'enui, E. J. (1995). Vocabulary acquisition: Synthesis of the research. Retrieved December 26, 2008, from *idea.uoregon.edu/~ncite/documents/te chrep/ tech13.html*

Barbetta, P. M., & Heward, W. L. (1993). Effects of active student response during error correction on the acquisition and maintenance of geography facts by elementary students with learning disabilities. *Journal of Behavioral Education, 3*(3), 217–233.

Beck, I. L., McKeown, M. G., & Kucan, L. (2002). *Bringing words to life: Robust vocabulary instruction.* New York: . Press.

Beck, I. L., Perfetti, C. A., & McKeown, M. G. (1982). Effects of long-term vocabulary instruction on lexical access and reading comprehension. *Journal of Educational Psychology, 74*(4), 506–521.

Beck, R., & Clement, R. (1991). The Great Falls Precision Teaching Project: An historical examination. *Journal of Precision Teaching, 8*(2), 8–12.

Berliner, D. C. (1980). Using research on teaching for the improvement of classroom practice. *Theory into Practice, 19*(4), 302–308.

Biemiller, A. (2001, Spring). Teaching vocabulary: Early, direct, and sequential. *American Educator,* pp. 24–28, 47.

279

Binder, C. (1996). Behavioral fluency: Evolution of a new paradigm. *The Behavior Analyst, 19*(2), 163–197.

Bloom, B. (1999). *Wolf.* New York: Orchard Books.

Bloom, B. S. (1956). *Taxonomy of educational objectives: The classification of educational goals. Handbook I: The cognitive domain.* New York: McKay.

Bloom, B. S. (1986). Automaticity: "The hands and feet of genius." *Educational Leadership, 43*(5), 70–77.

Brophy, J. (1981). Teacher praise: A functional analysis. *Review of Educational Research, 51,* 5–32.

Brophy, J. E. (1986). Teacher influences on student achievement. *American Psychologist, 41*(10), 1069–1077.

Brophy, J. E., & Evertson, C. (1976). *Learning from teaching: A developmental perspective.* Boston: Allyn & Bacon.

Brophy, J. E., & Good, T. L. (1986). Teacher behavior and student achievement. In M. C. Wittrock (Ed.), *Handbook of research on teaching* (3rd ed., pp. 328–377). New York: Macmillan.

Bryan, T., Burstein, K., & Bryan, J. (2001). Students with learning disabilities: Homework problems and promising practices. *Educational Psychologist, 36*(3), 167–180.

Bryan, T., Nelson, C., & Mathur, S. (1995). Homework: A survey of primary students in regular, resource, and self-contained special education classrooms. *Learning Disabilities Research and Practice, 10*(2), 85–90.

Cameron, J., Banko, K. M., & Pierce, W. D. (2001). Pervasive negative effects of rewards on intrinsic motivation: The myth continues. *The Behavior Analyst, 24,* 1–44.

Cameron, J., & Pierce, W. D. (1994). Reinforcement, reward and intrinsic motivation: A metaanalysis. *Review of Educational Research, 64,* 363–423.

Carle, E. (1996). *The grouchy ladybug* (2nd ed.). New York: HarperCollins.

Carlo, M. S., August, D., McLaughlin, B., Snow, C. E., Dressler, C., Lippman, D. N., et al. (2004). Closing the gap: Addressing the vocabulary needs of English-language learners in bilingual and mainstream classrooms. *Reading Research Quarterly, 39*(2), 188–215.

Carlson, N. S. (1986). *The family under the bridge.* New York: Scholastic. (Original work published 1958)

Carnine, D. W. (1976). Effects of two teacherpresentation rates on off-task behavior, answering correctly, and participation. *Journal of Applied Behavior Analysis, 9*(2), 199–206.

Carnine, D. W., Silbert, J., Kame'enui, E. J., & Tarver, S. G. (2009). *Direct instruction reading* (5th ed.). Upper Saddle River, NJ: Pearson.

Cavanaugh, R. A., Heward, W. L., & Donelson, F. (1996). Effects of response cards during lesson closure on the academic performance of second-ary students in an earth science course. *Journal of Applied Behavior Analysis, 29*(3), 403–406.

Chard, D. J., Vaughn, S., & Tyler, B. (2002). A synthesis of research on effective interventions for building reading fluency with elementary students with learning disabilities. *Journal of Learning Disabilities, 35*(5), 386–406.

Christenson, S. L., Ysseldyke, J. E., &

Thurlow, M. L. (1989). Critical instructional factors for students with mild handicaps: An integrative review. *Remedial and Special Education, 10*(5), 21–31.

Christle, C. A., & Schuster, J. W. (2003). The effects of using response cards on student participation, academic achievement, and on-task behavior during whole-class, math instruction. *Journal of Behavioral Education, 12*(3), 147–165.

Collins COBUILD student's dictionary plus grammar (3rd ed.). (2005). Boston: Heinle ELT.

Colvin, G., & Sugai, G. (1988). Proactive strategies for managing social behavior problems: An instructional approach. *Education and Treatment of Children, 11*(4), 341–348.

Colvin, G., Sugai, G., & Patching, B. (1993). Precorrection: An instructional approach for managing predictable problem behaviors. *Intervention in School and Clinic, 28*(3), 143–150.

Cooper, H. (1989). Synthesis of research on homework. *Educational Leadership, 47*(3), 85–91.

Cooper, H., Lindsay, J. J., Nye, B., & Greathouse, S. (1998). Relationships among attitudes about homework, amount of homework assigned and completed, and students achievement. *Journal of Educational Psychology, 90*(1), 70–83.

Cooper, H., & Nye, B. (1994). Homework for students with learning disabilities. *Journal of Learning Disabilities, 27*(8), 470–479.

Cooper, H., & Valentine, J. C. (2001). Using research to answer practical questions about homework. *Educational Psychologist, 36*(3), 143–153.

Corpus, J. H., Love, K. E., & Ogle, C. M. (2005, April). *Social-comparison praise undermines intrinsic motivation when children later doubt their ability.* Poster presented at the biennial meeting of the Society for Research in Child Development, Atlanta, GA.

Cotton, K. (2001). Classroom questioning. *Northwest Regional Educational Laboratory.* Retrieved December 9, 2008, from *www.nwrel.org/scpd/ sirs/3/cu5.html*

Council for Exceptional Children. (1987). *Academy for Effective Instruction: Working with mildly handicapped students.* Reston, VA: Author.

Coxhead, A. (2000). A new academic word list. *TESOL Quarterly, 34*(2), 213–238.

Crissman, J. K. (2006). *The design and utilization of effective worked examples: A meta-analysis.* Unpublished doctoral dissertation, University of Nebraska.

Cummings, C. B. (2000). *Winning strategies for classroom management.* Alexandria, VA: Association for Supervision and Curriculum Development.

Curtis, M. E., & Longo, A. M. (1997). *FAME: The Boys Town reading curriculum.* Boys Town, NE: Father Flanagan's Boys' Home.

Dempster, F. N. (1991). Synthesis of research on reviews and tests. *Educational Leadership, 48*(7), 71–76.

Dempster, F. N., & Farris, R. (1990). The spacing effect: Research and practice. *Journal of Research and Development in Education, 23*(2), 97–101.

Diamond, L., & Gutlohn, L. (2006). *Vocabulary handbook.* Berkeley, CA: Consortium on Reading Excellence.

Donovan, J. J., & Radosevich, D. J. (1999). A metaanalytic review of the distribution of practice effect: Now you see it, now you don't. *Journal of Applied Psychology, 84*(5), 795–805.

Dweck, C. S. (2008). *Mindset: The new psychology of success.* New York: Ballantine.

Elbaum, B., Vaughn, S., Hughes, M. T., Moody, S. W., & Schumm, J. S. (2000). How reading outcomes of students with disabilites are related to instructional grouping formats: A meta-analytic review. In R. Gersten, E. Schiller, & S. Vaughn (Eds.), *Contemporary special education research: Syntheses of the knowledge base on critical instructional issues* (pp. 105–135). Mahwah, NJ:

Erlbaum.

Ellis, E. S., & Worthington, L. A. (1994). *Research synthesis on effective teaching principles and the design of quality tools for educators* (Technical Report No. 5). Eugene: University of Oregon, National Center to Improve the Tools of Educators. (ERIC Document Reproduction Service No. ED386853)

Emmer, E. T., & Stough, L. M. (2001). Classroom management: A critical part of educational psychology, with implications for teacher education. *Educational Psychologist, 36*(2), 103–112.

Engelmann, S., & Carnine, D. (1982). *Theory of instruction: Principles and applications.* New York: Irvington.

Epstein, M. H., Polloway, E. A., Foley, R. M., & Patton, J. R. (1993). Homework: A comparison of teachers' and parents' perceptions of the problems experienced by students identified as having behavioral disorders, learning disabilities, or no disabilities. *RASE: Remedial and Special Education, 14*(5), 40–50.

Ericsson, K. A., & Charness, N. (1994). Expert performance: Its structure and acquisition. *American Psychologist, 49*(8), 725–747.

Ericsson, K. A., Krampe, R. T., & Tesch-Römer, C. (1993). The role of deliberate practice in the acquisition of expert performance. *Psychological Review, 100*(3), 363–406.

Fisher, C., Filby, N., Marliave, R., Cahen, L., Dishaw, M., Moore, J., et al. (1978). *Teaching behaviors: Academic learning time and student achievement: Final report of Phase III-B, Beginning Teacher Evaluation Study.* San Francisco: Far West Laboratory for Educational Research and Development.

Frayer, D. A., Frederick, W. D., & Klausmeir, H. J. (1969). *A schema for testing the level of concept mastery* (Working Paper No. 16). Madison: Wisconsin Research and Development Center for Cognitive Learning.

Fuchs, D., Fuchs, L. S., Mathes, P. G., &

Simmons, D. C. (1996). *Peer-assisted learning strategies: Making classrooms more responsive to diversity.* Nashville, TN: Vanderbilt University. (ERIC Document Reproduction Service No. ED393269)

Fuchs, D., Fuchs, L. S., Mathes, P. G., & Simmons, D. C. (1997). Peer-assisted learning strategies: Making classrooms more responsive to diversity. *American Educational Research Journal, 34*(1), 174–206.

Fuchs, D., Mathes, P. G., & Fuchs, L. S. (1996). *Peerassisted learning strategies: Reading methods for grades 2–6.* Nashville, TN: Vanderbilt University.

Fuchs, L. S., & Fuchs, D. (1986, April). *Effects of long- and short-term goal assessment on student achievement.* Paper presented at the annual meeting of the American Educational Research Association, San Francisco. (ERIC Document Reproduction Service No. ED268169)

Fuchs, L. S., Fuchs, D., Hosp, M. K., & Jenkins, J. R. (2001). Oral reading fluency as an indicator of reading competence: A theoretical, empirical, and historical analysis. *Scientific Studies of Reading, 5*(3), 239–256.

Fuchs, L. S., Fuchs, D., & Kazdan, S. (1999). Effects of peer-assisted learning strategies on high school students with serious reading problems. *Remedial and Special Education, 20*(5), 309–318.

Fuchs, L. S., Fuchs, D., Yazdian, L., & Powell, S. R. (2002). Enhancing first-grade children's mathematical development with peer-assisted learning strategies. *School Psychology Review, 31*(4), 569–583.

Gage, N. L., & Needles, M. C. (1989). Process– product research on teaching: A review of criticisms. *Elementary School Journal, 89*, 253–300.

Gagne, R. (1985). *The conditions of learning* (4th ed.). New York: Holt, Rinehart & Winston.

Gersten, R., Beckmann, S., Clarke, B., Foegen, A., Marsh, L., Star, J. R., et al. (2009). *Assisting students struggling* with mathematics: Response to intervention (RtI) for elementary and middle schools (NCEE No. 2009-4060). Washington, DC: National Center for Education Evaluation and Regional Assistance, Institute of Education Sciences, U.S. Department of Education. (Available online at ies.ed.gov/ncee/wwc/publications/practiceguides)

Gersten, R.., Schiller, E. P., & Vaughn, S. (Eds.). (2000). Contemporary special education research: Syntheses of the knowledge base on critical instructional issues. Mahwah, NJ: Erlbaum.

Gersten R., Williams, J. P., Fuchs, L., Baker, S., Koppenhaver, D., Spadorcia, S., et al. (1998). Improving reading comprehension for children with disabilities: A review of research. Final report. Washington, DC: Special Education Programs (ED/OSERS). (ERIC Document Reproduction Service No. ED451650)

Good, T., & Brophy, J. (1997). Looking in classrooms (7th ed.). New York: Longman.

Graves, M. F. (2006). The vocabulary book: Learning and instruction. Newark, DE: International Reading Association.

Greenwood, C. R., Hart, B., Walker, D., & Risley, T. R. (1994). The opportunity to respond revisited: A behavioral theory of developmental retardation and its prevention. In R. Gardner, D. M. Sainato, J. O. Cooper, T. E. Heron, W. L. Heward, J. W. Eshleman, et al. (Eds.), Behavior analysis in education: Focus on measurably superior instruction (pp. 213–223). Pacific Grove, CA: Brooks/Cole.

Gunter, P. L., Denny, R. K., Jack, S. L., Shores, R. E., & Nelson, C. M. (1993). Aversive stimuli in academic interactions between students with serious emotional disturbance and their teachers. Behavior Disorders, 18, 265–274.

Gunter, P. L., Shores, R. E., Jack, S. L., Denny, R. K., & DePaepe, P. A. (1994). A case study of the effects of altering instructional interactions on the disruptive behavior of a child identified with severe behavior disorders. Education and Treatment of Children, 17, 435–444.

Hall, T. E., Hughes, C. A., & Filbert, M. (2000). Computer assisted instruction in reading for students with learning disabilities: A research synthesis. Education and Treatment of Children, 23(2), 173–193.

Hamlin, D. W., Lee, D. L., & Ruhl, K. L. (2008). Unison responding: A quantitative synthesis of applied research. Manuscript in preparation.

Harmin, M. (1994). Inspiring active learning: A handbook for teachers. Alexandria, VA: Association for Supervision and Curriculum Development.

Hasbrouck, J., & Tindal, G. A. (2006). Oral reading fluency norms: A valuable assessment tool for reading teachers. The Reading Teacher, 59(7), 636–644.

Hattie, J. A. C. (2009). Visible learning: A synthesis of over 800 meta-analyses relating to achievement. New York: Routledge.

Hattie, J. A. C., & Timperley, H. (2007). The power of feedback. Review of Educational Research, 77(1), 81–112.

Haynes, M. C., & Jenkins, J. R. (1986). Reading instruction in special education resource rooms. American Educational Research Journal, 23(2), 161–190.

Heimlich, J. E., & Pittelman, S. D. (1986). Semantic mapping: Classroom applications. Newark, DE: International Reading Association.

Herschell, A. D., Greco, L. A., Filcheck, H. A., & McNeil, C. B. (2002). Who is testing whom?: Ten suggestions for managing the disruptive behavior of young children during testing. Intervention in School and Clinic, 37, 140–148.

Heward, W. L. (1997). Four validated instructional strategies. Behavior and Social Issues, 7(1), 43–51.

Heward, W. L. (2003). Ten faulty notions about teaching and learning that hinder the effectiveness of special education. Journal of Special Education, 36(4),

186–205.

Heward, W. L., Courson, F. H., & Narayan, J. S. (1989). Using choral responding to increase active student response during group instruction. *Teaching Exceptional Children, 21*(3), (72–75).

Heward, W. L., Gardner, R., III, R., Cavanaugh, R. A., Courson, F. H., Grossi, T. A., & Barbetta, P. M. (1996). Everyone participates in this class: Using response cards to increase active student response. *Teaching Exceptional Children, 28*(2), 4–10.

Hiebert, E. H., & Kamil, M. L. (Eds.). (2005). *Teaching and learning vocabulary: Bringing research to practice.* Mahwah, NJ: Erlbaum.

Hughes, C. A. (1998). Effective instruction for adults with learning disabilities. In B. K. Lenz, N. A. Sturomski, & M. A. Corley (Eds.), *Serving adults with learning disabilities: Implications for effective practice* (pp. 27–43). Washington, DC: National Adult Literacy and Learning Disabilities Center.

Hughes, C. A., & Maccini, P. (1997). Computerassisted mathematics instruction for students with learning disabilities: A research review. *Learning Disabilities: A Multidisciplinary Journal, 8*(3), 155–166.

Hughes, C. A., Maccini, P., & Gagnon, J. C. (2003). Interventions that positively impact the performance of students with learning disabilities in secondary general education classes. *Learning Disabilities: A Multidisciplinary Journal, 12*(3), 101–111.

Hughes, C. A., & Macy, M. M. (2010). *A metaanalysis of interventions that improve the academic performance of students with learning disabilities in general education classrooms.* Unpublished manuscript, Penn State University.

Hughes, C. A., Ruhl, K. L., Schumaker, J. B., & Deshler, D. D. (1995). *The assignment completion strategy.* Lawrence, KS: EDGE Enterprises.

Hughes, C. A., Ruhl, K. L., Schumaker, J. B.,

& Deshler, D. D. (2002). Effects of instruction in an assignment completion strategy on the homework performance of students with learning disabilities in general education classes. *Learning Disabilities Research and Practice, 17*(1), 1–18.

Hughes, C. A., & Suritsky, S. K. (1994). Notetaking skills of university students with and without learning disabilities. *Journal of Learning Disabilities, 27*(1), 20–24.

Hunter, M. (1982). *Mastery teaching.* El Segundo, CA: TIP Publications.

Jenkins, J. R., Matlock, B., & Slocum, T. A. (1989). Approaches to vocabulary instruction: The teaching of individual word meanings and practice in deriving word meaning from context. *Reading Research Quarterly, 24*(2), 215–235.

Jenkins, J. R., Stein, M., & Wysocki, K. (1984). Learning vocabulary through reading. *American Educational Research Journal, 21,* 767–787.

Johnson, D. W., Johnson, R. T., & Holubec, E. J. (1993). *Circles of learning: Cooperation in the classroom* (4th ed.). Edina, MN: Interaction Book.

Johnson, D. W., Johnson, R. T., & Smith, K. A. (1991). *Active learning: Cooperation in the college classroom.* Edina, MN: Interaction Book.

Jones, F. H. (2007). *Tools for teaching: Discipline, instruction, motivation.* Santa Cruz, CA: Fredric H. Jones & Associates.

Kagan, S. (1989). The structural approach to cooperative learning. *Educational Leadership, 47*(4), 12–15.

Kagan, S. (1992). *Cooperative learning* (7th ed.). San Juan Capistrano, CA: Resources for Teachers.

Kame'enui, E. J., & Carnine, D. W. (1998). *Effective teaching strategies that accommodate diverse learners.* Columbus, OH: Merrill.

Kame'enui, E. J., Carnine, D. W., Dixon, R. C., Simmons, D. C., & Coyne, M. D. (2002). *Effective teaching strategies that accommodate diverse learners.* Upper Saddle River, NJ: Merrill Prentice Hall.

Kame'enui, E. J., & Simmons, D. C. (1990). *Designing instructional strategies: The prevention of academic learning problems.* Columbus, OH: Merrill.

Kamil, M. L., Borman, G. D., Dole, J., Kral, C. C., Salinger, T., & Torgesen, J. (2008). *Improving adolescent literacy: Effective classroom and intervention practices: A practice guide* (NCEE No. 2008-4027). Washington, DC: National Center for Education Evaluation and Regional Assistance, Institute of Education Sciences, U.S. Department of Education. (Available online at *ies.ed.gov/ncee/ wwc/publications/practiceguides*)

Kamps, D., Dugan, E., Leonard, B., & Daoust, P. (1994). Enhanced small group instruction using choral responding and student interaction for children with autism and developmental disabilities. *American Journal on Mental Retardation, 99,* 60–73.

Keith, T. Z. (1992). Time spent on homework and high school grades: A large-sample path analysis. *Journal of Educational Psychology, 74*(2), 248–253.

Kirschner, P. A., Sweller, J., & Clark, R. E. (2006). Why minimal guidance during instruction does not work: An analysis of the failure of constructivist, discovery, problem-based, experiential, and inquiry-based teaching. *Educational Psychologist, 41*(2), 75–86.

Kluger, A. N., & DeNisi, A. (1996). The effects of feedback interventions on performance: A historical review, a meta-analysis, and a preliminary feedback intervention theory. *Psychological Bulletin, 119*(2), 254–284.

Kohn, A. (1993). *Punished by rewards: The trouble with gold stars, incentive plans, A's, praise, and other bribes.* Boston: Houghton Mifflin.

Kohn, A. (1998). *What to look for in a classroom.* San Francisco: Jossey-Bass.

Kroesbergen, E. H., & Van Luit, J. E. H. (2003). Mathematics interventions for children with special educational needs: A meta-analysis. *Remedial and Special Education, 24*(2), 97–114.

Kubina, R. M., & Hughes, C. A. (2008). *Reading fluency* (Practice Alert No. 9).

Arlington, VA: Council for Exceptional Children's Division for Learning Disabilities and Division for Research.

Lambert, M. C., Cartledge, G., Heward, W. L., & Lo, Y. (2006). Effects of response cards on behavior and academic responding during math lessons by fourth grade urban students. *Journal of Positive Behavioral Interventions, 8,* 88–99.

Lampi, A. R., Fenty, N. S., & Beaunae, C. (2005). Making the three Ps easier: Praise, proximity, and precorrection. *Beyond Behavior, 15,* 8–12.

Lenz, B. K., Alley, G. R., & Schumaker, J. B. (1987). Activating the inactive learner: Advance organizers in the secondary content classroom. *Learning Disability Quarterly, 10*(1), 53–67.

Lenz, B. K., Ehren, B. J., & Smiley, L. R. (1991). A goal attainment approach to improve completion of project-type assignments by adolescents with learning disabilities. *Learning Disabilities Research and Practice, 6*(3), 166–176.

Lenz, B. K., Ellis, E. S., & Scanlon, D. (1996). *Teaching learning strategies to adolescents and adults with learning disabilities.* Austin, TX: PRO-ED.

Locke, E. A., & Latham, G. P. (1990). *A theory of goal setting and task performance.* Englewood Cliffs, NJ: Prentice-Hall.

Longman dictionary of American English (3rd ed.). (2006). Harlow, UK: Pearson Education.

Lovitt, T. C. (2000). *Preventing school failure: Tactics for teaching adolescents* (2nd ed.). Austin, TX: PRO-ED.

Lubliner, S., & Hiebert, E. H. (2008). *An analysis of English–Spanish cognates.* Paper presented at the annual meeting of the American Educational Research Association, New York.

Lyman, F. T. (1981). The responsive classroom discussion: The inclusion of all students. In A. Anderson (Ed.), *Mainstreaming digest* (pp. 109–113). College Park: University of Maryland Press.

Maccini, P., Gagnon, J. C., & Hughes, C. A. (2002). Technology-based practices for secondary students with learning disabilities in general education classrooms. *Learning Disability Quarterly, 25*(4), 247–262.

Maheady, L., Mallette, B., Harper, G. F., & Sacca, K. (1991). Heads Together: A peer-mediated option for improving the academic achievement of heterogeneous learning groups. *Remedial and Special Education, 12,* 25–33.

Maheady, L., Michielli-Pendl, J., Harper, G. F., & Mallette, B. (2006). The effects of numbered heads together with and without an incentive package on the science test performance of a diverse group of sixth graders. *Journal of Behavioral Education, 15*(1), 25–39.

Maheady, L., Michielli-Pendl, J., Mallette, B., & Harper, G. F. (2002). A collaborative research project to improve the academic performance of a diverse sixth grade science class. *Teacher Education and Special Education, 25*(1), 55–70.

Maheady, L., Sacca, K. M., & Harper, G. F. (1988). Classwide peer tutoring with mildly handicapped high school students. *Exceptional Children, 55*(1), 52–59.

Marchand-Martella, N. E., Slocum, T. A., & Martella, R. C. (Eds.). (2004). *Introduction to direct instruction.* Boston: Pearson Education.

Marzano, R. J. (2000). Twentieth century advances in instruction. In R. Brandt (Ed.), *Education in a new era* (pp. 67–95). Alexandria, VA: Association for Supervision and Curriculum Development.

Marzano, R. J., & Pickering, D. J. (2005). *Building academic vocabulary: Teacher's manual.* Alexandria, VA: Association for Supervision and Curriculum Development.

Mastropieri, M. A., Scruggs, T. E., Bakken, J. P., & Whedon, C. (1996). Reading comprehension: A synthesis of research in learning disabilities. In T. E. Scruggs &

M. A. Mastropieri (Eds.), *Advances in learning and behavioral disabilities* (Vol. 10B, pp. 201–227). Greenwich, CT: JAI Press.

Mathes, P. G., Torgesen, J. K., & Allor, J. H. (2001). The effects of peer assisted learning strategies for first grade readers with and without additional computer assisted instruction in phonological awareness. *American Educational Research Journal, 38,* 371–410.

Mayfield, K. H., & Chase, P. N. (2002). The effects of cumulative practice on mathematics problem solving. *Journal of Applied Behavior Analysis, 35*(2), 105–123.

McEwan, E. K. (2006). *How to survive and thrive in the first three weeks of school.* Thousand Oaks, CA: Corwin Press.

McIntosh, K., Herman, K., Sanford, A., McGraw, K., & Florence, K. (2004). Teaching transitions: Techniques for promoting success between lessons. *Teaching Exceptional Children, 37*(1), 32–38.

McKeown, M. G., Beck, I. L., Omanson, R. C., & Pople, M. T. (1985). Some effects of the nature and frequency of vocabulary instruction on the knowledge and use of words. *Reading Research Quarterly, 20*(5), 522–535.

McTighe, J., & Lyman, F. T., Jr. (1988). Cueing thinking in the classroom: The promise of theoryembedded tools. *Educational Leadership, 45*(7), 18–24.

Meese, R. L. (2001). *Teaching learners with mild disabilities: Integrating research and practice* (2nd ed.). Belmont, CA: Wadsworth Thomson Learning.

Miao, Y., Darch, C., & Rabren, K. (2002). Use of precorrection strategies to enhance reading performance of students with learning and behavior problems. *Journal of Instructional Psychology, 29*(3), 162–174.

Munson, D. (2000). *Enemy pie.* San Francisco: Chronicle Books.

Nagy, W. E. (1988). *Teaching vocabulary to improve reading comprehension.*

Newark, DE: International Reading Association.

Nagy, W. E., & Anderson, R. C. (1984). The number of words in printed school English. *Reading Research Quarterly*, *19*(3), 304–330.

Nagy, W. E., García, G. E., Durgunoglu, A. Y., & Hancin-Bhatt, B. (1993). Spanish–English bilingual students' use of cognates in English reading. *Journal of Reading Behavior*, *25*(3), 241–259.

Narayan, J. S., Heward, W. L., Gardner, R., III, Courson, F. H., & Omness, C. K. (1990). Using response cards to increase student participation in an elementary classroom. *Journal of Applied Behavior Analysis*, *23*(4), 483–490.

Nash, R. (1997). *NTC's dictionary of Spanish cognates.* Lincolnwood, IL: NTC Publishing Group.

National Mathematics Advisory Panel. (2008). *Foundations for success: The final report of the National Mathematics Advisory Panel.* Washington, DC: U.S. Department of Education.

National Reading Panel. (2000). *Teaching children to read: An evidence-based assessment of the scientific research literature on reading and its implications for reading instruction: Reports of the subgroups* (NIH Publication No. 00-4754). Washington, DC: National Institutes of Health and National Institute of Child Health and Human Development.

Nelson, J. S., Alber, S. R., & Gordy, A. (2004). Effects of systematic error correction and repeated readings on the reading accuracy and proficiency of second graders with disabilities. *Education and Treatment of Children, 27*(3), 186–198.

Novak, J. D. (1993). How do we learn our lesson?: Taking students through the process. *Science Teacher, 60*(3), 50–55.

Paschal, R. A., Weinstein, T., & Walberg, H. J. (1984). The effects of homework on learning: A quantitative synthesis. *Journal of Educational Research, 78*(2), 97–104.

Pierce, D. W., & Cameron, J. (2002). A summary of the effects of reward contingencies on interest and performance. *The Behavior Analyst Today, 3*(2), 221–228.

Polloway, E. A., Foley, R. M., & Epstein, M. H. (1992). A comparison of the homework problems of students with learning disabilities and nonhandicapped students. *Learning Disabilities Research and Practice, 7*(4), 203–209.

Poplin, M. S. (1988). Holistic/constructivist principles of the teaching/learning process: Implications for the field of learning disabilities. *Journal of Learning Disabilities, 21*(7), 401–416.

Pratton, J., & Hales, L. W. (1986). The effects of active participation on student learning. *Journal of Educational Research, 79*(4), 210–215.

Putnam, M. L., Deshler, D. D., & Schumaker, J. B. (1993). The investigation of setting demands: A missing link in learning strategy instruction. In L. J. Meltzer (Ed.), *Strategy assessment and instruction for students with learning disabilities: From theory to practice* (pp. 325–354). Austin, TX: Pro-Ed.

Rademacher, J. A., Deshler, D. D., Schumaker, J. B., & Lenz, B. K. (1998). *The quality assignment routine.* Lawrence, KS: Edge Enterprises.

Rademacher, J. A., Schumaker, J. B., & Deshler, D. D. (1996). Development and validation of a classroom assignment routine for inclusive settings. *Learning Disabilitiy Quarterly, 19*(3), 163–178.

Randolph, J. J. (2007). Meta-analysis of the research on response cards. *Journal of Positive Behavior Interventions, 9*(2), 113–128.

Rosenshine, B. (1987). Explicit teaching and teacher training. *Journal of Teacher Education, 38*(3), 34–36.

Rosenshine, B. (1995). Advances in research on instruction. *Journal of Educational Research, 88*(5), 262–268.

Rosenshine, B. (1997). Advances in research on instruction. In J. W. Lloyd, E. J. Kame'enui, & D. Chard (Eds.), *Issues in educating students with disabilities* (pp. 197–221). Mahwah, NJ: Erlbaum.

Rosenshine, B., & Stevens, R. (1986).

Teaching functions. In M. C. Wittrock (Ed.), *Handbook of research on teaching* (3rd ed., pp. 326–391). New York: Macmillan.

Ruhl, K. L., & Hughes, C. A. (2005). *Effective homework practices with students with learning disabilities: A tutorial.* TeachingLD.org.

Ruhl, K. L., Hughes, C. A., & Gajar, A. H. (1990). Efficacy of the pause procedure for enhancing learning disabled and nondisabled college students' long- and short-term recall of facts presented through lecture. *Learning Disability Quarterly, 13,* 55–64.

Ruhl, K. L., Hughes, C. A., & Schloss, P. A. (1987). Using the pause procedure to enhance lecture recall. *Teacher Education and Special Education, 10,* 14–18.

Salend, S. J., & Gajria, M. (1995). Increasing the homework completion rates of students with mild disabilities. *Remedial and Special Education, 16*(5), 271–278.

Schumaker, J. B., Denton, P. H., & Deshler, D. D. (1984). *The paraphrasing strategy.* Lawrence: University of Kansas.

Schwartz, R. M., & Raphael, T. E. (1985). Concept of definition: A key to improving students' vocabulary. *The Reading Teacher, 39*(2), 198–205.

Simmons, D. C., Fuchs, L. S., Fuchs, D., Mathes, P., & Hodge, J. P. (1995). Effects of explicit teaching and peer tutoring on the reading achievement of learning-disabled and low-performing students in regular classrooms. *Elementary School Journal, 95*(5), 387–408.

Skinner, C. H., Fletcher, P. A., & Henington, C. (1996). Increasing learning trial rates by increasing student response rates. *School Psychology Quarterly, 11,* 313–325.

Slavin, R. E. (1984). Team-assisted individualization: Cooperative learning and individualized instruction in the mainstreamed classroom. *Remedial and Special Education (RASE), 5*(6), 33–42.

Slavin, R. E. (2008). *Educational psychology: Theory and practice* (9th ed.). Upper Saddle River, NJ: Pearson.

Slavin, R. E., Madden, N. A., & Leavey, M. (1984). Effects of team assisted individualization on the mathematics achievement of academically handicapped and nonhandicapped students. *Journal of Educational Psychology, 76*(5), 813–819.

Slavin, R. E., Madden, N. A., & Stevens, R. J. (1989/1990). Cooperative learning models for the 3 R's. *Educational Leadership, 47*(4), 22–28.

Sprick, R. S. (2006). *Discipline in the secondary classroom: A positive approach to behavior management.* San Francisco: Jossey-Bass.

Sprick, R. S., Garrison, M., & Howard, L. M. (1998). *CHAMPs: A proactive and positive approach to classroom management.* Longmont, CO: Sopris West.

Stahl, S., & Kapinus, B. (2001). *Word power: What every educator needs to know about teaching vocabulary.* Washington, DC: National Education Association.

Stahl, S. A. (1999). *Vocabulary development.* Brookline, MA: Brookline Books.

Stahl, S. A., & Fairbanks, M. M. (1986). The effects of vocabulary instruction: A model-based meta-analysis. *Review of Educational Research, 56,* 72–110.

Stahl, S. A., & Nagy, W. E. (2006). *Teaching word meanings.* Mahwah, NJ: Erlbaum.

Stainback, S., & Stainback, W. (Eds.). (1992). *Curriculum considerations in inclusive classrooms: Facilitating learning for all students.* Baltimore: Brookes.

Steffe, L., & Gale, J. (Eds.). (1995). *Constructivism in education.* Hillsdale, NJ: Erlbaum.

Stein, M., Carnine, D., & Dixon, R. (1998). Direct instruction: Integrating curriculum design and effective teaching practice. *Intervention in School and Clinic, 33*(4), 227–233.

Stronge, J. H. (2002). *Qualities of effective teachers.* Alexandria, VA: Association for Supervision and Curriculum Development.

Sutherland, K. S., & Wehby, J. H. (2001).

Exploring the relationship between increased opportunities to respond to academic requests and the academic and behavioral outcomes of students with EBD: A review. *Remedial and Special Education, 22*(2), 113–121.

Swanson, H. L. (1999). Instructional components that predict treatment outcomes for students with learning disabilities: Support for a combined strategy and direct instruction model. *Learning Disabilities Research and Practice, 14*(3), 129–140.

Swanson, H. L. (2001). Searching for the best model for instructing students with learning disabilities. *Focus on Exceptional Children, 34*(2), 1–14.

Swanson, H. L., & Hoskyn, M. (1998). Experimental intervention research on students with learning disabilities: A meta-analysis of treatment outcomes. *Review of Educational Research, 68*(3), 277–321.

Swanson, H. L., & Sachse-Lee, C. (2000). A metaanalysis of single-subject-design intervention research for students with LD. *Journal of Learning Disabilities, 33*(2), 114–136.

Swanson, H. L., & Siegel, L. (2001). Learning disabilities as a working memory deficit. *Issues in Education: Contributions of Educational Psychology, 7*(1), 1–48.

Sweller, J., Kirschner, P. A., & Clark, R. E. (2007). Why minimally guided teaching techniques do not work: A reply to commentaries. *Educational Psychologist, 42*(2), 115–121.

Thalheimer, W. (2008a). Providing learners with feedback: Part 1. Research-based recommendations for training, education, and e-learning. Retrieved December 11, 2008, from *www.worklearning.com/catalog*

Thalheimer, W. (2008b). Providing learners with feedback: Part 2. Peer-reviewed research compiled for training, education, and e-learning. Retrieved December 11, 2008, from *www.worklearning.com/catalog*

Titherington, J. (1990). *Pumpkin, pumpkin.* New York: Greenwillow Books.

Tomesen, M., & Aarnoutse, C. (1998). Effects of an instructional programme for deriving word meanings. *Educational Studies, 24*(1), 107–128.

Torrance, M., & Galbraith, D. (2006). The processing demands of writing. In C. A. MacArthur, S. Graham, & J. Fitzgerald (Eds.), *Handbook of writing research* (pp. 67–80). New York: . Press.

Trammel, D. L., Schloss, P. J., & Alper, S. (1994). Interventions: Using self-recording, evaluation, and graphing to increase completion of homework assignments. *Journal of Learning Disabilites, 27*(2), 75–81.

Vaughn, S., Gersten, R., & Chard, D. J. (2000). The underlying message in LD intervention research: Findings from research syntheses. *Exceptional Children, 67*(1), 99–114.

Viorst, J. (1972). *Alexander and the terrible, horrible, no good, very bad day.* New York: Simon & Schuster.

Walberg, H. J. (1986). Synthesis of research on teaching. In M. C. Wittrock (Ed.), *Handbook of research on teaching* (3rd ed., pp. 214–239). New York: Macmillan.

Wannarka, R., & Ruhl, K. (2008). Seating arrangements that promote positive academic and behavioural outcomes: A review of empirical research. *Support for Learning, 23*(2), 89–93.

Watkins, C. L. (n.d.) *Follow through: Why didn't we?* Retrieved from *www.uoregon.edu/~adiep/ft/watkins.htm*

Watkins, C. L., & Slocum, T. A. (2004). The components of direct instruction. In N. E. MarchandMartella, T. A. Slocum, & R. C. Martella (Eds.), *Introduction to direct instruction.* Boston: Allyn & Bacon.

White, T. G., Graves, M. F., & Slater, W. H. (1990). Growth of reading vocabulary in diverse elementary schools: Decoding and word meaning. *Journal of Educational Psychology, 82*, 281–290.

White, T. G., Sowell, J., & Yanagihara, A. (1989). Teaching elementary students to use word-part clues. *The Reading Teacher, 42*, 302–308.

Willingham, D. T. (2002). Allocating student study time: "Massed" versus "distributed" practice. *American Educator, 26*(2), 37–39, 47.

Wittrock, M. C. (Ed.). (1986). *Handbook of research on teaching* (3rd ed.). New York: Macmillan.

Wong, H. K., & Wong, R. T. (2009). *The first days of school: How to be an effective teacher.* Mountain View, CA: Harry K. Wong.

Wood, C. L., & Heward, W. L. (2005). *Good noise! Using choral responding to increase the effectiveness of group instruction.* Manuscript submitted for publication. (Available online at *education. osu.edu/wheward/PAES831.htm*)

Woodward, J. (2006). Developing automaticity in multiplication facts: Integrating strategy instruction with timed practice drills. *Learning Disability Quarterly, 29*(4), 269–289.

World cultures and geography. (2005). Geneva, IL: McDougal Littell.

Index

Pages followed by *f* indicate figures.

289

Made in the USA
Columbia, SC
10 October 2024

44107613R00241